I0084018

Alfred Edward Woodley Mason

The Courtship of Morrice Buckler

A Romance

Alfred Edward Woodley Mason

The Courtship of Morrice Buckler
A Romance

ISBN/EAN: 9783744673921

Printed in Europe, USA, Canada, Australia, Japan

Cover: Foto ©Thomas Meinert / pixelio.de

More available books at **www.hansebooks.com**

THE COURTSHIP

OF

MORRICE BUCKLER

THE COURTSHIP

OF

MORRICE BUCKLER

A Romance

*Being a Record of the Growth of an English Gentleman
during the years 1685–1687, under strange and difficult circumstances,
written some while afterwards in his own hand, and now edited by*

A. E. W. MASON

AUTHOR OF "A ROMANCE OF WASTDALE"

London
MACMILLAN AND CO., Ltd.
NEW YORK: MACMILLAN & CO.
1896

First Edition, February, 1896.
Second Edition, May, 1896.
Third Edition, June, 1896.

CONTENTS.

CHAPTER I.

PAGE

TELLS OF AN INTERRUPTED MESSAGE 1

CHAPTER II.

I REACH LONDON, AND THERE MAKE AN ACQUAINT-
ANCE 15

CHAPTER III.

TELLS HOW I REACH BRISTOL, AND IN WHAT STRANGE
GUISE I GO TO MEET MY FRIEND 38

CHAPTER IV.

SIR JULIAN HARNWOOD 67

CHAPTER V.

I JOURNEY TO THE TYROL, AND HAVE SOME DIS-
COURSE WITH COUNT LUKSTEIN 84

CHAPTER VI.

PAGE

SWORDS TAKE UP THE DISCOURSE 116

CHAPTER VII.

I RETURN HOME AND HEAR NEWS OF COUNTESS
LUKSTEIN 125

CHAPTER VIII.

I MAKE A BOW TO COUNTESS LUKSTEIN . . . 134

CHAPTER IX.

I RENEW AN ACQUAINTANCESHIP 152

CHAPTER X.

DOUBTS, PERPLEXITIES, AND A COMPROMISE . . . 164

CHAPTER XI.

THE COUNTESS EXPLAINS, AND SHOWS ME A PICTURE . 182

CHAPTER XII.

LADY TRACY 201

CHAPTER XIII.

PAGE

COUNTESS LUKSTEIN IS CONVINCED 216

CHAPTER XIV.

A GAME OF HIDE-AND-SEEK 228

CHAPTER XV.

THE HALF-WAY HOUSE AGAIN 251

CHAPTER XVI.

CONCERNING AN INVITATION AND A LOCKED DOOR . 265

CHAPTER XVII.

FATHER SPAUR 271

CHAPTER XVIII.

AT LUKSTEIN 287

CHAPTER XIX.

IN THE PAVILION. I EXPLAIN 296

viii CONTENTS.

CHAPTER XX.

PAGE

IN THE PAVILION. COUNTESS LUKSTEIN EXPLAINS . 310

CHAPTER XXI.

IN CAPTIVITY HOLLOW 328

CHAPTER XXII.

A TALK WITH OTTO. I ESCAPE TO INNSPRUCK . . 353

CHAPTER XXIII.

THE LAST 366

COURTSHIP OF MORRICE BUCKLER

CHAPTER I.

TELLS OF AN INTERRUPTED MESSAGE.

IT chanced that as I was shifting the volumes in my library this morning, more from sheer fatigue of idleness than with any set intention—for, alas! this long time since I have lost the savour of books—a little Elzevir copy of Horace fell from the back of a shelf between my hands. It lay in my palm, soiled and faded with the dust of twenty years; and as I swept clean its cover and the edges of the leaves, the look and feel of it unlocked my mind to such an inrush of glistening memories that I seemed to be sweeping those years and the overlay of their experience from off my consciousness. I lived again in that brief but eventful period which laid upon the unaccustomed shoulders of a bookish student a heavy burden of deeds, but gave him in compensation wherewith to reckon the burden light.

The book fell open of its own accord at the Palinodia at Tyndaridem. On the stained and fingered leaf facing the ode I could still decipher the plan of Lukstein Castle, and as I gazed, that blurred outline filled until it became a picture. I

B

looked into the book as into a magician's crystal. The great angle of the building, the level row of windows, the red roofs of the turrets, the terrace, and the little pinewood pavilion, all were clearly limned before my eyes, and were overswept by changing waves of colour. I saw the Castle as on the first occasion of my coming, hung disconsolately on a hillside in a far-away corner of the Tyrol, a black stain upon a sloping wilderness of snow; I saw it again under a waning moon in the stern silence of a frosty night, as each window grew angry with a tossing glare of links; but chiefly I saw it as when I rode thither on my last memorable visit, sleeping peacefully above the cornfields in the droning sabbath of a summer afternoon. I turned my eyes to the ode. The score of my pencil was visible against the last verse :

> Nunc ego mitibus
> Mutare quæro tristia dum mihi
> Fias recantatis amica
> Opprobriis animumque reddas.

On the margin beside the first line was the date, Sept. 14, 1685, and beneath the verse yet another date, Sept. 12, 1687. And as I looked, it came upon me that I would set down with what clearness I might the record of those two years, in the hope that my memories might warm and cheer these later days of loneliness, much as the afterglow lingers purple on yonder summit rocks when the sun has already sunk behind the Cumberland fells. For indeed that short interspace of time shines out in my remembrance like a thick thread of gold in a

woof of homespun.   I would not, however, be understood to therefore deprecate the quiet years of
happiness which followed.   The two years of which
I speak in their actual passage occasioned me more
anxiety and suffering than happiness.   But they have
a history of their own.   They mark out a portion of
my life whereof the two dates in my Horace were
the beginning and the end, and the verse between
the dates, strangely enough, its best epitome.

It was, then, the fourteenth day of September,
1685, and the time a few minutes past noon.   Jack
Larke, my fellow-student at the University of Leyden,
and myself had but just returned to our lodging in
that street of the town which they call the Pape-
Graft.   We were both fairly wearied, for the weather
was drowsy and hot, and one had little stomach for
the Magnificus Professor, the more particularly when
he discoursed concerning the natural philosophy of
Pliny.

"'Tis all lies, every jot of it!" cried Larke.   "If
I wrote such nonsense I should be whipped for a
heretic.   And yet I must sit there and listen and
take notes until my brain reels."

"You sit there but seldom, Jack," said I, "and
never played yourself so false as to listen; while as
for the notes—— !"

I took up his book which he had flung upon the
table.   It contained naught but pictures of the
Professor in divers humiliating attitudes, with John
Larke ever towering above him, his honest features
twisted into so heroical an expression of scorn as
set me laughing till my sides ached.

He snatched the book from my hand, and flung

B 2

it into a corner. "There!" said he. "It may go to the dust-hole and Pliny with it, to rot in company." And the Latin volume followed the note-book. Whereupon, with a sigh of relief, he lifted a brace of pistols from a shelf, and began industriously to scour and polish them, though indeed their locks and barrels shone like silver as it was. For my part, I plumped myself down before this very ode of Horace; and so for a while, each in his own way, we worked silently. Ever and again, however, he would look up and towards me, and then, with an impatient shrug, settle to his task again. At last he could contain no longer.

"Lord!" he burst out, "what a sick world it is! Here am I, fitted for a roving life under open skies, and plucked out of God's design by the want of a few pence."

"You may yet sit on the bench," said I, to console him.

"Ay, lad," he answered, "I might if I had sufficient roguery to supply my lack of wits." Then he suddenly turned on me. "And here are you," he said, "who could journey east and west, and never sleep twice beneath the same roof, breaking your back mewed up over a copy of Horace!"

At that moment I was indeed stretched full-length upon a sofa, but I had no mind to set him right. The tirade was passing old to me, and replies were but fresh fuel to keep it flickering. However, he had not yet done.

"I believe," he continued, "you would sooner solve a knot in Aristotle than lead out the finest lady in Europe to dance a pavan with you."

"That is true," I replied. "I should be no less afraid of her than you of Aristotle."

"Morrice," said he solemnly, "I do verily believe you have naught but fish-blood in your veins."

Whereat I laughed, and he, coming over to me :

"Why, man," he cried, "had I your fortune on my back——"

"You would soon find it a ragged cloak," I interposed.

"And your sword at my side——"

"You would still lack my skill in using it."

Larke stopped short in his speech, and his face darkened. I had touched him in the tenderest part of his pride. Proficiency in manly exercises was the single quality on which he plumed himself, and so he had made it his daily habit to repair to the fencing-rooms of a noted French master, who dwelt in Noort-Eynde by the Witte Poort. Thither also, by dint of much pertinacity, for which I had grave reason to thank him afterwards, he had haled me for instruction in the art. Once I got there, however, the play fascinated me. The delicate intricacy of the movements so absorbed brain and muscle in a common service as to produce in me an inward sense of completeness, very sweet and strange to one of my halting diffidence. In consequence I applied myself with considerable enthusiasm, and in the end acquired some nimbleness with the rapier, or, to speak more truly, the foil. For as yet my skill had never been put to the test of a serious encounter.

Now, on the previous day Larke and I had fenced together throughout the afternoon, and fortune had sided with me in every bout ; and it was, I think, the

recollection of this which rankled within him.   However, the fit soon passed—'twas not in his nature to
be silent long—and he broke out again, seating himself in a chair by the table.

"Dost never dream of adventures, Morrice?" he
asked.   "A life brimful of them, and a quick death
at the end?"

"I had as lief die in my bed," said I.

"To be sure, to be sure," he replied with a sneer.
"Men ever wish to die in the place they are most
fond of;" and then he leant forward upon the table
and said, with a curious wonder: "Hast never a
regret that thy sword rusted in June?"

"Nay," I answered him quickly.   "Monmouth
was broken and captured before we had even heard
he had raised his flag.   And, besides, the King had
stouter swords than mine, and yet no use for them."

But none the less I turned my face to the wall,
for I felt my cheeks blazing.   My words were indeed
the truth.   The same packet which brought to us the
news of Monmouth's rising in the west, brought to
us also the news of his defeat at Sedgemoor.   But I
might easily have divined his project some while ago.
For early in the spring I had received a visit from
one Ferguson, a Scot, who, after uttering many fantastical lies concerning the "Duke of York," as he
impudently styled the King, had warned me that
such as failed to assist the true monarch out of the
funds they possessed might well find themselves
sorely burdened in the near future.   At the time I
had merely laughed at the menace, and slipped it
from my thoughts.   Afterwards, however, the remembrance of his visit came back to me, and with

it a feeling of shame that I had lain thus sluggishly
at Leyden while this monstrous web of rebellion was
a-weaving about me in the neighbouring towns of
Holland.

"'Art more of a woman than a man, Morrice,
I fear me," said Jack.

I had heard some foolish talk of this kind more
than once before, and it ever angered me. I rose
quickly from the couch; but Jack skipped round the
table, and jeered yet the more.

"'Wilt never win a wife by fair means, lad," says
he. "The Muses are women, and women have no
liking for them. 'Must buy a wife when the time
comes."

Perceiving that his aim was but to provoke my
anger, I refrained from answering him and got me
back to my ode. The day was in truth too hot for
quarrelling. Larke, however, was not so easily put off.
He returned to his chair, which was close to my couch.

"Horace!" he said gravely, wagging his head at
me. "Horace! There are wise sayings in his book."

"What know you of them?" I laughed.

"I know one," he answered. "I learnt it yester-
night for thy special delectation. It begins in this
way:

"Quem si puellarum choro inseres."

He got no further in his quotation. For he tilted
his chair at this moment, and I thrusting at it with
my foot, he tumbled over backwards and sprawled
on the ground, swearing at great length.

"'Wilt never win a wife by fair means for all
that," he spluttered.

"Then 'tis no more than prudence in me to wed my books."

So I spake, and hot on the heels of my saying came the message which divorced me from them for good and all. For as Larke still lay upon the floor, a clatter of horse's hoofs came to us through the open window. The sound stopped at our door. Larke rose hastily, and leaned out across the sill.

"It is an Englishman," he cried. "He comes to us."

The next moment a noise of altercation filled the air. I could hear the shrill speech of our worthy landlady, and above it a man's voice in the English dialect, growing ever louder and louder as though the violence of his tone would translate his meaning. I followed Larke to the window. The quiet street was alive with peeping faces, and just beneath us stood the reason of the brawl, a short, thick-set man, whose face was hidden by a large flapping hat. His horse stood in the roadway in a lather of spume. For some reason, doubtless the excitement of his manner, our hostess would not let him pass into the house. She stood solidly filling the doorway, and for a little it amused us to watch the man's vehement gesticulations ; so little thought had we of the many strange events which were to follow from his visit. In a minute, however, he turned his face towards us, and I recognised him as Nicholas Swasfield, the body-servant of my good friend, Sir Julian Harnwood.

"Let him up!" I cried. "Let him up!"

"Yes, woman, let him up!" repeated Larke, and turning to me : "He hath many choice and wonderful oaths. and I fain would add them to my store."

Thereupon the woman drew reluctantly aside, and Swasfield bounded past her into the passage. We heard him tumble heavily up the dark stairway, cursing the country and its natives, and then with a great bump of his body he burst open the door and lurched into the room. At the sight of me he brake into a glad cry:

"Sir Julian, my master," he gasped, and stopped dead.

"Well, what of him?" I asked eagerly.

But he answered never a word; he stood mopping his brows with a great blue handkerchief, which hid his face from us. 'Tis strange how clearly I remember that handkerchief. It was embroidered at the corners with anchors in white cotton, and it recurred to me with a quaint irrelevancy that the man had been a sailor in his youth.

"Well, what of him?" I asked again with some sharpness. "Speak, man! You had words and to spare below."

"He lies in Bristol gaol," at last he said, heaving great breaths between his words, "and none but you can serve his turn."

With that he tore at his shirt above his heart, and made a little tripping run to the table. He clutched at its edge and swayed forward above it, his head loosely swinging between his shoulders.

"Hurry!" he said in a thick, strangled voice. "Assizes—twenty-first—Jeffries."

And with a sudden convulsion he straightened himself, stood for a second on the tips of his toes, with the veins ridged on his livid face like purple weals, and then fell in a huddled lump upon the floor.

I sprang to the stair-head and shouted for some one to run for a doctor. Jack was already loosening the man's shirt.

"It is a fit," he said, clasping a hand to his heart.

Luckily my bedroom gave onto the parlour, and between us we carried him within and laid him gently on my bed. His eyelids were open and his eyes fixed, but turned inwards, so that one saw but the whites of them, while a light froth oozed through his locked teeth.

"He will die," I cried.

A ewer of water stood by the bedside, and this I emptied over his head and shoulders, drowning the sheets, but to no other purpose. Our landlady fetched up a bottle of Dutch schnapps, which was the only spirit the house contained, but his jaws were too fast closed for us to open them. So we stood all three watching him helplessly, while those last words of his drummed at my heart. Jeffries! I knew enough of the bloody work he had taken in hand that summer to assure me there would be short shrift for Julian had he meddled in Monmouth's affairs. On the other hand, I reflected, if such indeed was my friend's case, wherein could I prove of effectual help? "None but you can serve his turn," the fellow had said. Could Julian have fallen under another charge? I was the more inclined to this conjecture, for that Julian had been always staunchly loyal to the King, and, moreover, a constant figure at the Court.

However, 'twas all idle guess-work, and there before my eyes was stretched the one man, who could have disclosed the truth, struck down in the very telling of his story ! I began to fear that he would die before the surgeon came. For he breathed heavily with a horrid sound like a dog snoring.

All at once à thought flashed into my mind. He might have brought a letter from Julian's hand. I searched his pockets on the instant ; they held nothing but a few English coins and some metal charms, such as the ignorant are wont to carry on their persons to preserve them from misadventure.

While I was thus engaged, the doctor was ushered into the room, very deliberate in manner, and magnificent in his dress. Erudition was marked in the very cock of his wig. I sprang towards him.

"Make him speak, Mynheer ! " I implored. " He hath a message to deliver, and it cannot wait."

But he put me aside with a wave of his hand and advanced towards the bed, pursing his lips and frowning as one sunk in a profundity of thought.

" Can you make him speak ? " I asked again with some impatience. But again he merely waved his hand, and taking a gilt box from his pocket, inhaled a large pinch of snuff. Then he turned to Larke, who stood holding the bottle of schnapps.

" Tell me, young gentleman," he said severely, " what time the fit took him, and the manner of his seizure ! "

Larke informed him hastily of what had passed, and he listened with much sage bobbing of his head. Then to our hostess :

" My assistant is below, and hath my instruments. Send him up ! "

He turned to us.

"I will bleed him," he said. "For what saith the learned Hippocrates?" Whereupon he mouthed out a rigmarole of Latin phrases, wherein I could detect neither cohesion nor significance.

"Leave him to me, gentlemen!" he continued with a third flourish of his wrist. "Leave him to me and Hippocrates!"

"Which we do," I replied, "with the more confidence in that Hippocrates had so much fore-knowledge of the Latin tongue."

And so we got us back to the parlour. How the minutes dragged! Through the door I could still hear the noise of the man's breathing; and now and again the light clink of instruments and a trickling sound as of blood dripping into a bason. I paced impatiently about the room, while Jack sat him down at the table and began loading his pistols.

"The twenty-first!" I exclaimed, "and this day is the fourteenth. Seven days, Jack! I have but seven days to win from here to Bristol."

I went to the window and leaned out. Swasfield's horse was standing quietly in the road, tethered by the bridle to a tree.

"'Canst do it, Morrice, if the wind holds fair," replied Jack. "Heaven send a wind!" and he rose from the table and joined me. Together we stretched out to catch the least hint of a breeze. But not a breath came to us; not a tree shimmered, not a shadow stirred. The world slumbered in a hot stupor. It seemed you might have felt the air vibrate with the passage of a single bird.

Of a sudden Larke cried out:

"Art sure 'tis the fourteenth to-day?"

With that we scrambled back into the room and searched for a calendar.

"Ay, lad!" he said ruefully as he discovered it; "'tis the fourteenth, not a doubt of it."

I flung myself dejectedly on the couch. The volume of Horace lay open by my hand, and I took it up, and quite idly, with no thought of what I was doing, I wrote this date and the name of the month and the date of the year on the margin of the page.

"Lord!" exclaimed Jack, flinging up his hands. "At the books again? Hast no boots and spurs?"

I slipped the book into my pocket, and sprang to my feet. In the heat of my anxiety I had forgotten everything but this half-spoken message. But, or ever I could make a step, the door of the bedroom opened and the surgeon stepped into the room.

"Can he speak now?" I asked.

"The fit has not passed," says he.

"Then in God's name, what ails the man?" cries Larke.

"It is a visitation," says the doctor, with an upward cast of his eyes.

"It is a canting ass of a doctor," I yelled in a fury, and I clapped my hat on my head.

"Your boots?" cried Larke.

"I'll e'en go in my shoes," I shouted back.

I snatched up one of Jack's pistols, rammed it into my pocket, and so clattered downstairs and into the street. I untied Swasfield's horse and sprang on to its back.

"Morrice!"

I looked up. Jack was leaning out from the window.

"Morrice," he said whimsically, and with a very winning smile, "'art not so much of a woman after all."

I dug my heels into the horse's flanks and so rode out at a gallop beneath the lime-trees to Rotterdam.

CHAPTER II.

AT Rotterdam I was fortunate enough to light upon a Dutch skipper whose ship was anchored in the Texel, and who purposed sailing that very night for the Port of London. For a while, indeed, he scrupled to set me over, my lack of equipment—for I had not so much with me as a clean shirt—and my great haste to be quit of the country firing his suspicions. However, I sold Swasfield's horse to the keeper of a tavern by the waterside, and adding the money I got thereby to what I held in my pockets, I presently persuaded him; and a light wind springing up about midnight, we weighed anchor and stood out for the sea.

That my purse was now empty occasioned me no great concern, since my cousin, Lord Elmscott, lived at London, in a fine house in Monmouth Square, and I doubted not but what I could instantly procure from him the means to enable me to continue my journey. I was, in truth, infinitely more distressed by the tardiness of our voyage, for towards sunrise the wind died utterly away, and during the next two days we lay becalmed, rocking lazily upon the swell. On the afternoon of the third, being the seventeenth day of the month, a breeze filled our sheets, and we made some progress, although our vessel, which was a ketch and heavily loaded, was a slow sailer at the best. But during the night the breeze quickened into a storm, and, blowing for twelve hours without intermission or abatement, drove us clean from our course, so that on the morning of the eighteenth we were scurrying northwards before it along the coast of Essex.

This last misadventure cast me into the very bottom of despair. I knew that if I were to prove of timely help in Julian's deliverance, I must needs reach Bristol before his trial commenced, the which seemed now plainly impossible; and, atop of this piece of knowledge, my ignorance of the nature of his calamity, and of the service he desired of me, worked in my blood like a fever.

For Julian and myself were linked together in a very sweet and intimate love. I could not, an I tried, point to its beginning. It seemed to have been native within us from our births. We took it from our fathers before us, and when they died we counted it no small part of our inheritance. Our estates, you should know, lay in contiguous valleys of the remote county of Cumberland, and thus we lived out our boyhood in a secluded comradeship. Seldom a day passed but we found a way to meet. Mostly Julian would come swinging across the fells, his otter-dogs yapping at his heels, and all the fresh morning in his voice. Together we would ramble over the slopes, bathe in the tarns and kelds, hunt,

climb, argue, ay, and fight too, when we were gravelled
for lack of arguments; so that even now, each time
that I turn my feet homewards after a period of
absence, and catch the first glimpse of these brown
hillsides, they become bright and populous with the
rich pageantry of our boyish fancies.

But my clearest recollections of those days centre
about Scafell, and a certain rock upon the Pillar
Mountain in Ennerdale. A common share of peril
is surely the stoutest bond of comradeship. You
may find exemplars in the story of well-nigh every
battle. But to hang half-way up a sheer cliff in
the chill eerie silence, where a slip of the heel, a
falter of the numbed fingers, would hurl both your
companion and yourself upon the stones a hundred
yards below—ah, that turns the friend into something
closer than even a *frère d'armes*. At least, so it was
with Julian and me.

I think, too, that the very difference between us
helped to fortify our love. Each felt the other the
complement of his nature. And in later times, when
Julian would come down from the Court to Oxford,
tricked out in some new French fashion, and with
all sorts of fantastical conceits upon his tongue, my
rooms seemed to glow as with a sudden shaft of
sunlight; and after that he had gone I was ever in
two minds whether to send for a tailor, and follow
him to Whitehall.

But to return to my journey. On the nineteenth
we changed our course, and tacked back to the
mouth of the Thames. But it was not until the
evening of the twentieth that we cast anchor by
London Bridge. From the ship I hurried straight

C

to the house of my cousin, Lord Elmscott, who resided in Monmouth Square, to the north of the town, being minded to borrow a horse of him and some money, and ride forthwith to Bristol. The windows, however, were dark, not a light glimmercd anywhere; and knock with what noise I might, for a while I could get no answer to my summons.

At last, just as I was turning away in no little distress of mind—for the town was all strange to me, and I knew no one else to whom I could apply at that late hour—a feeble shuffling step sounded in the passage. I knocked again, and as loudly as I could; the steps drew nearer, the bolts were slowly drawn from their sockets, and the door opened. I was faced by an old man in a faded livery, who held a lighted candle in his hand. Behind him the hall showed black and solitary.

"I am Mr. Morrice Buckler," said I, "and I would have a word with my cousin, Lord Elmscott."

The old man shook his head dolefully.

"Nay, sir," he replied in a thin, quavering voice, "you do ill to seck him here. At White's perchance you may light on him, or at Wood's, in Pall Mall—I know not. But never in his own house while there is a pack of cards abroad."

I waited not to hear the rest of his complaint, but dashed down the steps and set off westwards at a run. I crossed a lonely and noisome plain which I have since heard is named the pest-field, for that many of the sufferers in the late plague are buried there, and came out at the top of St. James' Street. There a stranger pointed out to me White's coffee-house.

"Is Lord Elmscott within?" I asked of an attendant as I entered.

For reply he looked me over coolly from head to foot.

"And what may be your business with Lord Elmscott?" he asked, with a sneer.

In truth I must have cut but a sorry figure in his eyes, for I was all dusty and begrimed with my five days' travel. But I thought not of that at the time.

"Tell him," said I, "that his cousin, Morrice Buckler, is here, and must needs speak with him." Whereupon the man's look changed to one of pure astonishment. "Be quick, fellow," I cried, stamping my foot; and with a humble "I crave your pardon," he hurried off upon the message. A door stood at the far end of the room, and through this he entered, leaving it ajar. In a moment I heard my cousin's voice, loud and boisterous:

"Show him in! 'Od's wounds, he may change my luck."

With that I followed him. 'Twas a strange sight to me. The room was small, and the floor so thickly littered with cards that it needed the feel of your foot to assure you it was carpeted. A number of gallants in a great disorder of dress stood about a little table whereat were seated a youth barely, I should guess, out of his teens, his face pale, but very indifferent and composed, and over against him my cousin. Elmscott's black peruke was all awry, his cheeks flushed, and his eyes bloodshot and staring.

"Morrice," he cried, "what brings you here in

this plight? I believe the fellow took you for a
bailiff, and, on my life," he added, surveying me, "I
have not the impudence to blame him." Thereupon
he addressed himself to the company. "This,
gentlemen," says he, "is my cousin, Mr. Morrice
Buckler, a very worthy—bookworm."

They all laughed as though there was some wit
in the ill-mannered sally; but I had no time to spare
for taking heed of their foolishness.

"You can do me a service," I said eagerly.

"You give me news," Elmscott laughed. "'Tis a
strange service that I can render. Well, what may
it be?"

"I need money for one thing, and——" A roar
of laughter broke in upon my words.

"Money!" cries Elmscott. "Lord, that any one
should come to me for money!" and he leaned back
in his chair laughing as heartily as the best of them.
"Why, Morrice, it's all gone—all gone into the devil's
whirlpool. Howbeit," he went on, growing suddenly
serious, "I will make a bargain with you. Stand by
my side here. I have it in my mind that you will
bring me luck. Stand by my side, and in return, if
I win, I will lend you what help I may."

"Nay, cousin," said I, "my business will not wait."

"Nor mine," he replied, "nor mine. Stand by
me! I shall not be long. My last stake's on the
table."

He seized hold of my arm as he spoke with
something of prayer in his eyes, and reluctantly I
consented. In truth, I knew not what else to do.
'Twas plain he was in no mood to hearken to my
request, even if he had the means to grant it.

"That's right, lad!" he bawled, and then to the
servant: "Brandy! Brandy, d'ye hear! And a
great deal of it! Now, gentlemen, you will see.
Mr. Buckler is a student of Leyden. 'Tis full time
that some good luck should come to us from
Holland."

And he turned him again to the table. His
pleasantry was received with an uproarious merriment, which methought it hardly merited. But I
have noted since that round a gaming-table, so tense
is the spirit which it engenders, the poorest jest
takes the currency of wit.

I was at first perplexed by the difference of the
stakes. Before my cousin lay a pair of diamond
buckles, but no gold, not so much as a single guinea-
piece. All that there was of that metal lay in
scattered heaps beside his opponent.

Lord Elmscott dealt the hands—the game was
écarté—and the other nodded his request for cards.
Looking over my cousin's shoulder I could see that
he held but one trump, the ten, and a tierce to the
king in another suit. For a little he remained
without answering, glancing indecisively from his
cards to the face of his player. At last, with a touch
of defiance in his voice :

"No!" he said. "'Tis no hand to play on, but
I'll trust to chance."

"As you will," nodded the other, and he led
directly into Elmscott's suit. Every one leaned
eagerly forward, but each trick fell to my cousin, and
he obtained the vole.

"There! I told you," he cries.

His opponent said never a word, but carelessly

pushed a tinkling pile of coins across the table. And
so the play went on; at the finish of each game a
stream of gold drifted over to Lord Elmscott. It
seemed that he could not lose. If he played the
eight, his companion would follow with the seven.

"He hath the devil at his back now," said one of
the bystanders."

"Pardon me!" replied my cousin very politely.
"You insult Mr. Buckler. I am merely fortified with
the learning of Leyden;" and he straightway marked
the king. After a time the room fell to utter silence,
even Elmscott stopped his outbursts. A strange
fascination caught and enmeshed us all; we strained
forward, holding our breaths as we watched the hands,
though each man, I think, was certain what the end
would be. For myself, I honestly struggled against
this devilish enchantment, but to little purpose. The
flutter of the cards made my heart leap. I sought
to picture to myself the long dark road I had to
traverse, and Julian in his prison at the end of it. I
saw nothing but the faces of the players, Elmscott's
flushed and purple, his opponent's growing paler and
paler, while his eyes seemed to retreat into his head
and the pupils of them to burn like points of fire. I
loaded myself with reproaches and abuse, but the
words ran through my head in a meaningless
sequence, and were tuned to a clink of gold.

And then an odd fancy came over me. In the
midst of the yellow heap, ever increasing, on our side
of the table, lay the pair of diamond buckles. I could
see rays of an infinite variety of colours spirting out
like little jets of flame, as the light caught the stones,
and I felt a queer conviction that Elmscott's luck was in

some way bound up with them. So strongly did the whim possess me that I lifted them from the table to test my thought. For so long as took the players to play two games, I held the buckles in my hands; and both games my cousin lost. I replaced them on the table, and he began to win once more with the old regularity, the heaps dwindling there and growing here, until at length all the money lay silted at my cousin's hand. You might have believed that a spell had been suddenly lifted from the company. Faces relaxed and softened, eyes lost their keen light, feet shuffled in a new freedom, and the heavy silence was torn by a Babel of voices. Strangely enough, all joined with Elmscott in attributing his change of fortune to my presence. Snuff-boxes were opened and their contents pressed upon me, and I think that I might have dined at no cost of myself for a full twelve months had I accepted the invitations I received. But the cessation of the play had waked me to my own necessities, and I turned to my cousin.

"Now," said I, but I got no further, for he exclaimed :

"Not yet, Morrice ! There's my house in Monmouth Square."

"Your house ? " I repeated.

"There's the manor of Silverdale."

"You have not lost that ? " I cried.

"Every brick of it," says he.

"Then," says I in a quick passion, "you must win them back as best you may. I'll bide no longer."

"Nay, lad !" he entreated, laying hold of my sleeve. "You cannot mean that. See, when you came in, I had but these poor buckles left. They were all my fortune. Stay but for a little. For if you go you take all my luck with you. 'Am deadly sure of it."

"I have stayed too long as it is," I replied, and wrenched myself free from his grasp.

"Well, take what money you need! But you are no more than a stone," he whimpered.

"The philosopher's stone, then," said I, and I caught up a couple of handsfull of gold and turned on my heel. But with a sudden cry I stopped. For as I turned, I glanced across the table to his opponent, and I saw his face change all in a moment to a strangely grey and livid colour. And to make the sight yet more ghastly, he still sat bolt upright in his chair, without a gesture, without a motion, a figure of marble, save that his eyes still burned steadily beneath his brows.

"Great God!" I cried. "He is dying."

"It is the morning," he said in a quiet voice, which had yet a very thrilling resonance, and it flashed across me with a singular uneasiness that this was the first time that he had spoken during all those hours.

I turned towards the window, which was behind my cousin's chair. Through a chink of the curtains a pale beam of twilight streamed full on to the youth's face. So long as I had stood by Elmscott's side, my back had intercepted it; but as I moved away I had uncovered the window, and it was the grey light streaming from it which had given to him a complexion of so deathly and ashen a colour. I flung the curtains apart, and the chill morning flooded the room. One shiver ran through the company like a breeze through

a group of aspens, and it seemed to me that on the
instant every one had grown old. The heavy gildings,
the yellow glare of the candles, the gaudy hangings
about the walls, seen in that pitiless light, appeared
inexpressibly pretentious and vulgar ; and the gentlemen with their leaden cheeks, their disordered
perukes, and the soiled finery of their laces and
ruffles, no more than the room's fitting complement.
A sickening qualm of disgust shot through me ; the
very air seemed to have grown acrid and stale ; and
yet, in spite of all I stayed—to my shame be it said, I
stayed. However, I paid for the fault—ay, ten times
over, in the years that were to come. For as I
halted at the door to make my bow—my fingers were
on the very handle—I perceived Lord Elmscott with
one foot upon his chair, and the buckles in his hand.
My presentiment came back to me with the conviction
of a creed. I knew—I knew that if he failed to add
those jewels to his stake, he would leave the coffee-
house as empty a beggar as when I entered it. I
strode back across the room, took them from his
hand, and laid them on the table. For a moment
Elmscott stared at me in astonishment. Then I must
think he read my superstition in my looks, for he
said, clapping me on the back :

"You will make a gambler yet, Morrice," and
he sat him down on his chair. I took my former
stand beside him.

"You will stay, Mr. Buckler?" asked his opponent.

"Yes," I replied.

"Then," he continued, in the same even voice, "I
have a plan in my head which I fancy will best suit
the purposes of the three of us. Lord Elmscott is

naturally anxious to follow his luck; you, Mr. Buckler, have overstayed your time ; and as for me— well, it is now Wednesday morning, and a damned dirty morning, too, if I may judge from the counte- nances of my friends.   We have sat playing here since six by the clock on Monday night, and I am weary.   My bed calls for me.   I propose then that we settle the bout with two casts of the dice.   On the first throw I will stake your house in Monmouth Square against the money you have before you.   If I win there's an end.   If you win, I will set the manor of Silverdale against your London house and your previous stake."

A complete silence followed upon his words. Even Lord Elmscott was taken aback by the magni- tude of the stakes.   The youth's proposal gained, moreover, on the mind by contrast with his tone of tired indifference.   He seemed the least occupied of all that company.

" I trust you will accept," he continued, speaking to my cousin with courteous gentleness.   " As I have said, I am very tired.   Luck is on your side, and, if I may be permitted to add, the advantage of the stakes."

Elmscott glanced at me, paused for a second, and then, with a forced laugh :

" Very well ; so be it," he said.   The dice were brought ; he rattled them vigorously, and flung them down.

" Four ! " cried one of the gentlemen.

" Damn ! " said my cousin, and he mopped his forehead with his handkerchief.   His antagonist picked up the dice with inimitable nonchalance,

barely shook them in the cup, and let them roll
idly out on to the table.

"Three!"

Elmscott heaved a sigh of relief. The other
stretched his arms above his head and yawned.

"'Tis a noble house, your house in Monmouth
Square," he remarked.

At the second throw, Elmscott discovered a most
nervous anxiety. He held the cup so long in his
hand that I feared he would lose the courage to
complete the game. I felt, in truth, a personal
shame at his indecision, and I gazed around with
the full expectation of seeing a like feeling expressed
upon the features of those who watched. But they
wore one common look of strained expectancy. At
last Elmscott threw.

"Nine!" cried one, and a low murmur of voices
buzzed for an instant and suddenly ceased as the
other took up the dice.

"Two!"

Both players rose as with one motion. Elmscott
tossed down his throat the brandy in his tumbler—it
had stood by his side untasted since the early part
of the night—and then turned to me with an almost
hysterical outburst.

"One moment."

It was the youth who spoke, and his voice rang
loud and strong. His weariness had slipped from
him like a mask. He bent across the table and
stretched out his arm, with his forefinger pointing at
my cousin.

"I will play you one more bout, Lord Elmscott.
Against all that you have won back from me

to-night—the money, your house, your estate—I will pit my docks in the city of Bristol. But I claim one condition," and he glanced at me and paused.

"If it affects my cousin's presence——" Elmscott began.

"It does not," the other interrupted. "'Tis a trivial condition—a whim of mine, a mere whim."

"What is it, then?" I asked, for in some unaccountable way I was much disquieted by his change of manner, and dreaded the event of his proposal.

"That while your cousin throws you hold his buckles in your hands."

It were impossible to describe the effect which this extraordinary request produced. At any other time it would have seemed no more than laughable. But after these long hours of play we were all tinder to a spark of superstition. Nothing seemed too whimsical for belief. Luck had proved so tricksy a sprite that the most trivial object might well take its fancy and overset the balance of its favours. The fierce vehemence of the speaker, besides, breaking thus unexpectedly through a crust of equanimity, carried conviction past the porches of the ears. So each man hung upon Elmscott's answer as upon the arbitrament of his own fortune.

For myself, I took a quick step towards my cousin; but the youth shot a glance of such imperious menace at me that I stopped shamefaced like a faulty schoolboy. However, Elmscott caught my movement and, I think, the look which arrested me.

"Not to-day," he said, "if you will pardon me. I am over-tired myself, and would fain keep to our bargain." Thereupon he came over to me. "Now,

Morrice," he exclaimed, "it is your turn. You have the money. What else d'ye lack? What else d'ye lack?"

"I need the swiftest horse in your stables," I replied.

Elmscott burst into a laugh.

"You shall have it—the swiftest horse in my stables. You shall e'en take it as a gift. Only I fear 'twill leave your desires unsatisfied." And he chuckled again.

"Then," I replied, with some severity, for in truth his merriment struck me as ill-conditioned, "then I shall take the liberty of leaving it behind at the first post on the Bristol Road."

"The Bristol Road?" interposed the youth. "You journey to Bristol?"

I merely bowed assent, for I was in no mood to disclose my purpose to that company, and caught up my hat; but he gently took my arm and drew me into the window.

"Mr. Buckler," he said, gazing at me the while with quiet eyes, "Fortune has brought us into an odd conjunction this night. I have so much of the gambler within me as to believe that she will repeat the trick, and I hope for my revenge."

He held out his hand courteously. I could not but take it. For a moment we stood with clasped hands, and I felt mine tremble within his.

"Ah!" he said, smiling curiously, "you believe so, too." And he made me a bow and turned back into the room.

I remained where he left me, gazing blindly out of the window; for the shadow of a great trouble had fallen across my spirit. His words and the concise certainty of his tone had been the perfect voicing of my own forebodings. I did indeed believe that Fortune would some day pit us in a fresh antagonism ; that somewhere in the future she had already set up the lists, and that clasp of the hands I felt to be our bond and surety that we would keep faith with her and answer to our names.

"Morrice," said Elmscott at my elbow, and I started like one waked from his sleep, "we'll go saddle your horse."

And he laughed to himself again as though savouring a jest. He slipped an arm through mine and walked to the door.

"Good morning, gentlemen," he said. "Marston, *au revoir !*" And with a twirl of his hat, he stepped into the outer room. His servant was sleeping upon a bench, and he woke him up and bade him fetch the money and follow home.

The morning was cold, and we set off at a brisk pace towards Monmouth Square, Elmscott chatting loudly the while, with ever and again, I thought, a covert laugh at me.

I only pressed on the harder. It was not merely that I was vexed by his quizzing demeanour ; but the moment I was free from that tawdry hell, and began to breathe fresh air in place of the heavy reek of perfumes and wine, the fulness of my disloyalty rolled in upon my conscience, so that Elmscott's idle talk made me sicken with repulsion ; for he babbled ever about cards and dice and the feminine caprice of luck.

"What ails you, Morrice ? " at length he inquired,

seeing that I had no stomach for his mirth. "You look as spiritless as a Quaker."

"I was thinking," I replied, in some irritation, for he clapped me on the back as he spoke, "that it must be sorely humiliating for a man of your age either to win money or lose it when you have a mere stripling to oppose you."

"A man of my age, indeed!" he exclaimed. "And what age do you take to be mine, Mr. Buckler?"

He turned his face angrily towards me, and I scanned it with great deliberation.

"It would not be fair," I answered, with a shake of the head. "It would not be fair for me to hazard a guess. Two nights at play may well stamp middle-age upon youth, and decrepitude upon middle-age."

At this he knew not whether to be mollified or yet more indignant, and so did the very thing I had been aiming at—he held his tongue. Thus we proceeded in a moody silence until we were hard by Soho. Then he asked suddenly:

"What drags you in such a scurry to Bristol?"

"I would give much to know myself," I answered. "I journey thither at the instance of a friend who lies in dire peril. But that is the whole sum of my knowledge. I have not so much as a hint of the purport of my service."

"A friend! What friend?" he inquired with something of a start, and looked at me earnestly.

"Sir Julian Harnwood," said I, and he stopped abruptly in his walk.

"Ah!" he said; then he looked on the ground, and swore a little to himself.

"You know what threatens him?" said I; but he made me no answer and resumed his walk, quickening his pace. "Tell me!" I entreated. "His servant came to me at Leyden six days ago, but was seized by a fit or ever he could out with his message. So I learnt no more than this—that Julian lies in Bristol gaol and hath need of me."

"But the assizes begin to-day," he interrupted, with an air of triumph. "You are over-late to help him."

"Ah, no!" I pleaded. "I may yet reach there in time. Julian may haply be amongst the last to come to trial?"

"'Twere most unlikely," returned he, with a snap of his teeth. "My Lord Jeffries wastes no time in weighing evidence. Why, at Taunton, but a fortnight ago, one hundred and forty-five prisoners were disposed of within three days. The man does not try; he executes. There's but one outlook for your friend, and that's through the noose of a rope. Jeffries holds a strict mandate from the King, I tell you, for the King's heart is full of anger against the rebels."

"But Julian was no rebel," I exclaimed.

"Tut, tut, lad!" he replied. "If he was no rebel himself, he harboured rebels. If he didn't flesh his sword at Sedgemoor, he gave shelter to those that did. And 'tis all one crime, I tell you. Hair-splitting is held in little favour at the Western Assizes."

"But are you sure of this?" I asked. "Or is it pure town gossip?"

"Nay," said he, "I have the news hot from Marston. He should know, eh?"

"Marston?" said I.

"Yes! The"—and he paused for a second, and smiled at me—"the *man* who played with me. 'Tis his sister that's betrothed to Harnwood."

His sister! The blood chilled in my veins. I had been aware, of course, that Julian was affianced to a certain Miss Marston of the county of Gloucestershire. But I had never set eyes upon her person and knew little of her history, beyond that she had been one of the ladies in attendance upon the Queen prior to her accession to the throne; I mean when she was still the Duchess of York. Miss Marston was, in fact, a mere name to me; and since consequently she held no place in my thoughts, it had not occurred to me to connect her in any way with this chance acquaintance of the gaming-table. Now, however, the relationship struck me with a peculiar and even menacing significance. It recalled to me the few words Marston had spoken in the window; and, lo! not half an hour after their utterance, here was, as it were, a guarantee of their fulfilment. Between Marston and myself there already existed, then, a certain faint accidental connection. I felt that I had caught a glimpse of the cord which was to draw us together.

Elmscott's voice broke in upon my imaginings.

"So, Morrice, I have sure knowledge to back my words. No good can come of your journey, though harm may, and it will fall on you. 'Twere best to stay quietly in London. You may think your hair grey, but you will never save Julian Harnwood from the gallows."

My cheeks burned as I heard him, for my thoughts

D

had been humming busily about my own affairs, and not at all about Julian's; and with a bitter shame, "God!" I cried, "that I should fail him so! Surely never was a man so misused as my poor friend! He is the very sport and shuttlecock of disaster. First his messenger must needs fall sick; then my boat must take five days to cross to England. And to cap it all, I must waste yet another night in a tavern or ever I can borrow a horse to help me on my way."

By this time we had got to Elmscott's house. He drew a key from his pocket and mounted the steps thoughtfully, and I after him. On the last step, however, he turned, and laying a hand upon my shoulder, as I stood below him, said, with a very solemn gravity: "There is God's hand in all this. He doth not intend you should go. In His great wisdom He doth not intend it. He would punish the guilty, and He would spare you who are innocent."

"But what harm can come to me?" I cried, with a laugh; though, indeed, the laugh was hollow as the echo of an empty house.

"That lies in the dark," said he. "But 'tis no common aid Julian Harnwood asks from you. He has friends enough in England. Why should he send to Holland when his time's so short?" And then he added with more insistent earnestness: "Don't go, lad! If any one could avail, 'twould be Marston. He has power in Bristol. And you see, he bides quietly in London."

"But methinks he was never well-disposed to Julian," said I, remembering certain half-forgotten phrases of my friend. "He looked but sourly on the marriage."

"Very well," said he, with a shrug of the shoulders. "Must make your own bed;" and he opened the door, and led me through the hall and into a garden at the back. At the far end of this the stables were built, and we crossed to them. "The rascals are still asleep," he remarked, and proceeded to waken them with much clanging of the bell and shouts of abuse. In a while we heard a heavy step stumbling down the stair.

"I had meant to have a fine laugh at you over this," said Elmscott, with a rueful smile. "But I have no heart for it now that I know your errand."

An ostler, still blinking and drowsy, opened the door. He rubbed his eyes at the sight of his master.

"Don't stand gaping, you fish!" cried my cousin. "Whom else did you expect to see? Show us to the stables."

The fellow led us silently into the stables. A long row of boxes stood against the wall, all neatly littered with straw, but to my astonishment and dismay, so far as I could see, not one of them held a horse.

"She's at the end, sir," said the groom; and we walked down the length of the boxes, and halted before the last.

"Get up, lass!" and after a few pokes the animal rose stiffly from its bed. For a moment I well-nigh cried from sheer mortification. Never in all my comings and goings since have I seen such a parody of Nature, not even in the booths of a country fair. 'Twas of a piebald colour, and stood very high, with long thin legs. Its knees were, moreover, broken. It had a neck of extraordinary length, and a huge, absurd head which swung pendulous at the end of it,

D 2

and seemed by its weight to have dragged the beast
out of shape, for the line of its back slanted downwards from its buttocks to its shoulders.

"This is no fair treatment," I exclaimed hotly.
"Elmscott, I deserve better at your hands. 'Tis an
untimely jest, and you might well have spared yourself the pleasure of it."

"And the name of her's Phœbe," he replied
musingly. "'Tis her one good point."

He spoke with so droll a melancholy that I had
some ado to refrain from laughing, in spite of my
vexation.

"But," said I, "surely this is not all your
equipage?"

"Nay," returned he proudly, "I have its saddle
and bridle. But for the rest of my horses, I lost
them all playing basset with Lord Culverton. He
took them away only yesterday morning, but left
me the mare, saying that he had no cart for her
conveyance."

"Well," said I, "I must e'en make shift with her.
She may carry me one stage."

And I walked out of the stables and back into the
hall. Elmscott bade his groom saddle the mare and
followed me, but I was too angry to speak with him,
and seated myself sullenly at a table. However, he
fetched a pie from the pantry and a bottle of wine,
and set them before me. I had eaten nothing since
I had disembarked the night before, and knowing,
besides, that I had a weary day in store, I fell to with
a good appetite. Elmscott opened the door. The
sun had just risen, and a warm flood of light poured
into the hall and brightened the dark panels of the

walls. With that entered the sound of birds singing, the rustle of trees, and all the pleasant garden-smells of a fresh September morning. And at once a great hope sprang up in my heart that I might yet be in time to prove the minister of Julian's need. I heard the sound of hoofs on the road outside.

"Lend me a whip!" I cried.

"You are still set on going?"

"Lend me a whip!"

He offered me an oak cudgel.

"Phœbe has passed her climacteric, and her perceptions are dull," he said; and then with a sudden change of manner he laid his hand on my shoulder. "'Twere best not to go," he declared earnestly. "Those who bring luck to others seldom find great store of it themselves."

But in the sweet clearness of the morning such thoughts seemed to me no more than night vapours, and I sprang down the steps with a laugh. The mare shivered as I mounted, and swung her head around as though she would ask me what in the devil's name I was doing on her back. But I thwacked her flanks with the cudgel, and she ambled heavily through the square. I turned to look behind me. Elmscott was still standing on the steps.

"Morrice," he called out, "be kind to her! She is an heirloom."

CHAPTER III.

AT length, then, I was fairly started on my way to
Bristol. For my direction over this first stage of my
journey I had made inquiries of Elmscott, and I
rode westwards towards the village of Knightsbridge,
thanking Providence most heartily for that the city
still slept. For what with my disordered dress, my
oak cudgel, and the weedy screw which I bestrode—
I scruple to dignify her with the name of mare, for
I have owned mares since which I loved, and would
not willingly affront them—I could not hope to pass
unnoticed were any one abroad, and, indeed, should
esteem myself well-used to be counted no worse
than a mountebank. Thus I crossed Hounslow
Heath and reached Brentford without misadventure.
There I joyfully parted with my Rosinante, and hiring
a horse, rode post. The way, however, was ill-suited
for speedy travelling, and my hope of seeing Julian
that night dwindled with my shadow as the sun rose
higher and higher behind my shoulders. Ruts deep
and broad as new furrows trenched the road, and
here and there some slough would make a wide

miry gap, wherein my horse sank over the fetlocks.
Some blame, moreover, must attach to me, for I
chose a false turn at the hamlet of Colnbrook, and
journeyed ten miles clean from my path to Datchet ;
so that in the end night found me blundering on the
edge of Wickham Heath, some sixty-one miles from
London. I had changed horses at Newbury, and
I determined to press on at least so far as Hungerford. But I had not counted with myself. I was
indeed overwrought with want of sleep, and the last
few stages I had ridden with dulled senses in a
lethargy of fatigue. At what point exactly I wandered from the road I could not tell. But the
darkness had closed in before I began to notice a
welcome ease and restfulness in the motion of the
gallop. I was wondering idly at the change, when of
a sudden my horse pops his foot into a hole. The
reins were hanging loose on his neck ; I myself was
rocking in the saddle, so that I shot clean over his
shoulder, turned a somersault in mid-air, and came
down flat on my back in the centre of the Heath.
For a while I lay there without an effort or desire to
move. I felt as if Mother Earth had taken pity
on my weariness, and had thus unceremoniously
put me to bed. The trample of hoofs, however,
somewhat too close to my legs, roused me to wakefulness, and I started up and prepared to remount.
To my dismay I found that my horse was badly
lamed ; he could barely set his foreleg to the ground.
The accident was the climax of my misfortunes. I
looked eagerly about me. The night was moonless,
but very clear and soft with the light of the stars. I
could see the common stretching away on every

side empty and desolate ; here a cluster of trees,
there a patch of bushes, but never a house, never
the kindly twinkle of a lamp, never a sign of a living
thing.   What it behoved me to do, I could not come
at, think as hard as I might.   But whatever that
might have been, what I did, alas ! was far different.
For I plumped myself down on the grass and cried
like a child.   It seemed to me that God's hand was
indeed turned against my friend and his deliverance.

But somehow into the midst of my lament there
slipped a remembrance of Jack Larke.   On the
instant his face took shape and life before me,
shining out as it were from a frame of darkness.
I saw an honest scorn kindle in his eyes, and his
lips shot " woman " at me.   The visionary picture
of him braced me like the cut of a whip.   At all
events, I thought, I would make a pretence of manhood, and I ceased from my blubbering, and laying
hold of the horse by the bridle, led him forward over
the Heath.

I kept a sharp watch about me as I walked, but
it must have been a full two hours afterwards when
I caught a glimpse of a light far away on my left
hand, glimmering in a little thicket upon a swell
of the turf.   At first I was minded to reckon it a
star, for the Heath at that point was ridged up
against the sky.   But it shone with a beam too
warm and homely to match the silver radiance of
the planets.   I turned joyfully in its direction, and
quickening my pace, came at length to the back of a
house.   The light shone from a window on the
ground floor facing me.   I looked into it over a little
paling, and saw that it was furnished as a kitchen.

Plates and pewter-pots gleamed orderly upon the shelves, and a row of noble hams hung from the rafters.

I hurried round the side of the house and found myself, to my great satisfaction, on a bank which overlooked the road. I scrambled down the side of it and knocked loudly at the door. It was opened by an elderly man, who stared at me in some surprise.

"You travel late, young sir," said he, holding the door ajar.

"I have need to," I replied. "I should have been in Bristol long ere this."

"'Tis strange," he went on, eyeing me a thought suspiciously. "I caught no sound of your horse's hoofs upon the road."

"'Twould have been stranger if you had," said I. "For I missed my way soon after sundown, and have been wandering since on the Heath. I saw the light of your house some half an hour agone over yonder," and I pointed in the direction whence I had come.

"Then you are main lucky, sir," he returned, but in a more civil tone. "This is the 'Half-way House,' and it has no neighbours. In another hour we should have gone to bed—for we have no guests to-night— and you might have wandered until dawn."

With that he set the door back against the wall, and stood aside for me to pass.

"You must pardon my surliness," he said. "But few honest travellers cross Wickham Heath by dark, and at first I mistook you. I have never held truck with the gentry of the road, though, indeed, my pockets suffer for the ease of my conscience. However, if you will step within, my wife will get you supper while I lead your horse to the stables."

"The beast is lame," said I, "and I would fain continue my way to-night. Have you a horse for hire?"

"Nay, sir," said he, shaking his head. "I have but one horse here besides your own, and that is not mine."

"I need it only for a day," I urged eagerly; "for less than a day. I could reach Bristol in the morning, and would send it you back forthwith."

I plunged my hand into my fob, and pulled out a handful of money as I spoke.

"It is no use," he declared. "The horse is not mine. 'Twas left here for a purpose, and I may not part with it."

"It would be with you again to-morrow," I repeated.

"It may be needed in the meanwhile," said he. "It may be needed in an hour. I know not."

I let the coins run from my right hand into the palm of my left, so that they fell clinking one on the top of the other. For a second he stood undecided ; then he spoke in a low voice like a man arguing with himself.

"I will not do it. The horse was left with me in trust—in trust. Moreover, I was well paid for the trust." And he turned to me.

"Put up your money, sir," said he stubbornly. "You should think shame to tempt poor folk. You will get no horse 'twixt here and Hungerford."

I slipped the money back into my pocket while

he moved away with the horse. It limped worse than
ever, and he stopped and picked up its foreleg.

" It is no more than a strain, I think," he called
out. " The wife shall make a poultice for it to-night,
and you can start betimes in the morning."

It was a poor consolation, but the only one. So
I made the best of it, and, taking my supper in the
kitchen, went forthwith to bed. I was indeed so
spent and tired that I fell asleep in the corner by the
fire while my ham was being fried, and after it, was
almost carried upstairs in the arms of my landlord.
I had not lain in a bed since I left Leyden, and few
sights, I think, have ever affected me with so pleasant
a sense of rest and comfort as that of the little inn-
chamber, with its white dimity curtains and lavender-
scented sheets. I have, in truth, always loved the
scent of lavender since.

The next morning I was early afoot, and, des-
patching a hasty breakfast, made my way to the
stables. The innkeeper had preceded me in order
to have all ready for my start ; but he stood in the
yard with the horse unsaddled.

" 'Tis no use, sir," he said. " You must e'en walk
to Hungerford."

I had but to see the horse take one step to realise
the truth of his words, for it limped yet worse than
the evening before. The foot, moreover, was exceeding hot and inflamed.

" Take it back," said I. " The poor beast must
bide here till I return."

I followed him into the stable, and inquired of
the road.

" You go straight," he said, "till you come to

Barton Court, opposite the village of Kintbury—"
when of a sudden I stopped him. There were but
two stalls in the building, and I had just caught a
glimpse of the horse which was tied up in the second.
It was of a light chestnut in colour, with white
stockings, and a fleck of white in its coat at the joint
of the hip. The patch was like a star in shape, and
very unusual.

"Why, this is Sir Julian Harnwood's horse," I
cried, leaping towards it—"his favourite horse!"

"Yes," he said, looking at me with some surprise,
"that was the name—Sir Julian Harnwood. 'Tis the
horse I told you of last night."

And in a flash the truth came upon me.

"It waits for me," I said. "Quick, man, saddle
it! Sir Julian's life hangs upon your speed."

But he planted himself sturdily before me.

"Not so fast, young master," he said. "That
trick will not serve your turn. 'Tis Sir Julian's horse,
sure enough, and it waits its rider, sure enough; but
that you are he, I must have some better warrant
than your word."

"My name may prove it," I replied. "It is
Buckler—Morrice Buckler. Sir Julian's servant came
to me in Holland."

"Buckler!" the man repeated, as though he heard
it for the first time. "Morrice Buckler! Yes, sir,
that may be your name. I have nothing against it
beyond that it is unfamiliar in these parts. But a
strange name is a poor thing to persuade a man to
forego his trust."

I looked at the man. Though elderly and somewhat bent, he was of a large frame, and the sinews

stood out in knots upon his bared arms. Plainly I was no match for him if it came to a struggle; and a sickening feeling of impotence and futility surged up within me. At every turn of the road destiny had built up its barrier. I understood that the clue to the matter lay hidden in that untold message which had been vainly conveyed to Leyden; that Swasfield had some pass-word, some token to impart whereby I might make myself known along the road.

" The horse waits for me," I cried, my voice rising as I beseeched him. " In very truth it waits for me. Doubtless I should have some proof of that. But the man that bid me come fell in a swoon or ever he could hand it me."

The innkeeper smiled, and sat him down on a corn-bin. Indeed, the explanation sounded weak enough to me, who was witness of its truth. I should hardly have credited it from another's lips.

" Oh, can't you see," I entreated, in an extremity of despair, "can't you feel that I am telling you God's truth?"

" No, master," he answered slowly, shaking his head, " I feel nought of that sort."

His words and stolid bumpkin air threw me into a frenzy of rage.

" Then," cried I, " may the devil's curse light on you and yours! That horse was left with you in trust. You have dinned the word into my ears; there's no gainsaying it. And I claim the fulfilment of your trust. Understand, fellow!" I went on, shaking my hand at him, for I saw his mouth open and his whole face broaden out into a laugh. " It's not a horse you are stealing; it is a life—a man's innocent life!"

Thereupon he broke in upon my passion with a
great gust of mirth that shook him from head to foot.
"Lord, master!" said he, "that be mighty fine
play-acting. I don't know that I ever saw better
in Newberry Market"—and he slapped a great fist
upon his thigh. "No, I'll be danged if I did. Go
on! go on! Lord, I could sit here and laugh till
dinner." And he thrust his feet forward, plunged
his hands in his breeches pockets, and rolled back
against the wall. I watched him in an utter vacancy
of mind. For his stupid laughter had quenched me
like a pailful of cold water. I searched for some
device by which I might outwit his stubbornness.
Not the smallest seed of a plan could I discover. I
sent my thoughts back to the morning of the fourteenth, and cudgelled my memory in the hope that
Swasfield might have dropped some hint which had
passed unnoticed. But he had said so little, and I
remembered his every word. Then in a twinkling I
recollected the charms which I had found upon his
person. Perchance one of them was the needed
token. No idea was too extravagant for me to grasp
at it. What had I done with them? I thought. I
clapped my hand into the pocket of my coat, and
my fingers closed, not on the charms, but on the
barrel of the pistol which Larke had handed to me
at the moment of my setting out. In an instant my
mind was made up. I must have that horse, cost
what it might. 'Twas useless to argue with my
landlord. Money I had made trial of the night
before. And here were the minutes running by, and
each one of them, it might be, a drop of Julian's
blood!

I walked quickly to the door, at once to disengage
the pistol secretly and to hide any change in my
countenance. But the cock must needs catch in the
flap of my pocket as I drew the weapon out. I
heard a startled cry behind me, a rattle of the corn-
bin, and a clatter of heavy shoes on the ground. I
took one spring out of the stable, turned, and levelled
the barrel through the doorway. For a moment
we stood watching one another, he crouched for a
leap, I covering his eyes with the pistol.

"Saddle that horse," I commanded, "and bring
it out into the road!"

It was his turn now to argue and entreat, but I
had no taste at the moment for "play-acting."

"Be quick, man!" I said. "You have wasted
time enough. Be quick, else I'll splatter your head
against the wall!"

The fellow rose erect and did as I bid, while
I stood in the doorway and railed at him. For,
alas! I was never over-generous by nature.

"Hurry, you potatoe!" I exclaimed. Why that
word above all other and more definite terms of
abuse should have pained him I know not. But so it
was; "Potatoe" grieved him immeasurably, and
noting that, I repeated it more often, I fear me, than
fitted my dignity. At length the horse was saddled.

"Lead it out!" I said, and walked backwards to
the road with my pistol still levelled.

He followed me with the horse, and I bade him
go back into the stable and close the door. Then I
put up my pistol, sprang into the saddle, and started
at a gallop past the inn. I had ridden little more
than a hundred yards when I chanced to look back.

My host was standing in the centre of the way, his legs firmly apart, and a huge blunderbuss at his shoulder. I flung my body forward on the neck of the horse, and a shower of slugs whistled through the air above my head. I felt for my pistol to return the compliment, but 'twould have been mere waste of the shot; I should never have hit him. So I just curved my hand about my mouth and bawled "Potatoe" at the top of my voice. It could have done no less hurt than his slugs.

The horse, fresh from its long confinement, answered gladly to my call upon its speed, and settled into a steady gallop. But for all that, though I pressed on quickly through Marlborough and Chippenham, the nearer I came to Bristol the more lively did my anxieties become. I began to ponder with an increasing apprehension on the business which Julian might have in store for me. The urgency of his need had been proved yet more clearly that morning. The horse which I bestrode was a fresh and convincing evidence; and I could not but believe that similar relays were waiting behind me the whole length of the road from London.

At the same time, as Elmscott had urged, I could bring him no solace of help in the matter of his trial. It would need greater authority than mine to rescue him from Jeffries' clutches. I realised that there must be some secret trouble at the back, and the more earnestly I groped after a hint of its nature, the more dark and awesome the riddle grew.

For, to my lasting shame I own it, Elmscott's forebodings recurred to me with the mystical force of a prophecy:

"There is God's hand in all this. He doth not mean you should go."

The warning seemed traced in black letters on the air before me ; fear whispered it at my heart, and the very hoofs of the horse beat it out in a ringing menace from the ground.

At last, when I was well-nigh in the grips of a panic, over the brow of a hill I saw a cluster of church-spires traced like needles against the sun, and in a sudden impulse to outstrip my cowardice I drove my heels into my horse's flanks, and an hour later rode through Lawford's Gate into Bristol town. I inquired of the first person I met where the Court was sitting. At the Guildhall, he told me, and pointed out the way. A clock struck four as he spoke, and I hurriedly thanked him and hastened on.

About the Guildhall a great rabble of people swung and pressed, and I reined up on the farther side of the street, but as nearly opposite to the entrance as I could force my way. In front of the building stood a carriage very magnificently equipped, with four horses, and footmen in powdered wigs and glistening liveries.

From such converse as went on about me, I sought to learn what prisoners had been tried that day. But so great was the confusion of voices, curses, lamentations, and rejoicings being mixed and blended in a common uproar, that I could gather no knowledge that was particular to my purpose. Then from the shadow of the vestibule shot a gleam of scarlet and white, and at once a deep hush fell upon the crowd. Preceded by his officers, my lord Jeffries stepped out to his carriage, a man of a royal

E

mien, with wonderfully dark and piercing eyes, though
the beauty of his face was much marred by spots
and blotches, and an evil smile that played incessantly
about his lips.   He seemed in truth in high good-
humour, and laughed boisterously with those that
attended him ; and bethinking me of his savage
cruelty, and the unholy lustfulness wherewith he
was wont to indulge it, my heart sank in fear for
Julian.

The departure of his carriage seemed to lift a
weight from every tongue, and the clamour recom-
menced.   I cast about for some one to approach,
when I beheld a little man with a face as wrinkled
and withered as a dry pippin, pressing through the
throng in my direction.   I thought at first that he
intended speech with me, for he looked me over with
some care.   But he came straight on to the horse's
head, and without pausing walked briskly along its
side to my right hand and disappeared behind me.
A minute after I heard the noise of a dispute on my
left.   There was my little friend again.   He had
turned on his steps, and moving in the contrary
direction had come up with me once more.   In the
hurry of his movements he had knocked up against a
passer-by, and the pair straightway fell loudly to
argument, each one accusing the other of clumsiness.
I turned in my saddle to watch the quarrel, and
immediately the little man, with profuse apologies,
took the blame upon himself and continued his way.
I followed him with my eyes.   He had proceeded
but ten yards when his pace began to slacken, then
he dropped into a saunter, and finally stood still
in a musing attitude with his eyes on the ground, as

though he was debating some newly-remembered
question. Of a sudden he raised his head, shot one
quick glance towards me, and resumed his walk.
The street was thinning rapidly, and I was able to
pursue him without difficulty. For half a mile we
went on, keeping the same distance between us, when
he sharply turned a corner and dived into a narrow
side-street. I checked my horse, thinking that I had
mistaken his look; for he had never so much as
turned round since. But the next minute he reappeared, and stood loitering in his former attitude
of reflection. There could be no doubt of the man's
intention, and I gathered up the reins again and
followed him. This side-street was narrow and
exceeding dark, for the storeys of the houses on each
side projected one above the other until the gables
nearly met at the top. The little man was waiting
for me about twenty yards from the entrance, in an
angle of the wall.

"It is Mr. Buckler?" he asked shortly.

"Yes," I answered. "What news of Julian?"

"You have but just arrived?"

"The clock struck four as I rode through Lawford's Gate. What news of Julian?"

He gave a sharp, sneering laugh.

"Ay, ay," he said. "No one so flustered as
your loiterer." And he stepped out from the shadow
of the house. "Sir Julian?" he cried hastily. "Sir
Julian will be hanged at noon to-morrow."

I swayed in the saddle; the houses spun round
me. I felt the man's arm catch at and steady me.

"It is my fault?" I whispered.

"No, lad!" he returned, with a new touch of kind-

E 2

liness in his tone. "Nothing could have saved him.
I should know; I am his attorney. Maybe I spoke
too harshly, but this last week he has been eating his
heart out for the sight of you, and your tardiness
plagued me. There, there ! Lay hold of your pluck !
It is a man your friend needs, not a weak girl."

There was a pitying contempt in the tone of these
last words which stung me inexpressibly. I sat up
erect, and said, with such firmness as I could force
into my voice :

"Where does Sir Julian lie ? "

"In the Bridewell to-night. But you must not go
there in this plight," he added quickly, for I was
already turning the horse. "You would ruin all."

He glanced sharply up and down the lane, and
went on :

"We have been together over-long as it is." Then
he tapped with his foot for a moment on the pavement. "I have it," said he. "Go to the 'Thatched
House Tavern,' in Lime Kiln Lane. I will seek you
there. Wait for me ; and, mind this, let no one else
have talk with you! Tell the people of the house I
sent you—Mr. Joseph Vincott. It will commend
you to their care."

With that he turned on his heel, ran up to the
opening of the street, and after a cautious look this
side and that, strolled carelessly away. I gave him a
few moments' grace, and then hurried with all despatch to the tavern, asking my direction as I went.
There I ordered a private room, and planting myself
at the window, waited impatiently for Vincott's
coming.

It must have been an hour afterwards that I saw

him turn into the lane from a passage almost opposite to where I stood. I expected him to cross the road, but he cast not so much as a glance towards the inn, and walked slowly past on the further side. I flung up the window, thinking that he had forgotten his errand, and leaned out to call him. But or ever I could speak he banged his stick angrily on the ground, raised it with a quick jerk and pointed twice over his shoulder behind him. The movement was full of significance, and I drew back into the shadow of the curtain. Mr. Vincott mounted the steps of a house, knocked at the door, and was admitted. No sooner had he entered than a man stepped out from the passage. He was of a large, heavy build, and yet, as I surmised from the litheness of his walk, very close-knit. His face was swarthy and bronzed, and he wore ear-rings in his ears. I should have taken him for an English sailor but that there was a singular compactness in his bearing, and his gait was that of a man perfectly balanced. For awhile he stood loitering at the entrance to the passage, and then noticing the inn, crossed quickly over and passed through the door beneath me.

My senses were now strained into activity, and I watched with a quivering eagerness for the end of this strange game of hide-and-seek. I had not long to wait. The little lawyer came down the steps, stopped at the bottom, took a pinch of snuff with great deliberation, and blowing his nose with unnecessary noise and vehemence, walked down the street. He had nearly reached the end of it before his pursuer lounged out of the inn and strolled in the same direction. The moment Vincott turned the corner, however, he lengthened his stride; I saw him pause at the last house and peep round the angle, draw back for a few seconds, and then follow stealthily on the trail.

The incident reawakened all my perplexed conjectures as to the business on which I was engaged. Why should the fact of my arrival in the town be so studiously concealed? Or again, what reason could there be for any one to suspect or fear it? The questions circled through my mind in an endless repetition. There was but one man who could answer them, and he lay helpless in his cell, adding to the torture of his last hours the belief that his friend had played him false. The thought stung me like Ino's gadfly. I paced up and down the room with my eyes ever on the street for Vincott's return. My heart rose on each sound of a nearing step, only to sink giddily with its dying reverberation. The daylight fell, a fog rolled up from the river in billows of white smoke, and still Vincott did not come. The very clock by the chimney seemed to tick off the seconds faster and faster until I began to fancy that the sounds would catch one another and run by in one continuous note. At last I heard a quick pattering noise of feet on the pavement below, and Vincott dashed up the stairs and burst into the room.

"I have shaken the rascal off," he gasped, falling into a chair; "but curse me if it's lawyer's work. We live too sedentary a life to go dragging herrings across a scent with any profit to our bodies."

"Then we can go," said I, taking my hat. But he struck it from my hands with his cane.

"And you!" he blazed out at me. "You must

poke your stupid yellow head out of the window as if you wanted all Bristol to notice it ! Sit down ! "

" Mr. Vincott ! " I exclaimed angrily.

" Mr. Buckler ! " he returned, mimicking my tone, and pulling a grimace. There was indeed no dignity about the man. " It may not have escaped your perceptions that I have some desire to conceal your visit to this town. Would it be too much to ask you to believe that there are reasons for that desire ? "

He spoke with a mocking politeness, and waited for me to answer him.

" I suppose there are," I replied ; " but I am in the dark as to their nature."

" The chief of them," said he, " is your own security."

" I will risk that," said I, stooping for my hat. " 'Tis not worth the suffering which it costs Julian."

" Dear, dear ! " he gibed. " 'Tis strange that so much heart should tarry so long. Let me see ! It must be full eight days since Swasfield came to you at Leyden." And he struck my hat once more out of my grasp.

" Mr. Vincott," said I—and my voice trembled as I spoke—" if you have a mind to quarrel with me, I will endeavour to gratify you at a more seasonable time. But I cannot wrangle over the body of my friend. I came hither with all the speed that God vouchsafed me." And I informed him of my journey, and the hindrances which had beset my path.

" Well, well," he said, when I had done, " I perceive that my thoughts have done you some injustice. And, after all, I am not sure but what your late coming is for the best. It has caused your friend no small anxiety, I admit. But against that we may set a gain of greater secrecy."

He picked up my hat from the floor, and placed it on the table.

" So," he continued, "you will pardon my roughness, but I have formed some affection for Sir Julian. 'Tis an unbusinesslike quality, and I trust to be well ashamed of it in a week's time. At the present, however, it angered me against you." He held out his hand with a genuine cordiality, and we made our peace.

" Now," said he, " the gist of the matter is this. It is all-essential that you be not observed and marked as a visitor to Sir Julian. Therefore 'twere best to wait until it is quite dark; and meanwhile we must think of some disguise."

" A disguise ? " I exclaimed.

" Yes," said he. " You must have noticed from that window that there are others awake beside ourselves."

I stood silent for a moment, reluctantly considering a plan which had just flashed into my head. Vincott drew a flint and steel from his pocket, and lighted the candles—for the dusk was filling the room—and drew the curtains close. All at once the dizzy faintness which had come over me in the side-street near the Guildhall returned, and set the room spinning about me. I clutched at a chair to save myself from falling. Vincott snatched up a candle, and looked shrewdly into my face.

" When did you dine ? " he asked.

" At breakfast-time," said I.

He opened the door, and rang a bell which stood

on a side-table. "Lucy!" he bawled over the bannisters.

A great buxom wench with a cheery face answered the summons, and he bade her cook what meats they had with all celerity.

"Meantime," said he, "we will while away the interval over a posset of Bristol milk. You have never tasted that, Mr. Buckler? I would that I could say the same. I envy you the pleasure of your first acquaintance with its merit."

The "milk," as he termed it, was a strong brewage of Spanish wine, singularly luxurious and palatable. Mr. Vincott held up his glass to the light, and the liquid sparkled like a clear ruby.

"'Tis a generous drink," he said. "It gives nimbleness to the body, wealth to the blood, and lightness to the heart. The true Promethean fire!" And he drained the glass, and smacked his lips.

"That is a fine strapping wench," said I. "She must be of my height, or thereabouts."

The lawyer cocked his head at me. "Ah!" said he drily, "a wonderful thing is Bristol milk."

But I was thinking of something totally different.

The girl fetched in a stew of beef, steaming hot, and we sat down to it, though indeed I had little inclination for the meal.

"Now, Mr. Vincott," said I, "I will pray you, while we are eating, to help me to the history of Julian's calamities." I think that my voice broke somewhat on the word, for he laid his hand gently upon my arm. "I know nothing of it myself beyond what you have told me, and a rumour that came to me in London."

The lawyer sat silent for a time, drumming with his fingers on the table.

"Your story," I urged, "will save much valuable time when I visit Julian."

"I was thinking," he replied, "how much I should tell you. You see, merely the facts are known to me. Of what lies underneath them—I mean the motives and passions which have ordered their sequence—I may have surmised something" (here his eyes twinkled cunningly), "but I have no certitude. That part of the business concerns you, not me. 'Twere best, then, that I show you no more than the plain face of the matter."

He pushed away his plate, leaned both arms upon the table, and, with a certain wariness in his manner, told me the following tale:

"In the spring of the year, Miss Enid Marston fell sick at Court. The air of St. James's is hardly the best tonic for invalids, and she came with her uncle and guardian to the family house at Bristol to recruit. Sir Julian Harnwood must, of course, follow her; and, in order that he may enjoy her company without encroaching upon her hospitality, he hires him a house in the suburbs, upon Brandon Hill. One night, during the second week of August, came two fugitives from Sedgemoor to his door. Sir Julian had some knowledge of the men, and the story of their sufferings so worked upon his pity that he promised to shelter them until such time as he could discover means of conveying them out of the country. To that end he hid them in one of his cellars, brought their food with his own hands, and generally used such precautions as he thought must avert suspicion.

But on the morning of the 10th September he was
arrested, his house searched, and the rebels discovered. The rest you know. Sir Julian was tried
this afternoon with the two fugitives, and pays the
penalty to-morrow. 'Tis the only result that could
have been looked for. His best friends despaired
from the outset—even Miss Marston."

" I had not thought of her," I broke in. " Poor
girl l "

" Poor girl l " he repeated, gazing intently at the
ceiling. " She was indeed so put back in her health,
that her physician advised her instant removal to a
less afflicting neighbourhood."

As he ended, he glanced sideways at me from
under half-closed lids ; but I chanced to be watching
him, and our eyes crossed. It seemed to me that he
coloured slightly, and sent his gaze travelling idly
about the room, anywhere, in short, but in my
direction, the while he hummed the refrain of a
song.

"You mean she has deserted Julian ?" I exclaimed.

" I have no recollection that I suggested that, or
indeed anything whatsoever," he returned blandly.
" As I mentioned to you before, I merely relate the
facts."

" There is one fact," said I, after a moment's
thought, " on which you have not touched."

" There are two," he replied ; " but specify if
you please. I will satisfy you to the limit of my
powers."

" The part which I shall play in this business."

He wagged his head sorrowfully at me.

"I perceive," says he, "with great regret that they

teach you no logic at the University of Leyden.
You are speaking, not of a fact, but of an hypothesis.
The part which you will play, indeed! You ask me
to read the future, and I am not qualified for the
task."

It became plain to me that I should win no profit
out of my questioning; there could be but one
result to a quibbling match with an attorney; so I
bade him roughly tell me what he would.

"There are two facts," he resumed, "which are
perhaps of interest. But I would premise that they
are 'in no way connected. I would have you bear
that in mind, Mr. Buckler. The first is this: it has
never been disclosed whence the information came
which led to the discovery of the fugitives. Sir
Julian, as I told you, used great precautions. His
loyalty, moreover, had never been suspected up till
then."

"From his servants, most like," I interposed.

"Most like!" he sneered. "The remark does
scanty credit to your perspicacity, and hardly
flatters me. I examined them with some care, and
satisfied myself on the score of their devotion to
their master. 'Tis doubtful even whether they were
aware of Sir Julian's folly. 'Tis most certain that
they never betrayed him. Besides, my lord Jeffries
rated them all most unmercifully this afternoon. He
would not have done that had they helped the
prosecution. No, the secret must have leaked out
if the information had come from them."

"And you could gather no clue?"

"Say, rather, that I did gather no clue. For my
client forbad me to pursue my inquiries. 'Tis strange

that, eh? 'Tis passing strange. It points, I think,
beyond the servants."

"Then Julian himself must know," I cried.

"'Tis a simple thought," said he. "If you will
pardon the hint, you discover what is obvious with a
singular freshness."

I understood that I had brought the rejoinder
upon myself by my interruption, and so digested it
in silence.

"The second point," he continued, "is interesting
as a——" he made the slightest possible pause—"a
coincidence. Sir Julian Harnwood was arrested at
six o'clock in the morning, not in his house, but
something like a mile away, on the King's down.
'Tis a quaint fancy for a gentleman to take it into
his head to stroll about the King's down in the rain
at six o'clock of the morning; almost as quaint as
for an officer to go thither at that hour to search
for him."

An idea sprang through my mind, and was up to
the tip of my tongue. But I remembered the fate
of my previous suggestions, and checked it on the
verge of utterance.

"You were about to proffer a remark," said Mr.
Vincott very politely.

"No!" said I, in a tone of indifference, and he
smiled.

Then his manner changed, and he began to speak
quickly, rapping with his fist upon the table as
though to drive home his words.

"The truth of the matter is, Mr. Buckler, Sir
Julian went out that morning to fight a duel, and his
antagonist was Count Lukstein, who came over to

England six months ago in the train of the Emperor
Leopold's ambassador. Ah! you know him!"
"No!" I replied. "I know of him from Julian."
"They were friends, it appears."
"Julian made the Count's acquaintance some
while ago in Paris, and has, I believe, visited his
home in the Tyrol."
"However that may be, they quarrelled in Bristol.
Count Lukstein came down from London to take
the waters at the Hotwell, by St. Vincent's rock,
and has resided there for the last three months.
'Twas a trumpery dispute, but nought would content
Sir Julian but that they must settle it with swords.
He was on the way to the trysting-place when he
was taken."

And with a final rap on the table, Mr. Vincott
leaned back in his chair, and froze again to a cold
deliberation.

"That," said he, "is the second fact I have to
bring to your notice."

"And the first," I cried, pressing the point on
him, "the first is that no one knows who gave the
information!"

"I observed, I believe," he replied, returning my
gaze with a mild rebuke, "that between those two
facts there is no connection."

At the time it seemed to me that he was bent
on fobbing me off. But I have since thought that
he was answering after his fashion the innuendo
which my words wrapped up. He took out his
snuff-box as he spoke, and inhaled a great pinch.
The action suddenly recalled to me the manœuvres
which I had watched from the window.

"It was a foreigner," I said, starting up in my excitement, "it was a foreigner who dogged your steps this afternoon."

"I like the ornaments of the ceiling," says he (for thither had his eyes returned); and, as though he were continuing the sentence : "I may tell you, Mr. Buckler, that Count Lukstein left Bristol eleven days ago."

"Did he take his servants with him?" I asked; and then, a new thought striking me : "Eleven days ago! That is, Mr. Vincott, the day after Julian's arrest."

"Mr. Buckler," says he, "you appear to me to lack discretion."

"I only re-state your facts," I answered, with some heat.

"The facts themselves are perhaps a trifle indiscreet," he admitted. "I shall certainly have that ceiling copied in my own house." And with that he rose from his chair. "'Tis close on eight by the clock, and we must hit upon some disguise. But, Lord! how it is to be contrived with that canary poll of yours I know not, unless you shave your head and wear my peruke."

"I have a better device than that," said I.

"Well, man, out with it!"

For I spoke with hesitation, fearing his irony.

"You can trust the people of the inn?"

He nodded his head.

"Else I should not have sent you hither. They are bound to me in gratitude. I saved them last year from some pother with the Excise."

"And Lucy—what of her?"

"She is the landlord's daughter."

Thus assured, I delivered to him my plan—that I would mask my person beneath one of Lucy's gowns.

Vincott leapt at the notion. "'Od rabbit me!" he cried, "I misliked your face at first, but I begin to love it dearly now. For I see 'twas given you for some purpose."

Once more he summoned Lucy, invented some story of a jest to be played, and bound her to the straitest secrecy. She gained no inkling from him, you may be sure, of the business which we had in hand. I stripped off my coat, and with much lacing and compressing, much exercise of vigour on Vincott's part, much panting on mine, and more roguish giggling upon Lucy's, I was at last squeezed into the girl's Sunday frock. It had a yellow bodice bedecked with red ribbons, and a red canvas skirt.

"But, la!" she exclaimed, "your feet! Sure you must have a long cloak to hide them." And she whipped out of the room and fetched one. My feet did indeed but poorly match the dress, which descended no lower than my ankles.

By good fortune the cloak had a hood attached, which could be drawn well forward, and blurred my features in its shadow.

"So!" said I. "I am ready." And I strode quickly to the door. For Lucy's glee and my masquerading weighed with equal heaviness upon me. I was full-charged with sorrow for the coming interview. The old days in Cumberland lived and beat within my heart; the old dreams of a linked future voiced themselves again with a very bitter

irony. 'Twas the last time my eyes were to be
gladdened with the sight of my loved friend and
playmate. I looked upon this visit as the sacred
visit to a death-bed; nay, as something yet more
sad than that, for Julian lay a-dying in the very
bloom of health and youth, and the grotesque
guise in which I went forth to him seemed to
mock and flout the solemnity of the occasion.

"Stop, lad!" said Vincott. "You must never
walk like that. Your first step would betray you.
Watch me!"

With a peacock air, which at another time
would have appeared to me inimitably ludicrous,
the little attorney minced across the room on
the tips of his toes. Lucy leaned against the wall
holding her sides, and fairly screamed with delight.

"What ails you, lass?" said he very sternly.

"La, Mr. Vincott," she gulped out between
bubbles of laughter, "I think you have but few
honest women among your clients."

Mr. Vincott rebuked her at some length for
her sauciness, and would have prolonged his lecture
yet further, but that my impatience mastered me
and I haled him from the room. The girl let us
out by a small door which gave on to an alley
at the back of the house. The night was pitch-
dark, and the streets deserted; not even a lamp
swung from a porch.

"Stay here for a moment," whispered Vincott.
"I will move ahead and reconnoitre."

His feet echoed on the cobbles with a strange
lonely sound. In a minute or so a low whistle
reached my ears, and I followed him.

F

" All's clear," he said. " I little thought the time would ever come when I should bless his late Majesty King Charles for forbidding the citizens of Bristol to light their streets."

We stepped quickly forward, threading the quiet roads as noiselessly as we could, until Vincott stopped before a large building. Lights streamed from the windows, piercing the mirk of the night with brownish rays, and a dull muffled clamour rang through the gateway.

" The Bridewell," whispered Vincott. " Keep your face well shrouded, and for God's sake hide your feet ! "

He drew a long breath. I did the same, and we crossed the road and passed beneath the arch.

CHAPTER IV.

MR. VINCOTT knocked at the great door within the arch, and we were presently admitted and handed over to the guidance of a gaoler.

The fellow led us across a courtyard and into a long room clouded and heavy with the smoke of tobacco.

"Keep the hood close!" whispered my companion a second time.

I muffled my face and bent my head towards the ground. For a noisy clamour of drunken songs and coarse merriment, and, mingled with that, a ceaseless rattle of drinking-cans, rose about me on all sides. It seemed that the Bridewell kept open house that night.

We traversed the room, picking out a path among the captives, for even the floor was littered with men in all imaginable attitudes, some playing cards, some asleep, and most of them drunk. My presence served to redouble the uproar, and each moment I feared that my disguise would be detected. I felt that every eye in the room was centred upon my hood. One fellow, indeed, that

F 2

sat talking to himself upon a bench, got unsteadily to his feet and reeled towards us. But or ever he came near, the gaoler cut him across the shoulders with his stick and sent him back howling and cursing.

"Back to your kennel!" he shouted. "'Tis an uncommon wench that would visit the lousy likes o' you."

At the far end of the room he unlocked a door which opened on to a narrow flight of stairs. On the landing above he halted before a second door of a more solid make, the panels being strengthened by cross-beams, and secured with iron bars and a massive lock. The gaoler unfastened it and threw it open.

"You have half an hour, mistress," he said, civilly enough. A startled cry of pain broke from the inside, I heard a sharp clink of fetters, and Julian confronted me through the doorway, his eyes ablaze with passion, and every limb strained and quivering.

"What more? What more, madam?" he asked, in a hoarse, trembling voice. "Are you not satisfied?"

He stopped suddenly with a gasping intake of the breath, and let his head roll forward on his breast like a fainting man. Vincott pushed me gently within the room, and I heard the door clang behind me. For a moment I could not speak. The tears rose in my throat and drowned the words. Julian was the first to recover his composure.

"I crave your pardon," he said, and his voice

sounded in my ears with a sad familiarity like the
echo of our boyhood. "I mistook you for another."
And he sat down on a bench and covered his face
with his hands.

"Julian!" I said, finding at length my voice,
and I held out my hands to him. He uncovered
his face and stared at me in sheer incredulity.
Then with a cry of joy he sprang forwards, stumbling
pitifully from the hindrance of his fetters.

"Morrice at last!" He lifted his hands and
clapped them down into mine, and the quick
movement jerked the chain between his handlocks
so that it fell cold across my wrists. So we stood
silent, memory speeding to and fro between our
eyes and telling the same wistful tale within the
heart of each of us. But in that brumous cell, lit only
by a smoky lamp which served rather to deepen
the shadows of the space which it left obscure
than to illumine the circle immediately about it,
such thoughts could not beguile one long; and
a strange, unaccountable fear began to creep up
in my mind like a mist. It seemed to me that
the chain pressed ever tighter and tighter about
my wrists, and grew cold like a ring of ice. The
chill of it slipped into the marrow of my bones. I
came almost to believe that I myself was manacled,
and with that I felt once again that premonition
of evil drawing near, which had numbed my spirit
in the grey dawn at London. Now, however, the
warning came to me with a clearer and more
particular message. I had a penetrating conviction
that this cell prefigured some scene in the years
to come wherein I should fill the place of Julian;

and, seeing him, I saw a dim image of myself as
when a man looks into a clouded mirror. So
thoroughly, indeed, did the fancy master me that
I too became, as it were, the shadow and reflex
of another, a mere counter and symbol representing
one as yet unknown to me.

"I thought you would never come," said my
friend, and I woke out of my trance.

"I started at once from Leyden," I replied;
but Julian cut short my explanation.

"I am sure of it. I never doubted you.
We have but half an hour, and I have much to
tell."

He turned away and flung himself down on
the bench, which was broad and had a rail at the
back, such as you may see outside a village ale-
house.

"Vincott has told you the history of my arrest?"

"Yes!" said I. The lamp stood upon a stool
beside the bench, and I lifted it up and placed
it on a rough bracket which was fixed to the wall
above. The light fell full upon his face, which
had grown extraordinary thin, with the skin very
bloodless and tight about his jaws, so that the
bones looked to have sharpened. Only around his
eyes was there any colour, and that of a heavy
purple. I sat down upon the stool, and Julian
gave something like a sigh of content.

"I am glad you have come, Morrice," he said.
"It has tired me so, waiting for you."

He closed his eyes wearily, and appeared to be
falling asleep. I touched him on the shoulder,
and he sprang to his feet like one dazed, brush-

ing against the bracket and making the flame of the lamp spirt up with a sudden flare. Once or twice he walked to and fro in the room, as though ordering his speech.

"Here is the kernel of the matter," said he at last, coming back to the bench. "I was arrested to serve no ends of justice, but the vilest treachery and cowardice that man ever heard of. The tale, in truth, seems well-nigh inconceivable. Even I, who have sounding evidence of its truth," and he kicked one of his feet, so that the links of the fetters rattled on the floor, "even I find it hard to believe that 'tis more than a monstrous fable. The man called himself my friend."

"It was Count Lukstein, then?"

"How did you find out that? Vincott could not have told you."

"He did not tell me, but yet he gave me to know it."

"Yes, it was Count Lukstein. He laid the information to spare himself a duel and to get rid of—well, of an obstacle. I meant to kill him. I should have killed him, and he knew it. The duel was arranged secretly on the afternoon of Saturday, the ninth; the spot chosen—a dip in the hill, solitary and unfrequented even at midday, for the descent is steep—and the time six o'clock on the Sunday morning. And yet there I was taken, on the very ground, at six o'clock on a Sunday morning—raining, too!"

"There seems little doubt."

"There is no doubt. 'Twas his life or mine.

The dispute was the mere pretext and occasion of the duel."

" So I understood."

I was beginning to understand, besides, that the facts which Mr. Vincott had intended to impart to me were somewhat more numerous than he thought fit to admit.

" The cause—but I can't speak of that. In any case, 'twas his life or mine, and he knew it, so deemed it prudent to take mine, since he had the power, without risking his own."

" But," I objected, " could you trust your seconds? They knew the time, the place——"

" But they did not know I was sheltering Monmouth's fugitives. Lukstein knew it."

" You told him ? "

" No ! "

He stopped abruptly, and his eyes fell from my face to the ground. And then he said, in a very sad and quiet voice :

" But I have none the less sure proof he knew."

He sat silent with bowed head, labouring his breath, and his hands lying clasped together upon his knees. I noticed that the tips of his fingers were pressed tight into the backs of his palms, so that the flesh about them looked dead.

I leaned forward and took him gently by the arm.

" You must deliver me that proof, Julian," said I. For I began to have a pretty sure inkling of the service he had it in his mind to require of me.

He shifted his eyes to my face and then back again to the floor.

"I know, I know," he replied unsteadily. "I
disclosed my secret to but one person in the world."
And as I held my peace wondering, he flashed on
me a tortured face. "Don't force me to give the
name!" he cried. "Think! Think, Morrice!
Who should I have told? Who should I have
told?"

The words seemed wrung from his soul. I
understood what that first outburst meant when
the gaoler had bidden me enter, and my gorge rose
against this woman who could make such foul sport
of her lover's trust. He read my thought in my face,
and though he might upbraid his mistress himself,
he would not suffer me to do the same.

"You must not blame her," he said earnestly,
laying a hand upon my knee. "Blame me! Blame
us who wantoned the days away at Whitehall, and
cloyed the very air with our flatteries. You chose
the right part, Morrice, a man's part—work. As for
us," he resumed his restless walk about the chamber,
beating one clenched fist into the palm of the other,
"as for us, a new fashion, a new dance, were our
studies, cajoling women our work. The divine laws
were sneered at, trampled down. They were meet
for the ragged who had nought but hope in the
next world to comfort them for their humiliation
in this. But we—we who had silk to wear and
money to spend, we needed a different creed. Sin
was our God, and we worshipped and honoured it
openly. When I think of it I, a Catholic, can
find it in my heart to wish that Monmouth's cause
had won. No, Morrice, you must not blame her.
The fault is ours, and I am rightly punished for my

share in it. Constancy was a burgess virtue, fit
for a tradesman. We despised it in ourselves; what
right had we to expect it in the women we sur-
rounded ? "

He checked his vehement flow abruptly, and came
and stood over me.

"And yet, Morrice," he said, with a smile that
was infinitely tender and sad, "and yet I loved her,
with a sweet purity in the love, and a humble
thankfulness for the knowledge of it, loved her as any
country bumpkin might love the girl who rakes
a furrow at his side."

"And in return," I said bitterly, "she betrayed
you to Count Lukstein ? "

He nodded "yes," and sat down again on his
bench.

" Why ? "

"Long before the duel. She had no suspicion
of the consequences of her words," he said hastily.
" She had no hand in this plot."

" Why ? " I repeated.

He looked at me, imploring mercy.

" I understand," said I.

"Ah, no ! " he said quickly ; "your suspicions
outstrip the truth. I think so," and again with
a curiously pleading voice, " I think so. The man
purred more softly than the rest, and so she——"

He broke off in the middle of the sentence and
began anew.

"I must lay the whole truth bare, I see that.
Only the shame of it cuts into me like a knife."

He paused, and great beads of sweat broke out
upon his forehead.

"I have told you that my dispute with Lukstein was no more than the pretext of our quarrel. She was the cause. How long their acquaintance had lasted I know not, or to what length of intimacy it had gone. Lukstein was as secret as a cat, and he taught her his duplicity. 'Twas I, myself, presented him to her formally when he came first to the Hotwell, but I think now the pair had met before in London. 'Twere too long to describe how my fears were aroused—an exchange of glances noted here, a letter in his hand dropped from a sachet there, a certain guarded hesitation she evinced when Lukstein and I were both with her, a word carelessly dropped showing knowledge of his movements; all trifles in themselves, but summed together a very weighty argument. So on the morning of the ninth, worn out with disquiet, I resolved to bring the matter to an issue, and I rode over to St. Vincent's rock. Lukstein was seated at an escritoire as I entered the room. I saw his face blanch and his hand fly to an open drawer, close, and lock it. He rose to greet me, and drew me to the window, which pleased me the more for that a bell stood upon the escritoire. I got between him and the bell and taxed him with his treachery. He denied it, larding me with friendly protestations. I backed to the escritoire and repeated the charge. He laughed at me for my unmanly lack of faith. With a sudden wrench I tore open the locked drawer. He bounded towards the bell; my sword was at his breast, and we stood watching one another while I rummaged with my left hand in the drawer.

"'You shall pay for this,' says he, very softly.

"'One of us will pay,' says I.

"'Yes, you! You!' and he smiled, with his lips drawn back so that I saw the gums of his teeth on both jaws. If only I had known what he meant! I had him there at my sword's point. I had but to lean forward on my arm!

"'Get back to the window!' I ordered, and he obeyed me with an affected jauntiness. Out of the drawer I drew a small gold box of an oval shape. I had given it but a fortnight agone to—to—— you will understand; and it contained my miniature. The box fastened with a lock, and I forgot to ask him for the key. He has it still. There were letters besides in the drawer, and I made him burn them before my eyes. Then I took my leave, and sent my seconds."

"Are you sure the box was the same?" I asked, when he had done. He slipped his hand into his pocket, and brought it out and placed it in my hand. His coat of arms was emblazoned on the cover.

"Keep it!" he said. I tried the lid, but the box was locked.

"Until I recover the key," I answered, and we clasped hands.

"Thank you!" he said simply. "Thank you!"

The smell of the Cumberland gorse was in my nostrils, my friend lay before me traitorously fettered, and this poor, belated adjustment of his wrong seemed the very right and fitting function of the love I bore for him. There was, however, still one point on which I still felt need to be assured.

For I knew the timidity of my nature, and I was minded to leave no fissure in this wall of evidence through which after-doubts might leak to sap my resolution.

"And the proof?" I asked. "The proof that she informed Count Lukstein."

"She confessed that to me herself. She came to me here on the evening of the day that I was taken."

I placed the gold box in the fob of my waist-coat, and as I did so I felt a book. I drew it out, wondering what it might be. 'Twas the small copy of Horace which I had thrust there unwittingly when I waited for the doctor's report at Leyden. I held it in my hands and turned over the pages idly.

"Count Lukstein has left Bristol," I said.

"Ay; he got little good out of his treachery beyond the saving of his carcase. But he left his servant here—Otto Krax. That is why I bade you come disguised. He knew I could not make the matter public for—for her sake. But I suppose that he feared I might reveal it to some friend if the trial went against me, entrust to him the just work I am forced to leave undone. Perchance he had some hint of Swasfield's departure; I know not. This only I know: Krax has been at Vincott's heels, keeping close watch on all who passed in with him to me; and should he find out that you had come from Holland in this great haste, it might prove an ill day's work for you, and, in any case, Lukstein would be forewarned."

"He lives in the Tyrol?"

"At Schloss Lukstein, six miles to the east of Glurns, in the valley of the Adige. But, Morrice, he is master there. The spot is remote, there's no one to gainsay him. You must needs be careful. He hath no love for honest dealing, and you had best take him privately."

He spoke with so sombre a warning in his tone that the shadows appeared to darken about the room.

"He is cunning," Julian went on; "you must match him in cunning. Nay, over-match him, for he has power as well."

"You have visited this castle?"

"Yes. 'Tis built in two wings which run from east to west, and north to south, and form a right angle at the north-east corner. At the extreme end of the latter wing there is a tower; a window opens on to the terrace from a small room in this tower. There are but two doors in the room; that on the left gives on to a passage which leads to the main hall. The servants sleep on the far side of the hall. The other door opens on to a narrow stairway which mounts to the Count's bedroom. 'Tis his habit of a night to sit in this small room."

"I understand. And the entrance to this terrace?"

"That is the danger, for the place is built upon a rock sheer and precipitous. However, there is one spot where the ascent may be contrived. I discovered the way by chance. The climb is hazardous, yet not more so than some that we attacked out of mere sport on Scafell crags. Ah, me! Morrice, those were the best days of my life. I wonder whether 'twill be the same with you!"

Something like a shiver ran through me, but before I could answer him the key grated in the lock and the door was flung open. I turned, and saw in the shadow of the entrance the sombre figure of a priest. He was tall, and the cassock which robed him in black from head to foot made him show yet taller. In his hand he held a gleaming crucifix. He raised it above his head as he crossed the threshold, and in the twilight of the room it shone like a silver flame.

Julian sprang from his bench; his shoulder caught the bracket, the lamp rocked once or twice, and then crashed to the ground. In the darkness no one spoke; the rustle of our breathing was marked like the ticking of a clock.

After a while the gaoler fetched in a taper. Julian looked at me in some embarrassment. The priest waited patiently by the door, and it was impossible for us to renew our discourse. In rising, however, I had let fall the Horace on to the floor, and the book lay open at my feet. Julian caught sight of it, and a plan occurred to him. He fumbled in his pocket for a pencil, picked the volume up, and drew a rapid sketch upon the open page.

"That will make all clear," he remarked.

I took the book from him, and we clasped hands for the last time.

"At this hour to-morrow?" he said, with a little catch in his voice. I was still holding his hand. I could feel the blood beating in his fingers. At

this hour to - morrow! It seemed incredible.
"Morrice!" he cried, clinging to me, and his
voice was the voice of a child crying out in the
black of the night. In a moment he recovered his
calm, and dropped my hand. I made my reverence
to the priest, and the door clanged to between us.

Vincott was waiting for me at the foot of the
stairs, and we hurried silently to the gates. The
porter came forward to let us out, but I noticed
that he fumbled with his keys which he carried
upon an iron ring. He tried first one and then
another in the lock, as though he knew not which
fitted it. His ignorance struck me as strange until
Vincott pulled me by the sleeve.

"Turn your back to the hutch," he whispered
suddenly. Instinct made me face it instead, and
I perceived, gazing curiously into my face, the
very man who had tracked Vincott in the afternoon :
Otto Krax, as I now knew him to be, Count
Lukstein's servant. So startled was I by the unexpected sight of him that I let the volume of
Horace fall from my fingers to the ground.
On the instant he ran forward and picked it up.
I snatched it from his hand before he could do
more than glance at its cover, whereupon he made
me a polite bow and returned to the embrasure.
At last the porter succeeded in opening the door,
and we got us into the street. Vincott was for
upbraiding me at first in that I followed not his
directions, but I cut him short roughly, and bade
him hold his peace. For the world seemed very
strange and empty, and I had no heart for talking.
So we walked in silence back towards the inn.

Of a sudden, however, Vincott stopped.

"Listen!" he whispered.

I strained my ears until they ached. Behind us, in the quiet of the night, I could hear footsteps creeping and stealthy, not very far away. Vincott drew me into an angle of the wall, and we waited there holding our breaths. The footsteps slid nearer and nearer. Never since have I heard a sound which so filled me with terror. The haunting secrecy of their approach had something in it which chilled the blood—the sound of a man on the trail. He passed no more than six feet from where we stood. It was Otto Krax; and we remained until we could hear him no more. Vincott wiped his forehead.

"If he had stopped in front of us," I said, "I should have cried out."

"And by the Lord," said he, "I should have done no less."

A hundred yards further on, Vincott stopped again.

"He has found out his mistake," he exclaimed in a low, quavering voice.

We listened again; the footsteps were returning swiftly, but with the same quiet stealth.

"Quick!" said Vincott, "against the wall!"

"No," said I, "he is tracking along the side of it. Let us face and pass him."

We walked on at a good pace, and made no effort at concealment. The man stopped as soon as we had gone by, turned, and came after us. My heart raced in my breast. He quickened his pace and drew level.

C

"'Tis a strange time for women to run these streets." He spoke with a guttural accent, and his face leered over my shoulder. In a passion of fear I swung my arm free from the cloak, and hit at the face with all my strength. The dress I was wearing ripped at the shoulder as though you had torn a sheet of brown paper. My blow by good fortune caught him in the neck at the point where the jaw curves up into the cheek, and he fell heavily to the ground, his head striking full upon a rounded cobble. I waited to see no more, but tucked up my skirts and ran as though the fiend were at my heels, with Vincott panting behind me. We never halted until we had reached the alley which led to the back-door of the inn.

I invited Vincott to come in with me and recruit his energies with a second dose of Bristol milk.

"No! no!" he returned. "'Tis late already, and you have to start betimes in the morning."

"There is the ceiling," I suggested.

He laughed softly.

"Mr. Buckler, I exaggerated its beauties," he said, "and I fear me if I went in with you I should be forced to repeat my error. It is just that which I wish to avoid."

"There are other and indifferent topics," I replied, "on which we might speak frankly." For a change had come over my spirit, and I dreaded to be left alone. Vincott shook his head.

"We should not find our tongues would talk of them."

However, he made no motion of departure, but

stood scraping a toe between the stones. Then
I heard him chuckle to himself.

"That was a good blow, my friend," he said;
"a good, clean blow, pat on the angle of the jaw.
I would never have credited you with the strength
for it. The man has been a plaguy nuisance to
me, and the blow was a very soothing compensation.
Only conduct your undertaking with the like energy
throughout, and I do believe——" He pulled
himself up suddenly.

"What do you believe?" I asked.

"I believe," he replied sententiously, "that
Lucy will need a new Sunday gown;" and he
turned on his heel and marched out of the
alley.

The next morning came a foreigner to the
inn, and made inquiry concerning a woman who
had stayed there over-night. Lucy, faithful to her
promise, stoutly declared that no woman had rested
in the house for so little as an hour, and, not
content with that asseveration, she must needs go
on to enforce her point by assuring him that the
inn had given shelter to but one traveller, and
that traveller a man. But the traveller by this
time was well upon his way to London, and so
learnt nothing of the inquiry until long afterwards.

CHAPTER V.

DEW jewelling the grasses in the fields, the chatter
of birds among the trees, a sparkling freshness in
the air, and before me the road, running white
into the gold of the rising sun. But behind! On
the top of St. Michael's hill, outlined black against
the pearly western sky, rose the gaunt cross-trees
of the gallows. 'Twas the last glimpse I had of
Bristol, and I lingered as one horribly fascinated
until the picture was embedded in my heart.

In London I tarried but so long as sufficed
for me to repair the deficiencies of my dress, since
my very linen was now become unsightly and foul,
and, riding to Gravesend, took ship for Rotterdam.

I had determined to join Larke with me in
my undertaking, for I bethought me of his craving
for strange paths and adventures, and hoped to
discover in him a readiness of wit which would
counteract my own scrupulous hesitancy. For this
I implicitly believed : that it was not so much the
wariness that Julian bespoke which would procure
success, as the instinct of opportunity, the power,

I mean, at once to grasp the fitting occasion when it presented, and to predispose one's movements in the way best calculated to bring about its presentment. In this quality I knew myself to be deficient. 'Twas ever my misfortune to confuse the by-ways with the high-road. I would waste the vital moment in deliberation as to which was shortest, and alas! the path I chose in the end more often than not turned out to be a *cul-de-sac.*

In the particular business in which I was engaged such overweening prudence would be like to nullify my purpose, and further, destroy both Jack and myself. For beyond a description of Count Lukstein's person which I had from Julian some while ago, I knew nothing but what he had told me in the prison ; and that knowledge was too scanty to serve as the foundation for even the flimsiest plan. The region, the Castle, the aggregate of servants, and their manner of life—it behoved me to have certain information on all these particulars were I to prearrange a mode of attack. As things were, I must needs lie in ambush for chance, and seize it with all speed when it passed our way.

At Leyden I found Jack, very glum and melancholy, poring over a folio of Shakespeare. 'Twas the single author whom he favoured, and he read his works with perpetual interest and delight. "This is the book of deeds," he would say, smacking a fist upon the cover. "There is but one bad play in it, and that is the tragedy of *Hamlet.* The good Prince is too speculative a personage."

"You reached Bristol in time?" he asked, springing up as I entered the room.

"In time; but not a moment too soon," I
replied, and sat mum.

"Then Sir Julian Harnwood is safe?"

"No! There was never a hope of that."

The old smile, half amusement, half contempt,
flashed upon his lips; the old envy looked out
from his eyes. I, of course, had bungled where
a man of vigour might have accomplished.

"It was not for that end that he sent for me,"
I hastened to add, and then I stuck. I had
determined to relate to Jack forthwith the story
of my mission, and to engage his assistance, but
the actual sight of him overturned my intentions.
I felt tongue-tied; I dared not tell him lest my
resolution should trickle away in the telling; for
I read upon his face his poor estimation of my
powers, and I dreaded the ridicule of his comments
upon my unfitness for the task to which I had
set my hand. I had sufficient doubts of my own
upon that score. Indeed, since I had entered
the room, they had buzzed about me importunate
as a cloud of gnats; for Larke had never been
sparing of his homilies upon my incapacity. I
think every article I possessed, at one time or
another, had been twisted into a text for them;
and now they all came flocking back to me, as
my eyes ranged over the familiar objects they
had been based upon. They seemed, in truth, to
saturate the very air.

Hence, I confided to Larke no more than the
fact of our journey into the Tyrol; its reason and
purpose I kept secret to myself. And to this
self-distrust, trivial matter though it was, I owed

my subsequent misfortunes. It was the first link in the chain of disaster, and I forged it myself unwittingly.

"Jack," said I, "you were ever fond of adventures. One lies at your door."

"Of what kind?" he asked.

"A journey into the Tyrol."

"For what purpose?"

"I cannot tell you. You must trust me if you come."

He looked at me doubtfully.

"Your life will be risked," I urged; "I can gratify you so far."

He closed the Shakespeare with a bang.

"When do we start?"

"As soon as ever we are prepared. To-morrow."

"'Twere a pity to waste a day."

I assured him that so far from wasting it, we should have much ado to get off even the next morning. For there were a couple of stout horses to be purchased, besides numberless other arrangements to be made. The horses we bought of a dealer in the Rapenburg, and then, enlisting the fencing-master to aid us, we sought the shop of an armourer in the Hout-Straat. From him we bought a long sword and a brace of pistols each, whereupon Larke declared that we were equipped cap-à-pie, and loudly protested against further hindrance. I insisted, however, in adding a pair of long cloaks of a heavier cloth than any we possessed, and divers other warm garments. For we were now in the last days of September, and I knew that winter comes apace in upland countries

like the Tyrol. Then there were maps to be pro-
cured, and a route to be pricked out, so that it
was late in the evening before we had completed
our preparations.

Meanwhile I inquired of Larke how it had
fared with Swasfield. It appeared that it was not
until some hours after I had ridden off that the
man regained his senses, and then he was still
too weak to amplify his tidings ; in fact, he had
only recovered sufficiently to depart from Leyden
two days before I returned. Doubtless to some
extent his convalescence was retarded by grief for
that he had not fulfilled his errand. For he was
ever lamenting the omission of his message, and
more particularly of that portion which referred to
the road between Bristol and London. For swift
horses had been stabled at intervals of fifteen miles
along the whole stretch, and in order to make sure
that no one but myself should have the profit of
them, as Swasfield said, or rather, as I think, in
order that my name might not transpire if Count
Lukstein's spies were watching the road and became
suspicious at this posting of relays, it was arranged
that they should be delivered only to the man who
passed the word "Wastwater," that being the name
of the lake in Cumberland on which my lands
abutted.

Of our journey into the Tyrol I have but faint
recollections. We set off the next morning with
no more impediments than we could carry in valises
fixed upon our saddles. Even Udal, my body-
servant, I left behind, for he had neither liking nor
aptitude for foreign tongues, a few scraps of French

and a meagre knowledge of Dutch forced on him by his residence in the country, being all· that he possessed. He would, therefore, have only hindered our progress, and, besides, I had no great faith in his discretion. I was minded, accordingly, to secure some foreigner in Strasbourg who would think we were engaged upon a tour of pleasure; which I did, and dismissed him at Innspruck.

For the rest I rode with little attention or regard for the provinces through which we passed. The very cities wherein we slept seemed the cities of a dream, so that now I am like one who strives to piece together memories of a journey taken in early childhood. An alley of trees recurs to me, the shine of stars in a midnight sky, or, again, the comfortable figure of a Boniface; but the images are confused and void of suggestion, for I rode eyes shut and hands clenched, as a coward rides in the press of battle.

At times, indeed, when we halted, I would turn industriously to my Horace. The book had fallen open at the Palinodia when I dropped it in the prison, so that Julian's sketch was on the page opposite to the date September 14. I append here the diagram which was to enable me to find an entrance into the Castle, and it will be seen that I had much excuse for studying it. In truth, I could make neither head nor tail of its significa-tion.

'Twas ever this outline of Lukstein Castle that I pondered, though Jack knew it not, and when he beheld the book in my hands would gaze at me with a troubled look of distrust. On the instant

I would fall miserably to taking count of myself.
"Here are you," I would object to myself, "a
bookish student of a mean stature and a dilatory

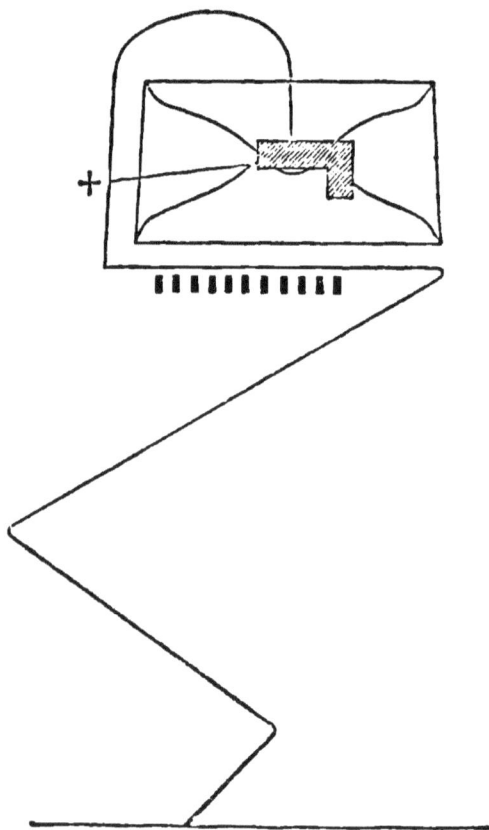

mind.   You have faced no weapon more deadly
than a buttoned foil, and you would compel a man
of great strength and indubitable cunning to a mortal
encounter in the privacy of his own house, that is,

supposing you are not previously done to death
by his serfs, which is most like to happen." Then
would my courage, a very ricketty bantling, make
weak protest: "You faced a blunderbuss and a
volley of slugs, and you were not afraid." "But,"
I would answer hotly, "you did not face them, you
were running away. Besides, you had called your
assailant a potatoe, and therefore had already a
contempt for him. This time it is you who will
be the potatoe, as you will most surely discover
when Count Lukstein spits you on his skewer;"
and so I would get me wretchedly to bed.

There were, indeed, but two thoughts which
served to console me. In the first place, I was
sensible that I had acquired some dexterity with the
foils, and if I could but imagine a button on the point
of the Count's sword I might hope to hold my own.
In the second, I remembered very clearly a remark
of Julian's. "The man's a coward," he had said,
and I hugged the sentence to my breast. I repeated
the words, indeed, until they fell into the cadence
of a rhythm and lost all meaning and comfort for
me, sounding hollow, like the tapping of an empty
nut.

Of what Larke suffered during that period I had
no suspicion, but from subsequent hints I gather
that his distress, though based upon far other
grounds, was no whit inferior to my own. His
behaviour, indeed, when I came to consider it,
revealed to me new and amiable aspects of his
character; for while he firmly disbelieved in my
ability to captain an expedition, he never once
pestered me for an explanation. I had entrusted

the purse to his care, and at each town he made
the arrangements for our stay, looked after the
welfare of our horses, and in short, took modestly
upon himself the troublesome conduct of our travels.
Knowing nothing of my purpose but its danger, and
distrustful of its achievement, he yet rode patiently
forward, humming ever a French song, of which the
refrain ran, I remember:

> Que toutes joies et toutes honneurs
> Viennent d'armes et d'amours.

For he possessed that delicate gift of sympathy
which keeps the friend silent when the acquaintance
multiplies his questions.

Thus we journeyed for over a month. It was,
I fancy, on the 12th November that we reached
the town of Innspruck, the weather very shrewd and
bitter, for snow had fallen in great quantities, and
a cutting wind blew from the hills. That night I
told my companion of our destination, but disclosed
no more of the business than that I had a private
message for Count Lukstein's ear, which must
needs be delivered secretly if we were to save our
lives. We stayed here for two days that we might
rest our horses, and early on the 14th set off
for Glurns, which lay some eighty miles away in
a broad valley they called the Vintschgau. The
snow, however, was massed very deep, and though
the road was sound, for it was the highway into
Italy, we did not come up with the village until
two o'clock on the third afternoon. Beyond Glurns
the road traversed the valley in a diagonal line
through a dreary avenue of stunted limes, which in

their naked leaflessness looked in the distance like a palisade. Into this avenue we passed, and were well-nigh across the dale and under its northern barrier of mountains, when Larke suddenly reined up.

"'Childe Roland to the dark tower came,'" he sang out. "Heaven send there be no one to complete the quotation!"

I followed the direction of his gaze. Right ahead of us the Castle, the rock whereon it was pinnacled, and the village, huddled on a little plateau at its base, stood out from the hillside like a black stain upon the snow. A carriage-way, diverging from our road a hundred yards farther on, ran up towards it in long zigzags, and to this point we advanced.

"Look!" suddenly cried Larke. "We are not the first to visit the worthy Count to-day."

From both directions carriages or sledges had turned into this track, so that the snow at its entrance was trampled by the hoofs of horses, and cut by intersecting curves.

"'Tis not certain," I said, "that the marks were made to-day."

"It is," he replied, "else would the ruts have frozen."

The thought that the Count had company doubled my disquiet. For there was the less chance of finding him alone, and I was anxious to have done with the matter.

The first angle made by the zigzags was thickly covered with a boskage of pines. Into this we led our horses, and fastening them in the heart of it where the trees were most dense, we crept towards the west corner. At this point the track bent back upon itself and mounted eastwards to the border of the village, turned again, threading the houses at the bottom of the cliff, struck up thence at a right angle in a clear, open stretch beneath the west face of the rock, and finally curved round at the back to the gates. For the entrance to the Castle fronted the hillside and not the valley.

I took my Horace from my pocket, and in an instant the diagram became intelligible to me. The long curving line represented the road, and the way of ascent, marked by the cross, was to be found on the western wall of rock, and above the open stretch of road. Of this we now commanded an unimpeded view, for the corner of the road at which we stood was situate to the west of the Castle.

"I see it!" I exclaimed, and I handed the book to Larke.

"So this is the secret of the poet's fascination," he answered. "But I see no path. The cliff is as smooth as an egg-shell, save for that one projecting rib."

"That is the path," I replied.

A shoulder of rock with a ribbon of snow upon its ridge jutted out from the summit of the cliff, and descended in an unbroken line to the road.

"'Tis impossible to ascend that," said he. "We should break our necks for a surety or ever we were half-way up."

"It shows steeper than it is," I answered. "We are not well-placed for judging of its incline; for that we should see it in profile. But where snow lies, there a man may climb."

Jack raised no further objection; but ever and
again I noticed him gazing at me with a puzzled
expression upon his face. We crouched down in
the undergrowth until such time as the night should
fall, blowing on our fingers and pressing close
against each other for warmth's sake. But 'twas
of little use; my body tingled with cold, and I
began to think my muscles would be frozen stiff,
before the darkness gave us leave to move. The
valley, moreover, looked singularly mournful and
desolate in its shroud of white. As far as the
eye could travel not a living thing could be seen,
nor could the ear detect a sound. The region
brooded in a sinister silence. I verily believe
that I should have loosed my horse and fled but
for the presence of my companion.

Jack, however, was in no higher spirits than
myself, and from the continual glances of his
eyes I think that he was infected with a wholesome fear of the rib of rock. At last the dusk
fell; the lights began to twinkle in the village
and in the upper windows of the Castle. For a
wall, broken here and there by round turrets, circled
about the edge of the cliff and hid the lower storey
from our sight.

We looked to the priming of our pistols, buckled
our swords tighter about the waist, shook the
snow from our cloaks, and cautiously stepped out
on to the path. At the edge of the village we
stopped. 'Twas but one street; but that very
narrow and busy. Not a moment passed but a
door opened, and a panel of orange light was
thrown across the gloom, and the figures of men

and women were seen passing and repassing. The village was astir and humming like a hive. But there was no other way. For on our right rose the tooth of rock in a sheer scarp; on our left the ground broke steeply away at the backs of the houses.

"We must make a dash for it," said Larke. We waited until the street cleared for a moment, and then ran between the houses as fast as our legs would carry us. The snow deadened the sound of our feet, and we were well-nigh through the village when Larke tripped over a hillock and stumbled forward on his face with a curse. The next instant I dropped down beside him, and covering his mouth with my hand, forced him prone to the ground. For barely twenty feet ahead a door had suddenly opened, and a man dressed in the jacket and short breeches of the Tyroler came out on to the path. He stood with his back towards us and exchanged some jest with the inmates of the house, and I recognised his voice. I had heard it no more than once, it is true, but the occasion had fixed the sound of it for ever in my memories. It was the voice of the spy who had tracked us in the streets of Bristol. He turned towards the door, so that the light streamed full upon his face, shouted a "God be with you," and strode off in the direction of the Castle. The sight of him left me no room for doubt. That he had outstripped us caused me, indeed, little surprise, for we had travelled by a devious way, and had, moreover, delayed here and there upon the road.

Larke commenced to sputter and cough.

" Quiet ! " I whispered, for the man was yet within hearing.

" Loose your hand, then ! " he returned. " 'Tis easy enough to say quiet, but 'tis not so easy to choke quietly."

In my fluster I was holding his head tightly pressed into the snow, so that he could only have caught the barest glimpse of the man.

" Who was it ? " he asked.

" One of Lukstein's servants."

" You know him ? "

" I have seen him, and he has seen me. Maybe he would know me again."

We got safely quit of the houses and turned into the upward stretch of road, towards the buttress of rock. It jutted out across our path, and was plainly distinguishable, for the night was pure and clean, and appeared to be tinctured with a vague light from the snow-fields. I noticed, too, that on the far side of the valley a pale radiance was welling over the brim of the hills with promise of the moon. 'Twas a very sweet sight to me, since climbing an unknown rock-ridge in the dark hath little to commend it, unless it be necessity.

At the foot of the rib we halted and prepared to ascend. But nowhere could I find a cranny for my fingers or a knob for my boot. The surface was indeed, as Jack had said, as smooth as an egg-shell. I stepped back to the outer edge of the road and examined it as thoroughly as was possible.

For the first twelve feet it was absolutely per-pendicular; above that point it began to slope.

H

It was as though the lowest portion of the rib had been cut purposely away.

And then I remembered! Julian had spoken only of a descent. Now a man may drop twelve feet and come to no harm, but once at the bottom he must bide there. There was but one way out of the difficulty, and luckily Larke's shoulders were broad.

"You must lend me your back," I said. "I will haul you up after me."

He planted himself firmly against the rock, with his legs apart, and I climbed up his back on to his shoulders.

"You teach me mercy to my horse," he said quietly.

"Why? What have I done?" I asked.

"Jabbed your spurs into my thighs and stood on them," he replied in a matter-of-fact voice. "But 'tis all one. Blood was meant to be spilled."

Being now more than five feet from the ground, I was able to worm my fingers into a crack at the point where the ridge began to incline, and so hoist myself on to an insecure footing. But it was utterly beyond my power to drag Larke after me, for the snow was thin and shallow, and underneath it the rock loose and shattered. I should most surely have been pulled over had I made the attempt. I ascended the ridge in the hope of discovering a more stable position, whence I could lower my cloak to my companion. But 'twas all slabs at a pretty steep slope, with here and there little breaks and ledges. I could just crawl up on my belly, but I could do no more. There was never a yard of level where you could secure a solid grip of the feet. So I climbed back again and leaned over the edge.

"Jack," I said, "I can't give you a helping hand. It would mean a certain fall."

"I shall need little help, Morrice—very little," he answered, in a tone of entreaty.

"I can't even give you that. The ridge is too insecure."

"Ah! Don't say that!" he burst out. "You have not come all these miles to be turned back by a foot or two of rock. It is absurd! It is worse than absurd. It is cowardly."

"Hush!" I whispered gently. For I could gauge his disappointment, and gauging it, could pardon his railing. "I have no thought of turning back."

"Then what will you do? Morrice, this is no time for dreaming! What will you do?"

"Jack," I said, "you and I must part company. I must win through this trouble by myself."

I heard something like a sob; it was the only answer he made.

"Wait for me by the horses in the wood! Give me till dawn, but not a moment longer! If I am not with you then—well, 'tis the long good-bye betwixt you and me, Jack, and you had best ride for your life."

Again he made no answer. For a moment I fancied that he had stolen away in a fury, and I craned my head over the rock, so that I could look down into the road. He was standing motionless with bent shoulders just beneath me.

"Jack!" I called. For it might well be the last

time I should speak to him. We had been good friends, and I would not have him part from me in anger. " There is no other way. It can't be helped."

He turned up his face towards me, but it was too dark for me to read its expression.

" Very well, Morrice," he said, and there was no resentment in his tone. " I will wait for your coming, and God send you come ! "

And with a dull, heavy step he walked back along the path.

I turned and set my face to the cliff. After a while the ridge widened out, and the snow over-laid it more firmly, insomuch that a surefoot might have walked along by day. In the uncertain light, however—for the moon as yet hung low in a gap of the hills—I dared not venture. it, and crept up on my hands and knees, testing carefully each tooth of rock or ever I trusted my weight to its stability. Towards the summit the rib thinned again to a sharp edge, and I was forced to straddle up it as best I could, with a leg dangling on either side. Altogether, what with the obstacles which the climb presented, and the numbing of my fingers, since the snow quickly soaked through my gloves, I made my way but slowly.

At the top I found myself face to face with the Castle wall, which was some ten feet in height, and quite solid and uncrumbled. Between it and the rim of the crag, however, was a strip of level ground about half a yard broad, and I determined to follow it round until I should reach some angle at which it would be possible to climb the wall. On

this strip the snow was heavily piled, and for security's
sake I got me again to my hands and knees, flogging
a path before me with the scabbard of my sword.
I began to fear that I might be foiled in my
endeavour for want of a companion; for again I
bethought me, Julian only descended, and a man
might drop from any portion of the wall, whereas
the scaling of it was a different matter. I proceeded in the opposite direction to the Castle gates,
and so came out above the south face of the precipice.
Below me the houses of Lukstein village glimmered
like a cluster of glow-worms; I had merely to roll over
to fall dump among the roof-tops. I could even hear
a faint murmur of brawling voices, and once I caught
a plaintive snatch of song. For in that still, windless
air sounds rose like bubbles in a clear pool of water.

The wall on my left curved and twisted with
the indents of the cliff, and a little more than half-
way across the face I came to a spot where it ran
in and out at a sharp angle. Moreover, one of the
turrets which I had remarked from the wood bulged
out from the line, and made of this angle a sort of
crevice. Into the corner I thrust my back, and
working my elbows and knees, with some help from
the roughness of the stones, I managed to mount on
to the parapet. The Castle lay stretched before me.
In front stood the main body of the building; to my
right a shorter wing, ending in a tower, jutted off
towards the wall on which I lay. A broad terrace,
enclosing in the centre a patch of lawn, separated
me from the building.

I fixed my eyes upon the tower. The window of
the lower room was dark, and, strangely enough,

'twas the only window dark in the house. From the upper room there shone a faint gleam as of a lamp ill-trimmed. But all the other windows in the chief façade and the more distant part of this wing blazed out into the night. I could see passing figures shadowed upon the curtains, and music floated forth on a ripple of laughter, gavotte being linked to minuet and pavane in an endless melody.

Every now and then some couple dainty with ribbons and jewels would step out from the porch, and with low voices and pensive steps pace the terrace until the cold froze the sweetness from their talk. They were plain to me, for the moon was riding high, and revealed even the nooks of the garden. Indeed, the only obscure corner was that in which I lay concealed. For a little pavilion leaned against the wall hard by me, and cast a deep shadow over the coping.

But I hardly needed even that protection to screen me from these truants. I might have stood visible in the lawn's centre, and yet been asked no question. For such as braved the frost came not out to spy for strangers; their eyes sought each other with too intimate an insistance.

I had indeed timed my visit ill. The revels of the village were being repeated in the Castle.

The sharp contrast of my particular purpose forced its reality grimly upon me, and made this vigil one long agony. I had planned to tell Larke the true object of my coming during the hour or so we should have to wait, and to draw some solace from his companionship. Now, however, I was planted there alone with a message of death for my foe or for myself, and the glamour of life in my eyes, and it seemed to me that all the tedium of my journey had been held over for these hours of waiting.

To cap my discomfort I found occasion to prove to myself that I was a most indisputable prig. I had often discoursed to Larke concerning the consolations to be drawn from the classics in moments of distress. Now I sought to practise the precept, and to that end lowered a bucket into the well of my memories. But alas! I hauled up naught but tags about Cerberus and Charon, and passages from the sixth book of Vergil.

To tell the honest truth, I was dismally afraid. The very stars in the sky flashed sword-points at my breast, and the ice upon the hills glittered like breast-plates of steel. Moreover, my hands were swollen and clumsy with the cold, and I dreaded lest I might lose the nervous flexibility of their muscles, and so the nice command of my sword. I stripped off my gloves which were freezing on my fingers, and thrust my hands inside my shirt to keep them warm against my skin.

Somehow or another, however, the night wore through. The stars and the moon shifted across the mountains, the music began to falter into breaks, and the murmurs grew louder from the village. I heard sledges descend the road with a jingle of bells, first one, then another, then several in quick succession. Iron gates clanked on the far side of the Castle, the windows darkened, and finally a light sprang up in the lower of the chambers which I watched.

I turned over on my face and dropped on to the snow. But my spurs rattled and clinked as I touched the ground, and I stooped down and loosed them from my feet. I cast a hurried glance around me. Not a shadow moved ; the world seemed frozen to an eternal immobility. I crept across the lawn, up the terrace steps to the sill of the window, and peered into the room. It was small and luxuriously furnished, the roof, panels, and floor, being all of a polished and mellow pine-wood. Warm - coloured rugs and the skins of chamois were scattered on the floor, and four candles in heavy sconces blazed on the mantel. Sunning himself before the log-fire sat Count Lukstein. I knew him at once from Julian's account : a big, heavy-featured man with a loose dropping mouth. He was elaborately dressed in a suit of grey satin richly laced with silver, which seemed somewhat too airy and fanciful to befit the massive girth of his limbs. These he displayed to their full proportions, and the sight did little to enhearten me. For he sat with his legs stretched out and his arms clasped behind his head, the firelight playing gaily upon a sparkle of diamonds in his cravat.

I noted the two doors of which Julian had spoken—that on my right leading to the bedroom, that on my left to the hall—and in particular a small writing-table which stood against the wall facing me. For a silver bell upon it caught the light of the candles and reflected it into my eyes. And I remembered Julian's story of his visit to the Hotwell.

Whether it was that I rattled the frame of the window, or that chance turned the Count's looks my way, I know not; but he suddenly turned full towards me. My face was pressed flat to the glass.

I drew back hastily into the shadow of the wall. One minute passed, two, three; the window darkened, and the Count, lifting his hands to his temples to shut out the light at his back, laid his forehead to the pane. Instinctively I clapped my hand to the pistol in my pocket and cocked it. The click of the hammer sounded loud in my ears as though I had exploded the charge. Count Lukstein flung open the window and set one foot outside.

"Who is it?" he cried; and yet again, "who is it?"

I drew a deep breath, stepped quickly past him into the room, and turned about. The two doors and the writing-table were now behind me.

He staggered back from the window, and his hand dived at the hilt of his sword. But before he could draw it he raised his eyes to my face; he let go of his sword and stared in sheer bewilderment.

"And in the devil's name," he asked, "who are you?"

'Twas a humiliating moment for me. He spoke as a master might to an impudent schoolboy, and it was with a quavering schoolboy's treble that I answered him.

"I am Morrice Buckler."

"An Englishman?" he questioned, bending his brows suddenly; for we were speaking in German.

"Of the county of Cumberland," I replied meekly. I felt as if I was repeating my catechism.

"Then, Mr. Morrice Buckler, of the county of Cumberland," he began, with an exaggerated politeness. But I broke in upon him.

"I have some knowledge of the county of Bristol, too," I said, with as much bravado as I could muster. But 'twas no great matter. The display would have disgraced a tavern bully.

The words, however, served their turn. Just for a second, just long enough for me to perceive it, a startled look of fear flashed into his eyes, and his body seemed to shrink in bulk. Then he asked suddenly:

"How came you here?"

"By a path Sir Julian Harnwood told me of," says I.

He stretched a finger towards the window.

"Go!" he cried in a low voice. "Go!"

I stood my ground, for I noted with a lively satisfaction that the quaver had passed from my voice into his.

"Have a care, Master Buckler!" he continued. "You are no longer in England. You would do well to remember that. There are reasons why I would have no disturbance here to-night. There are reasons. But on my life, if you refuse to obey me, I will have you whipped from here by my servants."

"Ah!" says I, "this is not the first time, Count Lukstein, that some one has stood between you and the bell."

He cast a glance over my shoulder. I saw that he was going to shout, and I whipped out the pistol from my pocket.

"If you shout," I said, "the crack of this will add little to the noise."

"It would go ill with you if you fired it," he blustered.

"It would go yet worse with you," I answered.

And there we stood over against one another, the finest brace of cowards in Christendom, each seeking to overcome the other by a wordy braggadocio. Indeed, my forefinger so trembled on the trigger that I wonder the pistol did not go off and settle our quarrel out of hand.

"What does it mean?" he burst out, screwing himself to a note of passion. "What does it mean? You skulk into my house like a thief."

"The manner of my visit does in truth leave much to be desired," I conceded. "But for that you must thank your reputation."

"It does, in truth," he returned, ignoring my last words. "It leaves much—very much. You see that yourself, Mr. Buckler. So, to-morrow! Return by the way you came, and come to me again to-morrow. We can talk at leisure. It is over-late to-night."

"Nay, my lord," said I, drawing some solid comfort from the wheedling tone in which he spake. "Your servants will be abroad in the house to-morrow, and, as you were careful to remind me, I am not in England. I have waited for some six hours upon the parapet of your terrace, and I have no mind to let the matter drag to another day."

His eyes shifted uneasily about the room; but ever they returned to the shining barrel of my pistol.

"Well, well," said he at length, with a shrug of the shoulders, and a laugh that rang flat as a cracked guinea, "one must needs listen when the speaker holds a pistol at your head. Say your say and get it done."

He flung himself into a chair which stood in
the corner by the window. I sat me in the one
from which he had risen, drawing it closer to the
fire. A little table stood within arm's reach, and I
pulled it up between us and laid my pistol on the
edge.

" I have come," said I, " upon Sir Julian Harnwood's part."

" Pardon me ! " he interrupted. " You will oblige
me by speaking English, and by speaking it low."

The request seemed strange, but 'twas all one
to me what language we spoke so long as he
understood.

" Certainly," I answered. " I am here to under-
take his share in the quarrel which he had with
you, and to complete the engagement which was
interrupted on the Kingsdown."

" But, Mr. Buckler," he said, with some show
of perplexity, " the quarrel was a private one.
Wherein lies your right to meddle with the
matter ? "

" I was Sir Julian's friend," I replied. " He knew
the love I bore him, and laid this errand as his
last charge upon it."

" Really, really," said he, " both you and your
friend seem strangely ill-versed in the conduct of
gentlemen. You say Sir Julian laid this errand
upon you. But I have your bare word for that.
It is not enough. And even granting it to be true,
my quarrel was with Sir Julian, not with you. One
does not fight duels by proxy."

He had recovered his composure, and spoke with
an easy superciliousness.

"My lord," I answered, stung by his manner, "I must ask you to get the better of that scruple, as I have of one far more serious, for, after all, one does not as a rule fight duels with murderers."

He started forward in his chair as though he had been struck. I seized the butt of my pistol, for I fancied he was about to throw himself upon me.

"I know more than you think," said I, nodding at him, "and this will prove it to you."

I drew the oval gold box from my fob and tossed it on to his knees. His hands darted at it, and he turned it over and over in his palms, staring at the cover with white cheeks.

"How got you this?" he asked hoarsely, and then remembering himself, "I know nothing of it. I know nothing of it."

"Sir Julian gave it into my hands," said I. "I visited him in his prison on the evening of the 22nd September."

He stared at me for a while, repeating "the 22nd September" like one busy over a sum.

"The 22nd September," said I, "the 22nd September. It was the day of his trial."

At the words his face cleared wonderfully. He rose with an indescribable air of relief, flung the box carelessly on the table, and said with a contemptuous smile:

"Ah, Mr. Buckler! Mr. Buckler! You would have saved much time had you mentioned the date earlier. How much?" and he shook some imaginary coins in the cup of his hand.

"Count Lukstein!" I exclaimed.

I had not the faintest notion of what he was driving at, and the surprise which his change of manner occasioned me obscured the insult.

"Tut, tut, man!" he resumed, with a wave of the hand. "How much? Surely the farce drags."

"The farce," I replied hotly, "is one of those which are best played seriously. Remember that, Count Lukstein!"

"Well, well," he said indulgently, "have your own way. But, believe me, you are making a mistake. I have no wish to cheapen your wares. That you have picked up some fragments of the truth I am ready to agree; and I am equally ready to buy your silence. You have but to name your price."

"I have named it," I muttered, locking my teeth, for I was fast losing my temper, and feared lest I might raise my voice sufficiently to be heard beyond the room.

"Let me prove to you that you are wasting time," said he with insolent patience. "You have been ill-primed for your work. You say that you visited Sir Julian on the night of the 22nd. You say that you were Sir Julian's friend. I would not hurt your feelings, Mr. Buckler, but both those statements are, to put it coarsely, lies. You were never Sir Julian's friend, or you would have known better than to have fixed that date. But two people visited him on the 22nd, a priest and a woman, the most edifying company possible for a dying man." He ended with a smooth scorn.

I looked up at him and laughed.

"Ah!" said he, "we are beginning to understand each other."

I laughed a second time.

"She was over-tall for a woman, my lord," said I, "though of no great stature for a man."

I rose as I spoke the words and confronted him. We were standing on opposite sides of the little table. The smile died off his face; he leaned his hands upon the table and bent slowly over it, searching my looks; with horror-stricken eyes.

"What do you mean?" he asked in a hoarse whisper.

"I was the woman. How else should I have got that box?"

"You, you!" He spoke in a queer matter-of-fact tone of assent. All his feeling and passion seemed to have gathered in his eyes.

So we stood waging a battle of looks. And then of a sudden I noticed a crafty, indefinable change in his expression, and from the tail of my eye I saw his fingers working stealthily across the table. I dropped my hand on to the butt of my pistol. With a ready cunning he picked up the gold box and began to examine it with so natural an air of abstraction that I almost wondered whether I had not mistaken his design.

"And so," says he at length, "you would fight with me?"

"If it please you, yes," says I.

"Miss Marston, it seems, has more admirers than I knew of," he returned, with a cunning leer which made my stomach rise at him.

He seemed incapable of conceiving a plain open

purpose in any man. Yet for all that I could not but
admire the nimbleness of his wits. Not merely had
he recovered his easy demeanour, but he was already,
as I could see, working out another issue from the
impasse. I clung fast to the facts.

"I have never seen Miss Marston," said I. "I
fight for my friend."

"For your friend? For your dead, useless friend?"
He dropped the words slowly, one by one, with a
smiling disbelief. "Come, come, Mr. Buckler! Not
for your friend! We are both men of the world.
Be frank with me! Is it sensible that two gentlemen
should spill honest blood for the sake of a feather-
headed wanton?"

"If the name fits her, my lord," I replied, "who
is to blame for that? And as for the honest blood,
I have more hope of spilling it than faith in its
honesty."

The Count's face grew purple, and the veins
swelled out upon his ample throat. I snatched up
the pistol, and we both stood trembling with passion.
The next moment, I think, must have decided the
quarrel, but for a light sound which became distinctly
audible in the silence. It descended from the room
above. We both looked up to the ceiling, the Count
with a sudden softness on his face, and I understood,
or rather I thought I understood, why he had not
raised the alarm before I produced my pistol, and
why he bade me subsequently speak in English.
For the sound was a tapping, such as a woman's
heels may make upon a polished floor.

I waited, straining my ears to hear the little stair-

way creak behind the door at my back, and cudgelling my brains to think what I should do.   If
she came down into the room, it was all over with
my project and, most likely, with my life, too, unless I was prepared to shoot my opponent in cold
blood and make a bolt for it.   After a while, however, the sound ceased altogether, to my indescribable relief.   The Count was the first to break the
silence.

"Very well, Mr. Buckler," said he; "send your
friends to me in the morning.   Let them come like
men to the door and give me assurance that I may
meet you without loss of self-respect, and you shall
have your way."

"You force me to repeat," said I, "that the
matter must be disposed of to-night."

"To-night!" he said, and stared at me incredu-
lously.   "Mr. Buckler, you must be mad."

"To-night," I repeated stubbornly.   For, apart
from all considerations of safety, I felt that such
courage as I possessed was but the froth of my
anger, and would soon vanish if it were left to
stand.   The Count began to pace the room between
the writing-table and the window.   I set my chair
against the wall and leaned against the chimney,
and I noted that at each turn in his walk he drew,
as though unconsciously, nearer and nearer to the
bell.

"Mr. Buckler," he said, "what you propose is
quite out of the question.   I can but attribute it to
your youth.   You take too little thought of my side
of the case.   To fight with one whom I have never

I

so much as set eyes on before, who forces his way into my house in the dead of night—you must see for yourself that it fits not my dignity."

"You are too close to the bell, Count Lukstein, and you raise your voice," I broke in sharply. "That fits not my safety."

He stood still in the middle of the room and raised a clenched fist to his shoulder, glaring at me. In a moment, however, he resumed his former manner.

"Besides," he went on, "there is a particular reason why I would have no disturbance here to-night. You got some inkling of it a moment ago." He nodded to the ceiling.

I blush with shame now when I remember what I answered him. I took a leaf from his book, as the saying is, and could conceive no worthy strain in him.

"The good lady," I said, "whom you honour with your attentions now must wait until the affairs of her predecessor are arranged."

The Count came sliding over the floor with a sinuous movement of his body and a very dangerous light in his eyes.

"You insult my wife," he said softly, and as I reeled against the hood of the fireplace, struck out of my wits by his words, he of a sudden gave a low bellowing cry, plucked his sword from his sheath, and lunged at my body. I saw the steel flash in a line of light and sprang on one side. The sword quivered in the wood level with my left elbow. My leap upset the table, the pistol clattered on the floor.

I whipped out my sword, Count Lukstein wrenched his free, and in a twinkling we were set to it.   I think all fear vanished from both of us, for Count Lukstein's face was ablaze with passion, and I felt the blood in my veins running like strong wine.

CHAPTER VI.

By these movements we had completely reversed our positions, so that now I stood with my back to the window, while the Count held that end of the room in which the doors were set. Not that I took any thought of this alteration at the time, for the Count attacked me with extraordinary fury, and I needed all my wits to defend myself from his violence. He was, as I had dreaded, a skilled swordsman, and he pressed his skill to the service of his anger. Now the point of his rapier twirled and spun like a spark of fire; now the blade coiled about mine with a sharp hiss like some lithe, glittering serpent. Every moment I expected it to bite into my flesh. I gave ground until my hindmost foot was stopped against the framework of the window; and there I stayed parrying his thrusts until he slackened from the ardour of his assault. Then in my turn I began to attack; slowly and persistently I drove him back towards the centre of the room, when suddenly, glancing across his shoulder, I saw something that turned my blood cold. The door leading to the staircase was ajar. I had heard no click of the handle; it must have been open before, I argued to myself, but I knew the argument was false. The door had been shut; I noted that from the garden, and it could not have opened so silently of itself. I renewed my attack upon the Count, pressing him harder and harder in a veritable panic. I snatched a second glance across his shoulder. The door was not only ajar; 'twas opening—very slowly, very silently, and a yellow light streamed through onto the wall beside the door. The sight arrested me at the moment of lunging—held me petrified with horror. A savage snarl of joy from Lukstein's lips warned me; his sword darted at my heart, I parried it clumsily, and the next moment the point leapt into my left shoulder. The wound quickened my senses, and I settled to the combat again, giving thrust for thrust. Each second I expected a scream of terror, a rush of feet. But not a sound came to me. I dared not look from the Count's face any more; the hit which he had made seemed to have doubled his energies. I strained my ears to catch the fall of a foot, the rustle of a dress. But our own hard breathing, a light rattle of steel as swords lunged and parried, a muffled stamp as one or the other stepped forward upon the rugs—these were the only noises in the room, and for me they only served to deepen and mark the silence. Yet all the while I felt that the door was opening—opening ; I knew that some one must be standing in the doorway quietly watching us, and that some one a woman, and Count Lukstein's wife. There was something horrible, unnatural in the silence, and I felt fear run down my back like ice, unstringing my muscles, sucking my heart. I

summoned all my strength, compressed all my intelligence into a despairing effort, and flung myself at
Lukstein. He drew back out of reach, and behind
him I saw a flutter of white. Through the doorway,
holding a lighted candle above her head, Countess
Lukstein advanced noiselessly into the room. Her
eyes, dark and dilated, were fixed upon mine; still she
spoke never a word. She seemed not to perceive her
husband ; she seemed not even to see me, into whose
face she gazed. 'Twas as though she was looking
through me, at something that stood in the window
behind my head.

The Count, recovering from my assault, rushed at
me again. I made a few passes, thinking that my
brain would crack. I could feel her eyes burning
into mine. I was certain that some one *was* behind
me, and I experienced an almost irresistible desire to
turn my head and discover who it might be. The
strain had become intolerable. There was just room
for me to leap backwards.

" Look ! " I gasped, and I leaned back against the
window-pane, clutching at the folds of the curtain for
support.

Count Lukstein turned ; the woman was close
behind him. A couple of paces more, and she must
have touched him. He dropped his sword-point and
stepped quickly aside.

" My God ! " he said in a hoarse whisper. " She
is asleep ! "

My whole body was dripping with sweat. It
seemed to me that a full hour must have passed
since I had seen her first, and yet so brief had been

the interval that she was not half-way across the room.

Had she come straight towards me I could not have moved from her path. But she walked betwixt Count Lukstein and myself direct to the open window. She wore a loose white gown, gathered in a white girdle at the waist, and white slippers on her naked feet. Her face even then showed to me as incomparably beautiful, and her head was crowned with masses of waving hair, in colour like red corn. She passed between us without check or falter ; her gown brushed against the Count. Through the open window she walked across the snowy terrace towards the pavilion by the Castle wall. The night was very still, and the flame of the candle burnt pure and steady.

I looked at the Count. For a moment we gazed at one another in silence, and then without a word we stepped side by side to follow her. Our dispute appeared to have been swallowed up in this overmastering event, and I experienced almost a revulsion of friendliness for my opponent.

" 'Tis not the first time this has happened, I am told," said he, and as I looked at him inquiringly, he added, very softly : " We were only married to-day."

" Only to-day," I exclaimed, and not noticing where I trod, I stumbled over a wolf-skin that lay on the floor with the head attached. My foot slipped on the polished boards beside it, and I fell upon my left knee. The Count stopped and faced me, an ugly smile suddenly flashing about his mouth. I saw him draw back his arm as I was rising. I dropped again upon hand and knee, and his sword whizzed an inch above my shoulder. I was still holding my own sword in my right hand, and or ever he could recover I lunged upwards at his breast with all my force, springing from the ground as I lunged, to drive the thrust home. The blade pierced through his body until the hilt rang against the buttons of his coat. He fell backwards heavily, and I let go of my sword. The point stuck in the floor behind him as he fell, and he slid down the blade on to the ground. Something dropped from his hand and rolled away into a corner, where it lay shining. I gave no thought to that, however, but glanced through the window. To my horror I saw that Countess Lukstein was already returning across the lawn. The Count had fallen across the window, blocking it. I plucked my sword free, and lugged the body into the curtains at the side, cowering down myself behind it. I had just time to gather up his legs and so leave the entrance clear, when she stepped over the sill. A little stream of blood was running towards her, and I was seized with a mad terror lest it should reach her feet. She moved so slowly and the stream ran so quickly. Every moment I expected to see the white of her slippers grow red with the stain of it. But she passed beyond the line of its channel just a second before it reached so far. With the same even and steady gait she recrossed the room and turned into the little stairway, latching the door behind her.

For a while I remained kneeling by the body of the Count in a numbed stupor. All was so

quiet and peaceful that I could not credit what had
happened in this last hour, not though I held the
Count within my arms. Then from the floor of
the room above there came once more the light
tapping sound of a woman's heels. I looked about
me. The table lay overturned, the rugs were heaped
and scattered, and the barrel of my pistol winked
in the sputtering light of the fire. I rose, snatched
up my sword, and fled out on to the snow.

The moon was setting and the moonlight grey
upon the garden, with the snow under foot very crisp
and dry.

I sheathed my sword and clambered on to the
coping. I turned to look at the Castle—how quietly
it slept, and how brightly burned the lights in those
two rooms!—and then dropped to the ledge upon the
further side of the wall.

I had reached the top of the ridge of rock, when
a cry rang out into the night—a cry, shrill and
lonesome, in a woman's voice—a cry followed by a
great silence. I halted in an agony. 'Twas not fear
that I felt ; 'twas not even pity. The cry spoke of
suffering too great for pity, and I stood aghast at
the sound of it, aghast at the thought that my
handiwork had begotten it. 'Twas not repeated,
however, and I tore down the ridge in a frenzy
of haste, taking little care where I set my hands
or my feet. How it was that I did not break my
neck I have never been able to think.

The village, I remember, was dark and lifeless
save just at one house, whence came a murmur of
voices, and a red beam of light slipped through a

chink in the shutter and lay like a rillet of blood across the snow.

Once clear of the houses, I ran at full speed down the track. At the corner of the wood, I stopped and looked upwards before I plunged among the trees. The moon had set behind the mountains while I was descending the ridge, and the Castle loomed vaguely above me as though at that spot the night was denser than elsewhere. 'Twas plain that no alarm had been taken, that the cry had not been heard. I understood the reason of this afterwards. The two rooms in the tower were separated by a great interval from the other bedrooms. But what of the Countess, I thought? I pictured her in a swoon upon the corpse of her husband.

Within the coppice 'twas so black that I could not see my hand when I raised it before me, and I went groping my way by guesswork towards the trees to which we had tethered our horses. I dared not call out to Larke; I feared even the sound of my footsteps. Every rustle of the bushes seemed to betray a spy. In the end I began to fancy that I should wander about the coppice until dawn, when close to my elbow there rose a low crooning song:

> Que toutes joies et toutes honneurs
> Viennent d'armes et d'amours.

"Jack!" I whispered.

The undergrowth crackled as he crushed it beneath his feet.

"Morrice, is that you? Where are you?"

A groping hand knocked against my arm and tightened on it. I gave a groan.

"Are you hurt, Morrice? Oh, my God! I thought you would never come!"

"You have heard nothing?"

"Nothing."

"Not a sound? Not—not a cry?"

"Nothing."

"Quick, then!" said I. "We must be miles away by morning."

He led me to where our horses stood, and we untied them and threaded through the trees to the road.

"Help me to mount, Jack!" said I.

He pulled a flask from his pocket and held it to my lips. 'Twas neat brandy, but I gulped a draught of it as though it were so much water. Then he helped me into the saddle and settled my feet in the stirrups.

"Why, Morrice," he asked, "what have you done with your spurs?"

"I left them on the terrace," said I, remembering. "I left my spurs, my pistol, and—and something else. But quick, Jack, quick!"

'Twould have saved me much trouble had I brought that "something else" with me, or at least examined it more closely before I left it there.

He swung himself on to the back of his horse, and we set off at a canter. But we had not gone twenty yards when I cried, "Stop!" 'Twas as though the windows of the Castle sprang at us suddenly out of the darkness, each one alive with a tossing glare of links. It seemed to me that a hundred angry eyes were searching for me. I drove my heels into my horse's flanks and galloped madly down the road in the direction of

Italy. A quarter of a mile further, and a bend of the valley hid the Castle from our sight; but I knew that I should never get the face of Countess Lukstein from before my eyes, or the sound of her cry out of my ears.

CHAPTER VII.

FROM Lukstein we rode hot-foot down the Vintschgau Thal to Meran, and thence by easy stages to
Verona, in Italy. I had no great fear of pursuit or
detection after the first day, since the road was much
frequented by travellers, and neither my spurs, nor
my pistol, nor the miniature of Julian bore any marks
by which Jack or myself could be singled out. At
Verona an inflammation set up in my wounded
shoulder, very violent and severe, so that I lay in that
town for some weeks delirious and at death's door.
Indeed, but for Jack's assiduous care in nursing me,
I must infallibly have lost my life.

At length, however, being somewhat recovered, I
was carried southwards to Naples, and thence we
wandered from town to town through the provinces
of Italy until, in the year 1686, the fulness of the
spring renewed my blood and set my fancies in a tide
towards home. Jack accompanied me to England
and took up his abode in my house in Cumberland,
being persuaded without much difficulty to abandon
his pretence of studying the law, and to throw in his
lot with me for good and all.

"My estates need a steward," said I, "and I—God knows I need a friend." And with little more talk the bargain was struck.

During all this time, however, I had not so much as breathed a word to him concerning the doings of that night in Castle Lukstein. At first the matter was too hot in my thoughts, and even afterwards, when the horror of my memories had dimmed, I could not bring myself to the point of speech. Had it not been for the appearance and intervention of the Countess, doubtless I should have blurted out the tale long before. But with her face ever fixed within my view, I could not speak; I could only picture it desolate with grief, and washed with a pitiful rain of tears. Moreover, I knew that Jack would account my story as the story of a worthy exploit, and I shrank from his praise as from a burning iron.

'Twould have, nevertheless, been strange had not my ravings in my delirium disclosed some portion of the night's incidents, and that they did so I understood from a certain speech Jack once made me. 'Twas when I was yet lying sick at Verona. One morning, when I was come to my senses after a feverish night, he walked over to my bedside from the chair where he had been watching.

"I have been a common fool," says he, and repeats the remark, shifting a foot to and fro on the floor; and then he claps his hand upon mine.

"God send me such a friend as you, Morrice, if ever trouble comes to me!" says he, and so gets him quickly from the room.

Often did I wonder how much I had betrayed, but I had reason subsequently to believe that 'twas

very little; just enough to assure him that I had not
flinched from the conflict, with probably some
revelation of the fear in which I engaged upon it.

'Twas in the last days of March that I saw once
more the rolling slopes of Yewbarrow, streaked here
and there with a ribbon of snow, and my house at the
base of it, its grey tiles shining in the sunset like
glass ; and a homely restfulness settled upon my spirit,
and looking back upon the last months of purposeless
wandering, I resolved to pass my days henceforward
in a placid ordering of my estate.

This feeling of peace, however, stayed with me no
great while, the very monotony of a quiet life casting
me back upon my troubled recollections. As a relief,
I sought diversion with Jack's ready assistance in the
pleasures of the field. Hawking, hunting, and
climbing—for which somehow my companion never
acquired a taste—filled out the hours of daylight.
We chased the fox on foot along ridges of the hills ;
we hunted the red deer in the forests about Styhead ;
we walked miles across fell and valley to watch a
wrestling-match or attend a fair. In a word, we lived
a clean, open-air life of wholesome activity.

But alas! 'Twas of little profit to me. I would
get me tired to bed only to plunge into a whirlpool
of unrestful dreams, and toss there until the morning.
Sometimes it would be the door of the little staircase
to the Count's bedroom. I would see it opening and
opening perpetually, and yet never wide open; or
again, it would grow gigantic in size, and swing back
across the world as though it was hinged betwixt the
poles. Most often, however, it would be Count
Lukstein's wife. I beheld her now, tall and stately,

with her glorious aureole of hair and her dark,
unseeing eyes eating through me like a slow fire as
she advanced across the room; now I followed her as
she moved through the moonlit garden with the taper
burning clear and steady in her hand. But, however
the dream began, 'twould always end the same way.
The fiery windows of Castle Lukstein would leap
upon me out of the darkness, and I would wake in a
cold sweat, my body a-quiver, and her lone cry
knelling in my ears.

A strange feature of these nightmare fancies, and
a feature that greatly perplexed me, was that the
Count himself played no part in them. Were my
dreams the test and touchstone of the truth, I could
never so much as have set eyes upon him. The
encounter, the conversation which preceded it, the
last cowardly thrust, and the dead form huddled up
in my arms among the curtains—of these things I
had not even a hint. They became erased from my
memory the moment that I fell asleep. Then 'twas
always the woman who was pictured to me; in
no single instance the man. I wondered at this
omission the more, inasmuch as I frequently thought
of Count Lukstein during the day-time, remembering
with an odd sense of envy the softness of his voice
when he spoke concerning his wife.

Spent with the double fatigue of the day's
exertions and the night's phantasmal horrors, I
betook myself at length to my library, seeking rest,
if not forgetfulness, among my old companions.
But the delight and joy of books had gone out
from me, and nowise could I recover it. Once the
very covers had seemed to me to answer the pressure

of my fingers with a friendly welcome; now I applied myself straightway to the text as to a laborious and uncongenial task. I had looked so deeply into a tragic reality that these printed images of life appeared false and distorted, like reflections thrown from a convex mirror; and I understood how it is that those who act are but seldom their own historians, and when they are, content themselves with a simple register of deeds. However, I persevered in this course for a while, hoping that some time my former zest and liking would return to me, and I should taste again the fine flavour of a nicely-ordered sentence or of a discriminate sequence of thoughts.

But one May morning, coming into the study shortly after sunrise, I sat me down, with my limbs unrefreshed and aching, before the "Religio Medici" of the Norwich doctor, and I fell immediately across this passage :

"I have heard some with deep sighs lament the lost lines of Cicero; others with as many groans deplore the combustion of the library of Alexandria. For my own part, I think there be too many in the world, and could with patience behold the urn and ashes of the Vatican, could I, with a few others, recover the perished leaves of Solomon."

The words chimed so appositely with my thoughts that I resolved there and then to put the theory into practice, and closing the book, I made a beginning with Sir Thomas Browne. Outside the window the birds piped happily from vernal branches; the shadows played hide-and-seek upon the grass, and the beck babbled and laughed as it raced down

K

behind the house. I locked the door of the library,
and taking the key in my hand, walked to the side of
the beck. At this point the stream spouted in a
fountain from a cleft of rock, and fell some twelve
feet into a deep bason. A group of larches over-
hung the pool, and the sunlight, sprinkling between
the leaves, dappled the clear green surface with
an ever-shifting pattern. Into this bason I dropped
the key, and watched it sink with a sparkling tail of
bubbles to the bottom. 'Twas of a bright metal, so
that I could still see it distinctly as it rested on the
rock-bed. A large stone lay upon the bank beside
me, and with a sudden, uncontrollable impulse I
stripped off my clothes, picked up the stone, and
diving into the cool water, set it carefully atop of the
key. Many months passed before I came again to
the pool, and found the key still hidden safe beneath
the stone ; and during those months so much that was
strange occurred to me, and I wandered along such
new and devious paths, that when I held it again, all
rusty and corroded, in my hand, I felt as though it
could not have been myself who had dropped it there,
but some one whose memories had been transmitted
to me and incorporated in my being by a mysterious
alchemy.

It was on that very afternoon that the letter
was brought to me. Jack and I were sitting at
dinner in the big oak dining-room about four of the
clock ; the great windows were open, and the sunny air
streamed in laden with fresh perfumes. I can see
Jim Ritson now as he rode up the drive—'twas
part of his duty to meet the mail at the post-town of
Cockermouth—I can almost hear his voice as he

gave in the letter at the hall-door. "There's a letter for t' maister," he said.

Jim is grown to middle age by this time, and owns a comfortable fat face and a brood of children. But whenever I pass him in the lanes and fields I ever experience a lively awe and respect for him as for the accredited messenger of fate.

The letter came from Lord Elmscott and urged me to visit him in town.

"Come !" he wrote. "To the dust of Leyden you are superadding the mould of Cumberland. Come and brush yourself clean with the contact of wits ! There is much afoot that should interest you. What with Romish priests and English bishops, the town is in ferment. Moreover, a new beauty hath come to Court. There is nothing very strange in that. But she is a foreigner, and her rivals have as yet discovered no scandal to smirch her with. There is something very strange in that. Such a miracle is well worth a man's beholding. She hails from the Tyrol and is the widow of one Count Lukstein, who was in London last year. She wears no mourning for her husband, and hath many suitors. I have of late won much money at cards, and so readily forgive you for that you were the death of Phœbe."

The letter ran on to some considerable length, but I read no more of it. Indeed, I understood little of what I had read. The face of Countess Lukstein seemed stamped upon the page to the obscuring of the inscription. I passed it across to Jack without a word, and he perused it silently and tossed it back.

K 2

All that evening I sat smoking my pipe and pondering the proposal. An overmastering desire to see her features alive with the changing lights of expression, began to possess me. The more I thought, the more ardently I longed to behold her. If only I could see her eyes alert and glancing, if only I could hear her voice, I might free myself from the picture of the blank, impassive mask which she wore in my dreams. That way, I fancied, and that way alone, should I find peace.

"I shall go," I said at last, knocking the ashes from my pipe. "I shall go to-morrow."

"You shan't!" cried Jack vehemently, springing up and facing me. "She knows you. She has seen you."

"She has never seen me," I replied steadily, and he gazed into my face with a look of bewilderment which gradually changed into fear.

"Are you mad, Morrice?" he asked, in a broken whisper, and took a step or two backwards, keeping his eyes fixed upon mine.

"Nay, Jack," said I ; "but unless God helps me, I soon shall be. He may be helping me now. I trust so, for this visit alone can save me."

"She has never seen you?" he repeated. "Swear it ! Morrice ! Swear it ! "

I did as he bade me.

"What brings her to England?" he mused.

"What kept us wandering about Italy?" I answered. "The fear to return home."

"'Twill not serve," said he. "She wears no mourning for her husband."

I wondered at this myself, but could come at no

solution, and so got me to bed. That night, for the first time since I left Austria, I slept dreamlessly. In the morning I was yet more determined to go. I felt, indeed, as though I had no power to stay, and, hurrying on my servants, I prepared to set out at two of the afternoon. Udal and two other of my men I took with me.

"Morrice," said Jack, as he stood upon the steps of the porch, "don't stay with your cousin! Hire a lodging of your own!"

"Why?" I asked, in surprise.

"You talk overmuch in your sleep. Only two nights ago I heard you making such an outcry that I feared you would wake the house. I rushed into your room. You were crouched up among the bed-curtains at the head of the bed and gibbering : 'It will touch her. It flows so fast. Oh, my God! My God!'"

I made no answer to his words, and he asked again very earnestly :

"The Countess has never seen you? You are sure?"

"Quite!" said I firmly, and I shook him by the hand, and so started for London.

CHAPTER VIII.

I MAKE A BOW TO COUNTESS LUKSTEIN.

IN London I engaged a commodious lodging on the south side of St. James' Park, and with little delay, you may be sure, sought out my cousin in Monmouth, or rather Soho, Square—for the name had been altered since the execution of the Duke. 'Twas some half an hour after noon, and my cousin, but newly out of bed, was breakfasting upon a bottle of Burgundy in his nightcap and dressing-gown.

"So you have come, Morrice," said Elmscott languidly. "How do ye? Lord Culverton, this is my cousin of whom I have spoken."

He turned towards a little popinjay man who was fluttering about the room in a laced coat, and powdered periwig which hung so full about his face that it was difficult to distinguish any feature beyond a thin, prominent nose.

"You should know one another. For if you re-member, Morrice, it was Culverton you robbed of Phœbe."

"Phœbe?" simpered Lord Culverton. "I re-member no Phœbe. But in truth the pretty creatures pester one so impertinently that burn me if I don't jumble up their names. What was she like, Mr. Buckler ? "

" She was piebald," said I gravely, "and needed cudgelling before she would walk."

" And Morrice killed her," added Elmscott, with a laugh.

" Then he did very well to kill her, strike me speechless ! But there must be some mistake. I have met many women who needed cudgelling before they would walk, but never one that was piebald."

Elmscott explained the matter to him, and then, with some timidity, I began to inquire concerning the Countess Lukstein.

" What ! bitten already ? " cried my cousin. " Faith, I knew not I had so smart a hand for description."

" The most rapturous female, pink me ! " broke in Lord Culverton. " She is but newly come to London, and hath the town at her feet already. Egad ! I'm half-soused in love myself, split my windpipe ! " and he flicked a speck of powder from his velvet coat, and carefully arranged the curls of his periwig. " The most provoking creature ! " he went on. " A widow without a widow's on-coming disposition."

" Ay, but she hath discarded the weeds," said Elmscott.

" She is a widow none the less. And yet breathe but one word of tender adoration in her ear, and she strikes you dumb, O Lard ! with the most supercilious eyebrow. However, time may do much with the obstinate dear—time, a tolerable phrase, and a *je ne sçay quoi* in one's person and conversation."

He pointed a skinny leg before the mirror, and languished with a ludicrous extravagance at his own reflection.

I had much ado to restrain myself from laughing, the more especially when Elmscott cried, with a wink at me:

" Oh, if you have entered the lists, the rest of us may creep out with as little ignominy as we can. They say that every pretty woman has a devil at her elbow, and 'tis most true, so long as Culverton lives."

" You flatter me ! A devil, indeed ! You flatter me," replied the fop, skipping with delight. " You positively flatter me. The ladies use me—no more. I am only their humble servant in general, and the Countess Lukstein's in particular."

The remark had more truth in it than Culverton would have cared for us to believe. For the Countess did in very truth use this gossipy tittle-tattler, and with no more consideration than she showed to the humblest of her servants. However, he was born for naught else but to fetch and carry, and since he delighted in the work, 'twas common kindness to employ him.

" Then we'll drink a health to your success," says Elmscott, pouring out three glasses of his Burgundy.

" I never drink in the morning," objected Culverton. " 'Tis a most villainous habit, and ruins the complexion irretrievably, stap my vitals ! "

However, I was less squeamish on the subject of mine, and draining the glass, I asked :

" Is she come to London alone ? "

"She hath a companion, a very faded, nauseous person: a Frenchwoman, Mademoiselle Durette. She serves as a foil;" and Culverton launched forth into an affected estimation of Countess Lukstein's charms. Her eyes dethroned the planets, the brightness of her hair shamed the sunlight; for her mouth, 'twas a Cupid's bow that shot a deadly arrow with every word. When she danced, her foot was a snow-flake upon the floor, and the glint of the buckle on her instep, a flame threatening to melt it; when she played upon the harp, her fingers were the ivory plectrums of the ancients.

"You make me curious," I interrupted him, "to become acquainted with the lady."

"Then let me present you!" said he eagerly.

"You see, Morrice," said Elmscott, "he has such solid grounds for confidence that he has no fear of rivals."

"Nay, the truth is, she has a passion for fresh faces."

"Indeed!" said I.

"Oh, most extraordinary! A veritable passion, and no one so graciously received as he who brings a stranger to her side. For that reason," he added naïvely, "I would fain present you;" and then he suddenly stopped and surveyed me, shaking his head doubtfully the while.

"But Lard! Mr. Buckler," he said, "you must first get some new clothes."

"The clothes are good enough," I laughed, for I was dressed in my best suit, and though 'twas something more modest than my Lord Culverton's attire, I was none the less pleased with it on that account.

"Rabbit me, but I daren't!" he said. "I daren't introduce you in that suit. I daren't, indeed! My character would never survive the imputation, strike me purple if it would! 'Tis a very yeoman's habit, and reeks of the country. I can smell onions and all sorts of horrible things, burn me!"

"I will run the risk, Morrice," interposed Elmscott. "Dine with me to-day at Lockett's, and I will take you to the Countess' lodging in Pall Mall afterwards. But Culverton's right. You do look like a Quaker, and that's the truth."

However, I paid little attention to what they said or thought concerning my appearance. The knowledge that I was to meet Countess Lukstein and have speech with her no later than that very evening, engendered within me an indescribable excitement. I got free from my companions as speedily as I could, and passed the hours till dinner-time in a vague expectancy; though what it was that I expected, I could not have told even to myself.

About seven of the clock we repaired to her apartments. The rooms were already filled with a gay crowd of ladies and gentlemen dressed in the extreme of fashion, and at first I could get no glimpse of the Countess. But I looked towards the spot where the throng was thickest, and the tripping noise of pleasantries most loud, and then I saw her. Elmscott advanced; I followed close upon his heels, the circle opened, magically it seemed to me, and I stood face to face with her at last.

Yet for all that I was prepared for it, now that

I beheld her but six steps from me, now that I
looked straight into her eyes, a strange sense of
unreality stole over me, dimming my brain like
a mist; so incredible did it appear to me that we
who had met before in such a tragic conjunction
in that far-away nook of the Tyrol, should now be
presented each to the other like the merest strangers,
amidst the brightness and gaiety of London town. I
almost expected the candles to go out, and the
company to dissolve into air. I almost began to
dread that I should wake up in a moment to find
myself in the dark, crouched up upon my bed in
Cumberland. So powerfully did this fear possess
me that I was on the point of crying aloud, "Speak!
speak!" when Elmscott took me by the arm.

"Madame," said he, "I have taken the liberty
of bringing hither my cousin, Mr. Morrice Buckler,
who is anxious—as who is not?—for the honour of
your acquaintance."

"It is no liberty," she replied graciously, in a
voice that was exquisitely sweet, and she let her
eyes fall upon my face with a quick and watchful
scrutiny.

The next instant, however, the alertness died out
of them.

"Mr. Buckler is very welcome," she said quietly,
and it struck me that there was some hint of
disappointment in her tone, and maybe a touch of
weariness. If, indeed, what Culverton had said
was true, and she had a passion for fresh faces,
'twas evident that mine was to be exempted from
the rule.

It might have been the expression of her indifference, or perchance the mere sound of her voice broke the spell upon me, but all at once I became sensible to the full of my sober, sad-coloured clothes. I looked about me. Coats and dresses brilliant with gold and brocade mingled their colours in a flashing rainbow, jewels sparkled and winked as they caught the light, and I felt that every eye in this circle of elegant courtiers was fixed disdainfully upon the awkward intruder.

I faltered through a compliment, conscious the while that I had done better to have held my tongue. I heard a titter behind me, and here and there some fine lady or gentleman held a quizzing-glass to the eye, as though I was some strange natural from over-seas. All the blood in my body seemed to run tingling into my face. I half turned to flee away and take to my heels, but a second glance at the sneering countenances around me stung my pride into wakefulness, and resolving to put the best face on the matter I could, I attempted a sweeping bow. Whether my foot slipped, whether some one tripped me purposely with a sword, I know not—I was too flustered to think at the time or to remember afterwards—but whatever the cause, I found myself plumped down upon my knees before her, with the titter changed into an open laugh.

"Hush!" lisped one of the bystanders, "don't disturb the gentleman; he is saying his prayers."

I rose to my feet in the greatest confusion.

"Madame," I stammered, "I come to my knees no earlier than the rest of your acquaintance. Only being country-bred, I do it with the less discretion."

She laughed with a charming friendliness which
lifted me somewhat out of my humiliation.

"The adroitness of the recovery, Mr. Buckler,"
she said, "more than atones for the maladresse of
the attack."

"Nay," I protested, with what may well have
appeared excessive earnestness, "the simile does
me some injustice, for it hints of an antagonism
betwixt you and me."

She glanced at me with some surprise and more
amusement in her eyes.

"Are not all men a woman's antagonists?" she
said lightly.

But to me it seemed an ill-omened beginning.
There was something too apposite in her chance
phrase. I remembered, besides, that I had stumbled
to the ground in much the same way before her
husband, and I bethought me what had come of
the slip.

'Twas but for a little, however, that these gloomy
forebodings possessed me, and I retired to the outer
edge of the throng, whence I could observe her
motions and gestures undisturbed. And with a
growing contentment I perceived that ever and
again her eyes would stray towards me, and she
would drop some question into Elmscott's ear.

The Countess wore, I remember, a gown of purple
velvet fronted with yellow satin, which to my eyes
hung a trifle heavily upon her young figure and so
emphasized its slenderness, imparting even to her
neck and head a certain graceful fragility. The rich
colour of her hair was hidden beneath a mask of
powder after the fashion, and below it her face shone

pale, pale indeed as when I saw her last, but with a
wonderful clarity and pureness of complexion, so
that as she spoke the blood came and went very
prettily about her cheeks and temples. The two
attributes, however, which I noted with the greatest
admiration were her eyes and voice. For it seemed
to me well-nigh beyond belief that the eyes which
I now saw flashing with so lively a fire were the
same which had stared vacantly into mine at
Lukstein Castle, and that the voice which I now
heard musical with all the notes of laughter was
that which had sent the shrill, awful scream tearing
the night.

After a while the company sat down to basset
and quadrille, and I was left standing disconsolately
by myself. I looked around for Elmscott, being
minded to depart, when her voice sounded at my
elbow, and I forgot all but the sweetness of it.

"Mr. Buckler," she asked, "you do not play?"

"No," I replied. "I have seen but little of either
cards or dice, and that little has given me no liking
for them."

"Then I will make bold to claim your services,
for the room is hot, and my ears, perchance, a little
tired."

'Twas with no small pride, you may be sure,
that I gave my arm to the Countess; only I could
have wished that she had laid her hand less delicately
upon my sleeve. Indeed, I should hardly have
known that it rested there at all had I not felt
its touch more surely on the strings of my heart.

We went into a smaller apartment at the end
of the room, which was dimly lit, and very cool

and peaceful. The window stood open and showed
a little balcony with a couch. The Countess seated
herself upon it with a sigh of relief, and leaning
forward, plucked a sprig of flowers which grew in
a pot at her side.

"I love these flowers," said she, holding the
spray towards me.

'Twas the blue flower of the aconite plant, and I
answered :

" They remind you of your home."

" Then you know the Tyrol, and have travelled
there." She turned to me with a lively interest.

" I learnt that much of botany at school."

" There should be a fellow-feeling between us,
Mr. Buckler," she said after a pause ; "for we are
both strangers to London, waifs thrown together
for an hour."

"But there is a world of difference, for you
might have lived amongst these gallants all your
days, while I, alas! have no skill even to hide my
awkwardness."

" Nay, no excuses, for I like you the better for
the lack of that skill."

" Madame," I began, " such words from you——"

She turned to me with a whimsical entreaty.

"Prithee, no ! To tell the honest truth, I am
surfeited with compliments, and 'twould give me
a great pleasure if during these few minutes we
are together you would style me neither nymph,
divinity, nor angel, but would treat me as just a
woman. The fashion, indeed, is not worth copying,
the more especially when, to quote your own phrase,
one copies it without discretion."

She laughed pleasantly as she spake, and the words conveyed not so much a rebuke as the amiable raillery of an intimate.

"'Tis true," I replied, "I do envy these townsmen. I envy them their grace of bearing and the nimbleness of their wits, which ever reminds me of the sparkle in a bottle of Rhenish wine."

She shook her head, and made room for me by her side.

"The bottle has stood open for me these two months since, and I begin to find the wine is very flat."

She dropped her voice at the end of the sentence, and leaned wearily back upon the cushions.

"You see, Mr. Buckler," she explained, "I live amongst the hills," and there was a certain wistfulness in her tone as of one home-sick.

"Then there is a second bond between us, for I live amongst the hills as well."

"It is that," said she, "which makes us friends," and just for a second she laid a hand upon my sleeve. It seemed to me that no man ever heard sweeter words or more sweetly spoken from the lips of woman.

"But since you are here," I questioned eagerly, "you will stay—you will stay for a little?"

"I know not," she replied, smiling at my urgency; and then with a certain sadness, "some day I shall go back, I hope, but when, I know not. It might be in a week, it might be in a year, it might be never." Of a sudden she gave a low cry of pain. "I daren't go home," she cried, "I daren't until—until——"

"Until you have forgotten." The words were on the tip of my tongue, but I caught them back in time, and for a while we sat silent. The Countess appeared to grow all unconscious of my presence, and gazed steadily down the quiet street as though it stretched beyond and beyond in an avenue of leagues, and she could see waving at the end of it the cedars and pine-trees of her Tyrol.

Nor was I in any hurry to arouse her. A noisy rattle of voices streamed out on a flood of yellow light from the further windows on my left, and here she and I were alone in the starlit dusk of a summer night. Her very silence was sweet to me with the subtlest of flatteries. For I looked upon it as the recognition - of a tie of sympathy which raised me from the general throng of her courtiers into the narrow circle of her friends.

So I sat and watched her. The pure profile of her face was outlined against the night, the perfume of her hair stole into my nostrils, and every now and then her warm breath played upon my cheek. A fold of her train had fallen across my ankle, and the soft touch of the velvet thrilled me like a caress; I dared not move a muscle for fear lest I should displace it.

At length she spoke again—'twas almost in a whisper.

"I have told you more about myself than I have told to any one since I came to England. It is your turn now. Tell me where lies your home!"

"In the north. In Cumberland."

"In—in Cumberland," she repeated, with a little catch of her breath. "You have lived there long?"

L

" 'Twas the home of my fathers, and I spent my boyhood there. But between that time and this year's spring I have been a stranger to the country-side. For I was first for some years at Oxford, and thence I went to Leyden."

She rose abruptly from the couch, drawing her train clear of me with her hand, and leaned over the balcony, resting her elbow on its baluster, and propping her chin upon the palm of her hand.

" Leyden ! " she said carelessly. " 'Tis a town of great beauty, they tell me, and much visited by English students."

" There were but few English students there during the months of my residence," said I. " I could have wished there had been more."

A second period of silence interrupted our talk, and I sat wondering over that catch in her breath and the tremor of her voice when she repeated " Cumberland." Was it possible, I asked myself, that she could have learnt of Sir Julian Harnwood and of his quarrel with her husband ? If she did know, and if she attributed the duel in which her husband fell to a result of it, why, then—Cumberland was Julian's county, and the name might well strike with some pain upon her hearing. But who could have informed her ? Not the Count, surely ; 'twas hardly a matter of which a man could boast to his wife. I remembered, besides, that he had asked me to speak English, and to speak it low. There could have been but one motive for the request—a desire to keep the subject of our conversation a secret from the Countess.

I glanced towards her. Without changing her attitude she had turned her head sideways upon her palm, and was quietly looking me over from head to foot. Then she rose erect, and with a frank and winning smile, she said, as if in explanation :

"I was seeking to discover, Mr. Buckler, what it was in you that had beguiled me to forget the rest of my guests. However, if I have shown them but scant courtesy, I shall bid them reproach you, not me."

"Prithee, madame, no! Have some pity on me! The statement would get me a thousand deadly enemies."

"Hush!" said she, with a playful menace. "You go perilous near to a compliment;" and we went back into the glare and noise of the drawing-room.

"Ah, Ilga! I have missed you this half-hour."

'Twas a little woman of, I should say, forty years who bustled up to us on our entrance.

"You see?" said the Countess, turning to me with a whimsical reproach. "You must blame Mr. Buckler, Clemence, and I will make you acquainted that you may have the occasion."

She presented me thus to Mademoiselle Durette, and left us together. But I fear the good woman must have found me the poorest company, for I paid little heed to what she said, and carried away no recollection beyond that her chatter wearied me intolerably, and that once or twice I caught the word "convenances," whence I gather she was reading me a lecture.

L 2

I got rid of her as soon as I decently could, and took my leave of the Countess. She gave me her hand, and I bent over and kissed it. 'Twas only the glove I kissed, but the hand was within the glove, as I had reason to know, for I felt it tremble within my fingers and then tug quickly away.

"One compliment I will allow you to pay me," she said, "and that is a renewal of your visit."

" Madame permits," I exclaimed joyfully.

" Madame will be much beholden to you," says she, and drops me a mocking curtsey.

I walked down the staircase in a prodigious elation. Six steps from the floor of the hall it made a curve, and as I turned at the angle I stopped dead of a sudden with my heart leaping within my breast. For at the foot of the stairs, and looking at me now straight in the face, as he had looked at me in the archway of Bristol Bridewell, I saw Otto Krax, the servant of Count Lukstein. The unexpected sight of his massive figure came upon me like a blow. I had forgotten him completely. I staggered back into the angle of the wall. He must know me, I thought. He *must* know me. But he gazed with no more than the stolid attention of a lackey. There was not a trace of recognition in his face, not a start of his muscles ; and then I remembered the difference in my garb. 'Twould have been strange indeed if he had known me.

I recovered my composure, drew a long breath of relief, and was about to step down to him when I happened to glance up the stairway.

The Countess herself was leaning over the rail at

its head, with the light from the hall-lamp below
streaming up into her face. I 'had not heard her
come out on the landing.

"I knew not whether Otto Krax was there to let
you out." She smiled at me. "Good night!"

"Good night," said I, and looking at Otto, I
understood whence she might have got some
knowledge of Sir Julian Harnwood.

Once outside, I stood for a while loitering in front
of the house, and wondering how much 'twould cost
to buy it up. For I believed that it would be a
degradation should any other woman lodge in those
same rooms afterwards.

In a few minutes Elmscott came out to me.

"You have seen the Countess Lukstein before?"
he asked, and the words fairly startled me.

"What in Heaven's name makes you think that?"

"I fancied I read it in your looks. Your eyes
went straight to her before ever I presented you."

"That proves no more than the merit of your
description."

"Well, did I exaggerate? What think you?"

I drew a long breath. 'Twas the only description
I could give. There were no words in the language
equal to my thoughts.

"That will suffice," said Elmscott, and he turned
away.

"One moment," I cried. "I need a service of
you."

He burst out into a laugh.

"A thousand pounds to a guinea I know the
service. 'Tis the address of my tailor you need. I

saw you looking down at your clothes as though the wearing of them sullied you. Very well, one of my servants shall be with you in the morning with a complete list of my tradesmen." And he swung off in the direction of Piccadilly, laughing as he went, while I, filled with all sorts of romantical notions, walked back to my lodging. Though, indeed, to say that I walked, falls somewhat short of the truth ; to speak by the book, I fairly scampered, and arrived breathless at my doorstep.

My servants had unpacked my baggage, and with a momentary pang of misgiving, I observed, lying on the table, my ill-omened copy of Horace.

" How comes this here ? " I inquired sharply of Udal, taking the book in my hands.

It opened at once at the diagram, and the date upon the leaf opposite. So often had this outline been scanned and examined that the merest fingering of the cover served to make the book fall open at this particular page. I doubt, indeed, whether it had been possible to lift or move the volume at all without noticing the diagram.

Udal told me that Jack himself had placed the book in my trunk. He intended it as a hint for my conduct, I made certain, and, newly come as I was from the presence of Countess Lukstein, I felt no gratitude for his interference. I tossed the book on to a side-table by the chimney, where it lay henceforward forgotten, and proceeded to light my pipe.

'Twas late when I mounted to my bedroom. The moon was in its last quarter, and the park which my window overlooked lay very fair and quiet in the soft light. What nonsense does a man con over and ponder at such times! Yet 'tis very pleasant nonsense, and though it keeps him out of bed o' nights, he may yet draw good from it—ay, and more good than from quartos of philosophy.

CHAPTER IX.

THE next morning, and while I was still in bed drinking a cup of chocolate, came Elmscott's servant to me, and under his guidance I set forth to purchase such apparel as would enable me to cut a more passable figure in the eyes of Countess Lukstein. Seldom, I think, had the shopkeepers a customer so nice and difficult to please. Here the wares were too plain and insignificant ; there too gaudy and pretentious, for while I was resolved to go no longer dressed like a Quaker, I was in no way minded to ape the extravagance of my lord Culverton. At last I determined upon a dozen suits, rich but of a sober colour, and being measured for them, went from the tailor's to the hosier's, shoemaker's, lace-merchant's, and I know not what other tradesmen. Muslin jabots, Holland shirts, ruffles of Mechlin and point de Venise, silk stockings, shoes with high red heels, which I needed particularly, for I was of no great stature, laced gloves—I bought enough, in truth, to make fine gentlemen of a company of soldiers.

Needless to say, when once my purchases were delivered at my lodging, I let no long time slip by before I repeated my visit to the house in Pall Mall. The Countess welcomed me with the same kindliness, so that I returned again and again. She distinguished me besides by displaying an especial interest not merely in my present comings and goings, but in the past history of my uneventful days. Surely there is no flattery in the world so potent and bewitching as the questions which a woman puts to a man concerning those years of his life which were spent before their paths had crossed. And if the history be dull as mine was, a trivial, homely record of common acts and thoughts, why, then the flattery is doubled. I know that it intoxicated me like a heady wine, and I almost dared to hope that she grudged the time during which we had been strangers.

Her bearing, indeed, towards me struck me as little short of wonderful, for I observed that she evinced to the rest of her courtiers and friends a certain pride and stateliness which, while it sat gracefully upon her, tempered her courtesy with an unmistakable reserve.

The summer was now at its height, and the Countess—or Ilga, as I had come to style her in my thoughts—would be ever planning some new excursion. One day it would be a water-party to view the orangery and myrtelum of Sir Henry Capel at Kew; on another we would visit the new camp at Hounslow, which in truth, with its mountebanks and booths, resembled more nearly a country fair than a garrison of armed men; or again on a third we would attend a coursing match in the fields behind Montague House. In short, seldom a day passed but I saw her and had talk with her; and if it was but for

five minutes, well, the remaining hours went by to
the lilt of her voice like songs to the sweet accom-
paniment of a viol.

One afternoon Elmscott walked down to my
lodging, and carried me with him to see a famous
comedy by Mr. Farquhar which was that day
repeated by the Duke's players. The second act
was begun by the time we got to the theatre, and the
house, in spite of the heat, very crowded. For
awhile I watched with some interest the packed
company in the pit, the orange-girls hawking their
baskets amongst them, the masked women in the
upper boxes and the crowd of bloods upon the stage,
who were continually shifting their positions, bowing
to ladies in the side-boxes, ogling the actresses, and
airing their persons and dress to the great detriment
of the spectacle. Amongst these latter gentlemen
I observed Lord Culverton combing the curls of his
periwig with a little ivory comb so that a white cloud
of powder hung about his head, and I was wondering
how long his neighbours would put up with his
impertinence when Elmscott, who was standing
beside me, gave a start.

"So he has come back," said he. I followed the
direction of his gaze, and looked across the theatre.
The Countess Lukstein and Mademoiselle Durette
had just entered one of the lower boxes; behind them
in the shadow was the figure of a man.

"Who is it?" I asked.

"An acquaintance of yours."

The man came forward as Elmscott spoke to the
front of the box, and seated himself by the side of
Ilga. He was young, with a white face and very

deep-set eyes, and though his appearance was in some measure familiar to me, I could neither remember his name nor the occasion of our meeting.

"You have forgotten that night at the H. P.?" asked Elmscott.

In a flash I recollected.

"It is Marston," I said, and then after a pause: "And he knows the Countess!"

"As well as you do; maybe better."

"Then how comes it I have never seen him with her before?"

"He left London conveniently before you came hither. We all thought that he had received his dismissal. It rather looks as if we were out of our reckoning, eh?"

Marston and the Countess were engaged in some absorbing talk with their heads very close together, and a sharp pang of jealousy shot through me.

"'Tis strange that she has never mentioned his name," I stammered.

"Not so strange now that Hugh Marston has returned. Had he been no more than the discarded suitor we imagined him, then yes—you might expect her to boast to you of his devotion. 'Tis a way women have. But it seems rather that you are rivals."

Rivals! The word was like a white light flashed upon my memories. I recalled Marston's half-forgotten prophecy. Was this the contest, I wondered, which he had foretold in the chill dawn at the tavern? Were we to come to grips with Ilga for the victor's prize? On the heels of the thought a swift fear slipped through my veins like ice. He had foretold more than the struggle; he had forecast its outcome and result.

It was, I think, at this moment that I first understood all that the Countess Lukstein meant to me. I leaned forward over the edge of the box, and set my eyes upon her face. I noted little of its young beauty, little of its wonderful purity of outline; but I seemed to see more clearly than ever before the woman that lurked behind it, and I felt a new strength, a new courage, a new life, flow out from her to me, and lift my heart. My very sinews braced and tightened about my limbs. If Marston and I were to fight for Ilga, it should be hand to hand, and foot to foot, in the deadliest determination.

Meanwhile she still spoke earnestly with her companion. Of a sudden, however, she raised her eyes from him, and glanced across towards us. I was still leaning forward, a conspicuous mark, and I saw her face change. She gave an abrupt start of surprise; there appeared to me something of uneasiness in the movement. She looked apprehensively at Marston, and back again at me; then she turned away from him, and sat with downcast head plucking with nervous fingers at the fan which lay on the ledge before her, and shooting furtive glances in our direction.

Elmscott, for some reason, began to chuckle.

"Let us make our compliments to the Countess!" he said.

We walked round the circle of the theatre. At the door of the box I stopped him.

"Marston heard nothing from you of my journey to Sir Julian Harnwood?" I asked.

"Not a word! He knows you were travelling to Bristol; so much you said yourself. But for my part, I have never breathed a word of the matter to a living soul." And we went in. The Countess held out her hand to me with a conscious timidity.

"You are not angered?" she said, in a low voice.

The mere thought that she should take such heed of what I might feel, made my pulses leap with joy. She seemed to recognise, as I should never have dared to do myself, that I had a right to be jealous, and her words almost granted me a claim upon her conduct. For answer I bent over her hand and kissed it, and behind me again I heard Elmscott chuckling.

Hugh Marston had risen from his chair as we entered, and stood looking at me curiously.

"You have not met Mr. Marston," she said. "I must make my two best friends acquainted."

I would that she had omitted that word "best," the more especially since she laid some emphasis upon it. It undid some portion of her previous work, and set us both upon a level in her estimation.

"We have met before," said Marston, and he bowed coldly.

"Indeed? I had not heard of that."

Marston recounted to her the story of the gambling-match, but she listened with no apparent attention, fixing her eyes upon the stage.

"I fancied, Mr. Buckler, you had no taste for cards or dice," she said carelessly, when he had done.

"Mr. Buckler in truth only stayed there on compulsion," replied Marston. "He came from Leyden in a great fluster without any money in his pockets, and so must needs wait upon his cousin's pleasure before he could borrow a horse to help him on his way."

I threw a glance of appeal towards Elmscott, and he broke in quickly:

"'Twas Lord Culverton lent him the horse, after all."

But the next moment the Countess herself, to my great relief, brought the conversation to an end.

"Gentlemen, gentlemen!" she said abruptly, with a show of impatience. "I fear me I am as yet so far out of the fashion as to feel some slight interest in the unravelling of the play, and I find it difficult to catch what the players say."

After that there was no more to be said, and we sat watching the stage with what amusement we might, or conversing in the discreetest of whispers. For my part I remembered that Ilga had shown no great interest in the comedy while she was alone with Marston, and I began to wonder whether our intrusion had angered her. It was impossible for me to see her face, since she held up a hand on the side next to me and so screened her cheek.

Suddenly, however, she cried:

"Oh, there's Lord Culverton!" and she bowed to him with marked affability.

Now Culverton had ranged himself in full view with an eye ever turned upon our box, so that it seemed somewhat strange she had not observed him till now. He swept the boards with his hat, and looking about the theatre, his face one gratified smirk, as who should say, " 'Tis an every-day affair with me," immediately left his station, and disappearing behind the scenery, made his way into the box. The Countess received him graciously, and kept him behind her chair, asking many questions concerning the players, and laughing heartily at the pleasantries and innuendos with which he described them. It seemed to me, however, that there was more scandal than wit in his anecdotes, and, marvelling that she should take delight in them, I turned away and let my eyes wander idly about the boxes.

When I glanced again at my companions I perceived that though Culverton was still chattering in Countess Lukstein's ear, her gaze was bent upon me with the same scrutiny which I had noticed on the evening that we sat together in her balcony. It was as though she was taking curious stock of my person and weighing me in some balance of her thoughts. I fancied that she was contrasting me with Marston, and gained some confirmation of the fancy in that she coloured slightly, and said hastily, with a nod at the stage :

" What think you of the sentiment, Mr. Buckler ? "

" Madame," I replied, "for once I am in the fashion, for I gave no heed to it."

I had been, in truth, thinking of her lucky intervention in Marston's narrative, for by her impatience

she had prevented him from telling either the date
of the gambling-match or the name of the town
which I was in such great hurry to reach. Not that
I had any solid reason to fear she would discover
me on that account, for many a man might have
ridden from London to Bristol at the time of the
assizes and had naught to do with Sir Julian Harnwood. But I had so begun to dread the possibility
of her aversion and hatred, that my imagination
found a motive to suspicion lurking in the simplest
of remarks.

"'Twas that a man would venture more for his
friend than for his mistress," she explained. "What
think you of it?"

"Why, that the worthy author has never been
in love."

"You believe that?" she laughed.

"'Twixt friend and friend a man's first thought
is of himself. Shame on us that it should be so;
but, alas! my own experience has proved it. It
needs, I fear me, a woman's fingers to tune him to
the true note of sacrifice."

"And has your own experience proved that
too?" she asked with some hesitation, looking down
on the ground, and twisting a foot to and fro upon
its heel.

"Not so," I answered in a meaning whisper.
"I wait for the woman's fingers and the occasion
of the sacrifice."

She shot a shy glance sideways at me, and, as
though by accident, her hand fell lightly upon mine.
I believed, indeed, that 'twas no more than an

accident until she said quietly : " The occasion may come, too."

She rose from her chair.

" The play begins to weary me," she continued aloud.   " Besides, Mr. Buckler convinces me the playwright has never been in love, and 'tis an unpardonable fault in an author."

Marston and myself started forward to escort her to her carriage.   The Countess looked from one to the other of us as though in doubt, and we stood glaring across her.   Elmscott commenced to chuckle again in a way that was indescribably irritating and silly.

" If Lord Culverton will honour me," suggested the Countess.

The little man was overwhelmed with the favour accorded to him, and with a peacock air of triumph led her from the box.

" 'Tis a monkey, a damned monkey ! " said Marston, looking after him.

The phrase seemed to me a very accurate description of the fop, and I assented to it with great cordiality.   For a little Marston sat sullenly watching the play, and then picking up his hat and cloak, departed without a word.   His precipitate retreat only made my cousin laugh the more heartily ; but I chose to make no remark upon this merriment, believing that Elmscott indulged it chiefly to provoke me to question him.   I knew full well the sort of gibe that was burning on his tongue, and presently imitating Marston's example, I left him to amuse himself.

M

In the portico of the theatre Marston was waiting. A thick fog had fallen with the evening, and snatching a torch from one of the link-boys who stood gathered within the light of the entrance, he beckoned to me to follow him, and stepped quickly across the square into a deserted alley. There he waited for me to come up with him, holding the torch above his head so that the brown glare of the flame was reflected in his eyes.

" So," he said, "luck sets us on opposite sides of the table again, Mr. Buckler. But the game has not begun. You have still time to draw back."

For the moment his words and vehement manner fairly staggered me. I had not expected from him so frank an avowal of rivalry.

"The stakes are high," he went on, pressing his advantage, " and call for a player of more experience than you."

" None the less," said I, meeting his gaze squarely, " I play my hand."

Instantly his manner changed. He looked at me silently for a second, and then with a calmness which intimidated me far more than his passion :

"Are you wise ? Are you wise ? " he asked slowly. " Think l What will the loser keep ? "

" What will the winner gain ? "

We stood measuring each other for the space of a minute in the flare of the torch. Then he dropped it on the ground, and stamped out the sparks with his heel. 'Twas too dark for me to see his face, but I heard his voice at my elbow very smooth and soft, and I knew that he was stooping by my side.

"You will find this the very worst day's work," he said, "to which ever you set your hand;" and I heard his footsteps ring hollow down the street. He had certainly won the first trick in the game, for he left me to pay the link-boy.

CHAPTER X.

TWO days later the Countess payed her first visit to my lodging. I had looked forward to the moment with a great longing, deeming that her presence would in a measure consecrate the rooms, and that the memory of what she did and said would linger about them afterwards like a soft and tender light.

We had journeyed that morning in a party to view the Italian Glass-house at Greenwich, and dining at a hostelry in the neighbourhood, had returned by water. We disembarked at Westminster steps, and I induced the company to favour me with their presence and drink a dish of bohea in my apartment.

Now the sitting-rooms which I occupied were two in number and opened upon each other, the first, which was the larger, lying along the front of the house, and the second, an inner chamber, giving upon a little garden at the back. Ilga, I noticed, wandered from one room to the other, examining my possessions with an indefatigable curiosity. For, said she:

"It is only by such means that one discovers the true nature of one's friends. Conversation is but the pretty scabbard that hides the sword. The blade may be lath for all that we can tell."

"You distrust your friends so much?"

"Have I no reason to?" she exclaimed, suddenly bending her eyes upon me, and she paused in expectation of an answer. "But I forgot; you know nothing of my history."

I turned away, for I felt the blood rushing to my face.

"I would fain hear you tell it me," I managed to stammer out.

"Some time I will," she replied quietly, "but not to-day; the time is inopportune. For it is brimful of sorrow, and the telling of it will, I trust, sadden you."

The strangeness of the words, and a passionate tension in her voice, filled me with uneasiness, and I wheeled sharply round.

"For I take you for my friend," she explained softly, "and so count on your sympathy. Yet, after all, can I count on it?"

I protested with some confusion that she could count on far more than my sympathies.

"It may be," she replied. "But I believe, Mr. Buckler, the whole story of woman might be written in one phrase. 'Tis the continual mistaking of lath for steel."

"And never steel for lath?" I asked.

"At times, no doubt," she answered, recovering herself with an easy laugh. "But we only find that error out when the steel cuts us. So either way

are we unfortunate. Therefore, I will e'en pursue
my inquiries," and she stepped off into the inner
room, whither presently I went to join her.

" Well, what have you discovered ? " I asked.

" Nothing," she replied, with a plaintive shake of
the head. " You disappoint me sorely, Mr. Buckler.
A student from the University of Leyden should
line his walls with volumes and folios, and I have
found but one book of Latin poems in that room,
and not so much as a pamphlet in this."

I started. The book of poems could be no other
than my copy of Horace, and it contained the plan
of Lukstein Castle. I reflected, however, that the
plan was a mere diagram of lines, without even
a letter to explain it, and with only a cross at the
point of ascent. The Countess, moreover, had
spoken in all levity; her tone betrayed no hint of an
afterthought.

A small package fastened with string lay on
the table before her, and beside of it a letter in
Elmscott's handwriting. She picked up the
package.

" And what new purchase is this ? " she asked,
with a smile.

" I know nothing of it. It is no purchase, and
I gather from the inscription of the letter it comes
from my cousin."

" I shall open it," said she, " and you must blame
my sex for its inquisitiveness."

" Madame," I replied, " the inquisitiveness implies an interest in the object of it, and so pays me
a compliment."

" 'Tis the sweetest way of condoning a fault

that ever I met with," she laughed, and dropped me
a sweeping curtsey.

I broke the seal of Elmscott's letter while she
untied the parcel.

"Marston's conversation at the theatre," he
wrote, "reminded me of these buckles. They belong
of right to you, and since it seems your turn has
come to need luck's services, I send them gladly in
the hope that they may repeat their office on your
behalf."

The parcel contained a shagreen case which Ilga
unfastened. The diamond buckles from it flashed
with a thousand rays, and she tipped them to and
fro so that the stones might catch the light.

"Your cousin must have a great liking for you,"
she said. "For in truth they are very beautiful."

"Elmscott is a gambler," I laughed, "with all
a gambler's superstitions," and I handed her the
letter.

She read it through. "These buckles were
your cousin's last stake, Mr. Marston related,"
she said. "Do you believe that they will bring
you luck?"

"To believe would be presumption. I have no
more courage than suffices me to copy Elmscott's
example, and hope."

She returned me no answer, giving, so it seemed,
all her attention to the brilliant jewels in her hands.
But I saw the colour mounting in her cheeks.

"Meanwhile," she said, after a pause, with a little
nervous laugh, "you are copying my bad example,
and leaving your guests to divert themselves."

Not knowing surely whether I had offended her

or not, I deemed it best to add nothing further or more precise to my hints, and got me back into the larger room. Ilga remained standing where I left her, and through the doorway I could see her still flashing the buckles backwards and forwards. Her evident admiration raised an idea in my mind. My guests were amusing themselves without any need of help from me. Some new scandal concerning the King and the Countess of Dorchester was being discussed for the tenth time that day with an enthusiasm which expanded as the story grew, so that I was presently able to slip back unnoticed. The inner room, however, was empty; but the glass door which gave on to the garden stood open, and picking up the shagreen case, I stepped out on to the lawn. Ilga was seated in a low chair about the centre of the grass-plot, and the sun, which hung low and red just above the ivied wall, burnished her hair, and was rosy on her face.

"Madame," said I, advancing towards her, "I have discovered how best to dispose of the buckles so that they may bring me luck."

"Indeed?" she asked indifferently. "And which way is it?"

"They are too fine for a plain gentleman's wearing," said I. "Sweet looks and precious jewels go best together." With that, and awkwardly enough, I dare say, for I always stumbled at a compliment, I opened the case and offered it.

She looked at me for a space as though she had not understood, and then:

"No, no," she cried, with extraordinary vehemence, repulsing my gift so that the case flew out of my grasp, and the buckles sparkled through the air in two divergent arcs, and dropped some few feet away into the grass. She rose from her seat and drew herself up to her full height, her eyes flashing and her bosom heaving. " How dare you?" she exclaimed, and yet again, "How dare you?"

Conscious of no intention but to please her by a gift which she plainly admired, I stared dumbfounded at the outburst.

" Madame !" I faltered out at last ; and with a great effort she recovered a part of her self-control.

" Mr. Buckler," she said, speaking with difficulty, while the blood swirled in and out of her cheeks, " the present hurts me sorely, even though—nay, all the more *because*, it comes from you. It is the fashion, I know well, to believe that a few gems will bribe the good will of any woman. But I hardly thought that — that you held me in such poor esteem."

I protested that nothing could have been further from my designs than the notion which she attributed to me, and went so far as to hint that there was something extravagant and unreasonable in her anger. For, said I, the gift was no bribe but a tribute, and, I continued, with greater confidence as her pride diminished, if either of us had a right to feel hurt, it was myself, whom she insulted by the imputation of so mean a spirit.

" Then I am to humbly beg your pardon, I suppose," she cried, with another flash of anger.

" Oh, there's no arguing with you," I burst out in a heat no less violent than her own. " Who bids you beg my pardon ? What makes you suppose I need you should, unless it be your own proper and fitting compunction? There's no moderation in your thoughts. You jump from one extreme to the other as nimbly as—as——."

I was turning away with the sentence unfinished, when:

" I could supply the simile you want," she said, with a whimsical demureness as sudden and inexplicable as her wrath, "only 'tis something indelicate," and she broke into a ringing laugh.

To a man of my slow disposition, whose very passions have a certain œconomy which delays their growth, the rapid transitions of a woman's humours have ever been confusing, and now I stood stockish and dumb, gazing at the Countess open-mouthed, and vainly endeavouring, like a fool, to reduce the various emotions she had expressed into a logical continuity.

"And there!" she continued, " now I have shocked you by lack of breeding!"

And once more she commenced to laugh with a mirth so natural and infectious that presently it gained on me, and for no definite reason that I could name I found myself laughing to her tune and with equal heartiness. 'Twas none the less a wiser action than any deliberation could have prompted me to, for here was our quarrel ended decisively, and no words said.

For a while we strolled up and down the lawn, Ilga interspacing her talk with little spirts of laughter, as now and again she looked at my face, until we stopped at the end of the garden, just before a small postern-door in the wall.

"It leads into the Park?" she asked.

"Yes! Shall we slip out?"

She looked back at the house.

"The host can hardly run away from his guests."

"There is no one in the room to notice us."

"But the room above? 'Twould look strange, whoever saw us."

"Nay, there can be no one there, for it is my dressing-room."

She took hold of the handle doubtfully and tried it.

"It is locked."

"But the key is on the mantelshelf. I will get it."

"In this little room?"

"No, 'tis in the larger room, but——"

"Nay," she interrupted, "our absence will be enough remarked as it is. Clemence will read me a lecture on the proprieties all the way home."

Consequently we returned to the house, and the Countess took her leave shortly with the rest of the company; but as I conducted her to the door, she said a strange thing to me.

"Mr. Buckler," she said, "you should be angry more often," and so with another laugh she walked away.

That night, as I sat smoking a pipe upon the lawn, I saw something flash and sparkle in the rays of the moon, and I remembered that Elmscott's buckles still lay where they had fallen. Picking them up, I returned to my seat and fell straightway into a very bitter train of thought. 'Twas the

recollection of the Countess' indignation that set
me on it, for since the mere gift could provoke
so stormy and sincere an outburst, how would it
have been, I reflected, had she really known who
the giver was? The thought pressed in upon me
all the more heavily for the reason which she had
offered to account for her anger. She set a value
upon my esteem, and no small value either; so
much she had told me plainly. Now it had been
my lot hitherto to meet with a half-contemptuous
tolerance rather than esteem; so that this unwonted
appreciation shown by the one person from whom
I most desired it filled me with a deep gratitude,
and obliged me in her service. Yet here was I
requiting her with a calculating and continuous
deception. 'Twas no longer of any use to argue
that Count Lukstein had received no greater punishment than his treachery merited; that but for his
last coward thrust he would have escaped even
that; that the advantage of the encounter had been
on his side from first to last, since I was chilled
to the bone with my long vigil upon the terrace
parapet. Such excuses were the merest thistle-
down, and it needed but a breath from her to
blow them into air. The solid stalk of my thoughts
was: "I was deceiving her." And it was not merely
the knowledge of my concealments which tortured
me, but an anticipation of the disdain and contempt
into which her kindliness would turn, should she
ever discover the truth.

For so closely had the idea and notion of her
become inwoven in my being that I ever estimated
my actions and purposes by imagining the judgment

which she would be like to pass on them, and, indeed, saw no true image of myself at all save that which was reflected from the mirror of her thoughts.

I came then to consider what path I should follow. There were three ways open to my choice. I might go on as heretofore, practising my duplicity; or, again, I might pack my trunks and scurry ignominiously back to my estate; or I might take my courage between my two hands and tell the truth of the matter to the Countess, be the consequences what they might.

Doubtless the last was the only honest course, and if I did not bring myself to adopt it—well, I paid dearly enough for the fault. At the time, however, the objections appeared to me insurmountable. In the first place, my natural timidity cried out against this hazard of all my happiness upon a single throw. Then, again, how could I tell her the truth? For it was not merely myself that the story accused, nor indeed in the main, but her husband. His treachery towards me in the actual fighting of the duel I might conceal, but not his treachery to Julian, and I shrank from inflicting such shame upon her pride as the disclosure must inevitably bring.

I deem it right to set out here the questions which so troubled me, with a view to the proper understanding of this story. For on the very next day, while I was still debating the matter in great abasement and despondency, an incident occurred which determined me upon a compromise.

It happened in this way. I had ridden out into

the country early in the morning, hoping that a vigorous gallop might help me to some solution of my perplexities, and returning home in the evening, chanced to be in my dressing-room shortly after seven of the clock.

My valet announced that Lord Culverton and my cousin were below, and I sent word down that I would be with them in the space of a few minutes. Elmscott, however, followed the servant up the stairs, and coming into the room entertained me with the latest gossip, walking about the while that he talked. In the middle of a sentence he stopped before the window which, as I have said, overlooked the Park, and broke off his speech with a sudden exclamation. I crossed to where he stood, wishing to see what had brought him so abruptly to a stop. The walks, however, were empty and deserted, it being the fashion among the gentry of the town rather to favour Hyde Park at this hour. A chair, certainly, stood at no great distance, but the porters were smoking their pipes as they leaned against the poles, and I inferred from that that it had no occupant.

" Wait," said Elmscott; " the wall of your garden hides them for the moment."

As he spoke, two figures emerged from its shelter and walked into the open. I gave a start as I saw them, and gripped Elmscott by the arm.

"Lord I" said he, "are you in so deep as that?"

The woman I knew at the first glance. The easy carriage of her head, the light grace of her walk, were qualities which I had noted and admired too often to make the ghost of a doubt possible. The man, who was gaily dressed in a scarlet coat, an instinct of jealousy told me was Hugh Marston. Their backs were towards the house, and I waited for them to turn, which they did after they had walked some hundred paces. Sure enough my suspicions were correct. The Countess was escorted by Marston, her hand was upon his arm, and the pair sauntered slowly, stopping here and there in their walk as though greatly concerned with one another.

"Damn him!" I cried. "Damn him!"

Elmscott burst into a laugh.

"The pretty Countess," said he, "would be more discreet did she but know you overlooked her."

"But she does know," I returned. "She knows that I lodge in the house; she knows also that this room is mine."

"Oh!" he exclaimed, in a tone of comprehension, "she knows that!"

"Ay; and 'twas no further back than yesterday that she discovered it. I told her myself."

Elmscott remained silent for a while, watching their promenade. Again they disappeared within the shelter of the wall; again they emerged from it, and again they promenaded some hundred paces and turned.

"I thought so," he muttered; "'tis all of a piece."

I asked what his words meant.

"You remember the evening at the Duke's

Theatre, when she caught sight of you across the
pit? One might have imagined she would not
have had you see her on such close terms with
our friend; that she feared you might mistake her
courtesy for proof of some deeper feeling."

"Well?" I asked, remembering how he had
chuckled through the evening. For such in truth
had been my thought, and I had drawn no small
comfort from it.

"Well, she saw you long ere that; she saw
you the moment she entered the box, before I
pointed her out to you. For she looked straight
in your direction and spoke to the Frenchwoman,
nodding towards you."

"No, it is impossible!" I replied. I recollected
how her hand had fallen upon mine, and the musical
sound of her words—"the occasion may come, too."
"There is no trace of the coquette about her. This
must be a mistake."

"It is you who are making it. Add her behaviour
now," he waved his hand to the window, "to what
I have told you! See how the incidents fit together.
Yesterday she finds out your room commands the
Park, to-day she walks in Marston's company
underneath the window, and backwards and forwards, mark that! never moving out of range. 'Tis
all part of one purpose."

"But what purpose?" I cried passionately.
"What purpose could she serve?"

"The devil knows!" he replied, with a shrug
of his shoulders. "It is of a woman we are speaking
—you forget that."

I flung open the window noisily, in a desire to

attract their attention and observe how the Countess would take our discovery of her interview. But she paid not the slightest heed to the sound. Elmscott made a sudden dash to the door.

" Culverton ! " he cried over the baluster.

I tried to check him, for I had no wish that Culverton's meddlesome fingers should pry into the matter. I was too late, however ; he entered the room, and Elmscott drew him to the open window.

" Burn me, but 'tis the oddest thing ! " he smirked.

For a minute or so we stood watching the couple in silence. Then the Countess dropped her fan, and as Marston stooped to pick it up she shot one quick glance towards us. Her companion handed her the fan, and they resumed the promenade. But they took no more than half a turn before the Countess signalled to the porters, and getting into the chair, was carried off. Marston waited until she was out of sight, with his hat in his hand, and then cocking it jauntily on his head, marched off in the opposite direction. The satisfaction of his manner made my blood boil with rage.

" The conceited ass ! " I cried, stamping my feet.

" She heard the window open after all," said Elmscott.

As for Culverton, he tittered the more.

" The oddest thing ! " he repeated. " The very oddest thing ! Strike me purple if I know what to make of the delightful creature ! "

" 'Tis as plain as my hand," replied Elmscott

N

roughly. "No sooner did she perceive that you were watching her than she gave Marston his congé. He had done his work, and she had no further use for him. She is a woman—there's the top and bottom of it. A couple of men to frown at each other and grimace prettily to her! Her vanity demands no less. She is like one of our Indian planters who value their wealth by the number of their slaves ; so she her beauty."

"Nay," interposed the fop. "If that were the whole business, one would hear less concerning Mr. Buckler from her rapturous lips. But rat me if she ever talks about any one else."

"Do you mean that?" I asked eagerly.

"Oh, most inquisitive, on my honour! In truth, your name is growing plaguy wearisome to me. Why, but the other night, when she selected me to lead her to her carriage at the theatre, 'twas but to question me concerning you, and whether you gambled, and the horse of mine you rode, and what not. And there was I with a thousand tender nothings to whisper in her ear, and pink me if I could get one of 'em out!"

"Then I give the riddle up," rejoined Elmscott, though I would fain have heard more of this strain from Culverton. "I make neither head nor tail of the business, unless, Morrice, she would bring you on by a little wholesome jealousy." He looked at me shrewdly, and continued : "You are a timid wooer, I fancy. Why not go to her boldly? Tell her you are going away, and have had enough of her tricks! 'Twould bring your suit to a climax."

"One way or another," said I doubtfully.

" If Mr. Buckler would take the advice of one who has had some small experience of ladies' whims," interposed Culverton, "and some participation in their favours, he would buy some new clothes."

" These are new," I said. " I followed your advice before, and bought enough to stock a shop."

" But of such a desperate colour," he replied. " Lard, Mr. Buckler, you go dressed like a mute at a funeral! The ladies loathe it; stap me, but they loathe it! A scarlet coat, like our friend wears, a full periwig, an embroidered stocking, makes deeper inroads into their affections than a year's tedious love-making. The dear creatures' hearts, Mr. Buckler, are in their eyes."

With that the subject of Countess Lukstein dropped. For Culverton, once started upon his favourite topic, launched forth into a complete philosophy of clothes. The colour of each garment, according to him, had a particular effect upon the sex; the adjustment of each ribbon conveyed a particular meaning. He had, indeed, ingeniously classified the various coats, hats, breeches, vests, periwigs, ruffles, cravats and the other appurtenances of a gentleman's wardrobe, with the modes of wearing them, as expressions of feeling and emotion. The larger and more dominant emotions were voiced in the clothes, the delicate and subtler shades of feeling in the disposition of ornaments. In short, 'twould be a very profitable philosophy for a race which had neither tongues to speak nor faces and limbs to act their meaning.   . .

N 2

This incident, as I have said, determined me
upon a compromise, for it set my heart aflame with
jealousy. I had not taken Marston into my cal-
culations before; now I reflected that if I retired to
the North, I should be leaving a free field for him,
and that I was obstinately minded I would not do.
On the other hand, however, this promenade in front
of my windows, whether undertaken of set purpose
or from sheer carelessness, seemed to show that after
all I had no stable footing in Ilga's esteem, and I
feared that if I disclosed to her the deception which
I had used towards her, there could be but one
result and consequence.

I determined then to forward my suit with what
ardour and haste I might, and to unbosom myself of
my fault in the very hour that I pleaded my love.

The Countess, however, gave me no heart or
occasion for the work. Her manner towards me
changed completely of a sudden, and where I had
previously met with smiles and kindly words, I got
now disdainful looks and biting speeches. She
would ridicule my conversation, my person, and my
bearing, and that, too, before a room full of people,
so that I was filled with the deepest shame; or again,
she would shrink from me with all the appearances
of aversion. Mademoiselle Durette, it is true, sought
to lighten my suffering. "It is ever Love's way to
blow hot and cold," she would whisper in my ear.
But I thought that she spoke only out of compassion.
For 'twas the cold wind which continually blew
on me.

At times, indeed, though very rarely, she would
resume her old familiarity, but there was a note of

effort in her voice as though she subdued herself to a distasteful practice, and something hysterical in her merriment ; and as like as not, she would break off in the middle of a kindly sentence and load me with the extremity of scorn.

Moreover, Marston was perpetually at her side, and in his company she made more than one return to the Park ; so that at last, being fallen into a most tormenting despair, I made shift to follow Elmscott's advice, and called at her lodging one morning to inform her that I intended setting my face homewards that very afternoon.

CHAPTER XI.

IT was a full week since I had last waited on my cruel mistress, and I hoped, though with no great confidence, that this intermission of my visits might temper and moderate her scorn. I had besides taken to heart Culverton's advice as well as that of my cousin. For I was in great trepidation lest she should take me at my word, and carelessly bid me adieu, and so caught eagerly at any hint that seemed likely to help me, however trivial it might be, and from whatever source it came.

Consequently I had had my own hair cropped, and had purchased a cumbersome full-bottomed peruke of the latest mode. With that on my head, and habited in a fine new brocaded coat of green velvet and lemon-coloured silk breeches and stockings, I went timidly to confront my destiny. How many times did I walk up and down before her house, or ever I could summon courage to knock! How many phrases and dignified reproaches did I con over and rehearse, yet never one that seemed other than offensive and ridiculous! What in truth emboldened me in the end to enter was a cloud of dust which a passing carriage caused to settle on my coat. If I hesitated much longer, I reflected, all my bravery would be wasted, and dusting myself carefully with my handkerchief, I mounted the steps. Otto Krax opened the door, and preceded me up the staircase.

But while we were still ascending the steps, Mademoiselle Durette came from the parlour which gave on to the landing.

"Very well, Otto," she said, "I will announce Mr. Buckler."

She waited until the man had descended the stairs, and then turned to me with a meaning smile.

"She is alone. Take her by surprise!"

With that she softly turned the handle of the door, and opened it just so far as would enable me to slip through. I heard the voice of Ilga singing sweetly in a low key, and my heart trembled and jumped within me, so that I hesitated on the threshold.

"I have no patience with you," said Mademoiselle Durette, in an exasperated whisper. "Cowards don't win when they go a-wooing. Haven't you learnt that? Ridicule her, if you like, as she does you—abuse her, do anything but gape like a stock-fish, with a white face as though all your blood had run down into the heels of your shoes!"

She pushed me as she spoke into the room, and noiselessly closed the door. The Countess was seated at a spinnet in the far corner of the room, and sang in her native tongue. The song,

I gathered, was a plaint, and had a strange and outlandish melancholy, the voice now lifting into a wild, keening note, now sinking abruptly to a dreary monotone. It oppressed me with a peculiar sadness, making the singer seem very lonely and far-away; and I leaned silently against the wall, not daring to interrupt her. At last the notes began to quaver, the voice broke once and twice; she gave a little sob, and her head fell forward on her hands.

An inrush of pity swept all my diffidence away. I stepped hastily forward with outstretched hands. At the sound she sprang to her feet and faced me, the colour flaming in her cheeks.

"Madame," cried I, "if my intrusion lacks ceremony, believe me——"

But I got no further in my protestations. For with a sneer upon her lips and a biting accent of irony,

"So," she broke in, looking me over, "the crow has turned into a cockatoo." And she rang a bell which stood upon the spinnet. I stopped in confusion, and not knowing what to say or do, remained foolishly shifting from one foot to the other, the while Ilga watched me with a malicious pleasure.

In a minute Otto Krax came to the door.

"How comes it," she asked sternly, "that Mr. Buckler enters unannounced? Have I no servants?"

The fellow explained that Mademoiselle Durette had taken the duty to herself.

"Send Mademoiselle Durette to me!" said the Countess.

I was ready to sink through the floor with humiliation, and busied my wits in a search for a plausible excuse. I had not found one when the Frenchwoman appeared.

Countess Lukstein repeated her question.

Mademoiselle Durette was no readier than myself, and glanced with a frightened air from me to her mistress, and back again from her mistress to me. Remembering what she had said on the landing about my irresolution, I felt my shame doubled.

"Madame," I stammered out, "the fault is in no wise your companion's. The blame of it should fall on me."

"Oh!" said she, "really?" And turning to Mademoiselle Durette, she began to clap her hands. "I believe," she exclaimed in a mock excitement, "that Mr. Buckler is going to make me a present of a superb cockatoo. Clemence, you must buy a cage and a chain for its leg!"

Clemence stared in amazement, as well she might, and I, stung to a passion,

"Nay," I cried, and for once my voice rang firmly. "By the Lord, you count too readily upon Mr. Buckler's gift. Mr. Buckler has come to offer you no present, but to take his leave for good and all."

I made her a dignified bow and stepped towards the door.

"What do you mean?" she asked sharply.

"That I ride homewards this afternoon."

She shot a glance at Mademoiselle Durette, who slipped obediently out of the room.

"And why?" she asked, with an innocent assumption of surprise, coming towards me. "Why?"

"What, madame!" I replied, looking her straight in the face. "Surely your ingenuity can find a reason."

"My ingenuity?" She spoke in the same accent of wonderment. "My ingenuity? Mr. Buckler, you take a tone——" She came some paces nearer to me and asked very gently: "Am I to blame?"

The humility of the question, and a certain trembling of the lips that uttered it, well-nigh disarmed me; but I felt that did I answer her, did I venture the mildest reproach, I should give her my present advantage.

"No, no," I replied, with a show of indifference; "my own people need me."

She took another step, and spoke with lowered eyes. "Are there no people who need you here?"

I forgot my part.

"You mean——" I exclaimed impulsively, when a movement which she made brought me to a stop. For she drew back a step, and picking up her fan from a little table, began to pluck nervously at the feathers. Her action recalled to my mind her behaviour at the Duke's Theatre and Elmscott's commentary thereon.

"None that I know of," I resumed, "for even those whom I counted my friends find me undeserving of even common civility."

"Civility! Civility!" she cried out in scorn. "'Tis the very proof and attribute of indifference—

the crust one tosses carelessly to the first-comer because it costs nothing."

"But I go fasting even for that crust."

"Not always," she replied softly, shooting a glance at me. "Not always, Mr. Buckler; and have you not found at times some butter on the bread?"

She smiled as she spoke, but I hardened my heart against her and vouchsafed no answer. For a little while she stood with her eyes upon the ground, and then:

"Oh, very well, very well!" she said petulantly, and turning away from me, flung the fan on to the table. The table was of polished mahogany, and the fan slid across its surface and dropped to the floor. I stepped forward, and knelt down to pick it up.

"What, Mr. Buckler!" she said bitterly, turning again to me, "you condescend to kneel. Surely it is not you; it must be some one else."

I thought that I had never heard sarcasm so unjust, for in truth kneeling to her had been my chief occupation this many a day, and I replied hotly, bethinking me of Marston and the episode which I had witnessed in the Park.

"Indeed, madame, and you may well think it strange, for have I not seen you drop your fan in order to deceive the man who picks it up?" With that I got to my feet and laid the fan on the table.

She flushed very red, and exclaimed hurriedly:

"All that can be explained."

"No doubt! no doubt!" I replied. "I have never doubted the subtlety of madame's invention."

She drew herself up with great pride, and bowed to me.

I walked to the door. As I opened it, I turned to take one last look at the face which I had so worshipped. It was very white; even the lips were bloodless, and oddly enough I noticed that she wore a loose white gown as on the occasion of our first meeting.

"Adieu," I said, and stepped behind the door.

From the other side of it her voice came to me quietly:

"Does this prove the sword to be lath or steel?"

I shut the door, and went slowly down the stairs, slowly and yet more slowly. For her last question drummed at my heart.

"Lath or steel?" Was I playing a man's part, or was I the mere bond-slave of a petty pride? "That can be explained," she had said. What if it could? Then the sword would be proved lath indeed! Just to salve my vanity I should have wasted my life—and only *my* life? I saw her lips trembling as the thought shot through me.

What if those walks with my rival beneath my window had been devised in some strange way for a test—a woman's test and touchstone to essay the metal of the sword, a test perhaps intelligible to a woman, though an enigma to me? If only I knew a woman whom I could consult!

My feet lagged more and more, but I reached the bottom of the stairs in the end. The hall was empty. I looked up towards the landing with a wild hope that she would come out and lean over the balustrade, as on the evening when Elmscott first brought me to

the house. But there was no stir or movement from
garret to cellar. I might have stood in the hall of
the Sleeping Palace. From a high window the
sunlight slanted athwart the cool gloom in a golden
pillar, and a fly buzzed against the pane. I crossed
the hall, and let myself out into the noonday. The
door clanged behind me with a hollow rattle; it
sounded to my hearing like the closing of the gates
of a tomb, and I felt it was myself that lay dead
behind it.

As I passed beneath the window, something hard
dropped upon the crown of my hat, and bounced
thence to the ground at my feet. I picked it up.
It was a crust of bread. For a space I stood looking
at it before I understood. Then I rushed back to the
entrance. The door stood open, but the hall was
empty and silent as when I left it. I sprang up the
stairs, and in my haste missed my footing about half-
way up, and rolled down some half-a-dozen steps. The
crash of my fall echoed up the well of the staircase,
and from behind the parlour door I heard some one
laugh. I got on to my legs, and burst into the room.

Ilga was seated before a frame of embroidery very
demure and busy. She paid no heed to me, keeping
her head bent over her work until I had approached
close to the frame. Then she looked up with her
eyes sparkling.

"How dare you?" she asked, in a mock accent
of injury.

"I don't know," I replied meekly.

She bent once more over her embroidery.

"Humours are the prerogative of my sex," she
said.

"I set you apart from it."

"Is that why you cannot trust me even a little?"

The gentle reproach made me hot with shame. I had no words to answer it. Then she laughed again, bending closer over her frame, in a low joyous note that gradually rose and trilled out sweet as music from a thrush.

"And so," she said, "you came all trim and spruce in your fine new clothes to show me what my discourtesy had lost me! What a child you are! And yet," she rose suddenly, her whole face changing, "and yet, are you a child? Would God I knew!" She ended with a passionate cry, clasping her hands together upon her breast; but before I could make head or tail of her meaning she was half-way through another mood. "Ah!" she cried, "you have brought my courtesy back with you." I had not noticed until then that I still held the crust in my hand. "You shall swallow it as a penance."

"Madame!" I laughed.

"Hush! you shall eat it. Yes, yes!" with a pretty imperious stamp of the foot. "Now! Before you speak a word!"

I obeyed her, but with some difficulty, for the crust was very dry.

"You see," she said, "courtesy is not always so tasteful a morsel. It sticks in the throat at times;" and crossing to a sideboard, she filled a goblet from a decanter of canary and brought it to me.

"You will pledge me first," I entreated.

Her face grew serious, and she balanced the cup doubtfully in her hand.

" Of a truth," she said, "of a truth I will." She raised it slowly to her lips; but at that moment the door opened.

" Oh ! " cried Mademoiselle Durette, with a start of surprise, " I fancied that Mr. Buckler had gone," and she was for whipping out of the room again, but Ilga called to her. The astonishment of the Frenchwoman made one point clear to me concerning which I felt some curiosity. I mean that 'twas not she who had set the hall-door open for my return.

" Clemence ! " said the Countess, setting down the wine untasted, as I noticed with regret, " will you bid Otto come to me ? I ransacked Mr. Buckler's rooms, and it is only fair that I should show him my poor treasures in return."

She handed a key to Otto, and bade him unlock a Japan cabinet which stood in a corner. He drew out a tray heaped up with curiosities, medals and trinkets, and bringing it over, laid it on a table in the window.

" I have bought them all since I came to London. You shall tell me whether I have been robbed."

" You come to the worst appraiser in the world," said I, " for these ornaments tell me nothing of their value though much of your industry."

" I have a great love for these trifles," said she, though her action seemed to belie her words, for she tossed and rattled them hither and thither upon the tray with rapid jerks of her fingers which would have made a virtuoso shiver. "They hint so much of bygone times, and tell so provokingly little."

"Their example, at all events, affords a lesson in discretion," I laughed.

"Which our poor sex is too trustful to learn, and yours too distrustful to forget."

There was a certain accent of appeal in her voice, very tender and sweet, as though she knew my story and was ready to forgive it. Had we been alone I believe that I should have blurted the whole truth out; only Otto Krax stood before me on the opposite side of the table, Mademoiselle Durette was seated in the room behind.

. Ilga had ceased to sort the articles, and now began to point out particular trinkets, describing their purposes and antiquity and the shops where she had discovered them. But I paid small heed to her words; that question—did she know?—pressed too urgently upon my thoughts. A glance at the stolid indifference of Otto Krax served to reassure me. Through him alone could suspicion have come, and I felt certain that he had as yet not recognised me.

Besides, I reflected, had she known, it was hardly in nature that she should have spoken so gently. I dismissed the suspicion from my mind, and turned me again to the inspection of the tray.

Just below my eyes lay a miniature of a girl, painted very delicately upon a thin oval slip of ivory. The face was dark in complexion, with black hair, the nose a trifle tip-tilted, and the lips full and red, but altogether a face very alluring and handsome. I was most struck, however, with the freshness of the colours; amongst those old curios the portrait shone like a gem. I took it up, and as I did so, Otto Krax leaned forward.

"Otto!" said Ilga sharply, "you stand between Mr. Buckler and the light."

The servant moved obediently from the window.

"This," said I, "hath less appearance of antiquity than the rest of your purchases."

"It was given to me," she replied. "The face is beautiful?"

Now it had been my custom of late to consider a face beautiful or not in proportion to its resemblance to that of Countess Lukstein. So I looked carefully at the miniature, and thence to Ilga. She was gazing closely at me with parted lips, and an odd intentness in her expression. I noticed this the more particularly, for that her eyes, which were violet in their natural hue, had a trick of growing dark when she was excited or absorbed.

"Why!" I exclaimed, in surprise. "One might think you fancy me acquainted with the lady."

"Well," she replied, laying a hand upon her heart, "what if I did—fancy that?" She stressed the word "fancy" with something of a sneer.

"Nay," said I, "the face is strange to me."

"Are you sure?" she asked. "Look again! Look again, Mr. Buckler!"

Disturbed by this recurrence of her irony, I fixed my eyes, as she bade me, upon the picture, and strangely enough, upon a closer scrutiny I began gradually to recognise it; but in so vague

o

and dim a fashion, that whether the familiarity
lay in the contour of the lineaments or merely
in the expression, I could by no effort of memory
determine.

"Well?" she asked, with a smile which had
nothing amiable or pleasant in it. "What say
you now?"

"Madame," I returned, completely at a loss,
"in truth I know not what to say. It may be
that I have seen the original. Indeed, I must
think that is the case——"

"Ah!" she cried, interrupting me as one who
convicts an opponent after much debate, and then,
in a hurried correction: "so at least I was
informed."

"Then tell me who informed you!" I said
earnestly, for I commenced to consider this miniature
as the cause of her recent resentment and scorn.
"For I have only seen this face—somewhere—for
a moment. Of one thing I am sure. I have
never had speech with it."

"Never?" she asked, in the same ironical tone.
"Look yet a third time, Mr. Buckler! For your
memory improves with each inspection."

She suddenly broke off, and "Otto!" she cried
sternly—it was almost a shout.

The fellow was standing just behind my shoulder,
and I swung round and eyed him. He came a step
forward, questioning his mistress with a look.

"Replace the tray in the cabinet!"

I kept the miniature in my hand, glancing ever
from it to the Countess and back again in pure
wonder and conjecture.

"Madame," I said firmly, "I have never had speech with the lady of this picture."

She looked into my eyes as though she would read my soul.

"It is God's truth!"

She signed a dismissal to Otto. Clemence Durette rose and followed the servant, and I thought that I had never fallen in with any one who showed such tact and discretion in the matter of leaving a room.

The Countess remained stock-still, facing me.

"And yet I have been told," she said, nodding her head with each word, "that she was very dear to you."

"Then," I replied hotly, "you were told a lie, a miserable calumny. I understand! 'Tis that that has poisoned your kind thoughts of me."

She turned away with a slight shrug of the shoulders.

"Oh, believe that!" I exclaimed, falling upon a knee and holding her by the hem of her dress. "You must believe it! I have told you what my life has been. Look at the picture yourself!" and I forced it into her hands. "What do you read there? Vanity and the love of conquest. Gaze into the eyes! What do they bespeak? Boldness that comes from the habit of conquest. Is it likely that such a woman would busy her head about an awkward, retiring student?"

"I am not so sure," she replied thoughtfully, though she seemed to relent a little at my vehemence; "women are capricious. You yourself have been complaining this morning of their caprice. And it might be that—I can imagine it—and for that very reason."

"Oh, compare us !" I cried. "Compare the painted figure there with me ! You must see it is impossible."

She laid a hand upon each of my shoulders as I knelt, and bent over me, staring into my eyes.

"I have been told," said she, "that the lady was so dear to you that for her sake you fought and killed your rival in love."

"You have been told that ? " I answered, in sheer incredulity; and then a flame of rage against my traducer kindling in my heart, I sprang to my feet.

"Who told you ? "

"I may not disclose his name."

"But you shall," said I, stepping in front of her. "You shall tell me ! He has lied to you foully, and you owe him therefore no consideration or respect. He has lied concerning me. I have a clear right to know his name, that I may convince you of the lie, and reckon with him for his slander. Confront us both, and yourself be present as the judge ! "

Of a sudden she held out her hand to me.

"Your sincerity convinces me. I need no other proof, and I crave your pardon for my suspicion."

I looked into her face, amazed at the sudden change. But there was no mistaking her conviction or the joy which it occasioned her. I saw a light in her eyes, dancing and sparkling, which I had never envisaged before, and which filled me with exquisite happiness.

"Still," I said, as I took her hand, "I would fain prove my words to you."

"Can you not trust me at all?"

She had a wonderful knack of putting me in the wrong when I was on the side of the right, and before I could find a suitable reply she slipped out of my grasp, and crossing the room, took in her hand the cup of wine.

"Now," said she, "I will pledge you, Mr. Buckler;" which she did very prettily, and handed the cup to me. As I raised it to my lips, however, an idea occurred to me.

"It is you who refuse to pledge me," she said.

"Nay, nay," said I, and I drained the cup. "But I have just guessed who my traducer is."

She looked perplexed for a moment.

"You have guessed who——" she began, in an accent of wonder.

"Who gave you the picture," I explained.

She stared at me in pure astonishment.

"You can hardly have guessed accurately, then," she remarked.

"Surely," said I, "it needs no magician to discover the giver. I know but one man in London who can hope to gain aught by slandering me to you."

Ilga gave a start of alarm. It seemed almost as though I were telling her news, as though she did not know herself who gave her the picture; and for the rest of my visit she appeared absent and anxious. This was particularly mortifying to me, since I thought the occasion too apt to be lost, and I was minded to open my heart to her.

Indeed, I began the preface of a love-speech in spite of her preoccupation, but sticking for lack of encouragement after half-a-dozen words or so, I perceived that she was not even listening to what I said. Consequently I took my leave with some irritation, marvelling at the flighty waywardness of a woman's thoughts, and rather inclined to believe that the properest age for a man to marry was his ninetieth year, for then he might perchance have sufficient experience to understand some portion of his wife's behaviour and whimsies.

My mortification was not of a lasting kind, for Ilga came out on to the landing while I was still descending the stairs.

"You do not know who gave me the picture," she said, entreating me; and she came down two of the steps.

"It would be exceeding strange if I did not," said I, stopping.

"You would seek him out and——" she began.

"I had that in my mind," said I, mounting two of the steps.

"Then you do not know him. Say you do not! There could be but one result, and I fear it."

A knock on the outer door rang through the hall; this time we took two steps up and down simultaneously.

"Swords !" she continued, "for you would fight ? "

I nodded.

"Oh !" she exclaimed, "swords are no true ordeal. Skill—it is skill, not justice, which directs the thrust."

I fancied that I comprehended the cause of her fear, and I laughed cheerfully.

"I have few good qualities," said I, "but amongst those few you may reckon some proficiency with the sword." I ascended two steps.

"So," she replied, with an indefinable change of tone, "you are skilled in the exercise?" But she stood where she was.

Otto Krax came from the inner part of the house and crossed to the door.

"It is my one qualification for a courtier."

Since Ilga had omitted to take the two steps down, I deemed it right to take four steps up.

She resumed her tone of entreaty.

"But chance may outwit skill; does—often."

We heard the chain rattle on the door as Krax unfastened it. Ilga bent forward hurriedly.

"You do not know the man!" and in a whisper she added: "For my sake—you do not!"

There were only four steps between us. I took them all in one spring.

"For your sake, is it?" and I caught her hand.

"Hush!" she said, disengaging herself. Marston's voice sounded in the entrance. "You do not know! Oh, you do not!" she beseeched in shaking tones. Then she drew back quickly, and leaned against the balustrade. I looked downwards. Otto was ushering in Marston, and the pair stood at the foot of the staircase. I glanced back at the Countess. There were tears in her eyes.

"Madame!" said I, "I have forgotten his name."

With a bow, I walked down the steps as Marston mounted them.

" 'Tis a fine day," says I, coming to a halt when we were level.

" Is it ?" says he, continuing the ascent.

" It seems to me wonderfully bright and clear," said the Countess from the head of the stairs.

CHAPTER XII.

LADY TRACY.

OUTSIDE the house I came face to face with the original of the miniature. So startled and surprised was I by her unexpected appearance that I could not repress an exclamation, and she turned her eyes full upon me. She was seated upon a horse, while a mounted groom behind her held the bridle of a third horse, saddled, but riderless. 'Twas evident that she had come to the house in Marston's company, and now waited his return. My conviction that Marston had handed the miniature to Ilga was, I thought, confirmed beyond possibility of doubt, and I scanned her face with more eagerness than courtesy, hoping to discover by those means a clue to her identity. For a moment or so she returned my stare without giving a sign of recognition, and then she turned her head away. It was clear, at all events, that she had no knowledge or remembrance of me, and though her lips curved with a gratified smile, and she glanced occasionally in my direction from the tail of her eye, I could not doubt that she considered my exclamation as merely a stranger's spontaneous tribute to her looks.

Indeed, the more closely I regarded her, the less certain did I myself become that I had ever set eyes on her before. I was sensible of a vague familiarity in her appearance, but I was not certain but what I ought to attribute it to my long examination of her likeness. However, since Providence had brought us thus opportunely together, I was minded to use the occasion in order to resolve my perplexities, and advancing towards her :

"Madam," I said, "you will, I trust, pardon my lack of ceremony when I assure you that it is no small matter which leads me to address you. I only ask of you the answer to a simple question. Have we met before to-day?"

"The excuse is not very adroit," she replied, with a coquettish laugh, "for it implies that you are more like to live in my memory than I in yours."

"Believe me!" said I eagerly, "the question is no excuse, but one of some moment to me. I should not have had the courage to thrust myself wantonly upon your attention, even had I felt——"

I broke off suddenly and stopped, since I saw a frown overspread her face, and feared to miss the answer to my question.

"Well! Even had you felt the wish. That is your meaning, is it not? Why not frankly complete the sentence? I hear the sentiment so seldom, that of a truth I relish it for its rarity."

She gave an indignant toss of her head, and looked away from me, running her fingers through the mane of her horse. I understood that flattery alone would serve my turn with her, and I answered boldly :

"You are right, madam. You supply the words my tongue checked at, but not the reason which prompted them. In the old days, when a poor mortal intruded upon a goddess, he paid for his presumption with all the pangs of despair, and I feared that the experience might not be obsolete."

She appeared a trifle mollified by my adulation, and replied archly, making play with her eyebrows :

"'Tis a pretty interpretation to put upon the words, but the words came first, I fear, and suggested the explanation."

"You should not blame me for the words, but rather yourself. An awkward speech, madam, implies startled senses, and so should be reckoned a more genuine compliment than the most nicely-ordered eulogy."

"That makes your peace," said she, much to my relief, for this work of gallantry was ever discomforting to me, my flatteries being of the heaviest and causing me no small labour in the making. "That makes your peace. I accept the explanation."

"And will answer the question?" said I, returning to the charge.

"You deserve no less," she assented. "But indeed, I have no recollection of your face, and so can speak with no greater certainty than yourself. Perchance your name might jog my memory."

"I am called Morrice Buckler," said I.

At that she started in her saddle and gathered up the reins as though intending to ride off.

"Then I can assure you on the point," she said hurriedly. "You and I have never met."

I was greatly astonished by this sudden action

which she made. 'Twas as though she was frightened;
and I knew no reason why any one should fear me,
least of all a stranger. But what she did next
astonished me far more ; for she dropped the reins
and looked me over curiously, saying with a little
laugh :

" So you are Morrice Buckler. I gave you credit
for horn-spectacles at the very least."

Something about her—was it her manner or her
voice ?—struck me as singularly familiar to me, and I
exclaimed :

" Surely, surely, madam, it is true. Somewhere
we have met."

" Nowhere," she answered, enjoying my mysti-
fication. " Have you ever been presented to Lady
Tracy, wife of Sir William Tracy ? "

" Not that I remember," said I, still more puzzled,
"nor have I ever heard the name."

"Then you should be satisfied, for I am Lady
Tracy."

"But you spoke of horn-spectacles. How comes
it that you know so much concerning me ? "

" Nay," she laughed. " You go too fast, Mr.
Buckler. I know nothing concerning you save that
some injustice has been done you. I was told of
a homespun student, glum and musty as an old
book, and I find instead a town-gallant point-de-vice,
who will barter me compliments with the best of
them."

" You got your knowledge, doubtless, from Hugh
Marston," I replied, with a glance at the door;
"and I only wonder the description was not more
unflattering."

"I did not mean him," she said slowly. "For I did not even know that you were acquainted with "— she paused, and looked me straight in the face— "with my brother."

"Your brother!" I exclaimed. "Hugh Marston is your brother?" And I took a step towards her. Again I saw a passing look of apprehension in her face, but I did not stop to wonder at it then. I understood that the indefinable familiarity in her looks was due to the likeness which she bore her brother—a likeness consisting not so much of a distinct stamp of features as of an occasional and fleeting similarity of expression.

"I understand," said I, more to myself than to her.

She flushed very red in a way which was unaccountable, and broke in abruptly.

"So you see we have never seen one another before to-day. For the last year I have been travelling abroad with my husband, and only came to London unexpectedly this morning."

Her words revealed the whole plot to me, or so I thought. Secured from discovery by the pledge of secrecy which he had exacted from Ilga, Marston had shown this miniature of his absent sister, and invented a story which there was no one to disprove. Looking back upon the incident with the cooler reflection which a lapse of years induces, I marvel at the conviction with which I drew the inference. But although now I see clearly how incredible it was that a man of Marston's breeding and family should so villainously misuse the fair fame of one thus near to hand,

at the time I measured his jealousy by the violence
of my own, and was ready to believe that he would
check at no barriers of pride and honour which
stood between him and his intention. Events,
moreover, seemed to jump most aptly with my
conclusion.

So, full of my discovery of his plot, I said
a second time, "I understand;" and a second
time she flushed unaccountably. I spoke the
words with some bitterness and contempt, and
she took them to refer to herself.

"You blame me," she began nervously, "for
marrying so soon after Julian died. But it is
unfair to judge quickly."

The speech was little short of a revelation to
me. So busy had my thoughts been with my
own affairs, that I had not realised this was in
truth the woman who had been betrothed to Julian,
and who had betrayed him to his shameful death.
I looked at her for a moment, stunned by the
knowledge. She was, as her portrait showed her
to be, very pretty, with something of the petted
child about her; of a trim and supple figure, and
with wonderfully small hands. I remarked her
hands especially, because her fingers were playing
restlessly with the jewelled butt of her riding-whip;
and I did not wonder at her power over men's
hearts. A small, trembling hand laid in a man's
great palm! In truth, it coaxes him out of very
pity for its size. For my part, however, conscious
of the evil which her treachery had done to
Julian, ay, and to myself, too, I felt nothing but
aversion for her, and, taking off my hat, I bowed

to her silently. Just as I was turning away, an idea occurred to me. She knew nothing of her brother's plot to ruin me in Ilga's estimation. Why should I not use her to confound his designs?

"Lady Tracy," said I, returning to her side, "it is in your power to do me a service."

"Indeed?" she asked, her face clearing, and her manner changing to its former flippancy. "Is it the new fashion for ladies to render services to gentlemen? It used to be the other way about."

"As you have sure warrant for knowing," I added.

The look of fear which I had previously noticed sprang again into her eyes; now I appreciated the cause. She was afraid that I knew something of her share in Julian's death.

"It has been my great good fortune," she replied uneasily, "when I needed any small services, to meet with gentlemen who rendered them with readiness and forbearance."

She laid a little stress upon the last word, and I took a step closer to her.

"You cannot be aware, I think, who lodges in this house."

"I am not," she replied. "Why? Who lodges here?"

"Countess Lukstein."

She gave a little faltering cry, and turned white to the lips.

"You need have no fear," I continued. "I said Countess Lukstein, the wife, or rather, the widow. For a widow she has been this many a month."

"A widow!" she repeated. "A widow!" And she drew a long breath of relief, the colour returning to her cheeks. Then she turned defiantly on me. "And what, pray, is this Countess Lukstein to me?"

"God forbid that I should inquire into that!" said I sternly, and her eyes fell from my face. "Now, madam," I went on, "will you do me the favour I ask of you?"

"You ask it with such humility," she answered bitterly, "that I cannot find it in my heart to refuse you."

"I expected no less," I returned. "Let me assist you to dismount."

She drew quickly away.

"For what purpose? You would not take me to—to his wife."

"Even so!"

"Ah, not that! Not that! Mr. Buckler, I beseech you," she implored piteously, laying a trembling hand upon my shoulder. "I have not the courage."

"There is nothing to fear," I said, reassuring her. "Nothing whatsoever. Your brother is there. That guarantees no harm can come to you. But, besides, Countess Lukstein knows nothing of the affair. No one knows of it but you and I."

She still sat unconvinced upon her saddle.

"How is it you know, Mr. Buckler?" she asked, in a low tone.

"Julian told me," I answered, perceiving that I must needs go further than I intended if I meant to get my way. "Cannot you guess why?

I said the Count was dead. I did not tell you
how he died. He was killed in a duel."

She looked at me for a moment with a great
wonder in her eyes.

"You!" she whispered. "You killed Count
Lukstein?"

"It is the truth," I answered. "And the
Countess knows so little of the affair that she is
even ignorant of that."

"Are you sure?"

"Should I come here a-visiting, think you,
if she knew?"

The words seemed somewhat to relieve her
of apprehension, and she asked:

"To what end would you have me speak to
her? What am I to say?"

"Simply that you and I have met by chance,
for the first time this morning."

"Then she couples your name with mine," she
exclaimed, in a fresh alarm. "Without ground or
reason! Your name—for you killed him—with
mine. Don't you see? She must suspect!"

"Nay," I answered. "It is the strangest
accident which has led her to link us together in
her thoughts. She can have no suspicion."

"Then how comes it that she couples us who
are strangers?"

I saw no object in relating to her the device
of her brother, or in disclosing my own passion
for the Countess. Moreover, I bethought me that
at any moment Marston might take his leave, and
I was resolved that Lady Tracy should speak in
his presence, since by that means he would be

P

compelled to confirm her words.   So I broke in
abruptly upon her questioning.

"Lady Tracy, we are wasting time.   You must
be content with my assurances.   'Tis but a little
service that I claim of you, and one that may
haply repair in some slight measure the fatal
consequences of your disloyalty."

She slipped her foot from the stirrup, and,
without touching the hand I held out to assist
her, sprang lightly to the ground.   It may be that
I spoke with more earnestness than I intended.

"What mean cowards love makes of men!"
she said, looking at me scornfully.

The remark stung me sharply because I was
fully sensible that I played but a despicable part
in forcing her thus to bear testimony for me
against her will, and I answered angrily:

"Surely your memory provides you with one
instance to the contrary;" and I mounted the
steps and knocked at the door.

Otto Krax answered my summons, and for once
in his life he betrayed surprise.   At the sight of
Lady Tracy, he leaped backwards into the hall,
and stared from her to me.   Lady Tracy laid a
hand within my arm, and the fingers tightened
convulsively upon my sleeve; it seemed as though
she were on the point of fainting.   I bade the
fellow, roughly, to wait upon his mistress, and
inquire whether she would receive me, and a friend
whom I was most anxious to present to her.   With
a curiosity very unusual, he asked of me my
companion's name, that he might announce it.   But
since my design was to surprise Hugh Marston,

I ordered him to deliver the message in the precise terms which I had used.

So changed indeed was the man from his ordinary polite impassivity, that he abruptly left us standing in the hall, and departed on his errand with no more ceremony than a minister's servant shows to the needy place-seekers at his master's levée. We stood, I remember particularly, in a line with the high window of which I have already spoken, and the full light of the noontide sun fell athwart our faces. I set the circumstance down here inasmuch as it helped to bring about a very strange result.

"Who is the man?" whispered Lady Tracy, in an agitated voice. "Does he know me?"

"Nay," said I, reassuring her. "It may be that he has seen you before, at Bristol, for he was Count Lukstein's servant. But it is hardly probable that the Count shared his secret with him. And the matter was a secret kept most studiously."

"But his manner? How account for that?"

"Simply enough," said I. "The person who slandered us to the Countess, gave her, as a warrant and proof, a miniature of you."

"A miniature!" she exclaimed, clinging to me in terror. "Oh, no! no!"

"Gott im Himmel!"

The guttural cry rang hoarsely from the top of the stairs. I looked up; Otto was leaning against the wall, his mouth open, his face working with excitement, and his eyes protruding from their sockets. I had just sufficient time to notice that, strangely enough, his gaze was directed at me, and not at the woman by my side, when I felt the hand slacken on my arm, and with a little weak sigh, Lady Tracy slipped to the floor in a swoon.

I stooped down, and lifting her with some difficulty, carried, or rather dragged her to a couch. " Quick, booby ! " I shouted to Otto. " Fetch one of the women and some water ! "

My outcry brought Ilga onto the landing.

" What has befallen ? " she asked, leaning over the rail.

" 'Tis but a swoon," I replied ; " nothing more. " There is no cause for alarm."

" Poor creature ! " she said tenderly, and came running down the stairs. " Let me look, Mr. Buckler. Ailments, you know, are a woman's province."

I was kneeling by the couch, supporting Lady Tracy's head upon my arm, and I drew aside, but without removing my arm. Ilga caught sight of her face, and stopped.

" Oh ! " she cried, with a gasping intake of the breath ; then she turned on me, her countenance flashing with a savage fury, and her voice so bitter and harsh that, had I closed my eyes, I could not have believed that it was she who spoke.

" So you lied ! You lied to me ! You tell me one hour that you have never had speech with her, the next I find her in your arms."

" Madame," I replied, withdrawing my arm hastily, " I told you the truth."

The head fell heavily forward upon my breast, and I sought to arrange the body full-length upon the couch.

"Nay," said the Countess. "Let the head rest there. It knows its proper place."

"I told you the truth; believe it or not as you please!" I repeated, exasperated by her cruel indifference to Lady Tracy. "I never so much as set eyes upon this lady before to-day. I know that now. For the first time in my life, I saw her when I left you but a few minutes ago. She was waiting on horseback at your steps, and I persuaded her to dismount and bear me out with you."

"A very likely plausible story," sneered Ilga. "And whom did your friend await at my steps?"

"Her brother," I replied shortly. "Hugh Marston."

"Her brother!" she exclaimed. "We'll even test the truth of that."

She ran quickly to the foot of the stairs, as though she would ascend them. But seeing Otto still posted agape half-way up, she stopped and called to him.

"Tell Mr. Marston that his sister lies in the hall in a dead faint!"

Otto recovered his wits, and went slowly up to the parlour, while the Countess eyed me triumphantly. But in a moment Marston came flying down the stairs; he flung himself on his knees beside his sister.

"Betty!" he cried aloud, and again, whispering it into her ear with a caressing reproach, "Betty!" He shook her gently by the shoulders, like one that wakes a child from sleep. "Is there no help, no doctor near?"

One of the Countess's women came forward

and loosed the bodice of Lady Tracy's riding-habit at the throat, while another fetched a bottle of salts.

"It is the heat," they said. "She will soon recover."

Marston turned to me with a momentary friendliness.

"It was you who helped my sister. Thank you!" He spoke simply and with so genuine cordiality that I could not doubt his affection for Lady Tracy; and I wondered yet the more at the selfish use to which he had put her reputation.

After a while the remedies had their effect, and Lady Tracy opened her eyes. Ilga was standing in front of her a few paces off, her face set and cold, and I noticed that Lady Tracy shivered as their glances met.

"Send for a chair, Hugh!" she whispered, rising unsteadily to her feet.

"'Twere wiser for you to rest a little before you leave," said the Countess, but there was no kindliness in her voice to second the invitation, and she did not move a step towards her.

"I would not appear discourteous, madame," faltered Lady Tracy, "but I shall recover best at home."

"I will fetch a chair, Betty," said Marston, and made as though to go; but with a terrified "No, no!" Lady Tracy caught him by the coat and drew his arm about her waist, clasping her hand upon it to keep it there. 'Twas the frankest confession of fear that ever I chanced upon, and I marvelled not that Ilga smiled at it. However, she despatched

Otto upon the errand, and presently Marston accompanied his sister to her home.

Ilga and myself were thus left standing in the hall, looking each at the other. I was determined not to speak, being greatly angered for that she had not believed me when I informed her Lady Tracy was Marston's sister, and I took up my hat and cane and marched with my nose in the air to the door. But she came softly behind me, and said in the gentlest tone of contrition :

" I seem to spend half my life in giving you offence and the other half in begging your pardon."

And contrasting her sweet patience with me against the cold dislike which she had evinced to Lady Tracy, I, poor fool, carried home with me the fancy yet more firmly rooted than before, that her antagonism to the original of the miniature was no more than the outcome of a woman's jealousy.

CHAPTER XIII.

COUNTESS LUKSTEIN IS CONVINCED.

ONE detail of this mischancy episode occasioned me considerable perplexity. Conjecture as I might, I could hit upon no cause or explanation of it that seemed in any degree feasible. The astonishment of Otto Krax I attributed, and as I afterwards discovered rightly attributed, to the appearance of Lady Tracy so pat upon the discussion of her picture, and to my expressed desire to present her to the Countess within a few minutes of strenuously denying her acquaintance ; and I deemed it not extravagant. That he recognised her as the object of his master's capricious fancy at Bristol, I considered most improbable. For I remembered how successfully the intrigue had been concealed ; so that even Julian himself came over-late to the knowledge of it. His second exclamation on the stairs I set down to the probability that he had perceived Lady Tracy was on the point of swooning.

It was indeed the fact of the lady's swoon which troubled me. Her natural repugnance to meeting the Countess was not motive enough. Nor did I believe her sufficiently sensible to shame for

that feeling to work on her to such purpose. It
seemed of a piece with the terror which she had
subsequently shown on her recovery. The miniature,
I conjectured, had something, if not everything to do
with it. Resolving wisely that I had best ascertain
the top and bottom of the matter, I called upon
Marston at his house in Lincoln's Inn Fields, close
to the new college of Franciscans, and asked where
his sister stayed, on the plea that I would fain
pay my respects to her, and assure myself of her
convalescence.

"I can satisfy you on the latter point," he
returned cordially, " but at the cost of denying you
the pleasure of a visit. For my sister left London
on the next day, and has gone down into the
country."

"So soon ?" I asked in some surprise. For Lady
Tracy hardly impressed me as likely to find much
enjoyment in the felicities of a rural life.

"Her illness left her weak, and she thought the
country air would give her health."

For a moment I was in two minds whether to
inquire more precisely of her whereabouts and follow
her; but I reflected that I might encounter some
difficulty in compassing an interview, for it was
evident that she had fled from London in order to
avoid further trouble and concern in the matter. And
even if I succeeded so far, I saw no means of eliciting
the explanation I needed, without revealing to her
the unscrupulous use which her brother had made of
her miniature; and that I had not the heart to do.
The business seemed of insufficient importance to
warrant it. There was besides a final and convincing

argument which decided me to remain in London.
If I journeyed into the West, I should leave an open
field for my rival, and no ally with the Countess
to guard against his insinuations; and I reflected
further that there were few possible insinuations from
which he would refrain.

On this point of his conduct, however, I was
minded to teach him a lesson, which would make him
more discreet in the future, and at the same time
effect the purpose I had in view when Lady Tracy
inopportunely swooned. For when I came to think
over the events of that morning, I recollected that
after all Lady Tracy had not spoken as I asked her,
and though the last words Ilga had said to me as I
left the house seemed to show me that she no longer
believed the calumny, I was none the less anxious to
compel Marston to disavow it.

Now it was the fashion at the time of which I
write for the fine ladies and gentlemen of the town to
take the air of a morning in the Piazza of Covent
Garden; and choosing an occasion when Marston
was lounging there in the company of the Countess
and her attendant, Mdlle. Durette, I inquired of him
pointedly concerning his sister's health, meaning to
lead him from that starting-point to an admission
that Lady Tracy was until that chance meeting a
complete stranger to me.

But or ever he could reply, Ilga broke in with an
air of flurry, and calling to Lord Culverton, who was
approaching, engaged him in a rapid conversation.
She was afraid, I supposed, that I meant to break the
promise which I had given her upon the stairs, and
tax Marston with his treachery; and I was confirmed

in the supposition when I repeated the question.
For she shot at me a look of reproach, and said
quickly :

"I was telling your friend when you joined us,"
she said, "of my home in the Tyrol." She laid some
stress upon the word "friend." "'Twere hard, I
think, at any season to find a spot more beautiful."

"'Twere impossible," rejoined Culverton, with his
most elegant bow. "For no spot can be more
beautiful than that which owns Beauty for its
queen."

"The compliment," replied Ilga, with a bow,
"is worthy of the playhouse."

"Nay, nay," smirked my lord, mightily gratified ;
"the truth, madame, the truth extorted from me, let
me die! And yet it hath some wit. I cannot help
it, wit will out, the more certainly when it is truth
as well."

"Lady Tracy, then——" I began to Marston.

"But at this time of the year," interrupted the
Countess immediately, "Lukstein has no rival. Cornfields redden below it, beeches are marshalled green
up the hillside behind it, gentian picks out a mosaic
on the grass, and night and day waterfalls tumble their
music through the air. Yet even in winter, when the
ice binds it and gags its voices, it has a quiet charm
of silence whereof the memory makes one homesick."

As she proceeded the anxiety died out of her face,
and she grew absorbed in the picture which her
memories painted.

"Madame," said Marston, "I should appreciate
the description better if it spoke less of a longing to
return."

"It is my kingdom, you see," she replied.
"Barbarous no doubt, with a turbulent populace,
but still it is my kingdom, and very loyal to me."

Culverton paid her the obvious flattery, but she
took no heed of it.

"The tiniest, compactest kingdom," she went on
in a musing tone, "sequestered in a nook of the
world." She seated herself on a chair which stood
at the edge of the Piazza. "Indeed, I shall return
there, and that, I fancy, soon."

"Countess!" replied Culverton. "That were
too heartless. 'Twould decimate London, let me
perish! For never a gallant but would drink himself to death. Oh, fie!"

Marston joined eagerly in the other's protestations. For my part, however, I remained silent,
well content with what she had said. For I recollected the evening when I first had talk with her,
and the construction which I had placed upon her
words; how she would never return to Lukstein
until she was eased of the pain which her husband's
disaster had caused her. The notion that her
memories had lost their sting thrilled me to the
heart, and woke my vanity to conjecture of a
cause.

"Then," said the Countess, "would my friends
be proved heartless. For it is their turn to visit
me, and I would not be baulked of requiting them
for their kindness to me here. 'Tis not so tedious a
journey after all."

"I can warrant the truth of that," said Culverton.
"For I have been as far as Innspruck myself."

"Indeed?" said the Countess. She looked hard

at him for a second, and then laughed to herself. "When was that?" she asked.

"Some six years ago. I was on the grand tour with a tutor—a most obnoxious person, who was ever poring over statues and cold marble figures, but as for a fine woman, rabbit me if he ever knew one when he saw her. He dragged me with him from Italy to Innspruck to view some figures in the Cathedral."

"Then you must needs have passed beneath Lukstein," said the Countess, "for it hangs just above the high-road from Italy."

Culverton would not admit the statement. Some instinct, some angelic warning, he declared, would surely have bidden him stop and climb to the Castle as to a holy shrine. The Countess laughingly assured him that nevertheless he had passed her home, and with a fond minuteness she described to him its aspect and position.

Then the strangest thing occurred. She leaned forward in her chair, and with the tip of the stick she carried, drew a line on the gravel at the edge of the pavement.

"That represents the road from Meran," she explained. "The stone yonder is the Lukstein rock, on which the Castle stands." She briefly described the character of the village, and marked out the windings of the road from the gates at the back of the Castle down the hillside, until she had well-nigh completed a diagram in all essentials similar to that which Julian had sketched for me in my Horace.

"From the village," she said, "the road runs in a zigzag to join the highway."

She traced two long, distinct lines, but stopped of a sudden at the apex of the second angle, where the coppice runs to a point, with her face puckered up in a great perplexity. Culverton asked her what troubled her.

"I was forgetting," she said. "I was forgetting how often the road twisted," and very slowly she drew the final line to join with that which she had marked to represent the highway in the bed of the valley.

It struck me as peculiar for the moment, that with her great affection for Lukstein, she should forget so simple and prominent a detail as the number of angles which the road made in its descent. But I gave little thought to the matter, being rather engrossed in the strange coincidence of the diagram. It brought home to me with greater poignancy than ever before the deceit which I was practising upon my mistress. For I compared the use to which I had put my plan of the Castle with the motive which had led her unconsciously to reproduce it, I mean her desire that her friends should appreciate the home in which she took such manifest delight.

But while I was thus uneasily reproaching myself I perceived Marston separate from the group, and being obstinately determined that he should admit before Ilga the tenuity of my acquaintance with his sister, I called him back and asked him at what period Lady Tracy might be expected again in town.

This time the Countess made no effort to divert me. Indeed, she seemed barely to notice that I had put the question, but sat with her chin propped on the palms of her hands gazing with a thoughtful frown at the outline which she had drawn ; and I believed her to be engrossed in the picture which it evoked in her imagination.

"It appears that you feel great interest in my sister, Mr. Buckler," said Marston curiously. Doubtless my question was a clumsy one, for I was never an adept at finesse ; but this was the last answer which I desired to hear. "Nay, nay," I said hurriedly, and stopped at a loss, idly adding with my cane a line here and there to Countess Lukstein's diagram.

To my surprise, however, Ilga herself came to my rescue, and in a careless tone brought the matter to an issue.

"Perhaps Mr. Buckler," she remarked, "is an old friend of Lady Tracy's."

I raised my eyes from the Countess, fixing them upon Marston to note how he took the thrust, and with a quick sweep of her stick she smoothed the gravel, obliterating the lines. That I expected to see Marston disconcerted and in a pother to evade the question, I need not say, and 'twas with an amazement which fell little short of stupefaction that I heard him answer forthwith in a brusque, curt tone.

"That can hardly be. For my sister has been abroad all this year, and Mr. Buckler in the same case until this year."

I turned to Ilga. But she seemed more interested in Lady Tracy than in the fact of the admission.

"Ah! Lady Tracy was abroad," she said. "When did she leave England?"

"In September."

"The very month that I returned," I exclaimed triumphantly.

The Countess turned quickly towards me. "I fancied you only returned this spring."

"I was in England for a short while in September," said I, regretting the haste with which I had spoken.

"September of last year?"

"Of last year."

"Anno Domini 1685," laughed Culverton. "There seems to be some doubt about the date."

"September, 1685," repeated the Countess with a curious insistency.

"There is no doubt," returned Marston hotly. "I could wish for Betty's sake we had not such cause to remember it. She was betrothed to one of Monmouth's rebels, curse him! and Betty was so distressed by his capture that her health gave way."

I was upon tenterhooks lest Ilga should inquire the name of the rebel. But she merely remarked in an absent way, as though she attached no significance to his words:

"'Tis a sad story."

"In truth it is, and the only consolation we got from it was that the rebel swung for his treachery. Betty was ordered forthwith abroad, and she left England on the fourteenth of September. I remember the day particularly since it was her birthday."

"September the fourteenth!" said the Countess; and I, thinking to make out my case beyond dispute, cried triumphantly:

"The very day whereon I bade good-bye to Leyden."

The words were barely off my lips when Ilga rose to her feet. She stood for a moment with her eyes very wide and her bosom heaving.

"I am convinced," she whispered to me with an odd smile. "I ought not to have needed the proof. I am convinced."

With that she turned a little on one side, and Marston resumed :

"That proves how little Mr. Buckler is acquainted with Lady Tracy."

He spoke as though I had been endeavouring to persuade the company that I was intimate with his sister ; he almost challenged me to contradict him. I could not but admire the effrontery of the man in carrying off the exposure of his falsity with so high a head, and I surmised that he had some new contrivance in his mind whereby he might sub-sequently set himself right with Ilga. One thing, however, was apparent to me : that he had no suspicion of his sister's acquaintance with Count Lukstein.

"It was on the fourteenth that Betty set out for France," he once more declared, and so walked away.

"Where she married most happily three months later," sniggered Culverton. "As you say, madame, it is a very sad story."

The Countess laughed.

"She was not over-constant to her rebel."

"In the matter of the affections," replied Culverton, "Lady Tracy was ever my Lady Bountiful."

It seemed to me that the Countess turned a shade paler, but any inference which I might have

Q

drawn adverse to myself from that was prevented by
a proposal which she presently mooted. For some
other of our friends joining us about this time, she
proposed for a frolic that the party should take
chairs and immediately invade my lodgings. Needless to say, I most heartily seconded the proposition,
apologising at the same time for the poor hospitality
which the suddenness of the invitation compelled me
to offer.

Since by chance I had the key in my pocket, we
entered from the Park by the little door in the wall of
the garden. I mention this because I was waked up
about the middle of the night by the sound of this door
banging to and fro against the jambs, and I believed
that I must have failed to lock it after I had let my
friends into the garden, the door having neither
latch nor bolt, but was secured only by the lock.
For awhile I lay in bed striving to shut my ears to
the sound. But the wind was high, and, moreover,
blew straight into the room through the open
window, so that I could not but listen, and in the
end grew very wakeful. The sounds were irregularly
spaced according to the lulls of the wind. Now the
door would flap to three or four times in quick
succession, short and sharp as the crack of a pistol ;
now it would stand noiseless for a time while I
waited and waited for it to slam. At last I could
endure the worry of it no longer, and hastily donning
some clothes, I clattered downstairs.

The moon was shining fitfully through a scurrying rack of clouds, but as I always placed the key of
the door upon the mantel-shelf of the larger parlour,
and thus knew exactly where to lay my hand on it,

I did not trouble to strike a light, to which omission I owed my life, and, indeed, more than my life. I stumbled past the furniture, crossed the garden, locked the door, and got me back to bed.

In a few moments I fell asleep, but by a chance association of ideas—for I think that the banging of the postern must have set my thoughts that way—I began, for the first time since I came to London, to dream once more of the door in Lukstein Castle, and to see it open, and open noiselessly across the world. For the first time in the history of my nightmare fancies, that door swung back against the wall. It swung heavily, and the sound of the collision shook me to the centre. I woke trembling in every limb. It was early morning, the sun being risen, and, to my amazement, through the open window I heard the postern bang against the jamb.

CHAPTER XIV.

A GAME OF HIDE-AND-SEEK.

OUTSIDE the boughs tossed blithely in the golden air ; the wind piped among the leaves, and the birds called cheerily. But for me the morning was empty of comfort. For the recurrence of this dream filled me with an uncontrollable terror ; I felt like one who gets him to bed of a night in the pride of strength, and wakes in the morning to see the stains of an old disease upon his skin. I looked back upon those first months of agony in Italy; I remembered how I had dreaded the coming of night and the quiet shadows of evening ; how each day, from the moment I rose from bed, appeared to me as no more than night's forerunner. Into such desperate straits did I fall that I was seized with a wild foreboding that this period of torture was destined to return upon me again and again in some inevitable cycle of fate.

There seemed indeed but one chance for me : to secure the pardon of Ilga ! It was only on her account that I felt remorse. I had realised that from the beginning   And I determined to seek her out that very day, unbosom myself of my passion, and confess the injury which I had done her.

It may be remembered that I was on the brink of the confession when Marston ascended the stairs at the apartment of the Countess, and interrupted me. Since then, though I had enjoyed opportunities enough, I had kept silence; for it was always my habit, due, I fancy, to a certain retiring timidity which I had not as yet thoroughly mastered, to wait somewhat slavishly upon circumstances, rather than to direct my wits to disposing the circumstances in the conjunction best suited to my end. Before I spoke or acted, I needed ever "the confederate season," as Shakespeare has it. Now, however, I determined to take the matter into my own hands, and tarry no longer for the opportune accident. So, leaving orders with my servants that they should procure a locksmith and have the lock of the garden door repaired, I set out and walked to Pall Mall.

To my grief, I discovered that I had tarried too long. Countess Lukstein, the servant told me— he was not Otto—had left London early that morning on a visit into the country. A letter, however, had been written to me. It was handed to me at the door, since the messenger had not yet started to deliver it. With the handwriting I was unfamiliar, and I turned at once to the signature. It was only natural, I assured myself, that Mademoiselle Durette should write; Ilga would no doubt be busy over the arrangements for her departure. But none the less I experienced a lively disappointment that she had not spared a moment to pen the missive herself. Mademoiselle Durette informed me that news had arrived from Lukstein which compelled

them to return shortly to the Tyrol, and that
consequently they had journeyed that morning
into the country, in order to pay a visit which
they had already put off too long. The Countess
would be absent for the space of a fortnight, but
would return to London without fail to take fitting
leave of her friends.

The first three days of her absence lagged by
with a most tedious monotony. It seems to me
now that I spent them entirely in marching backwards and forwards on the pavement of Pall Mall.
Only one thing, indeed, afforded me any interest—
the door in my garden wall. For there was nothing
whatever amiss with the lock, and on no subsequent
night did it fly open. I closely examined my
servants to ascertain whether any one of them had
made use of it for egress, but they all strenuously
denied that they had left the house that night, and
I was driven to the conclusion that I had turned
the key before closing the door, so that the lock
had missed its socket in the post.

On the fourth day, however, an incident occurred
which made the next week fly like a single hour,
and brought me to long most ardently, not merely
that the Countess might lengthen her visit, but that
she would depart from England without so much
as passing through London on her way. For as I
waked that morning at a somewhat late hour, I
perceived Marston sitting patiently on the edge
of my bed. He was in riding-dress, with his boots
and breeches much stained with mud, and he carried
a switch in his hand. For a while I lay staring at
him in silent surprise. He did not notice that I

was awake, and sat absorbed in a moody reverie. At last I stirred, and he turned towards me. I noticed that his face was dirty and leaden, his eyes heavy and tired.

"You sleep very well," said he.

"Have you waited long?"

"An hour. I was anxious to speak to you, so I came up to your room."

"We can talk the matter over at breakfast," said I cheerfully, though, to tell the truth, I felt exceedingly uneasy at the strangeness of his manner. And I made a movement as though I would rise; but he budged not so much as an inch.

"I don't fancy we shall breakfast together," said he, with a slow smile, and after a pause: "you sleep very well," he repeated, "considering that you have a crime upon your conscience."

I started up in my bed.

"Lie down!" he snarled, with a sudden fierceness, and with a queer sense of helplessness I obeyed him.

"That's right," he continued, with a patronising smile. "Keep quiet and listen!"

For the moment, however, there was nothing for me to listen to, since Marston sat silent, watching with evident enjoyment the concern which I betrayed. He had chosen the easiest way with me. The least hint of condescension in another's voice always made me conscious in the extreme of my own shortcomings, and I felt that I lay helpless in some new toils of his weaving.

At last he spoke.

"You killed Count Lukstein."

I was prepared for the accusation by his previous words.

"Well?" I asked, in as natural a tone as I could command.

"Well," he returned, "I would not be too hard with you. What if you returned to Cumberland to-day, and stayed there? Your estates, I am sure, will thrive all the better for their master's supervision."

"My estates," I replied, "have a steward to supervise them. Their master will return to them at no man's bidding."

"It is a pity, a very great pity," said he thoughtfully, flicking his switch in the air. "For not only are you unwise in your own interests, but you drive me to a proceeding which I assure you is very repugnant and distasteful to my nature. Really, Mr. Buckler, you should have more consideration for others."

The smooth irony of his voice began to make my anger rise.

"And what is this proceeding?" I inquired.

"It would be my duty," he began, and I interrupted him.

"I can quite understand, then, that it is repugnant to your nature."

He smiled indulgently.

"It is a common fault of the very young to indulge in dialectics at inappropriate seasons. It would be my duty, unless you retired obediently to Cumberland, to share my knowledge with the lady you have widowed."

"I shall save you that trouble," said I, much

relieved, " for I am in the mind to inform the Countess
of the fact myself. Indeed, I called at her lodging
the other day with that very object."

" But the Countess had left, and you didn't."
He turned on me sharply; the words were more a
question than a statement. I remained silent, and
he smiled again. " As it is, I shall inform her. That
will make all the difference."

I needed no arguments to convince me of the
truth of what he said. The confession must come
from me, else was I utterly undone. I sat up and
looked at him defiantly.

" So be it, then ! It is a race between us which
shall reach her first."

" Pardon me," he explained, in the same unruffled,
condescending tone ; " there will be no race, for I
happen to know where the Countess is a-visiting, and
you, I fancy, do not. I have the advantage of you in
that respect."

I glanced at him doubtfully. Did he seek to bluff
me into yielding, I wondered ? But he sat on the
bedside, carelessly swinging a leg, with so easy a
composure that I could not hesitate to credit his
words. However, I feigned not to believe him, and
telling him as much, fell back upon my pillow with a
show of indifference, and turned my face from him to
the wall, as though I would go to sleep.

" You do believe me," he insisted suavely. " You
do indeed. Besides, I can give you proof of my
knowledge. I am so certain that I know the lady's
whereabouts, and that you do not, that I will grant
you four days' grace to think the matter over. As
I say, I have no desire to press you hard, and

to be frank with you, I am not quite satisfied as to how my information would be received." I turned back towards him, and noticing the movement, he continued : "Oh, make no mistake, Mr. Buckler ! The disclosure will ruin your chance most surely. But will it benefit me ? That is the point. However, I must take the risk, and will, if you persist in your unwisdom."

I lay without answering him, turning over in my mind the only plan I could think of, which offered me a chance of outwitting him.

"You might send word to me, four days from now, which alternative you prefer. To-day is Monday. On Thursday I shall expect to hear from you."

He uncrossed his legs as he spoke, and the scabbard of his sword rattled against the frame of the bed. The sound, chiming appositely to my thoughts, urged me to embrace my plan, and I did embrace it, though reluctantly. After all, I thought, 'twas a dishonourable wooing that Marston was about. So I said, with a sneer:

"Men have been called snivelling curs for better conduct than yours."

"By pedantic schoolboys," he replied calmly. "But then the schoolboys have been whipped for their impertinence."

With that he drew the bed-clothes from my chest, and raised his whip in the air. I clenched my fists, and did not stir a muscle. I could have asked for nothing that was more like to serve me. I made a mistake, however, in not feigning some slight resistance, and he suddenly flung back the clothes upon me.

"The ruse was ingenious," he said, with a smile, "but I cannot gratify you to the extent you wish. In a week's time I shall have the greatest pleasure in crossing swords with you. But until then we must be patient."

My patience was exhausted already, and raising myself upon my elbow, I loaded him with every vile epithet I could lay my tongue to. He listened with extraordinary composure and indifference, stripping off his gloves the while, until I stopped from sheer lack of breath.

"It's all very true," he remarked quietly. "I have nothing to urge against the matter of your speech. Your voice is, I think, unnecessarily loud, but that is a small defect, and easily reformed."

The utter failure of my endeavour to provoke him to an encounter, combined with the contemptuous insolence of his manner, lifted me to the highest pitch of fury.

"You own your cowardice, then!" I cried, fairly beside myself with rage. "You have plotted against me from the outset like a common, rascally intriguer. No device was too mean for you to adopt. Why, the mere lie about the miniature——"

I stopped abruptly, seeing that he turned on me a sudden questioning look.

"Miniature?" he exclaimed. "What miniature?"

I remembered the pledge which I had given to Ilga, and continued hurriedly, seeking to cover up my slip:

"I could not have believed there was such underhand treachery in the world."

"Then now," said he, "you are better informed,"

and on the instant his composure gave way. It seemed as though he could no longer endure the strain which his repression threw on him. Passion leaped into his face, and burned there like a flame; his voice vibrated and broke with the extremity of feeling; his very limbs trembled.

"'Tis all old talk to me—ages old and hackneyed. You are only repeating my thoughts, the thoughts I have lived with through this damned night. But I have killed them. Understand that!" His voice shrilled to a wild laugh. "I have killed them. Do you think I don't know it's cowardly? But there's a prize to be won, and I tell you"— he raised his hands above his head, and spoke with a sort of devilish exaltation—"I tell you, were my mother alive, and did she stand between Ilga and me, I would trample her as surely as I mean to trample you."

"Damn you!" I cried, wrought to a very hysteria by his manner. "Don't call her by that name!"

"And you!" he said, and with an effort he recovered his self-control. "And you, are your hands quite clean, my little parson? You kill the husband secretly, and then woo the wife with all the innocence and timidity in the world. Is there no treachery in that?"

I was completely staggered by his words and the contempt with which they were spoken. That any one should conceive my lack of assurance in paying my addresses to be a deliberate piece of deceit, had never so much as entered my head. I had always been too busy upbraiding myself upon that very score. Yet I could not but realise now how plausible the notion appeared. 'Twas plain that Marston believed I had been carefully playing a part; and I wondered:ˈ Would Ilga imagine that, too, when I told her my story? Would she believe that my deference and hesitation had been assumed to beguile her? I gazed at Marston, horror-stricken by the conjecture.

"Ay!" said he, nodding an answer to my look, "we have found each other out. Come, let us be frank! We are just a couple of dishonest scoundrels, and preaching befits neither of us."

He moved away from the bedside, and picked up his whip which he had dropped on to the floor. It lay close to the window, and as he raised himself again, he looked out across the garden.

"You overlook the Park," he said in an altered tone. "It is very strange."

At the time I was so overwhelmed by the construction which he had placed upon my behaviour, that I did not carefully consider what he meant. Thinking over the remark subsequently, however, I inferred from it, what indeed I had always suspected, that Marston had no knowledge his interviews and promenades with the Countess had taken place within sight of my windows.

He took up his hat, and opened the door.

"I told you fortune would give me my revenge," he said.

"You are leaving your gloves," said I, awakened to the necessity of action by his leave-taking.

The gloves were lying on the edge of the bed.

Thanking me politely, he returned, and stooped forward to take them. I gathered them in my hand and tossed them into his face. His head went back as though I had struck him a blow; he flushed to a dark crimson, and I saw his fingers tighten about his whip. The next moment, however, he gave a little amused laugh.

"There is much of the child lingering in you, Mr. Buckler," he said. "'Tis a very amiable quality, and I wonder not that it gets you friends. Indeed, I should have rejoiced to have been reckoned among them myself, had such a consummation been possible."

He spoke the last sentence with something of sincerity; but it only served to increase my rage.

"You cannot disregard the insult," I cried.

"Why not? There are no witnesses."

"There shall be witnesses and to spare on the next occasion," I replied, baffled by his coolness. He shrugged his shoulders.

"You have four days to bring about that occasion. Afterwards I shall seek it myself."

I had four days wherein to discover the whereabouts of Countess Lukstein, or to compel Marston to an encounter. The one alternative seemed impossible; the other, as I had evidence enough, little short of impossible. Four days! The words beat into my brain like dull strokes of a hammer. I could not think for their pressing repetition. I was, moreover, bitterly sensible that I had myself placed the weapon for my destruction into Marston's hand.

For there was no doubting that he had obtained his knowledge from his sister. I had plumed myself somewhat upon my diplomacy in revealing my secret to her, and in using it as a means to force her to deny my acquaintance. Now, when it was all too late, I saw what a mistake my cleverness had been. For not only through Lady Tracy's swoon had I missed my particular aim, but I had presented to my antagonist a veritable Excalibur, and kept not so much as a poniard for my own defence. Even then, however, I did not realise the entirety of the mistake, and had no inkling of the price I was to pay for it.

The first step which I took that morning was to make inquiries at the lodging of Countess Lukstein. The servants, however, whom she had left behind, knew—or rather pretended to know—nothing of their mistress' journey, beyond what they had previously told me.

Since, then, it was impossible to search the length and breadth of England within four days, I was thrown back upon my last resource. It was discreditable enough even to my fevered mind; but I could see no other way out of the difficulty, and at all costs I was resolved that Marston should not relate his story to the Countess until I had related mine. For even if he was minded to speak the truth, it would make all the difference, as he justly said, which of us twain spoke the first. I felt certain, moreover, that he would not speak the truth. For, to begin with, he would ascribe my timidity to a carefully-laid plan, since that was his genuine conviction; and again, remembering the story which I believed him to have invented concerning the miniature, I had no doubt

that he would so embroider his actual knowledge
that I should figure on the pattern as a common
assassin. How much of the real history of Count
Lukstein's death he knew, of course I was not aware,
nor did I trouble myself to consider.

My conclusion, accordingly, was to fix upon him
within the next four days an affront so public and
precise that he must needs put the business without
delay to the arbitrament of swords ; in which case, I
was determined, one or the other of us should find
his account.

To this end I spent the day amidst the favourite
resorts of the town, passing from the Piazza to the
Exchange in search of him ; thence back to St.
Paul's Church, thence to Hyde Park, from the Park
across the water to the Spring Garden at Lambeth,
and thence again to Barn Elms. By this time the
afternoon was far advanced, and bethinking me that
he might by chance be dining abroad, I sought out
the taverns which he most frequented : Pontac's in
Abchurch Lane, Locket's, and the " Rummer." But
this pursuit was as fruitless as the former, and without
waiting to bite a morsel myself, I hurried to make
the round of the chocolate-houses. Marston, however,
was not to be discovered in any of them, nor had
word been heard of him that day. At the " Spread
Eagle," in Covent Garden, however, I fell across
Lord Culverton, and framing an excuse persuaded
him to bear me company ; which he did with great
good-nature, for he was engaged at ombre, a game to
which he was much addicted. At the " Cocoa Tree "
in Pall Mall, I secured Elmscott by a like pretext,
and asked him if he knew of another who was

minded for a frolic, and would make the fourth. He
presented me immediately to a Mr. Aglionby, a
country gentleman of the neighbouring county to
my own, but newly come to town, and very boisterous
and talkative. I thought him the very man for my
purpose, since he would be like to spread the report
of the quarrel, and joining him to my company I
summoned a hackney coach, and we drove to the
Lincoln's Inn Fields. A hundred yards from
Marston's house I dismissed the coach and sent
Elmscott and the rest of the party forward, myself
following a little way behind. I had previously
instructed Elmscott in the part which I desired him
to play. Briefly, he was to inquire whether Marston
was within; and if, as I suspected, that was the case,
to seek admittance on the plea that he wished to
introduce a friend from the country, in the person
of Mr. Aglionby. Whereupon I was to join myself
quietly to the party, and so secure an entrance into
the house in company with sufficient witnesses to
render a duel inevitable upon any insult.

Marston, however, was prepared against all
contingencies, for four servants appeared in answer
to my cousin's knocking; and as they opened the
door no further than would allow one person to
enter at a time, it was impossible even to carry
the entrance by a rush. My friends, however, had
no thought of doing that, since one of the servants
came forward into the street and gravely informed
them that his master had fallen suddenly sick of
an infectious fever, and lay abed in a frenzy of
delirium. Even as the fellow spoke, a noise of
shouts and wild laughter came through the open

R

door. My companions shuddered at the sounds, and with a few hasty expressions of regret, hurried away from the neighbourhood. I ran after them, shouting out that it was all a lie; that Marston had not one-tenth of the fever which possessed me, and that his illness was a coward's dissimulation to avoid a just chastisement. However, I had better have spared my breath; for my words had no effect but to alienate their good-will, and they presently parted from me with every appearance of relief.

I walked home falling from depth to depth of despondency. The summer evening, pleasant with delicate colours, came down upon the town; the air was charged and lucent with a cool dew; the sweet odours of the country—nowhere, I think, so haunting, so bewitching to the senses as when one catches them astray in the heart of a city—were fragrant in the nostrils, so that the passers-by walked with a new alertness in their limbs, and a renewed youth in their faces; and as I stood at the door of my lodging, a great home-sickness swept in upon my soul, a longing for the dark fields in the starshine and the silent hills about them. I was seized with a masterful impulse to saddle my horse and ride out northwards through the night, while the lights grew blurred and misty behind me, and the fresh wind blew out of the heavens on my face. I doubt not, however, that the desire would have passed ere I had got far, and that I should have felt much the same desolate home-sickness for the cobbles and dust of London as I felt now for Cumberland.

However, I did not test the strength of my impulse; for while I stood upon the steps debating

whether I should go or stay, I perceived one of
Marston's servants coming towards me down the
street. With a grave deference, under which, rightly
or wrongly, I seemed to detect a certain irony,
he gave me his master's compliments, and handed
me a little stick of wood. There was a single notch
cut deep into the stick. I understood it to signify
that one day out of the four had passed, and—
so strangely is a man constituted — this gibing
menace determined me to stay. It turned my rage,
with its fitful alternatives of passion and despair,
into a steady hate, just as one may stir together
the scattered, spurting embers of a fire into one
glowing flame.

Late that evening came Lord Elmscott to see
me, and asked me with a concern which I little
expected, after his curt desertion of a few hours
agone, what dispute had arisen between Marston
and myself. I told him as much as I could without
revealing the ground of our quarrel; that Marston
had certain knowledge concerning myself which
he was minded to impart to Countess Lukstein;
that I was fully sensible the Countess ought to be
informed of the matter, but that I wished to carry
the information myself; that I doubted Marston
would not speak the truth, but would distort the
story to suit his own ends. The rest of the events
I related to him in the order in which they had
occurred.

"But it may be," he objected, "that Marston has
really fallen sick."

For reply, I handed him the stick of wood, and
told him how it had been delivered.

R 2

"The fellow's cunning," he observed, "for not only is he out of your reach, but he locks your mouth. You cannot urge that a man refuses to meet you when he lies abed with a fever, and you cannot prove that the sickness is feigned."

For awhile he sat silent, drumming with his fingers on the table. Then he asked:

"How comes it that Marston knows of this secret?"

"His sister must have told him," I replied.

"His sister!" he repeated. "Why, you never met her before this month."

"I told her on the first occasion that I met her. She was in some measure concerned in it."

He looked at me shrewdly.

"She was engaged to Sir Julian Harnwood," said he.

I nodded assent.

He brought his fist down on the table with a bang.

"The trouble springs from that cursed journey of yours to Bristol. I warned you harm would come of it. Had Lady Tracy any reason to fear you?"

"None," I replied promptly.

"Or any reason to fear Countess Lukstein?"

"None," I replied again; but after a moment's thought I added: "But she did fear her. I am sure of it."

He sprang to his feet.

"Three days!" he cried. "Three days! We may yet outwit him."

"How?" I asked, with the greatest eagerness.

"I'll not tell you now. 'Tis no more than a fancy. Wait you here your three days. Keep a strict watch on Marston's house. 'Tis unlikely that he will move before the time, since he would rather you spared him the telling of the story ; but there's no trusting him. On Thursday I will come to you here before midnight; so wait for me, unless, of course, Marston leaves before then. In that case, follow him, but send word here of your direction. You must be wary ; the fellow's cunning, and may get free from his house in some disguise."

With that he clapped his hat on his head, and rushed out into the street. For the next three days I saw no more of him. About Marston's house I kept strict watch as he enjoined. There were but two entrances : one in the façade of the building towards the Square, and the second in a little side-street which ran along a wall of the house. Few, however, either came in or out of these entrances, for the rumour of his sickness was spread abroad in the town, and even his tradesmen dreaded to catch the infection. I was, moreover, certain that he had not escaped, since each evening his servant came to my lodging and left a stick notched according to the number of days.

On the morning of the Thursday, being the fourth day and my last of grace, I doubled the sentinels about the house, hiring for the purpose some fellows of whom my people had cognizance. At the entrances, however, I planted my own men, and bidding them mark carefully the faces of such as passed out, in whatever dress they might be clothed, I retired to a coign of vantage at some distance whence I could keep an eye upon the house, and yet not obtrude myself upon the notice of those within it. In a little alley hard by I had stationed a groom with the swiftest horse that I possessed, so that I might be prepared to set off in pursuit of my antagonist the moment word of his departure was brought to me.

Thus, then, I waited, my heart throbbing faster and faster as the day wore on, and every nerve in my body a jerking pulse. At last my excitement mastered me; a clock in a neighbouring belfry chimed the hour of four, and I crept out of my corner and mingled with the gipsies and mountebanks who were encamped with their booths in the centre of the Square. Amongst this motley crowd I thought myself safe from detection, and moved, though still observing some caution, towards the front of Marston's house. It wore almost an air of desertion; over many of the windows the curtains were drawn, and never a face showed through the panes of the rest. I could see that my men were still stationed at their posts, and I began to think that we must needs prolong our vigil into the night. Shortly after six, however, the hall-door was opened, and the same servant who brought me the sticks of an evening came out on to the steps. He looked neither to the right nor to the left, but without a moment's hesitation stepped across the road, and threading the tents and booths, came directly towards me. It was evident that I had been remarked from some quarter of the house, and so I made no effort at further concealment, but rather went forward to meet him. With the same grave

politeness which had always characterised him, he
offered me a letter.

"My master," said he, "bade me deliver this
into your hand two hours after he had left."

"Two hours after he had left!" I gasped,
well-nigh stunned by his words.

"Two hours," he replied. "But I have been
a trifle remiss, I fear me, and for that I would
crave your pardon. It is now two hours and a
half since my master departed."

He made a low bow and went back to the
house, leaving me stupidly staring at the letter.

"My fever," it ran, "is happily so abated that
I am to be carried this instant into the country.
There will be no danger, I am assured, providing
that I am well wrapped up. Au revoir! Or is it
adieu?—HUGH MARSTON."

The sarcasm made my blood boil in my veins,
and I ran to the sentinels I had posted before the
entrances, rating them immeasurably for their
negligence. They heard me with all the marks of
surprise, and expostulated in some heat. No one,
they maintained, who in any way resembled Mr.
Marston had left the house; they had watched
most faithfully the day long, without a bite of food
to stay their stomachs. Somewhat relieved by their
words, I took no heed of their forward demeanour,
but gave them to understand that if their words
were true, they should eat themselves into a stupor
an they were so disposed. For I began to fancy
that the letter was a ruse to induce me to withdraw

my watchmen from the neighbourhood, and thus open a free passage for my rival's escape.

With the view of confirming the suspicion, I ordered them to give me a strict and particular account of all persons who had come from the house that day. For those who had kept guard before the front-door the task was simple enough. A few gentlemen had called; but of them only one, whom they imagined to be the physician, had entered the hall. He had reappeared again within half an hour or so of his going in, and, with that exception, no person had departed by this way.

The side-door, however, had been more frequently used. Now and again a servant had come out, or a tradesman had delivered his wares. At one time a cart had driven up, a bale of carpets had been carried into the house, and a second bale fetched out.

"What!" I cried, interrupting the speaker. "A bale of carpets? At what time?"

He knew not exactly, but 'twas between three and four, for he heard a clock chime the latter hour some while afterwards.

"You dolt!" I cried. "He was in the carpets."

"I know nought of that," he answered sullenly. "You only bade me note faces, and I noted them that carried the carpets. You said nothing about noting carpets."

The fellow was justly indignant, I felt; for, indeed, I doubt whether I should have suspected the bale myself but for Marston's letter. So I dismissed the men from their work, and rode slowly back to my lodging. Marston had three hours' start

of me already ; by midnight he would have nine,
even supposing that Elmscott arrived with trust-
worthy intelligence.   What chance had I of catching.
him ?

I walked about the room consumed with a fire
of impatience.   I seemed to hear the beat of hoofs
as Marston rode upon the way; and the further
he went into the distance, the louder and louder
grew the sound, until I was forced to sit down
and clasp my head between my hands in a mad
fear lest it should burst with the racket.   And then
I saw him—saw him, as in a crystal, spurring along
a white, winding road; and strangely enough the
road was familiar to me, so that I knew each stretch
that lay ahead of him, before it came in view and
was mirrored in my imaginings.   I followed him
through village and wood ; now a river would flash
for a second beneath a bridge; now a hill lift in
front, and I noticed the horse slacken speed and
the rider lean forward in the saddle.   Then for a
moment he would stand outlined against the sky
on the crest, then dip into a hollow, and out again
across a heath.   At last he came towards the gate
of a town.   How I prayed that the gate would be
barred !   We were too distant to ascertain that
as yet.   He drove his spurs deeper into the flanks
of his horse.   The gate was open !   He dashed at
full gallop down a street; turned into a broad lane
at right angles ; the beat of hoofs became louder
and louder in my ears.   Of a sudden he drew rein,
and the sound stopped.   He sprang from his horse,
mounted a staircase, and burst into a room.   I heard
the door rattle as it was flung open.   I knew the

room. I recognised the clock in the corner. I gazed about me for the Countess—and Elmscott's hand fell upon my shoulder.

"Why, lad, art all in the dark?"

"I have just reached the light," I cried, springing up in a frenzy of excitement. "The Countess Lukstein lies at the 'Thatched House Tavern,' in Bristol town."

"Damn!" said Elmscott. "I have just ridden thither and back to find that out."

And he fell swearing and cursing in a chair, whilst I rang for candles to be brought.

CHAPTER XV.

I HAD previously given orders that my horse should be kept ready saddled in the stable, and I now bade the servant bring it round to the door.

"Nay, there's no need to hurry," said Elmscott comfortably, throwing his legs across a chair. "Marston will never start before the morning."

"He has started," I replied. "He has seven hours to the good already. He started between three and four of the afternoon."

"But you were to follow him," he exclaimed, starting up. "You knew the road he was going. You were to follow him."

"He slipped through my fingers," said I, with some shame, for Elmscott was regarding me with the same doubtful look which I had noticed so frequently upon Jack Larke's face. "And as for knowing his road, 'twas a mere guess that flashed on me at the moment of your arrival."

"Well, well," said Elmscott, with a shrug, "order some supper, and if you can lend me a horse we will follow in half an hour."

Udal fetched a capon and a bottle of canary from

the larder, and together we made short work of the meal. For, in truth, I was no less famished than Elmscott, though it needed his appetite to remind me of the fact. Meanwhile, I related in what manner Marston had escaped me, and handed him the letter which the servant had delivered to me in the Lincoln's Inn Fields.

"In a bale of carpets!" cried Elmscott, with a fit of laughter which promised to choke him. "Gadsbud, but the fellow deserves to win! Well wrapped up! Morrice, Morrice, I fear me he'll trip up your heels!"

Elmscott's hilarity, it may easily be understood, had little in it which could commend it to me, and I asked him abruptly by what means he had discovered that the Countess Lukstein was visiting in Bristol.

"I'll tell you that as we go," said he, with a mouth full of capon. "At present I have but one object, to fill my stomach."

After we had set forth, which we did a short while before midnight—for I heard a clock tell that hour as we rode through the village of Knightsbridge— he explained how the conjecture had grown up in his mind.

"Marston came to you in the early morning, a week after the Countess had left London. He was muddied and soiled, as though he had ridden hard all night. In fact, he told you as much himself, and gave you the reason : that he had been fighting out his battle with himself. I reasoned, therefore, that he had only heard of this secret, whatever it may be, which put you at his mercy, the evening before,

Now that information came from his sister. It concerned Countess Lukstein. Lady Tracy, you told
me, for some reason feared the Countess. I argued
then that it could only be this fear which made
her write to her brother. But then she had been
in England a month already. How was it that she
had not revealed her anxiety before? And further,
how was it that Marston knew what you and every
one else was ignorant of—where Countess Lukstein
was staying? Lady Tracy, I was aware, had gone
down to the family estate near Bristol ; and I inferred in consequence that she had seen the Countess
in the neighbourhood, that her alarm had been
increased by the sight, and that she had promptly
communicated her fears to her brother; which fears
Marston made use of as a weapon against you. The
period of Countess Lukstein's departure jumped most
aptly with my conjecture, and I thought it would be
worth while to ride to Bristol and discover the truth."

The notion seemed to me, upon his recounting
it, so reasonable and clear that I wondered why it
had never occurred to me, and expressed as much
to Elmscott.

He laughed in reply.

"A man in love," said he, "is ever a damned
fool. He smothers his mind in a petticoat."

The night was very open, the moon being in
the last quarter, and the road, from the dry summer,
much harder than when I had travelled over it
in the previous year; so that we made a good pace,
and drew rein before the "Golden Crown" at Newbury about seven of the morning. There we
discovered that two travellers had arrived at the

inn a little after midnight with their horses very
wearied; but, since Thursday was market-day, and
the inn consequently full, they had remained but
a little while to water their beasts, and had then
pushed on towards Hungerford. Elmscott was for
breakfasting at the "Golden Crown," but I bethought
me that Hungerford was but nine miles distant, and
that Marston was most like to have lain the night
there. Consequently, if we pressed forward with
all speed, there was a good chance that we might
overtake my rival or ever he had started from
the town; in which case Elmscott, at all events,
would be able to take his meal at his leisure. To
this view my companion assented, though with some
reluctance, and we set off afresh across Wickham
Heath. In a short time we came in view of the
"Half-way House," and I related to Elmscott my
adventure with the landlord. As we rode past it,
however, I perceived the worthy man going towards
the stable with a bucket of water in his hand, and I
hastily reined up.

"What is it?" asked Elmscott.

"The fellow has no horses of his own," I replied.
"It follows he must needs have guests."

I dismounted as I spoke, and hailed the man.

"Potatoe!" I cried to him.

For a moment he looked at me in amazement,
and then:

"Dang it!" he shouted. "The play-actor!"
And he dropped the bucket, and ran towards me
doubling his fists.

"I have a pass-word for you," I said, when he
was near. "It lags a year behind the time, it's

true—Wastwater.   So you see the mare was meant
for me no less than your slugs."

He stopped, and answered doggedly :

"Well, 'twas your fault, master.   You should
have passed the word.   The mare was left with me
in strict trust, and you were ready enough with your
pistol to make an honest man believe you meant
no good."

Elmscott broke in impatiently upon his apology
with a demand for breakfast.   His wife, the landlord
assured us, was preparing breakfast even now for
two gentlemen who had come over-night, and we
might join them if they had no objection to our
company.   I asked him at what hour these gentlemen had ridden up to the inn, and he answered
about one of the morning.   I could not repress an
exclamation of joy.   Elmscott gave me a warning
look and dismounted ; he bade the landlord see
the horses groomed and fed, and joined me in the
road.

"Their faces will be a fine sight," said he,
rubbing his hands, "when we take our seats at the
table.   A guinea-piece will be white in comparison."
And he fell to devising plans by which our surprise
might produce the most startling effect.

Strangely enough, it occurred to neither of us
at the time that the surest method of outwitting
Marston was to leave him undisturbed to his breakfast and ride forward to Bristol.   But during these
last days the anxiety and tension of my mind
had so fanned my hatred of the man, that I could
think of nothing but crossing swords with him.
We were both, in a word, absorbed in a single quest ;

from wishing to outstrip, we had come to wish merely to overtake.

Elmscott gave orders to the innkeeper that he should inform us as soon as the two travellers were set down to their meal; and for the space of half an hour we strolled up and down, keeping the inn ever within our view. At the end of that time I perceived a cloud of dust at a bend of the road in the direction of Hungerford. It came rolling towards us, and we saw that it was raised by a berlin which was drawn at a great speed by six horses.

"They travel early," said Elmscott carelessly. I looked at the coach again, but this time with more attention.

"Quick!" I cried of a sudden, and drew Elmscott through an opening in the hedge into the field that bordered the road. The next moment the berlin dashed by.

"Did you see?" I asked. "Otto Krax was on the box."

"Ay!" he answered. "And Countess Lukstein within the carriage. What takes her back so fast, I wonder? She will be in London two days before her time."

We came out again from behind the hedge, and watched the carriage dwindling to a speck along the road.

"If you will, Morrice," said my cousin, with a great reluctance, "you can let Marston journey to Bristol, and yourself follow the Countess to town."

"Nay!" said I shortly. "I have a mind to settle my accounts with Marston, and not later than this morning."

He brightened wonderfully at the words.

"'Twere indeed more than a pity to miss so promising an occasion. But as I am your Mentor for the nonce, I deemed it right to mention the alternative—though I should have thought the less of you had you taken my advice. Here comes the landlord to summon us to breakfast."

We followed him along the passage towards the kitchen. The door stood half-opened, and peeping through the crack at the hinges, we could see Marston and his friend seated at a table.

"Gentlemen," said Elmscott, stepping in with the politest bow, "will you allow two friends to join your repast?"

Marston was in the act of raising a tankard to his lips; but save that his face turned a shade paler, and his hand trembled so that a few drops of the wine were spilled upon the cloth, he betrayed none of the disappointment which my cousin had fondly anticipated. He looked at us steadily for a second, and then drained the tankard. His companion — a Mr. Cuthbert Cliffe, with whom both Elmscott and myself were acquainted—rose from his seat and welcomed us heartily. It was evident that he was in the dark as to the object of our journey. We seated ourselves opposite them on the other side of the table. Elmscott was somewhat dashed by the prosaic nature of the reception, and seemed at a loss how to broach the subject of the duel, when Marston suddenly hissed at me:

" How the devil came you here?"

" On a magic carpet," replied Elmscott smoothly. " Like the Arabian, we came upon a magic carpet."

s

Marston rose from the table and walked to the fireplace, where he stood kicking the logs with the toe of his boot, and laughing to himself in a short, affected way, as men are used who seek to cover up a mortification.   Then he turned again to me.

"Very well," he said, with a nod, "and the sooner the better.   If Lord Elmscott and Mr. Cliffe will arrange the details, I am entirely at your service."

With that he set his hat carelessly on his head, and sauntered out of the room.   Mr. Cliffe looked at me in surprise.

"It is an old-standing quarrel between Mr. Buckler and your friend," Elmscott explained, "but certain matters, of which we need not speak, have brought it to a head.   Your friend would fain have deferred the settlement for another week, but Mr. Buckler's engagements forbade the delay."

So far he had got when a suspicion flashed into my head.   Leaving Elmscott to arrange the encounter with Mr. Cliffe, I hurried down the passage and out on to the road.   On neither side was Marston to be seen, but I perceived that the stable door stood open.   I looked quickly to the priming of my pistol — for, knowing that the Great West Road was infested by footpads and highwaymen, we had armed ourselves with some care before leaving London—and took my station in the middle of the way.   Another minute and I should have been too late ; for Marston dashed out of the stable door, already mounted upon his horse.   He drove his spurs into its flanks, and rode straight at me. I had just time to leap on one side.   His riding-

whip slashed across my face, I heard him laugh
with a triumphant mockery, and then I fired.
The horse bounded into the air with a scream of
pain, sank on its haunches, and rolled over on its
side.

The noise of the shot brought our seconds to the
door.

"Your friend seems in need of assistance," said
Elmscott. For Marston lay on the road struggling
to free himself from the weight of the horse. Cliffe
loosened the saddle and helped Marston to his feet.
Then he drew aside and stood silent, looking at
his companion with a questioning disdain. Marston
returned the look with a proud indifference, which,
in spite of myself, I could not but admire.

" There was more courage than cowardice in the
act," said I, "to those who understand it."

"I can do without your approbation," said
Marston, flushing, as he turned sharply upon me.
Catching sight of my face, he smiled. "Did the
whip sting?" he asked.

I unsheathed my sword, and without another
word we mounted the bank on the left side of the
road and passed on to the heath.

The seconds chose a spot about a hundred
yards from the highway, where the turf was level
and smooth, and set us facing north and south,
so that neither might get advantage from the sun.
The morning was very clear and bright, with just
here and there a feather of white cloud in the
blue of the sky ; and our swords shone in the sunlight like darting tongues of flame.

The encounter was of the shortest, since we were

in no condition to plan or execute the combinations
of a cool and subtle attack, but drove at each
other with the utmost fury. Marston wounded me
in the forearm before ever I touched him. But a
few seconds after that he had pinked me, he laid
his side open, and I passed my sword between his
ribs. He staggered backwards, swayed for a moment
to and fro in an effort to keep his feet; his knees
gave under him, and he sank down upon the heath,
his fingers clasping and unclasping convulsively
about the pommel of his sword. Cliffe lifted him
in his arms and strove to staunch the blood, which
was reddening through his shirt, while Elmscott ran
to the inn and hurried off to Hungerford for a
surgeon.

For awhile I stood on my ground, idly digging
holes in the grass with the point of my rapier.
Then Marston called me faintly, and I dropped the
sword and went to his side. His face was white
and sweaty, and the pupils of his eyes were con-
tracted to pin-points.

I knelt down and bent my head close to his.

"So," he whispered, "luck sides with you after
all. This time I thought that I had won the
vole."

He was silent for a minute or so, and then:

"I want to speak with you alone."

I took him from Cliffe's arms and supported his
head upon my knee, he pressing both his hands
tightly upon his side.

"Betty is afraid," he continued, with a gasp
between each word, as soon as Cliffe had left us.
"Betty is afraid, and her husband's a fool"

The implied request, even at that moment, struck me as wonderfully characteristic of the man. So long as his own desires were at stake he disregarded his sister's fears; but no sooner had all chance of gaining them failed, than his affection for her re-asserted itself, and even drove him to the length of asking help from his chief enemy.

" I will see that no harm comes to her."

" Promise ! "

I promised, somehow touched by his trust in me.

"I knew you would," he said gratefully; and then, with a smile : " I am sorry I hit you with my whip—Morrice. I could have loved you."

Again he lay silent, plucking at the grass with the fingers of his left hand.

" Lift me higher ! There is something else."

I raised his body as gently as I could; but nevertheless the rough bandage which Cliffe had fastened over the wound became displaced with the movement, and the blood burst out again, soaking through his shirt.

" You spoke of a miniature——" he began, and then with a little gasping sob he turned over in my arms, and fell forward on the grass upon his face.

I called to Cliffe, who stood with his back towards us a little distance off, and ran to where I had laid my coat and cravat before the duel commenced. For the cravat was of soft muslin, and might, I fancied, be of some use as lint. With this in my hand, I hurried back. Cliffe was lifting Marston from the ground.

" Best let him lie there quietly," I said.

He turned the body over upon its back.

"Aye!" he answered, "under God's sky."

I dropped on my knees beside the corpse, felt the pulse, laid my ear to the heart. The sun shone hot and bright upon his dead face. Cliffe took a handkerchief from his pocket, and gently placed it over Marston's eyes.

"This means a year on the Continent for you, my friend," he said.

When Elmscott and the surgeon arrived some half an hour later, they found me eating my breakfast in the kitchen.

"Where is he?" they asked.

"Who?" said I.

I remember vaguely that the surgeon looked at me with a certain anxiety, and made a remark to Elmscott. Then they went out of the room again. How long it was before they returned I have no notion. Elmscott brought in my coat, hat, and sword, and I got up to put them on; but the doctor checked him, and setting me again in my chair, bound up my arm, not without some resistance from me, for I saw that his hands were dabbled with Marston's blood.

"Now," said he to Elmscott, "if you will help, we will get him upstairs to bed."

"No!" said I, suddenly recollecting all that had occurred. "I made Marston a promise. I must keep it! I must ride to town and keep it!"

"It will be the best way, if he can," said Elmscott. "He will be taken here for a surety. I have sent a messenger to Bristol with the news."

The surgeon eased my arm into the sleeve of my coat, and made a sling about my shoulders with my cravat. Elmscott buckled on my sword and led me to the stables, leaving me outside while he went in and saddled a horse.

"This is Cliffe's horse," said he; "yours is too tired. I will explain to him."

He held the horse while I climbed into the saddle.

"Now, Morrice," he said, "you have no time to lose. You have got the start of the law ; keep it. Marston's family is of some power and weight. As soon as his death is known, there will be a hue and cry after you; so fly the country. I would say leave the promise unfulfilled, but that it were waste of breath. Fly the country as soon as you may, unless you have a mind for twelve months in Newgate gaol. I will follow you to town with all speed, but for your own sake 'twere best I find you gone."

He moved aside, and I galloped off towards Newberry. The misery of that ride I could not, if I would, describe. The pain of my wound, the utter weariness and dejection which came upon me as a reaction from the excitement of the last days, and the knowledge that I could no longer shirk my confession, so combined to weaken and distress me, that I had much ado to keep my seat in the saddle. 'Twas late in the evening when I rode up to Ilga's lodging. The door, by some chance, stood open, and without bethinking me to summon the servants, I walked straight up the staircase to the parlour, dragging myself from one step to the other by the help of the balustrade. The parlour door was shut, and I could not lay my fingers on the handle, but scratched blindly up and down the panels in an effort to find it. At last some one opened the door from within, and I staggered into the room. Mdlle. Durette—for it was she — set up a little scream, and then in the embrasure of the window I saw the Countess rise slowly to her feet. The last light of the day fell grey and wan across her face and hair. I saw her as through a mist, and she seemed to me more than ordinarily tall. I stumbled across the room, my limbs growing heavier every moment.

"Countess," I began, "I have a promise to fulfil. Lady Tracy——" There I stopped. The room commenced to swim round me. "Lady Tracy——" I repeated.

The Countess stood motionless as a statue, dumb as a statue. Yet in a strange way she appeared suddenly to come near and increase in stature— suddenly to dwindle and diminish.

"Ilga," I cried, stretching out my hands to her. She made no movement. I felt my legs bend beneath me, as if the bones of them were dissolved to water, and I sank heavily upon my knees. "Ilga," I cried again, but very faintly. She stirred not so much as a muscle to help me, and I fell forward swooning, with my head upon her feet.

CHAPTER XVI.

CONCERNING AN INVITATION AND A LOCKED DOOR.

WHEN consciousness returned to me, and I became sensible of where I lay, I perceived that Elmscott was in the room. He stood in the centre, slapping his boot continually with his riding-crop, and betraying every expression of impatience upon his face. But I gave little heed to him, for beside me knelt Ilga, a bottle of hartshorn salts in her hand. I was resting upon a couch, which stood before the spinet; the lamps were lighted, and the curtains drawn across the window, so that my swoon must have lasted some while.

As I let my eyes rest upon the Countess, she slipped an arm under my head and raised it, taking at the same time a cup of cordial, which Clemence Durette held ready. 'Twas of a very potent description, and filled me with a great sense of comfort. Ilga moved her arm as though to withdraw it. "No," I murmured to her, and she smiled and let it remain.

"Come, Morrice," said Elmscott. "You have but to walk downstairs. A carriage is waiting."

He moved towards the couch. I tried to raise my arm to warn him off, but found that it had been bandaged afresh, and was fastened in a sling. For a moment I could not remember how I had come by the hurt; then the history of it came back to me, and with that the promise I had made to my dying antagonist. For while I believed that Lady Tracy could have no grounds for her apprehensions, seeing that the Countess must needs be ignorant of her relations with the Count, whatever they might have been, I felt that the circumstances under which the request was uttered gave to it a special authority, and laid upon me a strict compulsion to obey it to the letter. The request, moreover, fitted exactly with my own intention. Ilga believed now that I had never seen Lady Tracy until that morning when she fainted, and so by merely confessing that the death of Count Lukstein lay at my door, and at my door alone, I should divert all possibilities of suspicion from approaching Lady Tracy ; so I whispered to Ilga :

"Send every one away ! "

"Nay," she replied ; "your cousin has told me."

"It is not that," said I. "There is something else—something my cousin could not know."

"Does it follow," she answered, lowering her eyes, "that I could not know it? Or do you think me blind ? "

The gentle, hesitating words nearly drove my purpose from my mind. It would have been so easy to say just, "I love you, and you know it." It became so difficult to say, "I killed your husband, and have deceived you." However, the confession

pressed urgently for utterance, and I said again:
"Send them away!"

"No," she replied, "you have no time for that
now. You must leave London to-night. Everything is ready; your cousin's carriage waits to take
you to the coast. To-morrow you must cross to
France. But if you still—still wish to unburden
your mind——"

"Heart," I could not refrain from whispering;
and, indeed, my heart leaped as she faltered and
blushed crimson.

"Then," she continued, "come to Lukstein!
You will be welcome," and with a quiet gravity she
repeated the phrase: "You will be very welcome!"

Every word she spoke made my task the harder.
I trust that the weakness of my body, the pain of
the wound, and my great fatigue, had something
to do with the sapping of my resolution. But whatever the cause, an overwhelming desire to cease
from effort, to let the whole world go, rushed in
upon me. The one real thing for me was this
woman who knelt beside the couch; the one real
need was to tell her of my love. I felt as though,
that once told, I could rest without compunction,
without a scruple of regret, just rest like a tired child.

"Come to Lukstein!" she repeated.

"Hear me now!" I replied with a last struggle,
and got to my feet. I was still so weak, however,
that the violence of the movement made me sick and
dizzy, and I tottered into Elmscott's arms.

"Come, Morrice!" he urged. "A little courage;
'tis only a few steps to descend."

I steadied myself against his shoulder. In a

corner of the room, rigid and impassive, was the tall figure of Otto Krax. How could I speak before him?

"I shall expect you, then," said the Countess, "and soon. I leave England to-morrow myself, and return straight home."

"You leave England to-morrow?" I asked eagerly.

"To-morrow!" she replied.

I drew a deep breath of relief. All danger to Lady Tracy, all her fears of danger, would vanish with the departure of the Countess; and as for my confession—it could wait.

"At Castle Lukstein, then," said I, and it seemed to me that she also drew a breath of relief.

From Pall Mall we drove to my lodging, where I found my trunks packed, and Udal fully dressed to accompany me in my flight; for Elmscott, who had started from the "Half-way House" some two hours later than myself, had ridden straight thither. On learning that my people had no news of me, he had immediately guessed where I should be discovered, and, instructing them to prepare instantly for a journey, had himself hastened to the apartment of the Countess.

My baggage was speedily placed in the boot, Udal mounted on the box, I directed my other servants to pay the bill and return to Cumberland, and we drove off quickly to the coast, just twenty-four hours after we had set out upon the great West Road on our desperate adventure.

As we rolled peacefully through the moonlit gardens of Kent, I had time to think over and

apportion the hurried events of the day, and I
recalled the half-spoken sentence which was on
Marston's lips at the moment of his death. I conjectured that he intended some expression of remorse
for the use to which he had put the likeness of
his sister, and I began again to wonder at the
strange inconsistency of the man. I had been
bewildered by it before in respect of this very
miniature, when I first observed his genuine devotion
to his sister. To-day he had afforded me a second
and corroborating instance, for no sooner had he
knowledge of his sister's fears, than he had used
the knowledge straightway as a weapon against me,
leaving it to his antagonist to secure her the safe-
guarding which she implored. And yet that his
anxiety on her account was very real it was impossible for me to doubt, for I had looked upon
his face when he bound me by a promise to protect
her.

At Dover we found a packet on the point of
sailing for Calais. Elmscott bade me good-bye
upon the quay, and declared that if I would keep
him informed of my movements, he would send me
word when the affair had blown over and I might
safely return. Then he asked:

" Morrice, did you tell Countess Lukstein of your
duel?"

" I had not the time," I replied. " But she said
you told her."

" Ay, I told the story, though I gave not the
reason for the encounter. But did you say nothing
to her, give her no hint by which she might
guess it?"

"Nay," said I; "I swooned or ever I got a word of it out. I spoke but two words to her: ' Lady Tracy.' She could have guessed little enough from that."

"Strange!" said he, in a tone of some perplexity. "And yet, some way or another, she must needs have known. For when I came to seek you, Otto denied you were there. I was positive, however, and ran past him up the stairs. The parlour door was locked, and they only gave me entrance when I bawled my name through the keyhole and declared that I knew you were within, and for your own sake must have immediate speech with you. I fancied that the Countess was aware of the duel and meant to conceal you."

I thought no more of his words at the time, and went presently aboard. A fair wind filled the sheets and hummed through the cordage of the rigging. The cliffs lessened and lessened until they shone in the sunlight like a silver rim about the bowl of the sea ; the gulls swooped and circled in our wake ; and thus I sailed out upon my strange pilgrimage, which was to last so many weary months and set me amid such perilous surroundings.

CHAPTER XVII.

IT was on the sixth day of June that I arrived in London from Cumberland; it was on the sixteenth of July that I landed at Calais; and so much that was new and bewildering to me had happened within this brief interspace of time, that I cannot wonder how little I understood of all which it portended. For here was I, accustomed to solitude, with small knowledge of men and a veritable fear of women, plumped of a sudden amidst the gayest company of the town, where thought and wit were struck out of converse sharply as sparks from a flint not reached by my slow methods, which, to carry on my simile, more resembled the practice of the Indians who produce fire, so travellers tell, by the laborious attrition of stick upon stick.

From Calais I journeyed to Paris, where I stayed until a bill of exchange upon some French merchants, which I had asked Elmscott to procure for me, came to hand. With it was enclosed a letter from my cousin and yet another from Jack Larke.

"This letter," wrote Elmscott, "was brought to your lodging the day after you left London. L'affaire

Marston has caused much astonishment. Your
friends almost refused to credit you with the exploit.
The family, however, is raised to a clamorous pitch
of anger against you ; it has influence at Court,
and the King has no liking for duels."

The letter from Larke recounted the homely
details of the country-side, and dwelt in particular
upon the plan of Sir J. Lowther of Stockbridge
to appoint a new carrier between Kendal and
Whitehaven, so that the shipment of Kendal cottons
to Virginia might be facilitated. The obstacle to
the scheme, he declared, was that the road ran
over Hard Knott, which in winter and spring is
frequently impassable for the snow. I wrote back
to him that he should refund to Elmscott with
all despatch the amount of the bill of exchange,
and relating shortly the causes which kept me
abroad, bade him, if he were so minded, join me
towards the end of September at Venice. Of my
visit to Lukstein I said never a word, the consequence of it was too doubtful. I shrank from
setting out my hopes and fears openly upon paper.
If I succeeded, I could better explain the matter
to him in speech, and take him back with me
again to the Castle. If I failed, I should avoid
the need of making any explanation whatsoever.

From Paris I travelled into Austria ; and so
one sunset, in the latter days of August, drove
up to the door of " Der Goldener Adler " at
Glurns. From this inn I sent Udal forward with
a note to Countess Lukstein, announcing my
arrival in the neighbourhood, and asking whether
she would be willing to receive me. The next

day he returned with Otto Krax, and brought
me a message of very kindly welcome. Otto
himself, for once, unbent from his grave demeanour,
saying that it was long since the Castle had
been brightened with a guest, and that for his part
he trusted I would be in no great hurry to
depart.

I gathered no little comfort from his greeting,
you may be sure, and I set off forthwith to the
Castle. The valley which, when I last rode through
it, showed stark and desolate in its snow drapery,
now lay basking in the lusty summer, and seemed
to smile upon my visit. The lime-trees were in
leaf along the road, wild strawberries, red as the
lips of my mistress, peeped from the grasses, on
either side cornfields spread up the lower slopes
to meet the serried pines, which were broken here
and there by a green gap, where the winter snows
had driven a track. Behind the ridge of the hills
I could see mountains towering up with bastions of
ice, which had a look peculiarly rich and soft, like
white velvet. The air was fragrant with the scent
of flowers, and musical with the voices of innumerable
streams. Even Lukstein, which had worn so bare
and menacing an aspect in the grey twilight of that
November afternoon, now nestled warmly upon its
tiny plateau, the red pointed roofs of its turrets
glowing against the green background of firs.

I was received at the Castle by a priest, who
informed me that the Countess was indisposed, and
wished him to express her regrets that she was
unable to welcome me in person. I was much
chapfallen and chilled by this vicarious greeting,

T

since on the way from Glurns I had given free
play to all sorts of foolish imaginings. The priest,
who was a kinsman of the Countess, conducted me
very politely to the rooms prepared for me.

"Mr. Buckler," said he, "it is only your face
that is strange to me; for I have heard so much
of you from your hostess that I made your acquaintance some while ago." Whereat I recovered
something of my spirits.

He led me through the great hall, paved with
roughish slabs of stone, and up a wide staircase to
a gallery which ran round the four sides of the
hall. From that he turned off into a corridor, which
ran, as I guessed, through the smaller wing of the
building towards the tower. At the extreme end
he opened a door and bowed me into a large room
lit by two windows opposite to one another. One
of these commanded the little ravine which pierced
backwards into the hills beside the Castle, and
was called the Senner Thal; the other window
looked out on to the garden. Moving towards this
last, I perceived, on the left hand, the arbour of
pinewood and the parapet on which I had lain
concealed; the main wing of the Castle stretched
out upon the right, and I realised, with an uneasy
shiver, that I had been given the bedroom of Count
Lukstein. The moment I realised this my eyes went
straight to that corner, where I knew the little
staircase to be. The door of it stood by the head
of the bed, and was almost concealed in the
hangings.

"It leads," said the priest, interpreting my glance,
"to a little room below; but the room gives only

on to the garden, and the door has not been used
this many a month."

He went over to it as he spoke, and tried the
handle. The door was locked, but the key remained
in the lock. It creaked and grated when he turned
it, as though it had rusted in the keyhole. Together
we went down the little winding stairway and into
the chamber at the bottom. What wonder that I
hesitated on the last step with a failing heart, and
needed the invitation of the priest to nerve me to
cross the threshold! Not a single thing had been
moved since I stood there last. But for the clouds
of dust, which rose at each movement that we made,
I could have believed this day was the morrow of
our deadly encounter. The table still lay overturned
upon the floor, the rugs and skins were heaped
and disordered by the trampling of our feet, the
curtain hung half-torn from the vallance, where I
had cowered in it with clutching hands as the
Countess passed through the window on to the
snow. Nothing had been touched. Yes, one thing ;
for as I glanced about the room, I saw my pistol
dangling from a nail upon the hood of the fireplace.

"The room, you think, Mr. Buckler, does little
credit to our housekeeping ?" said the priest. "But
'tis unswept and uncleansed of a set purpose. As
you see it now, so it was on the fifteenth night
of last November, and the Countess our mistress
wills that so it shall remain."

"There is some story," I replied, with such indifference as I could assume, "some story connected
with the room."

T 2

"Ay, a story of midnight crime—of crime that struck at the roots of the Lukstein race, that breaks the line of a family which has ruled here for centuries, and must in a few years make its very name to perish off the earth. Count Lukstein was the last of his race, and in this room was he slain upon his bridal night."

Sombre as were the words, the priest's voice seemed to have something of exultation in its tone, and unwarily I remarked on it.

"God works out His purposes by ways we cannot understand," he explained, with a humility that struck me as exaggerated and insincere. "Unless Countess Lukstein marries again, the Castle and its demesne will pass into the holy keeping of the Church."

He looked steadily at me while he spoke, and I wondered whether he meant his utterance to convey a menace and warning.

"What if the Countess married a true son of the Church?" I hastened to answer. "Would he not second and further her intention?"

"I think, Mr. Buckler, that you have more faith in mankind than knowledge of the world. But 'twas of the room that we were speaking. Until that crime is brought to light, the room may neither be swept nor cleansed."

"You hope, then, to discover——" I began.

"Nay, nay!" said he. "'Tis not with us that the discovery rests. Look you, sin is not a dead thing like these tables, to which each day adds a covering of dust; it is rather a plant that each day throws out fibres towards the sun, bury it deep as you will in the earth. Surely, surely it will make itself known—this very afternoon, maybe, or maybe in years to come; maybe not until the Day of Wrath. God chooses His own time."

Very solemnly he crossed himself, and led the way back to the bedroom above.

This conversation increased my anxiety to unburden myself to Ilga. For it was no crime that I had committed, but an act of common justice. But although the household, apart from the servants and retainers, who made indeed a veritable army, consisted only of the Countess, Mdlle. Durette, and Father Spaur, as the priest was named, I found it impossible to hit upon an occasion.

In the first place, the Countess herself was, without doubt, ailing and indisposed. She would come down late in the morning with heavy eyes and a weariful face, as though she slept but little. 'Twas no better, moreover, when she joined us, for she treated me, though ever with courtesy as befitted a hostess, still with a certain distance ; and at times, when she thought I was interested in some talk and had no eyes for her, I would catch a troubled look upon her face wherein anger and sorrow seemed equally mixed. Nor, indeed, could I ever come upon her alone, and such hints as I put forward to bring such a consummation about were purposely misunderstood. In truth, the priest stood between us. I set the changed manner of Countess Lukstein entirely to his account, believing that he was studiously poisoning her mind against me, and maybe persuading her that I did but pursue her wealth like any vulgar adventurer. I suggested as

much to Mdlle. Durette, who showed me great
kindness in this nadir of my fortunes.

"I know not what to make of it," she replied,
"for Ilga has shut me from her confidence of late.
But there is something of the kind afoot, I fear, for
Father Spaur is continually with her, and 'twas ever
his fashion to ascribe a secret and underhand motive
for all one's doings."

The Father, indeed, was perpetually with either
Ilga or myself. If he chanced not to be closeted
with the Countess, he would dance indefatigable
attendance upon me, devising excursions into the
mountains or in pursuit of the chamois, which
abounded in great numbers among the higher forests
of the ravine.

On these latter occasions he would depute
Otto Krax, who was, as I soon learned, the chief
huntsman of the Castle, to take his place with
me, pleading his own age with needless effusion
as an excuse for his absence. In the company
of Otto, then, I gained much knowledge of the
locality, and in particular of the great ice-clad
mountain which blocked the head of the ravine.
For the chase led us many a time high up the
slopes above the trees to where the ice lay in great
tongues all cracked and ridged across like waves
frozen at the crest; and at times, growing yet
more adventurous with the heat of our pursuit, we
would ascend still higher, making long circuits
and detours about the cliffs and gullies to get to
windward of our quarry; so that I saw this mountain from many points of view, and gained a know-

ledge of its character and formation which was afterwards to stand me in good stead. The natives termed it the "Wildthurm," and approached it ever with the greatest reluctance and with much commending of their souls to God. For the spirits of the lost, they said, circled in agony about its summit, and might be heard at noonday no less often than at night piercing the air with a wail of lamentation. It may be even as they held; but I was spared the manifestation of their presence when I invaded their abode, and found no denizens of that solitary region more terrible than the eagles which built their nests upon the topmost cliffs. Towards the ravine the "Wildthurm" towered in a stupendous wall of rock of thousands of feet, but so sheer that even the chamois, however encompassed, never sought escape that way. From the apex of this wall a ridge of ice ran backwards in a narrow line and sloped outwards on either side, so that it looked like nothing so much as a gipsy's tent of white canvas.

When we sought diversion upon lower ground, hawking or riding in the valley, Father Spaur himself would bear me company. In fact, I never seemed to journey a mile from the Castle without either Otto or the priest to keep me in surveillance.

Father Spaur, though past his climacteric, was of a tall, massive build, and, I judged, of great muscular strength. His hair was perfectly white, and threw into relief his broad, tanned face, which wore as a rule an uninterested bovine expression, as of one whom neither trouble nor thought had

ever touched. One afternoon, however, as we were
riding up the hillside towards the Castle, I chanced
to make mention of the persecution of the Protestants
in France, whereof I had been a witness during my
stay at Paris, and ventured, though a Catholic, to
criticise the French King's action in abrogating the
edict of Nantes.

"Cruelty, Mr. Buckler!" he exclaimed, reining
in his horse, with his eyes aglare, and his fleshy
face of a sudden shining with animation. 'Twas
as though some one had lit a lamp behind a curtain.
"Cruelty! 'Tis the idlest name that was ever
invented. Look you: a general throws a thousand
troops upon certain death. Is not that cruelty?
Yet if he faltered he would fail in his duty. If
the men shrank, they in theirs. Cruelty is the
law of life. Nay, more, for with that word the
wicked stigmatise the law of God. Never a spring
comes upon these hills but it buries numbers of
our villagers beneath its slipping snowdrifts. You
have seen the crosses on the slopes yourself. They
perish, and through no foolhardiness of their own.
Is not that what you term cruelty? Take a
wider view. Is there not cruelty in the very
making of man? We are born with minds curious
after knowledge, and yet we only gain knowledge
by much suffering and labour—an infinitesimal drop
after years of thirst. Take it yet higher. The
holy Church teaches us that God upon His throne
is happy; yet He condemns the guilty to torment.
With a smile, we must believe He condemns the
guilty. Judge that by our poor weak understanding;

is it not cruelty? What you term cruelty is a law
of God—difficult, unintelligible, but a law of God,
and therefore good."

'Twas a strange discourse, delivered with a ringing voice of exaltation, and thereafter my thoughts
did more justice to the subtlety of his intellect.

Meanwhile the days slipped on and brought me
no nearer to the fulfilment of my purpose. The
time had come, moreover, when I must set off into
Italy if I was to meet Larke at Venice as I had most
faithfully promised. I resolved, then, to put an end
to a visit which I saw brought no happiness to my
mistress, and wasted me with impatience and
despondency. I was minded to go down into Italy,
and taking Jack with me to set sail for the Indies,
and ease my heart, if so I might, with viewing of the
many wonders of those parts. So choosing an
occasion when we were all dining together in the
great parlour on the first floor of the Castle, I
thanked the Countess for the hospitality which
she had shown me, and fixed my departure for
the next day. For awhile there was silence, Ilga
rising suddenly from the table and walking over
to the wide-open windows, where she stood with
her back turned, and looked out across the waving
valley of the Adige.

"It seems that we have been guilty of some
discourtesy, Mr. Buckler, since you leave us so
abruptly," said Father Spaur with a great per-
turbation.

Upon that point I hastened to set him right;
for indeed I had been so hedged in by attention

and ceremony that I should have been well content
with a little neglect.

"Then," he continued with an easy laugh, "we
shall make bold to keep you. If we bring guests so
far to visit us, we cannot speed them away so soon.
Doubtless the Castle is dull to you who come fresh
from London and Paris——"

"Nay," said I with some impatience, for I
thought it unfair that he should attribute such
motives to me. "Madame will bear me out that
I have little liking for town pleasures." I turned
towards her, but she made no sign or movement,
and appeared not to have heard me. "I am pledged
to meet a friend at Venice, and, as it is, I have
overstayed my time."

"Oh! you have a friend awaiting you," said
the priest slowly. "You are very prudent, Mr.
Buckler."

The Countess turned swiftly about, her eyes wide
open and staring like one dismayed.

"Prudent?" I exclaimed in perplexity.

"I mean," said the priest, flushing a dark red
and dropping his voice, "I mean that if one fixes
so precise a limit to one's visit, one guards against
any inclination to prolong it." He spoke with a
meaning glance in the direction of the Countess,
who had turned away again. "The heart says
'stay,' prudence 'go.' Is it not the case?" he
whispered, and he smiled with an awkward effort at
archness, which, upon his heavy face, was little short
of grotesque.

Now his words and manner perplexed me greatly,

for at the moment of my coming to Lukstein, he had seemed most plainly to warn me against encouraging any passion for Ilga, and his conduct since in disparting us had assured me that I had rightly guessed his intention. Yet here was he urging me to extend my stay, and sneering at my prudence for not giving free play to that passion.

"Besides," he continued, raising his voice again, "if you go to-morrow you will miss the best entertainment that our poor domain provides. We are to have a great hunt, wherein some of our neighbours will join us, and Otto informs us that you have great partiality for the sport, and extraordinary skill and nimbleness upon mountains. In a week, moreover, the headsman of our village is to marry. 'Tis a great event in Lukstein, and, indeed, to a stranger well worth witnessing, for there are many quaint and curious customs to be observed which are not met with elsewhere."

He added many other inducements, so that at last I felt some shame at persisting in my refusal. But, after all, the Countess was my hostess, and she had said never a word, but had turned back again to the window as though she would not meddle in the matter. At last, however, she broke in upon the priest, keeping, however, her face still set towards the landscape.

"Could you not send forward your servant, Mr. Buckler, to meet your friend, and remain with us this week? As Father Spaur says, the marriage will be well worth seeing, and since you are so pressed, you may leave here that very night."

There was, however, no heartiness in her invitation; the words dropped reluctantly from her lips, as if compelled by mere politeness towards her guest.

"The most suitable plan!" cried the priest, starting up. "Send your man to Venice, and yourself follow afterwards."

I explained that Udal was little accustomed to travelling in strange countries, and had no knowledge of either the German or Italian tongues; and to put a close to the discussion, I rose from my seat and walked away to the end of the apartment, where I busied myself over some weapons that hung upon the wall. In a minute or so I heard the door close softly, and facing about, I saw that the priest and Mdlle. Durette, who had taken no part in any of this talk, had departed out of the room. The Countess came towards me.

"I sent them away," she said, with a wan smile, and a voice subdued to great gentleness. "I have no thought to—to part with you so soon. Stay out this week. You—you told me that you had something which you wished to say."

"Madame," said I, snatching eagerly at her hand, "you also told me that you had guessed it."

"Not now; not now." She slipped her hand from my grasp with an imploring cry, and held it outspread close before my face to check my words. "Not now. I could not bear it. Oh, I would that I had more strength to resist, or more weakness to succumb,"

Never have I heard such pain in a human voice:
never have I seen features so wrung with suffering.
The sight of her cut me to the heart.

"Listen," she went on, controlling herself after
a moment, though her voice still trembled with
agitation, and now and again ran upwards into an
odd laugh, the like of which I have never hearkened
to before or since. 'Twas the most pitiful sound
that ever jarred on a man's ears. "On the night
of the marriage the villagers will come to the Castle
to dance in the Great Hall. That night you shall
speak to me, and a carriage shall be ready to
take you away afterwards, if you will. Until that
night be 'prudent.'"

She gave me no time to answer her, but ran
to the door, and so out of the room. I could hear
her footsteps falling uncertainly along the gallery,
as though she stumbled while she ran, and a great
anger against the priest flamed up in my breast.
"Strength to resist, or weakness to succumb."
Doubtless the words would have bewildered me,
like the oracles of old Greece, but for what I sus-
picioned in the priest. Now, however, in the
blindness of my thoughts, I construed them as the
confirmation of my belief that he was practising
all his arts upon Ilga to secure Lukstein for the
Church. 'Twas Father Spaur, I imagined, whom
she had neither the strength to resist nor the
weakness to yield to, and I fancied that I was set
upon a second contest for the winning of her, though
this time with a more subtle and noteworthy antagonist.

And yet for all my fears, for all Ilga's trouble, with such selfish pertinacity do a lover's reflections seek to enhearten his love, I could not but feel a throb of joy for that she had so plainly shown to me what the struggle cost her.

CHAPTER XVIII.

IN accordance, then, with the suggestion of Ilga, I despatched Udal to Venice, bearing a letter wherein I requested Jack to bide there until such time as I arrived. To supply my servant's place Father Spaur offered me one, Michael Groder, whose assistance at the first sight I was strongly in a mind to decline; for he was more than common uncouth even for those parts, and with his scarred knees, tangled black hair, and gaunt, weather-roughened face, seemed more fitted for hewing wood upon the hillside than for the neater functions of a valet. The priest, however, pressed his services upon me with so importunate a courtesy that I thought it ungracious to persist in a refusal. Indeed, Michael Groder, though of a slight and wiry build, was the unhandiest man with his fingers that ever I had met with. There was not a servant in the Castle who could not have done the work better; and I came speedily to the conclusion that Father Spaur had selected him particularly out of some motive very different from a desire to oblige me; I mean, in order that he might keep a watch upon my actions, and see that I gained no secret advantage with the Countess.

However, had I entertained any such design, the hunting expedition would have effectually prevented its fulfilment. It lasted the greater part of the week, and we did not return to Lukstein until the eve of my departure. By this time my anxiety as to the answer which Ilga would make to my suit when she knew all that I had to tell her, had well-nigh worked me into a fever. I was for ever rehearsing and picturing the scene, inventing all sorts of womanly objections for her to urge, and disproving them succinctly to her satisfaction by Barbara, Celarent and all the rules of logic.

Under these speculations, bolster them up as I might, there lurked none the less a heavy and disheartening fear. 'Twas all vain labour to reckon up, as I did again and again, the few good qualities which I possessed, and to add to them those others which my friends attributed to me. I could not shut my eyes to the disparity between us; I could not believe but that she must be sensible of it herself. Such a woman, I conceived, should wed a warrior and hero; though, indeed, 'twas doubtful whether you could find even amongst them one whose deserts made him a fit mate for her. As for me, 'twas as though a clown should run a-wooing after a princess.

'Twill be readily understood that I had in consequence no great inclination for the hearty fellowship of the neighbours who joined in the hunt; and since my anxiety grew with every hour, by the time we came back to Lukstein—for many of them returned thither instead of to their own homes, meaning to stay over until the following night—'twas as much as I could do to answer with attention any civil question that was addressed to me.

The Countess, I found, was in an agitation no whit inferior to my own. I observed her that afternoon at dinner. At times she talked with a feverish excitement, at times she relapsed into long silences; but even during these pauses I noticed that her fingers were never still, but continually twitched and plucked at the cloth. I inferred from her manner that she had not yet decided on the course she would take, the more particularly because she sedulously avoided speech with me. If I spoke to her she replied politely enough, but at once drew those about her into the conversation, and herself withdrew from it; and if by accident our eyes met, she hastily turned her head away. I knew not what to make of these signs, and as soon as the company was risen from table I slipped away out of the Castle that I might con them over quietly and weigh whether they boded me good or ill.

The Castle, as I have said, stood upon a headland at the mouth of the Senner Thal, and turning a corner of this bluff, I wandered by a rough track some way along the side of the ravine, and flung myself down on my back on the turf. The sun had already sunk below the crest of the mountains, and the glow was fast fading out of the sky. The pines on the hillside opposite grew black in the deepening twilight; a star peeped over the shoulder of the Wildthurm; and here and there a grey scarf of cloud lay trailed along the slopes. From a hut

U

high above came clear and sweet the voice of a
woman singing a Tyrolese melody, and so softly did
the evening droop upon the mountains, shutting
as it were the very peace of the heavens into the
valleys, that the brooks seemed to laugh louder and
louder as they raced among the stones. The air
itself never stirred, save when some bat came flapping
blindly about my face. I became the more curious,
therefore, concerning a bush some twenty yards
below me, which now and again shivered and bent
as though with a gust of wind. I had been lying on
the grass some ten minutes before I noticed this
movement. The dwarf oaks and beeches which
studded the slopes about me were as still and
noiseless as though their leaves had been carved
from metal; only this one bush rustled and shook.
In a direct line with it, and within reach of my foot,
a small boulder hung insecurely on the turf. I
stretched out my foot and pushed it; the stone
rocked a little on its base. I pushed again and
harder; the stone tilted forwards and stuck. I
brought my other foot to help, set them both
flat against the stone, slid down on my back until
my legs were doubled, and then kicked with all my
strength. The boulder flew from the soles of my
feet, rolled over and over, bounded into the air,
dropped on to the slope about ten yards from the
bush, and then sprang at it like a dog at the throat.
I heard a startled cry; I saw the figure of a man
leap up from the centre of the bush. The stone
took him full in the pit of the stomach, and toppled
him backwards like a ninepin. He fell on the far
side of the shrub, and I heard the boulder go

XVIII.]   AT LUKSTEIN.   291

crash - crashing down the whole length of the incline. Who the man was I had not the time to perceive, and I made no effort to discover. The Countess had retired a few moments before I slipped away from the Hall, and I judged that he was no more than a spy sent by Father Spaur to ascertain whether I had some tryst with her. So deeming that he had got no more than his deserts, I left him lying where he fell and loitered back to the Castle.

The company I found gathered about a huge fire of logs at the end of the Great Hall. Beyond the glow of the flames the Hall was lost in shadow, and now and again from some corner would come a soft scuffling sound, as a dog moved lazily across the flags. Thereupon with one movement the heads would huddle closer together, and for a moment the voices would sink to a whisper. They were speaking, as men will who are girt with more of God's handiwork than of man's, concerning the spirits that haunted the countryside, and told many stories of the warnings they had vouchsafed to unheeding ears. In particular, they dwelt much upon a bell, which they declared rang out from the Wildthurm when good or ill-fortune approached the House of Lukstein, tolling as the presage of disaster, pealing joyously in the forefront of prosperity. One, indeed—with frequent glances across his shoulder into the gloom—averred that he had heard it tolling on the eve of Count Lukstein's marriage, and from that beginning the talk slid to the manner of his death. 'Twas altogether an eerie experience, and one that I would not willingly repeat, to listen to them debating that question in hushed whispers, with the darkness closing in around us, and the firelight playing upon mature, weather-hardened faces grown timorous with the awe of children. For this I remarked with some wonder, that no one made mention either of the things which I had left behind me, or of the track which I had flogged in the snow about the rim of the precipice. 'Twas evident that these details of the story had been kept carefully secret, though with what object I could not understand.

That evening I had no Michael Groder to assist me in my toilet, and so got me to bed with the saving of half an hour. I cannot say, however, that I gained half an hour's sleep thereby, for the thought of the morrow, and all that hung upon it, kept me tossing from side to side in a turmoil of unrest. It must have been near upon two hours that I lay thus uneasily cushioned upon disquiet, before a faint sound came to my ears, and made me start up in the darkness with my heart racing.

'Twas the sound that a man can never forget or mistake when once he has heard it—the sound of a woman sobbing. It rose from the little sitting-room immediately beneath me. The staircase door was close to my bedside, and I reached out my hand and, turning the handle cautiously, opened it. The sound was louder now, but still muffled, and I knew that the door at the bottom of the staircase was closed. For a little I remained propped on my elbow, and straining my ears to listen. The mourner must be either Clemence Durette or Ilga, and I could not doubt which of them it was. Why

she wept, I did not consider. 'Twas the noise of
her weeping, made yet more lonesome and sad by
the black dead of night, that occupied my senses
and filled me with an unbearable pain.

I got quietly out of my bed, and slipping on
some clothes crept down the staircase in my stockings. 'Twas pitch dark in this passage, and I felt
before me with my hands as I descended, fearing
lest I might unawares stumble against the door.
At the last step I paused and listened again. Then
very gently I groped for the handle. I had good
reason to know how noiselessly it turned, and I
opened the door for the space of an inch. A feeble
light flickered on the wall of the room at my side.
I waited with my fingers on the handle, but there
was no check in the sobbing. I pushed the door
wider open; the light upon the wall wavered and
shook, as though a draught took the flame of a
candle. But that was all. So I stepped silently
forward and looked into the room.

The sight made my heart bleed. Ilga lay face
downwards and prone upon the floor, her arms
outstretched, her hair unbound and rippling about
her shoulders. From head to foot she was robed
in black. It broke upon me suddenly that I had
never seen her so clad before, and I remembered
a remark that Elmscott had passed in London upon
that very score.

The window was open, and from the garden a
light wind brought the soughing of trees into the
room. A single candle guttered on the mantel-
shelf and heightened its general aspect of neglect.
Thus Ilga lay, abandoned to—what? Grief for her

husband, or remorse at forgetting him? That black dress might well be the fitting symbol of either sentiment. 'Twas for neither of these reasons that she wept, as I learned long afterwards, but for another of which I had no suspicion then.

I closed the door softly and sat me down in the darkness on the stairs, hearkening to that desolate sound of tears and praying for the morning to come and for the day to pass into night, that I might say my say and either bring her such rest and happiness as a man's love can bring to a woman, or slip out of her life and so trouble her no more.

'Twas a long while before she ceased from her distress, and to me it seemed far longer than it was. As soon as I heard her move I got me back to my room. The dawn was just breaking when, from a corner of my window, I saw her walk out across the lawn, and the dew was white upon the grass like a hoar-frost. With a weary, dragging step, and a head adroop like a broken flower, she walked to the parapet of the terrace, and hung on it for a little, gazing down upon the roofs of her sleeping village. Then she turned and fixed her eyes upon my window. I was hidden in the curtains so that she could not see me. For some minutes she gazed at it, her face very tired and sad. 'Twas her bridal chamber, or rather, would have been but for me, and I wondered much whether she was thinking of the husband or the guest. She turned away again, looked out across the valley paved with a grey floor of mist, and so walked back to the main wing of the Castle.

The light broadened out; starlings began to

twitter in the trees, and far away a white peak blushed rosy at the kiss of the sun. The one day of my life had come. By this time to-morrow, I thought, the world would have changed its colours for me, one way or another; and tired out with my vigil, I tumbled into bed and slept dreamlessly until Michael Groder roused me.

I asked him why he had failed me the night before.

" I was unwell," he replied.

" True ! " said I, with great friendliness. "You got a heavier load upon your stomach than it would stand."

The which was as unwise a remark as I could nave made; for Groder's ill-will towards me needed no stimulus to provoke it.

CHAPTER XIX.

THE marriage, with its odd customs of the Ehren-
gang and Ehrentanz, might at another time have
afforded me the entertainment which Father Spaur
promised; but, to speak the truth, the whole
ceremony wearied me beyond expression. My
thoughts were set in a tide towards the evening,
and I watched the sun loiter idly down the length
of the valley in a burning fever of impatience.

'Twas about seven of the clock when the villagers
flocked up to the Castle and began their antic
dances in the Hall and in the ball-room which
fronted the terrace. They aimed at a display of
agility rather than of elegance, leaping into the
air and falling crack upon their knees, slapping
their thighs and the soles of their feet, with many
other barbaric gambols; and all the while they kept
up such a noise of shouting, whistling, and singing,
as fairly deafened one.

Ilga, I observed with some heart-sinking, had
once more robed herself in black, and very simply;
but the colour so set off the brightness of her hair,
which was coiled in a coronal upon her head, and

the white beauty of her arms, that for all my fears I could not but think she had never looked so exquisitely fair. However, I had thought the same upon so many different occasions that I would not now assert it as an indisputable fact.

As you may be certain, I had not copied Ilga's simplicity, but had rather dressed in the opposite extreme. 'Twas no part of my policy to show her the disrespect of plain apparel. I had so little to offer that I must needs trick that little out to the best of advantage; indeed, even at this distance of time, I fairly laugh when I recall the extraordinary pains I spent that evening upon my adornment. My Lord Culverton could never have bettered them. A coat of white brocaded velvet, ruffles that reached to the tips of my fingers, a cravat of the finest Mechlin, pink breeches, silk stockings rolled above the knees, with gold clocks and garters, white Spanish leather shoes with red heels and Elmscott's buckles, a new heavy black peruke; so I attired myself for this momentous interview.

Father Spaur greeted me with a sour smile and a sneering compliment; but 'twas not his favour that I sought, and I cared little that he showed so plainly his resentment.

"A carriage," he added, "will be in waiting for you at eleven, if you are still minded to leave us."

I thanked him shortly, and passed on to Ilga, but for some while I could get no private speech with her. For though she took no part in the dancing, even when a quieter measure made a

break in the boisterous revelry, she moved continually from one to the other of her villagers
with a kindly smile and affable word for each in
a spirit of so sweet a condescension, that I had no
doubt that she had vaunted their loyalty most
truthfully. 'Twould have been strange, indeed, if
they had not greatly worshipped her.

In the midst of the clatter, however, and near
upon the hour of nine, a man burst wildly into the
room, faltering out that the "Wildthurm" bell was
even now ringing its message to Lukstein.

On the instant the music was stopped; a great
awe fell upon the noisy throng; women clung in
fear to men, and men crossed themselves with a
muttering of tremulous prayers; and then Ilga led
the way through the Hall into the courtyard of
the Castle.

The ice-fields of the mountain glittered like
silver in the moonlight, and we gazed upwards
towards them with our ears strained to catch the
sound. Many, I know, will scoff at and question
what I relate. Many have already done so,
attributing it to a delusion of the senses, a heated
imagination, or any other of the causes which are
held to absolve the spirits of the air from participation in men's affairs.

Against such unholy disbelief it is not for me
to argue or dispute, nor is this the fitting place and
opportunity. But this I do attest, and to it I do
solemnly put my name. 'Twas not I alone who
heard the bell ; every man and woman who danced
that night at Lukstein Castle heard it. The sound
was faint, but wonderfully pure and clear, the strokes

of the hammer coming briskly one upon the other as though the bell was tossed from side to side by willing hands.

"It speaks of happiness for Lukstein," said Father Spaur with an evil glance towards me.

For my part I just looked at Ilga.

"Come!" she said.

And we walked back through the empty echoing Hall, and across the lawn to the terrace.

A light wind was blowing from the south, but there were no clouds in the sky, and the valley lay beneath us with all its landmarks merged by the grey, tender light, so that it seemed to have widened to double its breadth.

The terrace, however, was for the most part in shadow, since the moon, hanging behind a cluster of trees at the east corner of the wall, only sprinkled its radiance through a tracery of boughs, and drew a dancing pattern about our feet. As I leaned upon the parapet there came before my eyes, raised by I know not what chance suggestion, a vivid picture of my little far-away hamlet in the country of the English lakes.

"You are thoughtful, Mr. Buckler!" said Ilga.

"I was thinking of the valley of Wastdale," I replied, "and of a carrier's cart stuck in a snowdrift on Hard Knot."

"Of your home? 'Twas of your home that you were thinking?" she asked curiously, and yet with something more than curiosity in her voice, with something of regret, something almost of pity.

"Not so much of my home," I replied, "but rather from what distant points our two lives have

drawn together." I was emboldened to the words
by the tone in which she had spoken. "A few
weeks ago you were here at Lukstein in the Tyrol,
I was at the Hall in Cumberland, and we had
never spoken to one another. How strange it all
seems!"

"Nay," she answered simply; "it was certain
you and I should meet. Is not God in His
heaven?"

My heart gave a great leap. We had come
now to the pavilion, which leaned against the Castle
wall, and Ilga opened the door and entered it. I
followed her, and closed the latch behind me.

In the side of the room there was a square
window with shutters, but no glass. The shutters
were open, and through a gap of the trees the
moonlight poured into the pavilion.

We stood facing one another silently. The time
had come for me to speak.

"Well," said she, and her voice was very calm,
"what is it, Mr. Buckler?"

All my fine arguments and protestations flew
out of my head like birds startled from a nest.
I forgot even the confession I had to make to
her, and

"I love you!" I said humbly, looking down
on the floor.

She gave me no answer. My heart fainted
within me; I feared that it would stop. But in
a little I dared to raise my eyes to her face. She
stood in the pillar of moonlight, her eyes glistening,
but with no expression on her face which could

give me a clue to her thoughts, and she softly opened and shut her fan, which hung on a girdle about her waist.

" How I do love you ! " I cried, and I made a step towards her. " But you know that."

She nodded her head.

" I took good care you should," she said.

I did not stop to consider the strangeness of the speech. My desire construed it without seeking help from the dictionary of thought.

" Then you wished it," I cried joyfully, and I threw myself down on my knee at her feet, and buried my face in my hands. " Ilga !   Ilga ! "

She made no movement, but replied in a low voice :

" With all my heart I wished it. How else could I have brought you to the Tyrol ? "

I felt the tears gathering into my eyes and my throat choking.   I lifted my face to hers, and, taking courage from her words, clipped my arms about her waist.

She gave a little trembling cry, and plucked at my fingers.   I but tightened my clasp.

" Ilga ! " I murmured.   'Twas the only word which came to my lips, but it summed the whole world for me then—ay, and has done ever since. " Ilga ! "

Again she plucked at my fingers, and for all the calmness which she had shown, I could feel her hands burning through her gloves.   Then a shadow darkened for an instant across the window, the moonlight faded, and her face was lost to me.

'Twas for no longer than an instant. I looked towards the window, but Ilga bent her head down between it and me.

"'Tis only the branches swinging in the wind," she said softly.

I rose to my feet and drew her towards me. She set her palms against my chest as if to repulse me, but she said no word, and I saw the necklace about her throat flashing and sparkling with the heave of her bosom.

It seemed to me that a light step sounded without the pavilion, and I turned my head aside to listen.

"'Tis only the leaves blowing along the terrace," she whispered, and I looked again at her and drew her closer.

For a time she resisted; then I heard her sigh, and her hand stole across my shoulder. Her head drooped forward until her hair touched my lips. I could feel her heart beating on my breast. Gently I turned her face upwards, and then with a loud clap the shutters were flung to and the room was plunged in darkness.

Ilga started away from me, drawing a deep breath as for some release. I groped my way to the window. The shutters opened outwards, and I pushed against them. They were held close and fast.

A wooden settle stood against the wall just beneath the window, and I knelt on it and drove at the shutters with my shoulder. They gave a little at first, and I heard a whispered call for help. The pressure from without was redoubled; I was forced back; a bar fell across them outside and was fitted into a socket. Thrust as I might I could not break it; the window was securely barricadoed.

Meanwhile Ilga had not spoken.

" Ilga ! " I called.

She did not answer me, nor in the blackness of the pavilion could I discover where she stood.

" Ilga ! "

The same empty silence. I could not even hear her breathing, and yet she was in the pavilion, within a few feet of me. There was something horrible in her quietude, and a great fear of I knew not what caught at my heart and turned my blood cold.

" This is the priest's doing," I cried, and I drew my sword and made towards the door.

A startled cry burst from the gloom behind me.

" Stop ! If you open it, you will be killed."

I stopped as she bade me, body and brain numbed in a common inaction. I could hear her breathing now plainly enough.

" This is not the priest's doing," she said, at length. " It is the wife's." Her voice steadied and became even as she spoke. " From the hour I found Count Lukstein dead I have lived only for this night."

I let my sword slip from my grasp, and it clattered and rang on the floor.

'Twas not surprise that I felt; ever since the shutters had been slammed I seemed to have known that she would speak those words. And 'twas no longer fear. Nor did I as yet wonder how she came by her knowledge. Indeed, I had but one

thought, one thought of overwhelming sadness, and
I voiced it in utter despondency.

"So all this time—in London, here, a minute
ago, you were tricking me! Tricking me into
loving you ; then tricking my love for you!"

"A minute ago!" she caught me up, and there
was a quiver in her voice of some deep feeling.
Then she broke off, and said, in a hard, clear tone:
"I was a woman, and alone. I used a woman's
weapons."

Again she paused, but I made no answer. I
had none to make. She resumed, with a flash of
anger, as though my silence accused her:

"And was there no trickery on your side, too?"

They were almost the same words as those
which Marston had levelled at me, and I imagined
that they conveyed the same charge. However, it
seemed of little use or profit to defend myself at
length, and I answered:

"I have played no part. It might have fared
better with me if I had. What deceit I have practised may be set down to love's account. 'Twas
my fear of losing you that locked my lips. Had
I not loved you, what need to tell you my secret?
'Twas no crime that I committed. But since I
loved you, I was bound in very truth to speak. I
have known that from the first, and I pledged
myself to speak at the moment that I told you of
my love. I dared not disclose the matter before.
There was so little chance that I should win your
favour, even had every circumstance seconded my
suit. But this very night I should have told you the
truth."

"No doubt! no doubt!" she answered, with the bitterest irony, and I understood what a fatal mistake I had made in pleading my passion before disclosing the story of the duel. I should have begun from the other end. "And no doubt you meant also to tell me, with the same open frankness, of the woman for whose sake you killed my—my husband?"

"I fought for no woman, but for my friend."

She laughed; surely the hardest, most biting laugh that ever man heard.

"Tell me your fine story now."

I sank down on the settle, feeling strangely helpless in the face of her contempt.

"This is the priest's doing," I repeated, more to myself than to her.

"It is my doing," she said again; "my doing from first to last."

"Then what was it?" I asked, with a dull, involuntary curiosity. "What was it you had neither the weakness to yield to nor the strength to resist?"

She did not answer me, but it seemed as though she suddenly put out a hand and steadied herself against the wall.

"Tell me your story," she said briefly; and sitting there in the darkness, unable to see my mistress, I began the history of that November night.

"It is true that I killed Count Lukstein; but I killed him in open encounter. I fought him fairly and honourably."

"At midnight!" she interrupted. "Without witnesses, upon his wedding-day."

x

"There was blood upon Count Lukstein's sword," I went on doggedly, "and that blood was mine. I fought him fairly and honourably. I own I compelled him to fight me."

"You and your—companion."

She stressed the word with an extraordinary contempt.

"My companion!" I repeated in surprise. "What know you of my companion? My companion watched our horses in the valley."

"You dare to tell me that?" she cried, ceasing from her contempt, and suddenly lifting her voice in an inexplicable passion.

"It is the truth."

"The truth! The truth!" she exclaimed, and then, with a stamp of her foot, and in a ringing tone of decision, "Otto!"

The door was flung open. Otto Krax and Michael Groder blocked the opening, and behind them stood Father Spaur, holding a lighted torch above his head. The Tyrolese servants carried hangers in their hands. I can see their blades flashing in the red light now!

Silently they filed into the pavilion. Father Spaur lifted his torch into a bracket, latched the door, and leaned his back against the panels. All three looked at the Countess, waiting her orders. 'Twas plain, from the priest's demeanour, that Ilga had spoken no more than truth. In this matter she was the mistress and the priest the servitor.

I turned and gazed at her. She stood erect against the wall opposite to me, meeting my gaze, her face stern and set, as though carven out of white marble, her eyes dark and glittering with menace.

For my part, I rose from the settle and stood with folded arms. I did not even stoop to pick up my rapier; it seemed to me not worth while.

" The proper attitude of heroical endurance,' sneered Father Spaur. "Perhaps a little more humility might become 'a true son of the Church.' Was not that the phrase ? "

The Countess nodded to Otto. He took Groder's sword and stood it with his own, by a low stool in the corner near the door.

" 'Tis your own fault," she said sternly. " Even now I would have spared you had you told me the truth. But you presume too much upon my folly."

The next moment the two men sprang at me. The manner of their attack took me by surprise, and in a twinkling they had me down upon the bench. Then, however, a savage fury flamed up within me. 'Twas one thing to be run through at the command of Ilga, and so perish decently by the sword ; 'twas quite another to be handled by her servants, and I fought against the indignity with all my strength. But the struggle was too unequal. I should have proved no match for Otto had he stood alone, and I before him, fairly planted on my legs. With the pair of them to master me I was well-nigh as powerless as a child. Moreover, they had already forced me down by the shoulders, so that the edge of the settle cut across my back just below the shoulder-blades, and I could get no more purchase or support than the soles of my feet on the rough flooring gave me.

X 2

My single chance lay in regaining possession of my rapier. It lay just within my reach, and struggling violently with my left arm, in order to the better conceal my design, I stretched out the other cautiously towards it.

My fingers were actually on the pommel, I was working it nearer to me so that I might grasp the blade short, before Groder perceived my intention. With an oath he kicked it behind him. Otto set a huge knee calmly upon my chest, and pressed his weight upon it until I thought my spine would snap. Then he seized my arms, jerked them upwards, and held them outstretched above my head, keeping his knee the while jammed down upon my ribs. Groder drew a cord from his pocket, and turning back my sleeves with an ironic deliberation, bound my wrists tightly together.

"'Twas not for nothing Groder went a-valeting," laughed Father Spaur; and then, seeing that I was assisted in my struggle by the pressure which I got from the floor, "'Twere wise to repeat the ceremony with his ankles."

"You, Groder!" said Otto.

"I have no more cord," growled Michael, as he tied the knots viciously about my wrists.

Something rattled lightly on the ground. 'Twas the girdle of the Countess, with the fan attached to the end of it.

Groder plucked the fan off, struck my heels from under me, and bound the girdle round and round my ankles until they jarred together and I felt the bones cracking.

Otto took his knee from my chest, and the

two men went back to their former stations by the
door.

Father Spaur came over to where I lay, rubbing
his hands gently together.

"Really, really!" said he in a silky voice, "so
the cockatoo has been caged after all."

The words, recalling that morning in London
when first I allowed myself to take heart in my
hopes, so stung me that, tied as I was, I struggled
on to my feet, and so stood tottering. Father
Spaur drew back a pace and glanced quickly about
him.

"Michael!" he called. But the next instant
I fell heavily forward upon his breast. He burst
into a loud laugh of relief, and flung me back upon
the settle.

I looked towards Ilga.

"What have you not told him?" I asked.

"Nothing!" she said coldly. "I, at all events,
had nothing to conceal."

She motioned Father Spaur to fall back. Otto
and Groder picked up their swords. Father Spaur
unlatched the door, rubbed out the torch upon the
boards, and one after another they stepped from
the pavilion. Ilga followed last, but she did not
turn her head as she went out. Through the open
doorway I could see the shadows dancing on the
terrace, I could hear the music pouring from the
Castle in a lilting measure. The door closed, the
pavilion became black once more, and I heard their
footsteps recede across the pavement and grow
silent upon the grass,

CHAPTER XX.

OF the horror which the next two hours brought to me, I find it difficult to speak, even at this distance of time. 'Twas not the fear of what might be in store for me that oppressed my mind, though God knows I do not say this to make a boast of it; for doubtless some fear upon that score would have argued me a better man; but in truth I barely sent a thought that way. The savour of life had become brine upon my lips, and I cared little what became of me, so that the ending was quick.

For the moment the door closed I was filled with an appalling sense of loneliness and isolation. Heart and brain it seized and possessed me. 'Twas the closing of a door upon all the hopes which had chattered and laughed and nestled at my heart for so long; and into such a vacancy of mind did I fall, that I did not trouble to speculate upon the nature of the story which Countess Lukstein believed to be true. That she had been led by I knew not what suspicions into some strange error, that she had got but a misshapen account of the duel between her husband and myself, was, of course, plain to me. But since her former kindliness and courtesy had been part of a deliberate and ordained plan for securing me within her power, since, in a word, she had cherished no favourable thoughts of me at any time, I deemed it idle to consider of the matter.

Moreover, the remoteness of these parts made my helplessness yet more bitter and overpowering; though, indeed, I was not like to forget my helplessness in any case, for the cords about my ankles and wrists bit into my flesh like coils of hot wire. "A sequestered nook of the world," so I remembered, had Ilga called this corner of the Tyrol, and for a second time that night my thoughts went back to my own distant valley. I saw it pleasant with the domestic serenity which a man discovers nowhere but in his native landscape.

And to crown, as it were, my loneliness, now and again a few stray notes of music or a noise of laughter would drift through the chinks into the pitch-dark hut, and tell of the lighted Hall and of Ilga, now, maybe, dancing among her guests.

'Twas a little short of eleven when she returned to the pavilion. I am able to fix the time from an incident which occurred shortly afterwards. At first, the steps falling light as they approached, I bethought me my visitor was either Otto or Groder coming stealthily upon his toes to complete his work with me; for I never expected to look upon her face again.

She carried no light with her, and paused on the sill of the door, her slight figure outlined against the twilight. She bent her head forward, peering into the gloom of the room, but she said no word; neither did I address her. So she stood for a little, and then, stepping again outside, she unbarred and opened the shutters of the window. Returning, she latched the door, locked it from within, and, fetching the stool from the corner, sat her down quietly before me.

The moon, which had previously shone into the room almost in a level bar, now slanted its beams, so that the Countess was bathed in them from head to foot, while I, being nearer to the window, lay half in shadow, half on the edge of the light.

She sat with her chin propped upon her hands, and her eyes steadily fixed upon mine, but she betrayed no resentment in her looks nor, indeed, feeling of any kind. Then, in a low, absent voice, she began to croon over to herself that odd, wailing elegy which I had once heard her sing in London. The tune had often haunted me since that day from its native melancholy, but now, as Ilga sang it in the moonlight, her eyes very big and dark, and fastened quietly upon mine, it gained a weird and eerie quality from her manner, and I felt my flesh begin to creep.

I stirred uneasily upon the settle, and Ilga stopped. I must think she mistook the reason of my restlessness, for a slow smile came upon her face, and, reaching out a hand, she tried the knots wherewith I was bound.

"It may well be," she suggested, "that you are better inclined to speak the truth, since now you know to what falsehood has brought you,"

" Madame," I replied wearily, " I know not what
you believe nor what you would have me say. It
matters little to me, nor can I see, since you have
reached the end for which you worked, that it need
greatly concern you. This only I know, that I have
already told you the truth."

"And the miniature you left behind you?" she
asked, with an ironic smile. " Am I to understand
it has no bearing on the duel?"

" Nay, madame," said I ; " 'tis the key to the
cause of our encounter."

" Ah ! " she interrupted, with a satisfaction which
I did not comprehend. "You have drawn some
profit from the reflection of these last hours."

" For," I continued, " it contained the likeness of
my friend, Sir Julian Harnwood, as, indeed, Otto
must needs have told you. 'Twas in his cause that
I came to Lukstein."

"'Twas the likeness of a woman," she replied
patiently.

I stared at her in amazement.

" Of a woman ! " I exclaimed.

She laughed with a quiet scorn.

" Of a woman," she repeated. " I showed it you
in my apartments at London."

" The portrait of Lady Tracy ? It is impossible!"
I cried, starting up. " Why, Marston gave it you.
You told me so."

" Oh, is there no end to it?" She burst out
into sudden passion, beating her hands together as
though to enforce her words. " Is there no end
to it ? I never told you so. 'Twas you who pretended that, You pretended you believed it, and

like a weak fool, I let your cunning deceive me. I was not sure then that you had killed the Count, and I believed you had never seen the likeness till that day. But now I know. You own you left the miniature behind you."

"But the case was locked," I said, "and I had not the key."

"I know not that."

I could have informed her who had possessed the key, but refrained, bethinking me that the knowledge might only add to her distress and yet do no real service to me.

"And so," I observed instead, "all your anxiety that I should not tax Marston with the giving of it was on your own account, and not at all on mine."

She was taken aback by the unexpected rejoinder. But to me 'twas no more than a corollary of my original thought that the Countess had been playing me like a silly fish during the entire period of our acquaintance.

"I showed you the portrait as a test," she said hurriedly. "I believed you guiltless, and I knew Mr. Marston and yourself had little liking for each other. Any pretext would have served you for a quarrel. Besides—besides——"

"Besides," I took her up, "you allowed me to believe that Marston had given you the miniature, and had I spoken of the matter to him I should have discovered you were playing me false."

"But you knew," she cried, whipping herself to anger, as it seemed to me, to make up for having given ground. "You knew how the miniature came into my hands. All the while you knew it, and you talk of my playing you false ! "

Suddenly she resumed her seat, and continued in a quieter voice :

" But the brother found out the shameful secret. You could overreach me, but not the brother ; and fresh from accounting to him for your conduct, you must needs stumble into my presence with Lady Tracy's name upon your lips, and doubtless some new explanation ready."

" Madame, that is not so. I came that evening to tell you what I have told you to-night, but you would not hear me. You bade me come to Lukstein. I know now why, and 'twas doubtless for the same reason that you locked the door when I had swooned."

She started as I mentioned that incident.

" 'Twas not on Lady Tracy's account, or because of any conduct of mine towards her, that I fought Marston. Against his will I compelled him to fight, as Lord Elmscott will bear out. He had learned by whose hand Count Lukstein died, and rode after you to Bristol that he might be the first to tell you ; and I was minded to tell you the story myself."

" Or, at all events, to prevent him telling it," she added, with a sneer. " But how came Mr. Marston to learn this fact ? "

I was silent. I could not but understand that the Countess presumed her husband, Lady Tracy, and myself to be bound together by some vulgar intrigue, and I saw how my answer must needs strengthen her suspicions.

"How did he find out?" she repeated. "Tell me that!"

"Lady Tracy informed him," I answered, in despair.

"Then you admit that Lady Tracy knew?"

"I told her of the duel myself, on the very morning that I first met her—on the morning that I introduced her into your house."

"And why did she carry the news to her brother?"

Again I was silent, and again she pressed the question.

"She was afraid of you, and she sought her brother's protection." Every word I uttered seemed to plead against me. "I understand now why she was afraid. I did not know her miniature was in that case, but doubtless she did, and she was afraid you should connect her with Count Lukstein's death."

"Whereas," replied the Countess, "she had nothing to do with it?"

I had made up my mind what answer I should make to this question when it was put. Since I had plainly lost Ilga beyond all hope, I was resolved to spare her the knowledge of her husband's treachery. 'Twould not better my case—for in truth I cared little what became of me—to relate that disgraceful episode to her, and 'twould only add to her unhappiness. So I answered boldly:

"She had nothing to do with it."

The Countess sat looking at me without a word, and I was bethinking me of some excuse by which I might explain how it came about that Lady

Tracy's portrait and not Julian's was in the box, when she bent forward, with her face quite close to mine, so that she might note every change in my expression

"And the footsteps in the snow; how do you account for them? The woman's footsteps that kept side by side with yours from the parapet to the window, and back again from the window to the parapet?"

I uttered a cry, and setting my feet to the ground, raised myself up in the settle.

"The footsteps in the snow? They were your own."

The Countess stared at me vacantly, and then I saw the horror growing in her eyes, and I knew that at last she believed me.

"They were your own," I went on. "I knew nothing of Count Lukstein's marriage. I had never set eyes on him at all. I knew not 'twas your wedding-day. I came hither hot-foot from Bristol to serve my friend Sir Julian Harnwood. He had quarrelled with the Count, and since he lay condemned to death as one of Monmouth's rebels, he charged me to take the quarrel up. In furtherance of that charge, I forced Count Lukstein to fight me. In the midst of the encounter you came down the little staircase into the room. I saw you across the Count's shoulder. The curtain by the window hangs now half-torn from the vallance. I tore it clutching its folds in my horror. We started asunder, and you passed between us. You walked out across the garden and to the Castle wall. Madame, as God is my witness, when once I had seen you, I wished for nothing so much as to leave the Count in peace. But—but——"

" Well ? " she asked breathlessly.

" 'Twas Count Lukstein's turn to compel me," I went on, recovering from a momentary hesitation. I had indeed nearly blurted out the truth about his final thrust. " And when you came back into the room, you passed within a foot of the dead body of your husband, and of myself, who was kneeling——"

She flung herself back, interrupting me with a shuddering cry. She covered her face with her hands, and swayed to and fro upon the stool, as though she would fall.

"Madame!" I exclaimed. " For God's sake! For if you swoon, alas ! I cannot help you."

She recovered herself in a moment, and taking her hands from before her face, looked at me with a strangely softened expression. She rose from her seat, and took a step or two thoughtfully towards the door. Then she stopped and turned to me.

" Lady Tracy, you say, had nothing to do with this quarrel, and yet her likeness was in the miniature case."

I had no doubt in my own mind as to how it came there. 'Twas the case which Lady Tracy had given to Count Lukstein, and doubtless she had substituted her portrait for that of Julian. But this I could not tell to the Countess.

" 'Twas a mistake of my friend," said I. " He gave me the case as a warrant and proof, which I might show to Count Lukstein, that I came on his part, telling me his portrait was within it. But 'twas on the night before he was executed, and his thoughts may well have gone astray."

"But since the case was locked, and you had not the key, who was to open it?"

"Count Lukstein," I replied, being thrown for a moment off my guard.

"Count Lukstein?" she asked, coming back to me. "Then he possessed the key. You fought for your friend, Sir Julian Harnwood. Lady Tracy was betrothed to Sir Julian. The case was given to you as a warrant of the cause in which you came. It contained Lady Tracy's likeness, and Count Lukstein held the key."

She spoke with great slowness and deliberation, adding sentence to sentence as links in a chain of testimony. I heard her with a great fear, perceiving how near she was to the truth. There was, however, one link missing to make the chain complete. She did not know that Lady Tracy had owned the case and had given it to Count Lukstein, and of that fact I was determined she should still remain ignorant.

"My husband loved me," she said quickly, with a curious challenge in her voice.

"I believe most sincerely that he did," I answered with vehemence. I was able to say so honestly, for I remembered how his face and tone had softened when he made mention of his wife.

"Then tell me the cause of this quarrel that induced you to break into this house at midnight, and, on a friend's behalf, force a stranger to fight you without even a witness?"

There was a return of suspicion in her tone, and

she came back into the moonlight. The tempta-
tion to speak out grew upon me as I watched
her. I longed to assure her that I was bound to
no other woman, but pledged heart and soul to
her, and the fear that if I kept silent she would
once more set this duel down to some rivalry in
intrigue, urged me well-nigh out of all restraint.
Why should I be so careful of the reputation of
Count Lukstein? 'Twas an unworthy thought, and
one that promised to mislead me ; for after all,
'twas not his good or ill repute that I had to consider, but rather whether Ilga held his memory in
such esteem and respect that my disclosures would
inflict great misery upon her and a lasting distress.
This postulate I could hardly bring myself to question. Had I not, indeed, ample surety in the care
and perseverance wherewith she had sought to
avenge his death? However, being hard pressed
by my inclinations, I determined to test that point
conclusively if by any means I might.

"Madame," I said, "last night, as I lay in my
bed, bethinking me of the morrow, and wondering
what it held in store for me, I heard the sound of
a woman weeping. It rose from the little room
beneath me; from the room wherein I fought
Count Lukstein. 'Twas the most desolate sound
that ever my ears have hearkened to—a woman
weeping alone in the black of the night. I stole
down the staircase and opened the door. I saw
that the woman who wept was yourself."

"'Twas for my husband," she interposed, very
sharp and quick, and my heart sank.

Yet her words seemed to quicken my desire to

reveal the truth. They woke in me a strange and morbid jealousy of the man. I longed to cry out: " He was a coward; false to you, false to his friend, false to me."

" And in London ? " I asked, temporising again. " The morning I came to you unannounced. You were at the spinnet."

" 'Twas for my husband," she repeated, with a certain stubbornness. " But we will keep to the question we have in hand, if you please—the cause of your dispute with Count Lukstein."

" I will not tell you it."

I spoke with no great firmness, and on that account most like I helped to confirm her reawakened suspicions.

" Will not ? " says she, her voice cold and sneering. " They are brave words though unbravely spoken. You forget I have the advantage and can compel you."

" Madame," I replied, " you overrate your powers. Your servants can bind me hand and foot, but they cannot compel me to speak what I will not."

" Have you no lie ready ? What ? Does your invention fail ? " and she suddenly rose from the stool in a whirlwind of passion. " God forgive me ! " she cried. " For even now I believed you."

She ceased abruptly and pushed her head forward, listening. The creak of wheels came faintly to our ears.

" You hear that ? It is Mr. Buckler's carriage, and Mr. Buckler rides within it. Do you understand ? The carriage takes you to Meran ; you will not be the first traveller who has disappeared on

Y

the borders of Italy. I am afraid your friend at
Venice will wait for you in vain."

The carriage rumbled down the hill, and we both
listened until the sound died away.

"For the future you shall labour as my peasant
on the hillside among the woods, with my peasants
for companionship, until your thoughts grow coarse
with your body, and your soul dwindles to the
soul of a peasant. So shall you live, and so shall
you die, for the wrong which you have done to
me." She towered above me in her outburst, her
eyes flashing with anger. "And you dared to
charge me with trickery! Why, what else has
your life been? From the night you went clothed
as a woman to Bristol Bridewell, what else has
your life been? A woman! The part fitted you
well; you have all the cunning. You need but
the addition of a petticoat."

The bitterness of her speech stung me into
a fury, and, forgetful of the continence I owed to
her:

"Madame!" I said, "I proved the contrary
to your husband."

"Silence!" she cried, and with her open hand
she struck me on the face. And then a strange
thing happened. It seemed as though we changed
places. For all my helplessness, I seemed to have
won the mastery over her. A feeling of power
and domination, such as I had never experienced
before, grew stronger and stronger within me, and
ran tingling through every vein. I forgot my
bonds; I forgot the contempt which she had poured
on me; I forgot the very diffidence with which

she had always inspired me. I felt somehow that I was her master, and exulted in the feeling. Whatever happened to me in the future, whether or no I was to labour as her bondslave for all my days, for that one moment I was her master. She could never hold me in lower esteem, in greater scorn than she did at this hour, and yet I was her master. Something told me indeed that she would never hold me in contempt at all again. She stood before me, her face dark with shame, her attitude one of shrinking humiliation. Twice she strove to raise her eyes to mine; twice she let them fall to the ground. She began a sentence, and broke off at the second word. She pulled fretfully at the laces of her gloves. Then she turned and walked to the door. She walked slowly at first, constraining herself; she quickened her pace, fumbled with the key in her hurry to unlock the door, and once out of the pavilion, without pausing to latch or lock it, fled like one pursued towards the house. And from the bottom of my heart I pitied her.

In a little while Father Spaur, with the two Tyrolese, returned, and they carried me quickly through the little parlour and up the staircase to my bedroom. There they flung me on the bed and locked the door and left me. Through the open window the dance-melodies rose to my ears. It seemed to me that I could distinguish particular tunes which I had heard when I crouched in the snow upon that November night.

> Que toutes joies et toutes honneurs
> Viennent d'armes et d'amours.

Jack's refrain, which he had hummed so continually during our ride to Austria, came into
my head, and set itself to the lilt of the music.
Well, I had made essay of both arms and love,
and I had got little joy and less honour therefrom,
unless it be joy to burn with anxieties, and honour
to labour as a peasant and be deemed a common
trickster!

The music ceased; the guests went homewards
down the hill, laughing and singing as they went;
the Castle gradually grew silent. The door of
my room was unlocked and flung open, and Groder
entered, bearing a candle in his hand. He set
it down upon the table, and drew a long knife
from a sheath which projected out of his pocket.
This he held and flourished before my eyes, seeking
like a child to terrify me with his antics, until Father
Spaur, following in upon his heels, bade him desist
from his buffoonery.

Groder cut the girdle which bound my ankles.

" March !" said he.

But my legs were so numbed with the tightness
of the cord that they refused their office. Father
Spaur ordered him to chafe my limbs with his
hands, which he did very unwillingly, and after
a little I was able to walk, though with uncertain
and wavering steps.

" Should you suffer at all at Groder's hands,"
said the priest pleasantly, " I beg you to console
yourself with certain reflections which I shared
with you one afternoon that we rode together."

We proceeded along the corridor and turned
into the gallery which ran round the hall. But

at the head of the great staircase I stopped and drew back. The priest's taunts and Groder's insolence I had endured in silence. What they had bidden me do, that I had done; for in the miscarriage of my fortunes I was minded to bear myself as a gentleman should, without pettish complaints or an unavailing resistance which could only entail upon me further indignities. But from this final humiliation I shrank.

Below me the entire household of servants was ranged in the hall, leaving a lane open from the foot of the stairs to the door. Every face was turned towards me—except one. One face was held aside and hidden in a handkerchief, and since that hour I have ever felt a special friendliness and gratitude for the withered little Frenchwoman, Clemence Durette. Alone of all that company she showed some pity for my plight. None the less, however, my eyes went wandering for another sight. What with the uncertain glare of the torches, that sent waves of red light and shadow in succession sweeping across the throng of faces, 'twas some while or ever I could discover the Countess. That she was present I had no doubt, and at last I saw her, standing by the door apart from her servants, her face white, and her eyelids closed over her eyes.

Groder pushed me roughly in the small of the back, and I stumbled down the topmost steps. There was no escape from the ordeal, and glancing neither to the right nor to the left, I walked between the silent rows of servants. I passed within a yard of Countess Lukstein, but she made no movement;

she never even raised her eyes. A carriage stood in the courtyard, and I got into it, and was followed by Michael Groder and Otto. As we drove off a hubbub arose within the hall, and it seemed to me that a ring was formed about the doorway, as though some one had fallen. But before I had time to take much note of it, a cloth was bound over my eyes, and the carriage rolled down the hill.

At the bottom, where the track from Lukstein debouches upon the main road, we turned eastwards in the direction of Meran, and thence again to the left, ascending an incline; so that I gathered we were entering a ravine parallel to the Senner Thal, but further east.

In a while the carriage stopped, and Otto, opening the door, told me civilly enough to descend. Then he took me by the arm and led me across a threshold into a room. A woman's voice was raised in astonishment.

"Wait till he's plucked of his feathers!" laughed Groder, and bade her close the shutters.

The bandage was removed from my eyes, and by the grey morning light which pierced through the crevices of the window, I perceived that I was in some rough cottage. An old woman stood gaping open-mouthed before me. Groder sharply bade her go and prepare breakfast. Otto unbound my wrists, and pointed to a heap of clothes which lay in a corner, and so they left me to myself.

I had some difficulty in putting on these clothes, since my wrists were swollen and well-nigh useless from their long confinement. Indeed, but for a threat which Groder shouted through the door, saying that he would come and assist me to make my toilet, I doubt whether I should have succeeded at all.

For breakfast they brought me a pannikin full of a greasy steaming gruel, which I constrained myself to swallow. Then they bound my hands again. Groder wrapped up the clothes which I had taken off in a bundle, and slung it on his back. Otto replaced the bandage on my eyes, and we set out, mounting upwards by a rough mountain track, along which they guided me. About noon Otto called a halt, and none too soon, for I was ready to drop with fatigue and pain. There we made a meal of some dry coarse bread, and washed it down with spirit of a very bitter flavour. 'Twas new to me at the time, but I know now that it was distilled from the gentian flower. Groder lit a fire and burned the bundle of clothes which he had brought with him, the two men sharing my jewels between them.

From that point we left the track and climbed up a grass slope, winding this way and that in the ascent. 'Twas as much as I could do to keep my feet, though Otto and Groder supported me upon either side. At the top we dipped down again for a little, crossed a level field of heather, but in what direction I know not, for by this I had lost all sense of our bearings, mounted again, descended again, and towards nightfall came to a hut. Groder thrust me inside, plucked the cloth from my face, and unbound my hands.

"'Tis a long day's journey," said he; "but what matters that if you make it only once?"

CHAPTER XXI.

IN CAPTIVITY HOLLOW.

THE hut wherein I passed the first month of my captivity was of a more solid construction than is customary at so great a height, and had been built by the order of Count Lukstein for a shelter when the chase brought him hitherwards. For the hillside was covered with a dense forest of fir-trees in which chamois abounded, and now and again, though 'twas never my lot to come across one, a bear might be discovered.

The hut had a sort of vestibule paved with cobble-stones and roofed with pine-wood. From this hall a room led out upon either side, though only that upon the right hand was used by the wood-cutters who dwelt here. Of these there were two, and they lived and slept in the one room, cooking the gruel or porridge, which formed our chief food, in a great cauldron slung over a rough fireplace of stones in the centre of the floor. There was no chimney to carry off the smoke, not so much as a hole in the wall; but the smoke found its way out as best it might through the door. From the hall a ladder led up through a trap-door

into a loft above, and as soon as we had supped,
Groder bade me mount it, and followed me himself. The wood-cutters below removed the ladder,
Groder closed the trap, and, spreading some
branches of fir upon it, laid him down and went
to sleep. I followed his example in the matter of
making my bed, but, as you may believe, I got little
sleep that night. For one thing my arms and legs
were now become so swollen and painful that it
tortured me even to move them, and it was full
two days before I was sufficiently recovered to be
able to descend from the loft. By that time Otto
had got him back to the valley, and I was left under
the authority of Groder, which he used without
scruple or intermission. Each morning at daybreak
the ladder was hoisted to the loft We descended
and despatched a hasty breakfast; thereupon I was
given an axe, and the four of us proceeded into
the forest, where we felled trees the day long.
Through the gaps in the clearings I would look
across the valley to the bleak rocks and naked
snow-fields, and thoughts of English meadows knee-
deep in grass, and of rooks cawing through a
summer afternoon, would force themselves into my
mind until I grew well-nigh daft with longing for
a sight of them. At nightfall we returned to the
hut and partook of a meal, and no words wasted.
When the meal was finished I was straightway
banished to my loft, where I lay in the dark,
and heard through the floor the wood-cutters
breaking into all sorts of rough jests and songs
now that I was no longer present to check their
merriment. For towards me they consistently

showed the greatest taciturnity and sullen reserve. 'Twas seldom that any one except Groder addressed a word to me, and in truth I would lief he had been as silent as the rest. For when he opened his mouth 'twas only to utter some command in a harsh, growling tone as though he spoke to a cur, and to couple thereto a coarse and unseemly oath.

For a time I endured this servitude in an extraordinary barrenness of mind. Not even the thought of escape stirred me to activity. The sudden misfortune which had befallen me seemed to have numbed and dulled all but my bodily faculties. Moreover the long and arduous labour, to which I was set, wearied me in the extreme, and each evening I came back so broken with fatigue that I wished for nothing so much as to climb into my loft and stretch myself out upon my branches in the dark, though even then I was often too tired to sleep, and so would lie hour after hour counting the seconds by the pulsing of my sinews.

After a couple of weeks had gone by, however, I began to take some notice of the place of my captivity, and to seek whether by any means I might compass my escape. For I recalled, with an apprehension which quickened speedily, as I dwelt upon it, into a panic of terror, the singular prophecy and sentence which the Countess had flung at me. I began to see myself already sinking into a dull apathy, performing my daily task, with no thought beyond my physical needs, until I became one with these coarse peasants in spirit and mind.

What else, I reflected, could happen? Remote from all intercourse or companionship, with not so much as a single book to divert me, labouring with my hands from dawn to dusk, and guarded ever by ignorant boors who reckoned me not worth even their speech—what else could I become? 'Twould need far less than a lifetime to work the transformation !

But, however carefully I watched, I could by no means come at the opportunity of an evasion. At night, as I have said, Groder shared the loft with me, and, slept over the trap-door ; nor was there any window or other opening through which I might drop to the ground, since the roof reached down to the flooring upon every side. This roof consisted of a thatch of boughs, and of large sheets of bark superimposed upon them, and weighted down by heavy stones. One night, indeed, when Groder lay snoring, I endeavoured to force an opening through the thatch ; but I had no help beyond what my hands afforded me—for they took my axe from me every night as soon as we got back to the hut— and I was compelled, moreover, to work with the greatest caution and quietude lest I should awaken my companion ; so that I got nothing for my pains but a few scratches and an additional fatigue to carry through the morrow.

Nor, indeed, was my case any better in the day-time. We all worked in the same clearing, and at no single moment was I out of sight of my gaolers.

But even had I succeeded in eluding them, I doubt whether at this time I should have been any

nearer the fulfilment of my desire. For I knew not
so much as the direction of Lukstein, and I should
only have wandered helpless amongst these heights
until either I was recaptured or perished miserably
upon the desolate wastes of snow.

The hut stood in the centre of a little hollow, on
the brink of a torrent, and was girt about by a
rim of hills. There was, indeed, but one outlet, and
that a precipitous gully, through which the water
rushed with a great roaring noise, and I gathered
from this that it fell pretty sheer. I was the more
inclined to this conjecture, since had the gully
afforded a path it would have been the natural
entrance into the hollow, and I knew that I had
not been brought that way, else I must needs have
remarked the roar of the stream sooner than I did.
For that sound only came to my ears when I was
but a short distance from the hut.

If you stood with your back to the door of the
hut, the noise came from directly behind you. On
your right rose the pine-forest wherein we laboured,
very steep and dense, to the crest of a hill; on
your left a barren wilderness, encumbered by stones,
sloped up to the foot of a great field of snow,
which grew steeper and steeper towards its summit.
Here and there great masses of ice bulged out from
the incline, like nothing so much as the bosses of
shields. I was rather apt to underrate the size and
danger of these, until one day a fragment, which
seemed in comparison no greater than a pea, broke
away from one of these bosses and dropped on to
the slope beneath, starting, as it were, a little rillet
of snow down the hillside. On the instant the

hollow was filled with a great thunder, as though
a battery of cannon had been discharged; and I
should hardly have believed this fragment could
have produced so great a disturbance, had not the
Tyrolese looked across the valley, and by their
words to one another assured me it was so.

In front of you, the head of this hollow was
blocked up by a tongue of ice, which wound downwards like some huge dragon, and the stream of
which I have spoken flowed from the tip of it, as
though the dragon spewed the water from its mouth.
It was then apparent to me from these observations
that I had been carried into this prison by some
track through the pine-forest, and I set myself to
the discovery of it. But whether the wood-cutters
kept aloof from it, or whether it was in reality
indistinguishable, I could perceive no trace of it.
At one point on the crest of the hill there was a
marked depression, and I judged that there lay the
true entrance; but through the gap I could see
nothing but a sea of white, with dark peaks of rock
tossed this way and that, and dreaded much
adventuring myself that way.

It soon came upon me, however, that in which-
ever way I determined to make my attempt, I must
needs delay the actual enterprise until the spring;
for we were now in the month of November, and
the snow falling very thickly, so that for some while
we worked knee-deep in snow. Then one morning
Groder and his comrades once more bound my
hands and bandaged my eyes, and we set off to
pass the winter in one of the lower valleys. On
this occasion I took such notice as I could of our

direction, and from the diminishing sound of the
waterfall, I understood that we marched for some
distance towards the head of the valley, and then
turned to the right through the pine-forest. Evidently
we were making for the gap in the ridge of the
hill, and I determined to pay particular heed to
the course which we followed down the other side.
Again, however, I was led in a continual zigzag,
first to the right, then to the left, and with such
irregular distances between each turn that it became
impossible to keep a clear notion of our direction.
At times, too, we would retrace our steps, at others
we seemed to be describing the greater part of a
circle; so that in the end, when we finally reached
our quarters, I was little wiser than at the moment
of setting out.

There were some five or six cottages in the
ravine whither we were come, and one of them
most undeniably an inn; for though I was not
suffered to go there myself — nor, indeed, had I
any inclination that way—my guardians frequently
brought back upon their tongues and in their faces
evidence as convincing as a sign swinging above
the door.   In truth if the house was not an inn,
it possessed the most hospitable master in the world.

None the less strictly, however, on this account
was the watch maintained upon me; for if Groder
and his fellows chanced to be incapacitated for
the time, there were ever some peasants from the
neighbouring cottages ready to fill their place;
though, indeed, there was but little necessity for
their zeal, for the snow lay many feet deep upon
the ground, and the only path along which one

could travel at all led down to the more populous parts of the valley, through which, at this time of the year, it would be impossible to escape. One could journey no faster than at a snail's pace, and would leave, besides, an unmistakable trail for the pursuers.

These winter months proved the most irksome of my captivity, my sole occupation being the plaiting of ropes from the flax which was grown about these parts. At this tedious and mechanic labour I toiled for many hours a day, in an exceeding great vacancy of spirit, until I hit upon a plan by which I might exercise my mind without hindering the work of my fingers. 'Twas my terror lest my wits should wither for lack of use that first set me on the device; since, indeed, it mattered little how or when Countess Ilga discovered that I had slain her husband. She *had* discovered it; that was the kernel of the matter, and the searching out of the means whereby she gained the knowledge no more than an idle cracking of the shell into little fragments after the kernel has been removed.

Many incidents, of course, became intelligible to me now that I knew whose portrait the miniature box contained. The sudden swoon of Lady Tracy in the hall at Pall Mall was now easily accounted for. The moment before I had been speaking of the miniature, and Lady Tracy knew—what I could not know— that Ilga held a proof of her acquaintanceship with the Count, and would be certain to attribute it as the cause of his death. It was doubtless, also, that piece of knowledge which drove her to such a pitch of fear that on seeing the Countess at Bristol she disclosed the story to her brother and besought his protection. I understood, moreover, the drift of the words which Marston was uttering when death took him. He meant to ask a question, not to make an explanation.

Concerning those events, however, which more nearly concerned myself I was not so clear. I had no clue whereby I could ascertain how the Countess first came to fix her suspicions upon me, and in the absence of that, my speculations were the merest conjectures. Much of course was significant to me which I had disregarded, as, for instance, the journey of Countess Lukstein to Bristol, the diagram which she had drawn on the gravel under the piazza of Covent Garden, the perplexity with which she had regarded the diagram, and the sudden start she had given when I mentioned the date of my departure from Leyden. For I remembered that she had previously remarked the Horace when she came to visit me; and in that volume the date "September 14, 1685," was inscribed on the page opposite to Julian's outline of Lukstein.

These details, now that I was aware she suspected me at that time, were full of significance, but they gave me no help towards the solving of that first question as to what directed her thoughts my way. It seemed to me, indeed, as I looked back upon the incidents of our acquaintance, that the Countess, almost from our first meeting, had begun to set her husband's death to my account.

One thing, however, I did clearly recognise, and for that recognition I shall ever be most gratefully thankful. 'Twas of far more importance to me than any academic speculations, and I do but cite them here that I may show how I came by it. I perceived that 'twas not so much any investigation on the part of the Countess which had betrayed me to her, as my own wilful and independent actions. Of my own free choice I came from Cumberland to seek her; of my own free choice I brought her to my rooms, where she saw the Horace ; of my own free choice I joined her in the box at the Duke's Theatre, and so led Marston to speak of my ride to Bristol ; and again of my own free choice I had persuaded Lady Tracy to enter the house in Pall Mall and confront my mistress. Even in the matter of the diagram, 'twas my anxiety and insistence to prove that Lady Tracy and I were strangers which induced me to dwell upon the date of my leaving Holland, and so gave to the Countess the clue to resolve her perplexity. In short, my very efforts at concealment were the means by which suspicion was ratified and assured, and I could not but believe that Providence in its great wisdom had so willed it. 'Tis that belief and conviction for which I have ever been most grateful; for it enheartened me with patience to endure my present sufferings, and saved me, in particular, from cherishing a petty rancour and resentment against the lady who inflicted them.

I had yet one other consolation during this winter. For at times Otto Krax would come up from the valley to inquire after the prisoner. At first he would but stay for the night and so get him back ; but his visits gradually lengthened and grew more frequent, an odd friendship springing up

z

between us.   For one thing, I was attracted to
him because he came from Lukstein, and, indeed,
might have had speech with Countess Ilga upon
the very day of his coming.   But, besides that,
there was a certain dignity about the man which
set him apart from these rude peasants, and made
his companionship very welcome.   He showed his
good-will towards me by recounting at great length
all that happened at Lukstein, and on the eve of
the Epiphany, which 'tis the fashion of this
people to celebrate with much rejoicing, he brought
me a pipe and a packet of tobacco.   No present
could have been more grateful, and it touched me
to notice his pleasure when I manifested my delight.
We went out of the cottage together, and sat
smoking in the starlight upon a boulder, and I
remember that he told me one might see upon
this evening a woman in white clothing, with a
train of little ragged children chattering · and
clattering behind her.   'Twas Procula, the wife of
Pontius Pilate, he explained.   'Twas her penance
to wander over the world until the · last day
attended by the souls of all children that died
before they had been baptized, and at the season
of the Epiphany she ever passed through the
valleys of the Tyrol.   However, we saw naught of
her that night.

   Early in May Groder carried me back to the
hollow, and I began seriously to consider in what
way I should be most like to effect my escape.
At any cost I was firmly resolved to venture the
attempt, and during this summer too, dreading

the thought of a second winter of such unendurable monotony as that through which I had passed.

We were now set to drag from the hillside to the brink of the torrent the wood which we had felled in the autumn, so that as the stream swelled with the melting of the snows we might send the timber floating down to the valley. 'Twas a task of great labour, and since we had to saw many of the trunks into logs before we could move them, one that occupied no inconsiderable time. Indeed we had not the wood fairly stacked upon the bank until we were well into the first days of June. Meanwhile I had turned over many projects in my mind, but not one that seemed to offer me a possibility of success. I realised especially that if I sought to escape by the way we had come, I should, even though I were so lucky as to hit upon the right path, nevertheless, have to pass through the most inhabited portion of the district. And did I succeed so far, I should then find myself in the valley, close by Castle Lukstein, with not so much as a penny piece in my pocket to help me further on my way. Besides, by that route would Groder be certain to pursue me the moment he discovered my escape, and being familiar with the windings of the ravines, he would most surely overtake me. Yet in no other direction could I discover the hint of an outlet. I was in truth like a fly with wetted wings in the hollow of a cup.

It was our custom to launch the trunks endwise into the torrent, but one of them, which was larger than the rest, being caught in a swirl, turned broadside to the stream, and floating down thus, stuck in the narrow defile, through which the water plunged out of the hollow. The barrier thus begun was strengthened by each succeeding log, so that in a very short time a solid dam was raised, the water running away underneath. To remedy this, Groder bade the peasants and myself take our axes to the spot and cut the wood free.

Now this defile was no more than a deep channel bored by the torrent, and on one side of it the cliff rose precipitously to the height of a hundred feet. On the other, however, a steep slope of grass and bushes, with here and there a dwarf-pine clinging to it, ran down to a rough platform of rock, only twenty feet or so above the surface of the current. To one of these trees we bound a couple of stout ropes, and two men were lowered on to the block of timber, while the third remained upon the platform to see that the ropes did not slip, and to haul the others up. So we worked all the day, taking turn and turn about on the platform.

To this lower end of the dale I had never come before, and when the time arrived for me to rest, I naturally commenced to look about me and consider whether or no I might escape that way. Beneath me the torrent leaped and foamed in a mist of spray, here sweeping along the cliff with a breaking crest like a wave, there circling in a whirlpool about a boulder, and all with such a prodigious roar that I could not hear my companions speak, though they shouted trumpet-wise through their hands. 'Twas indeed no less than I had expected; the stream filled the outlet from side to side.

Then I looked across to the great snow-slope opposite, and in an instant I understood the position of Captivity Hollow, as, for want of a better name, I termed the place of my confinement. The slope finished abruptly just over against me, as though it had been shorn by a knife, and I could see that the end face of it was a gigantic wall of rock. I saw this wall in profile, as one may say, and for that very reason I recognised it the more surely. 'Twas singularly flat, and unbroken by buttresses; not a patch of snow was to be discovered anywhere upon its face, and, moreover, the shape of its apex, which was like the cupola upon a church belfry, made any mistake impossible. In a word, the mountain was the Wildthurm; the wall of cliff blocked the head of the Senner Thal, and the slope on which I gazed was the eastern side, which I had likened to one of the canvas sides of a tent.

If I could but cross it, I thought! No one would look for me in that direction. I could strike into one of the many ravines that led into the Vintschgau Thal to the west of Lukstein, and thence make my way to Innspruck. If only I could cross it! But I gazed at the slope, and my heart died within me. It rose before my eyes vast and steep, flashing menace from a thousand glittering points. Besides, the early summer was upon us, and the sun hot in the sky, so that never an hour passed in the forenoon but blocks of ice would split off and thunder down the incline.

The notion, however, still worked in my head throughout the day, and as we returned to the hut I eagerly scanned the upper end of our ravine, for

at that point the slope of the Wildthurm declined
very greatly in height. Whilst the Tyrolese went in
to prepare supper I stayed by the door.

"Come!" shouted one of them at length — it
was not Groder. "Come, unless you prefer to sleep
fasting."

And I turned to go in, with my mind made up;
for I had perceived, running upwards beside the
tongue of ice which I have described, a long, narrow
ridge. 'Twas neither of ice nor snow, and in colour
a reddish brown, so that I imagined it to be a mound
of earth, thrown up in some way by the pressure
of the snow. Along that it seemed to me that I
might find a path.

Groder was crouched up close to the fire, shivering
by fits and starts, like a man with an ague. He
glanced evilly at me as I entered the room, but
said no word either to me or to his comrades, and
kept muttering to himself concerning "the Cold
Torment." I knew not what the man meant, but
'twas plain that he was shaken with a great fear;
and even during the night I heard him more than
once start from his sleep with a cry, and those same
words upon his lips, "the Cold Torment."

The next morning, hearing that the barrier
was well-nigh cut through, he ordered only one
of the peasants to take me with him and complete
the work. I was lowered on to the dam first,
and laboured at it with saw and axe for the
greater part of the morning. About noon, however,
I took my turn upon the platform, and after I
had been standing some little while, bent over
the torrent, with my hand ready upon the rope,

since at any moment the logs might give way, I suddenly raised myself to ease my back, and turned about.

Just above me on the slope I saw Groder's face peering over the edge of a boulder. 'Twas so contorted with malignancy and hatred that it had no human quality except its shape. 'Twas the face of a devil. For one moment I saw it; the next it dropped behind the stone. I pretended to have noticed nothing, and so stood looking everywhere except in his direction. The expression upon his face left me no doubt as to his intention. He was minded to take a leaf from my book, and precipitate the boulder upon me when my back was turned, in which case I should not come off so cheaply as he had done, for I should inevitably be swept into the torrent. The boulder, I observed, was in a line with the spot where I must stand in order to handle the rope.

What to do I could not determine. I dared not show him openly that I had detected his design, for I should most likely in that event provoke an open conflict, and I doubted not that the other peasant was within call to help him to an issue if help were needed; and even if I succeeded in avoiding a conflict, I should only put him upon his guard and make him use more precautions when next he attempted my life.

I turned me again to the torrent and took the rope in my hand, with my ears open for any sound behind me. I stooped slowly forwards, as if to watch my companion, thinking that Groder would launch the stone as soon as he deemed it impossible for me to recover in time to elude it. And so it proved. I heard a dull thud as the boulder fell forward upon the turf. I sprang quickly to one side, and not a moment too soon, for the boulder whizzed past me on a level with my shoulder, leaped across the stream, and was shattered into a thousand fragments against the opposite cliff. The man below, who had been almost startled from his footing, began to curse me roundly for my carelessness, and I answered him without casting a glance to my rear, deeming it prudent to give Groder the opportunity to crawl away into cover.

In that, however, I made a mistake, and one that went near to costing me my life, for when I did turn, after explaining that the boulder had slipped of its own weight and momentum, Groder was within ten feet of me. He had crept noiselessly down the bank, and now stood with one foot planted against it, the other upon the platform, his body all gathered together for a leap. His teeth were bared, his eyes very bright, and in his hand he held a long knife. I ran for my hatchet, which lay some yards distant, but he was upon me before I could stoop to pick it up. The knife flashed above my head; I caught at Groder's wrist as it descended and grappled him close, for I knew enough of their ways of fighting to feel assured that if I did but give his arms free play, my eyes would soon be lying on my cheeks.

Backwards and forwards we swayed upon the narrow platform with never a word spoken. Then

from the torrent came a great crack and a shout.
I knew well enough what was happening. The
barrier was giving, the water was bursting the
timber, and the peasant would of a surety be crushed
and ground to death between the loosened logs.
But I dared not relax my grip. Groder's breath
was hot upon my face, his knife ever quivering
towards my throat. I heard a few quick sounds
as of the snapping of twigs, and once, I think,
again the cry of a man in distress; but the roaring of the waters was in my ears and I could not
be sure.

The labours of my captivity had hardened my
limbs and sinews, else had Groder mastered me
more easily; but as it was, I felt my strength
ebbing, and twice the knife pricked into my shoulder
as he pressed it down. The din of the torrent
died away. I was sensible of a deathly stillness of
the elements. It seemed as though Nature held
its breath. Suddenly a look of terror sprang into
Groder's face. He redoubled his efforts, and I felt
my back give. Involuntarily I closed my eyes, and
then his fingers loosened their hold. He plucked
himself free with a jerk, and stood sullenly looking
up the slope. I followed the direction of his gaze,
and saw Otto Krax standing above me. Gradually
the torrent became audible to me again; there was a
rustling of leaves in the wind, and in a little I
understood that some one was speaking. Groder
advanced slowly across the grass and reached out
the hand which held the knife. Very calmly Otto
grasped it by the wrist, twisted the arm, and snapped
it across his knee. What he said I could not hear,

but Groder went up the slope holding his broken arm, and I saw his face no more.

Otto came down to me.

"You have never been nearer your death but once," he said.

I made no reply, but pointed to the rope at my feet. 'Twas dragging to and fro upon the platform, and the thought of what dangled and tossed in the water at the tag of it turned me sick. Otto walked to the edge and looked over. Then he drew his knife and cut the rope.

"I saw only the end of the struggle," said he. "How did it begin?"

I told him briefly what had occurred.

"'Twas you taught him the trick," he said, with a laugh; "and he bore you no good-will for the lesson."

"But what brought you so pat?" I asked.

"I was sent," he replied. "'Twas thought best I should follow."

"Follow? Follow whom?" said I.

He made no answer to my question, and continued hurriedly.

"I asked the fellow at the hut where you were, and he directed me here — not a minute too soon either. Were you working at the timber yesterday?"

"All day."

"Did Groder help?"

"No! He remained behind."

Otto gave a grunt.

"Alone?" he asked.

"Quite," I replied. "The others were with me."

We walked back to the hut together, and as on the evening before, I stopped in the doorway to examine the ridge on which my hopes were set. But I watched it to-day with a beating heart, and, let me own it, with a shrinking apprehension too, for within the last hour the possibility of my attempt had grown immeasurably real. Groder, I was certain, I should see no more. 'Twas equally certain that Otto would not remain to fill his place, and one of the peasants had been battered to death in the breaking of the dam. 'Twas doubtless an unworthy feeling, but, much as the nature of the man's end had horrified me at the time, I could not now find it in my heart to greatly regret it. I was too conscious of the fact that only a couple of gaolers were left to guard me.

Otto coming from the kitchen to join me, I deemed it prudent not to be particular in my gaze, and so taking my eyes off the ridge, which was become to me what Mahomet's bridge is to the Turk, I let them roam idly this way and that as we strolled forward over the turf. Hence it chanced that about twenty yards from the door I saw something bright winking in the verdure. I went towards it and picked it up. 'Twas a little gold cross, and, moreover, clean and unrusted. A sudden thought breaking in upon me, I turned to Otto and said:

"Otto, have you ever heard of the Cold Torment?"

Otto fell to crossing himself devoutly.

"The Cold Torment?" he asked, in awed tones. "What know you of it?" He turned towards the

gap in the hillside upon our right. "Look!" said
he. "You see the peak that stands apart like a
silver wedge. On its summit is buried an inex-
haustible treasure, and night and day through the
ages seven guilty souls keep ward about it in the
cold. Never may one be freed until another is condemned in its stead. The Virgin save us from the
Cold Torment!"

"Ah!" said I, remarking the fervour of his
prayer. "'Tis the text for a persuasive homily,
and Father Spaur, I fancy, preached from it
yesterday."

Otto started, and glanced about him with some
fear, as though he half expected to see the priest
start out of the earth.

"You know not what you say," he exclaimed.

"Who sent you to follow him?"

"Nay," he protested; "I came not to spy upon
Father Spaur. We know not that he has been
here. 'Twere wise not to know it."

I handed him the gold cross, and asked again:

"Who sent you after him?"

"I was not sent after him. I was bidden to
come hither by my mistress."

"Ah! she sent you!" I cried. "Give the cross
back to Father Spaur, and with it my most grateful
thanks. He has done me better service than ever
did my dearest friend."

I reasoned it out in this way. Father Spaur
was bent on appropriating Lukstein and its broad
lands to the Church. To that end, the Countess
must, at all costs, be hindered from a second
marriage. What motive could he have in prompting

Groder to make an end of me, unless—unless Ilga
now and again let her thoughts stray my way?
And to confirm my conjecture, to rid it of presumption, I had this certain knowledge that she
had sent Otto to see that I came to no harm at
his hands. I should add that my speculations
during the winter months had in some measure
prepared me to entertain this notion. From con-
stantly analysing and pondering all that she had
said to me in the pavilion, and bringing my
recollections of her change in manner to illumine
her words, I had come, though hesitatingly, to a
conclusion very different from that which I had
originally formed. I could not but perceive that
it made a great difference whether or no I had
been alone upon my first coming to the Castle.
Besides, I realised that there was a pregnant
meaning which might be placed to the sentence
which had so perplexed me: "Would that I had
the strength to resist, or the weakness to yield!"
And going yet further back, I had good grounds
from what she had let slip to believe that there
was something more than a regard for herself in
the entreaty which she had addressed to me in
London, that I should not tax Marston with
treachery in the matter of the miniature.

Otto gave me back the cross.

"It is a mistake," said he. "Father Spaur has
gone from Lukstein on a visit."

"Then," said I, "present it to your mistress.
She has more claim to it than I."

That night Otto slept in the loft in Groder's
place.

"You are sure," he asked, "that no one remained behind with Groder yesterday afternoon?"

"Quite," said I.

"None the less, I should sleep on the trap if I were you, and 'twere wise to carry your hatchet to bed for company."

"But they take it from me each night," I replied eagerly. "You must tell them."

"I will. But there's no cause for fear."

'Twas not at all fear which prompted my eagerness; but I bethought me if I had the loft to myself, and the axe ready to my hand, 'twould be a strange thing if I could not find a way out by the morning. Thereupon we fell to talking again of Groder's attempt upon my life, and he repeated the words which he had used at the time.

"You were never nearer your death but once."

"And when was that once?" I asked drowsily.

He laughed softly to himself for a little, and then he replied; and with his first sentence my drowsiness left me, just as a mist clears in a moment off the hills.

"Do you remember one night in London that your garden door kept slamming in the wind?"

"Well?" said I, starting up.

"You came downstairs in the dark, took the key from the mantelshelf, and went out into the garden and locked it. That occasion was the once."

"You were in the room!" I exclaimed. "I remember. The door was open again in the morning. I had a locksmith to it. There was nothing amiss with the lock, and I wondered how it happened."

Otto laughed again quietly.

"Right. I was in the room, and I was not alone either."

"The Countess was with you. Why?"

"There was a book in your rooms which she wished to see—a poetry book, eh?—with a date on one page, and a plan of Castle Lukstein on the page opposite. My mistress was at your lodging with some company that afternoon."

"True," said I, interrupting him. "She proposed the party herself."

"Well, it seems that she got no chance of examining the book then. But she unlocked the garden door. You had told her where you kept the key."

I recollected that I had done so on the occasion of her first visit.

"And so Countess Lukstein and yourself were in the room when I passed through th ^t night."

Otto began to chuckle again.

"'Twas lucky you came down in the dark, and didn't stumble over us. Lord! I thought that I should have burst with holding my breath."

"Otto," I said, "tell me the whole story; how your suspicions set towards me, and what confirmed them."

"Very well," said he, after a pause, "I will; for my mistress consulted me throughout. But you will get no sleep."

"I shall get less if you don't tell me."

"Wait a moment!"

He filled his tobacco-pipe and lighted it. I followed his example, and between the puffs he related the history of those far-away days in London. To me, lying back upon the boughs which formed my bed in the dark loft, it seemed like the weaving of a fairy tale. The house in Pall Mall—St. James's Park—the piazza of Covent Garden! How strange it all sounded, and how unreal!

The odour of pine-wood was in my nostrils, and I had but to raise my arm to touch the sloping thatch above my head.

CHAPTER XXII

"OF what happened at Bristol," he began, "you know well-nigh as much as I do, in a sense, maybe more; for I have never learnt to this day why my master, the late Count, left me behind there to keep an eye upon the old attorney and Sir Julian Harnwood's visitors. There's only one thing I need tell you. The night you came from the Bridewell, after—well, after——" He hesitated, seeming at a loss for a word. I understood what it was that he stuck at, and realising that my turn had come to chuckle, I said, with a laugh:

"The blow was a good one, Otto."

"'Twas not so good as you thought," he replied rather hotly, "not by a great deal; and for all that you ran away so fast," he repeated the phrase with considerable emphasis, "for all that you ran away so fast, I found out where you lodged. I passed the lawyer man as he was coming back alone, and remembering that I had traced him into Lime-kiln Lane in the afternoon, I returned there the next morning. The 'Thatched House' was the

2 A

only tavern in the street, and I inquired whether
a woman had stayed there overnight. They told
me no; they had only put up one traveller, and
he had left already. I thought no more of this at
the time, believing my suspicions to be wrong, and
so got me back to Lukstein. After the wedding-
night I told the Countess all that I knew."

" Wait !" I said, interrupting him.

There was a point I had long been anxious
to resolve, and I thought I should never get
so likely an opportunity for the question again.

" Was Count Lukstein betrothed at the time
that he came to the Hotwells ? "

" Most assuredly," he replied, and I wondered
greatly at the strange madness which should lead a
man astray to chase a pretty face, when all the while
he loved another, and was plighted to her.

Otto resumed his story.

"I told all that I knew: my master's anxiety
concerning Sir Julian, his relief when I brought him
the news hither that only a woman had visited the
captive on the night before his execution, and his
apparent fear of peril. My mistress broke open the gold
case which you had left behind, and asked whether
the likeness was the likeness of Sir Julian's visitor.
I assured her it was not, but she was convinced that
this Bristol pother was at the bottom of the trouble.
We could find no trace of you beyond your footsteps
in the snow, and the footsteps of the woman who
was with you. I have often wondered how she
climbed the Lukstein rock."

He paused as though expecting an answer. But
I had no inclination to argue my innocence in that

respect with one of Ilga's servants, and presently he continued :

" Well, a quiet tongue is wisdom where women are concerned. No one in the valley had seen you come; no one had seen you go. But my lady was set upon discovering the truth and punishing the assailant herself. So she said as little as she could to the neighbours, and the following spring took me with her to London."

"Where I promptly jumped into the trap," said I.

"You did that and more. You set the trap yourself before you jumped into it."

- 'Twas my own thought that he uttered, and I asked him how he came by it.

" I mean this. 'Twas my lady's hope to discover the original of the miniature, and so get at the . man who was with her. But we had not to wait for that. You left something else behind you besides the miniature."

" I did," I replied. " I left a pair of spurs and a pistol, but I see not how they could serve you."

" The spurs were of little profit in our search. You have worn them since, it is true, but one pair of spurs is like another. For the pistol, however— that was another matter. It had the gunmaker's name upon the barrel, and also the name of the town where it was made."

" Leyden ? " I exclaimed.

" That was the name—Leyden."

At last I understood. I recalled that evening when Elmscott presented me to Ilga, and how frankly I had spoken to her of my life.

2 A 2

"We journeyed to Leyden first of all," he resumed, "and sought out the gunmaker. But he
did not remember selling the pistol, or, perhaps,
would not—at all events, we got no help from him,
and went on to London. In the beginning I believe
Countess Lukstein was inclined to suspect Mr.
Marston. You see he came from Bristol, and so
completely did this search possess her that everything which concerned that city seemed to her to
have some bearing upon her disaster. But she
soon abandoned that idea, and—and—well, I know
not why, but Mr. Marston left London for a time.
Then you were brought to the house, and on your
first visit you told her that your home was in
Cumberland, where Sir Julian Harnwood lived ; that
you had been till recently a student at Leyden,
and that there were few other English students
there besides yourself. At first I think she did not
seriously accuse you of Count Lukstein's death.
It seemed little likely ; you had not the look of
it. I did not recognise you at all, and, further, my
mistress herself inquired much of you concerning
your actions, and you let slip no hint that could
convict you."

I remembered what interest the Countess had
seemed to take in my uneventful history, and how
her questions had delighted me, flattering my vanity
and lifting me to the topmasts of hope ; and the
irony of my recollections made me laugh aloud.

"Howbeit," he went on, paying no heed to my
interruption—there was no great merriment in my
laughter, and it may be that he understood—"Howbeit, her suspicions were alert, and then Mr. Marston

came back to London. She learnt from him that
you had passed through London in a great hurry
one night, and from Lord Culverton that the night
was in September and that your destination was
Bristol. I wanted to ride there and see what I could
discover, but my mistress would not allow me. I
don't know, but at that time I almost fancied she
regretted her resolve, and would fain have let the
matter lie."

'Twas at that time also, I remembered, that the
Countess treated me so waywardly, and I coupled
Otto's remark and my remembrance together, and
set them aside as food for future pondering.

"Then she showed you the miniature. You
faced it out and denied all knowledge of it. So far
so good. But that same morning you brought Lady
Tracy into the house, and that was the ruin of you.
Oh, I know," he went on as I sought to interrupt
him, "I know! You faced that matter out too.
You brought Lady Tracy to bear witness that you
and she were never acquainted. 'Twas a cunning
device and it deceived my mistress; but you did
not take me into account. I opened the door to
you, and I recognised Lady Tracy as the original
of the miniature. Well, I looked at her carefully,
wondering whether I could have made a mistake,
whether it was she whom I had seen at the Bristol
prison after all. I felt certain it was not, but all
the same I kept thinking about it as I went upstairs
to announce you. Lady Tracy was dark; the other
woman, I remembered, fair and over-tall for a
woman. So I went on comparing them, setting
the two faces side by side in my mind. Well, when

I came back again there were you and Lady Tracy
standing side by side—the two faces that were side
by side in my thoughts. The sunlight was full upon
you both. Lord! I was cluttered out of my senses.
I knew you at once. Height, face, everything fitted.
I told my mistress immediately after you had gone.
She would not believe it at first; but soon after she
informed me that Lady Tracy had been betrothed
to Sir Julian Harnwood. That night we visited your
rooms, as I have told you."

"Ay," said I, "Marston told her of his sister's
betrothal in Covent Garden."

'Twas indeed at the very time that the Countess
was tracing that diagram in the gravel.

"The visit to your rooms convinced Countess
Lukstein."

"No doubt," said I, and I explained to him
how she had traced the diagram, and my mention
of the date which had given her the clue to my
Horace.

"But that's not all," he laughed. "'Tis true that
my mistress knew that she had seen that same plan
somewhere. 'Tis true your mention of the date told
her where. But the plan which my lady drew on
the gravel was different from yours in one respect.
It lacked the line which showed your way of ascent,
the line which stood for the rib of rock."

"Well?"

"Well, you added that line yourself while you
were talking."

"I did!" I exclaimed.

I could not credit it; but then I recollected how

Ilga had suddenly stooped forward and obliterated
the diagram with a sweep of her stick.

" Ay, Otto ! " I said.   " You spoke truth indeed.
I set the traps myself."

" The next morning we started for Bristol.   We
drove to the ' Thatched House Tavern,' and with
the help of a few coins wormed the truth from the
chambermaid.   She had told me before that a man
had stayed at the inn on that particular night
and I had no doubt who was the man.   We knew
the story ; we merely needed her to confirm it."

With that he laid his pipe aside, and was for
settling to sleep.   But I had one more question to
ask him.

"When Lord Elmscott came to find me at
Countess Lukstein's apartments, he was informed I
was not there, and the door of the room in which I
lay was locked."

" We intended to convey you out of the country
ourselves," he laughed, " and that very night.
'Twould indeed have saved much trouble had Lord
Elmscott been delayed an hour or so upon the road.
A boat was in waiting for us on the river."

'Twas long before I could follow Otto's example
and compose myself to sleep.   Using his narrative
as a commentary, I read over and over again my
memories of those weeks in London, and each time
I felt yet more convinced that this deed had been
brought home to me through no cunning of the
Countess, through no great folly of mine, but simply
because Providence had so willed it.   As Otto said,
I had set the traps myself, and bethinking me of

this, I recalled a phrase which I had spoken to Count Lukstein. "I can fight you," I had said, "but I can't fight your wife." In what a strange way had the remark come true!

The next morning Otto departed from the hollow, and fearing lest he might presently despatch two other of Countess Lukstein's servants to fill up the complement of my guards, I determined to make my effort at enlargement that very night. I took my axe boldly from the corner of the room when the time came for me to mount to the loft. The peasants scowled but said nothing, and 'twas with a very great relief that I understood Otto had been as good as his word. It had been my habit of late to secrete about me at each meal some fragment of my portion of bread, so that I had now a good number of such morsels hidden away among the leaves of my bed. These I gathered together, and fastened inside my shirt, and then sat me down, with such patience as I might, to wait until the peasants beneath me were sound asleep. The delay would have been more endurable had there been some window or opening in the loft. But to sit there in the darkness, never knowing but what the sky was clouding over and a storm gathering upon the heights, 'twas the quintessence of suspense, and it wrought in me like a fever. I allowed two hours, as near as I could guess, to elapse, and then, working quietly with my axe, I cut a hole through the thatch at the corner most distant from the room of my gaolers, and dropped some twelve feet on to the ground. There was no moon to light me but the sparkle of innumerable stars, and the night was black in the valley and purple about the cheerless hills. Cautiously I made my way over the grass towards the ridge, taking the air into my lungs with an exquisite enjoyment like one that has long been cooped in a sick-room.

Whimsically enough, I thought not at all of the dangers which were like to beset me, but rather of Ilga in her Castle of Lukstein; and walking forwards in the lonely quiet, I wondered ˉwhether at that moment she was asleep.

The ridge, as I had hoped, was entirely compacted of earth and stones. 'Twas thrown up to a considerable height above the ice, and resembled a great earthwork raised for defence, such as I have seen since about the walls of Londonderry. I was able to walk along the crest for some way with no more peril than was occasioned by the darkness and the narrow limits of my path, and taking to some rocks which jutted out from the snow, about two hours after daybreak, I reached the top of the hill at noon. To my great delight I perceived that I stood, as it were, upon a neck of the mountain. To my left the Wildthurm rose in a sweeping line of ice, ever higher and higher towards the peak; to my right it terminated in a ridge of rocks which again rose upwards, and circled about the head of the ravine. I had nothing to do but to descend; so I lay down to rest myself for a while, and take my last look at Captivity Hollow and the hut wherein I had been imprisoned. The descent, however, was not so easy a matter as I believed it would be. For some distance, it is true, I could walk without

much difficulty, kicking a sort of staircase in the
snow with my feet; but after a while the incline
became steeper, and, moreover, was inlaid with
strips of ice, wherein I had to cut holes with my
hatchet before I could secure a footing. Indeed,
I doubt whether I should have come safe off from
this adventure but for the many crags and rocks
which studded the slope. By keeping close to these,
however, I was able to get solid hold for my hands,
the while I stepped upon the treacherous ice.
Towards the foot of the mountain, moreover, the
ice was split with great gashes and chasms, so
deep that I could see no bottom to them, but
only an azure haze; and I was often compelled
to make long circuits before I could discover a
passage. Once or twice, besides, when the ground
seemed perfectly firm, I slipped a leg through the
crust and felt it touch nothing; and taking warning
from these accidents, I proceeded henceforth more
cautiously, tapping the snow in front of me with
the hatchet at each step.

These hindrances did so delay me that I was
still upon the mountain when night fell, and not
daring to continue this perilous journey in the dark,
I crept under the shelter of a rock, and so lay
shivering until the morning. However, I bethought
me of my loft and its thatch-roof, and contrasting
it with the open sky, passed the night pleasantly
enough. I had still enough of my bread left over
to serve me for breakfast in the morning, and since
there was no water to be got, I made shift to
moisten my throat by sucking lumps of ice. Late
that afternoon I came down into a desolate valley,

and felt the green turf once more spring beneath
my feet. 'Twas closing in very dark and black.
In front of me I could see the rain stretched across
the hills like a diaphanous veil, shot here and
there by a stray thread of sunlight; while behind,
the heights of the Wildthurm were hidden by a
white crawling mist. Looking at this mist, I could
not but be sensible of the dangers from which
I had escaped, and with a heart full of gratitude
I knelt down and thanked God for that He had
reached out His hand above me to save my
life.

For many days I journeyed among these upland
valleys, passing from hut to hut and from ravine
to ravine, moving ever westwards from Lukstein,
and descended finally into the high-road close to
the village of Nauders. Thence I proceeded along
the Inn Thal to Innspruck, earning my food each
day by cutting wood into logs at the various
taverns, or by some such service; and as for
lodging, 'twas no great hardship to sleep in the
fields at this season of the year. At Innspruck,
however, whither I came in the first days of July,
I was sore put to it to find employment, which
should keep me from starving until such time as I
could receive letters of credit from England. My
first thought was to obtain the position of usher or
master in one of the many schools and colleges of
the town. But wherever I applied they only laughed
in my face, and unceremoniously closed the door
upon my entreaties. Nor, indeed, could I wonder
at their behaviour, for what with my torn peasant's
clothes, my bare, scarred knees, and my face, which

was burnt to the colour of a ripe apple, I looked the most unlikely tutor that ever ruined a boy's education. At one school—'twas the last at which I sought employment—the master informed me that he "did his own whipping," and wandering thence in a great despondency of spirit, I came into the Neustadt, which is the principal street of the town. There I chanced to espy the sign of a fencing-master, and realising what little profit I was like to make of such rusty book-learning as I still retained, I crossed the road and proffered him the assistance of my services. At the onset he was inclined to treat my offer with no less hilarity than the schoolmasters had shown ; but being now at my wits' end, I persisted, and perhaps vaunted my skill more than befitted a gentleman. 'Twas, I think, chiefly to disprove my words, and so rid himself of me, that he bade me take a foil and stand on guard. In the first bout, however, I was lucky enough to secure the advantage, as also in the second. In a fluster of anger he insisted that I should engage upon a third, and thereupon I deemed it prudent to allow him to get the better of me, though not by so much as would give him the right to accuse me of a lack of skill. The ruse was entirely successful ; for he was so delighted with his success that he hired me straightway as his lieutenant, and was pleased to compliment me upon my mastery of the weapon ; not but what he declared I had many faults in the matter of style, which I might correct under his tuition.

In this occupation I remained for some three months. I wrote a letter immediately to Jack Larke, but received no answer whatsoever. Each week, however, I put by a certain sum out of my wages until I had accumulated sufficient to carry me, if I practised economy, to England. In the beginning of September, then, I gave up my position ; a pupil, on hearing of my purposed journey, most generously presented me with a horse, which I accepted as a loan, and one fine morning I mounted on to the animal's back and rode out towards the gates of the town.

CHAPTER XXIII.

THE LAST.

Now the road which I chose led past the Hofgarten, a great open space of lawns and shrubberies which had been enclosed and presented to the town by Leopold, the late Archduke of Styria. Opposite to the gates of this garden stood the "Black Stag," at that time the principal inn, and I noticed ahead of me four or five mounted men waiting at the door. Drawing nearer I perceived that these men wore the livery of Countess Lukstein.

My first impulse was to turn my horse's head and ride off with all speed in the contrary direction ; but bethinking me that they would never dare to make an attempt upon my liberty in the streets of an orderly city, I resolved to continue on my way, and pay no heed to them as I passed. And this I began to do, walking my horse slowly, so that they might not think I had any fear of them. Otto was stationed at the head of the troop, a few paces in advance of the rest, and I was well-nigh abreast of him before any of the servants perceived who passed them. Even then 'twas myself who invited their attention. For turning my head I saw the Countess just within the gates of the garden. She was habited in a riding-dress, and was taking leave of a gentleman who was with her.

On the instant I stopped my horse.

"Here, Otto!" I cried, and flinging the reins to him, I jumped to the ground.

I heard him give a startled exclamation, but I stayed not to cast a glance at him, and walked instantly forwards to where Ilga stood. I was within two paces of her before she turned and saw me. She reached out a hand to the gate, and so steadying herself looked at me for a little without a word. I bowed low, and took another step towards her, whereupon she turned again to her companion and began to speak very volubly, the colour going and coming quickly upon her face. For my part I made no effort to interrupt her. I had schooled myself to think of her as one whom I should never see again, and here we were face to face. I remained contentedly waiting with my hat in my hand.

"You have been long in Innspruck?" she asked of me at length, and added, with some hesitation, "Mr. Buckler?"

"Three months, madame," I replied.

"But you are leaving?"

She looked across to my horse, which Otto was holding. A small valise, containing the few necessaries I possessed, was slung to the saddle-bow.

"I return to England," said I.

She presented me to the gentleman who talked with her, but I did not catch his name any more than the conversation they resumed. 'Twas enough for me to hear the sweet sound of her voice; as, when a singer sings, one is charmed by the music of his tones, and recks little of the words of his song. At last, however, her companion made his bow. Ilga stretched out her hand to him and said:

"You will come, then, to Lukstein?" and detaining him, as it seemed to me, she added, "I would ask Mr. Buckler to come, too, only I fear that he has no great opinion of our hospitality."

"Madame," I replied simply, "if you ask me, I will come."

She stood for the space of some twenty seconds with her eyes bent upon the ground. Then, raising her face with a look which was wonderfully timid and shy, she said:

"You are a brave man, Mr. Buckler"; and after another pause, " I do ask you."

With that she crossed the road and mounted upon her horse. I did the same, and the little cavalcade rode out from Innspruck along the highway to Landeck. The Countess pressed on ahead, and thinking that she had no wish to speak with me, I rode some paces behind her. Behind me came Otto and the servants. Otto, I should say, had resumed his old impenetrable air. He was once more the servant, and seemed to have completely forgotten our companionship in Captivity Hollow. Thus we travelled until we came near to the village of Silz.

Now all this morning one regretful thought had been buzzing in my head. 'Twas an old thought, one that I had lived with many a month. Yet

never had it become familiar to me; the pain which
it brought was always fresh and sharp. But now,
since I saw Countess Lukstein again, since she rode
in front of me, since each moment my eyes beheld
her, this regret grew and grew until it was lost in
a great longing to speak out my mind, and, if so
I might, ease myself of my burden. Consequently I
spurred my horse lightly, and as we entered Silz
I drew level with the Countess.

"Madame," I said, "I see plainly enough that
you have no heart for my company, neither do
I intend any idle intrusion. I would but say two
words to you. They have been on my lips ever
since I caught sight of you on the Hofgarten; they
have been in my heart for the weariest span of
days. When I told you that I entered Castle
Lukstein alone, God is my witness that I spoke
the truth. No woman was with me. I championed
no woman; by no ties was I bound to any woman
in this world. This I would have you believe;
for it is the truth. I could not lie to you if I
would; it is the truth."

She made me no answer, but bowed her head
down on her horse's mane, so that I could see
nothing of her face, and thinking sadly that she
would not credit me, I tightened my reins that
I might fall back behind her. It may be that she
noticed the movement of my hands. I know not,
nor, indeed, shall I be at any pains to speculate
upon her motive. 'Twas her action which occupied
my thoughts then and for hours afterwards. She
suddenly lifted her face towards me, all rosy with
blushes and wearing that sweet look which I had

· 2 B

once and once only remarked before. I mean when she pledged me in her apartments in Pall Mall.

"Then," says she, "we will travel no further afield to-day," and she drew rein before the first inn we came to.

I was greatly perplexed by this precipitate action, also by the word she used, inasmuch as we were not travelling afield at all, but on the contrary directly towards her home. Besides, 'twas still early in the afternoon. Howbeit, there we stayed, and the Countess retiring privately to her room, I saw no more of her until the night was come. 'Twas about eleven of the clock when I heard a light tap upon my door, and opening it, I perceived that she was my visitor. She laid a finger upon her lip and slipped quietly into the room. In her hand she held her hat and whip, and these she laid upon the table.

"You have not inquired," she began, "why I asked you to return with me to Lukstein, what end I had in view."

"In truth, madame," I replied, "I gave no thought to it ; only—only——"

"Only I asked you, and you came," she said in a voice that broke and faltered. "Even after all you had suffered at my hands, even in spite of what you still might suffer, I asked you, and you came."

She spoke in a low wondering tone, and with a queer feeling of shame I hastened to reply:

"Madame, if you were in my place, you would understand that there is little strange in that."

"Let me finish!" she said. "Lord Elmscott
and your friend, Mr. Larke, are awaiting you at
Lukstein. When your friend returned to England
without you, he could hear no word of you. He
had no acquaintance with Lord Elmscott, and did
not know of him at all. He met Lord Elmscott
in London this spring for the first time. It appears
that your cousin suspected something of the trouble
that stood between you and me, but until he met
Mr. Larke he believed you were travelling in Italy.
Mr. Larke gave him the account of your first journey
into the Tyrol. They found out Sir Julian's attorney
at Bristol, and learned the cause of it from him.
They came to Lukstein two months ago, and told
me what you would not. I went up to the hills
myself to bring you home; you had escaped, and
your—the men had concealed your flight in fear
of my anger. Lord Elmscott went to Meran, I
came to Innspruck; and we arranged to return
after we had searched a month. The month is gone.
They will be at Lukstein now."

So much she said, though with many a pause
and with so keen a self-reproach in her tone that
I could hardly bear to hear her, when I interrupted:

"And you have been a month searching for me
in Innspruck?"

She took no heed of my interruption.

"So, you see," she continued, "I know the whole
truth. I know, too, that you hid the truth out
of kindness to me, and—and——"

She was wearing the gold cross which I had
sent to her by Otto s hand. It hung on a long

chain about her neck, and I took it gently into my palm.

"And is there nothing more you know?" I asked.

"I know that you love me," she whispered, "that you love me still. Oh! how is it possible?" And then she raised her eyes to mine and laid two trembling hands upon my shoulders. "But it is true. You told me so this afternoon."

"I told you?" I asked in some surprise.

"Ay, and more surely than if you had spoken it out. That is why I stopped our horses in the village. It is why I am with you now."

She glanced towards her hat and whip, and I understood. I realised what it would cost her to carry me back as her guest to Lukstein after all that had passed there.

I opened the door and stepped out on to the landing. A panel of moonlight was marked out upon the floor. 'Twas the only light in the passage, and the house was still as an empty cave. When I came back into the room Ilga was standing with her hat upon her head.

"And what of Lukstein?"

"A sop to Father Spaur," she said with a happy laugh, and reaching out a hand to me she blew out the candle. I guided her to the landing, and there stopped and kissed her.

"I have hungered for that," said I, "for a year and more."

"And I too," she whispered, "dear heart, and I too," and I felt her arms tighten about my neck. "Oh, how you must have hated me!" she said.

"I called you no harder name than 'la belle dame sans merci,'" said I.

We crept down the stairs a true couple of runaways. The door was secured by a wooden bar. I removed the bar, and we went out into the road. The stables lay to the right of the inn, and leaving Ilga where she stood, I crossed over to them and rapped quietly at the window. The ostler let me in, and we saddled quickly Ilga's horse and mine. I gave the fellow all of my three months' savings, and bidding him go back to his bed, brought the horses into the road.

I lifted Ilga into the saddle.

"So," she said, bending over me, and her heart looked through her eyes, "the lath was steel after all, and I only found it out when the steel cut me."

And that night we rode hand in hand to Innspruck. Once she trilled out a snatch of song, and I knew indeed that Jack Larke was waiting for me at Lukstein. For the words she sang were from an old ballad of Froissart :

> Que toutes joies et toutes honneurs
> Viennent d'armes et d'amours.

THE END.

F M. EVANS AND CO., LIMITED, PRINTERS, CRYSTAL PALACE, S.E.

A CLASSIFIED

CATALOGUE OF BOOKS

IN GENERAL LITERATURE

PUBLISHED BY

MACMILLAN AND CO., LTD.

BEDFORD STREET, STRAND, LONDON, W.C.

For purely Educational Works see MACMILLAN AND CO.'s *Educational Catalogue.*

AGRICULTURE.

(*See also* BOTANY; GARDENING.)

FRANKLAND (Prof. P. F.).—A HANDBOOK OF AGRICULTURAL CHEMICAL ANALYSIS. Cr. 8vo. 7s. 6d.

KING (F. H.).—THE SOIL, ITS NATURE, ETC. Fcp. 8vo. 3s. net.

LAURIE (A. P.).—PRIMER OF AGRICULTURAL CHEMISTRY, or THE FOOD OF PLANTS. Pott 8vo. 1s.

MUIR (J.).—MANUAL OF DAIRY WORK. Pott 8vo. 1s.

—— AGRICULTURE, PRACTICAL AND SCIENTIFIC. Cr. 8vo. 4s. 6d.

NICHOLLS (H. A. A.).—TEXT BOOK OF TROPICAL AGRICULTURE. Cr. 8vo. 6s.

TANNER (Henry).—ELEMENTARY LESSONS IN THE SCIENCE OF AGRICULTURAL PRACTICE. Fcp. 8vo. 3s. 6d.

—— FIRST PRINCIPLES OF AGRICULTURE. Pott 8vo. 1s.

—— THE PRINCIPLES OF AGRICULTURE. For Use in Elementary Schools. Ext. fcp. 8vo.— THE ALPHABET OF THE PRINCIPLES OF AGRICULTURE. 6d.—FURTHER STEPS IN THE PRINCIPLES OF AGRICULTURE. 1s.— ELEMENTARY SCHOOL READINGS ON THE PRINCIPLES OF AGRICULTURE FOR THE THIRD STAGE. 1s.

—— THE ABBOT'S FARM; or, Practice with Science. Cr. 8vo. 3s. 6d.

ANATOMY, Human. (*See* PHYSIOLOGY.)

ANTHROPOLOGY.

BROWN (J. Allen).—PALÆOLITHIC MAN IN NORTH-WEST MIDDLESEX. 8vo. 7s. 6d.

DAWKINS (Prof. W. Boyd).—EARLY MAN IN BRITAIN AND HIS PLACE IN THE TERTIARY PERIOD. Med. 8vo. 25s.

DE QUATREFAGES (A.).—THE PYGMIES. Translated by F. STARR. Cr. 8vo. 6s. net.

FINCK (Henry T.).—ROMANTIC LOVE AND PERSONAL BEAUTY. 2 vols. Cr. 8vo. 18s.

FISON (L.) and HOWITT (A. W.).—KAMILAROI AND KURNAI GROUP. Group-Marriage and Relationship, and Marriage by Elopement. 8vo. 15s.

FRAZER (J. G.).—THE GOLDEN BOUGH: A Study in Comparative Religion. 2 vols. 8vo. 28s.

GALTON (Francis).—ENGLISH MEN OF SCIENCE: THEIR NATURE AND NURTURE. 8vo. 8s. 6d.

GALTON (Francis).—NATURAL INHERITANCE. 8vo. 9s.

—— INQUIRIES INTO HUMAN FACULTY AND ITS DEVELOPMENT. 8vo. 16s.

—— LIFE-HISTORY ALBUM: Being a Personal Note-book, combining Diary, Photograph Album, a Register of Height, Weight, and other Anthropometrical Observations, and a Record of Illnesses. 4to. 3s. 6d.—Or with Cards of Wool for Testing Colour Vision. 4s. 6d.

—— RECORD OF FAMILY FACULTIES. Consisting of Tabular Forms and Directions for Entering Data. 4to. 2s. 6d.

—— HEREDITARY GENIUS: An Enquiry into its Laws and Consequences. Ext. cr. 8vo. 7s. net.

—— FINGER PRINTS. 8vo. 6s. net.

—— BLURRED FINGER PRINTS. 8vo. 2s. 6d. net.

—— FINGERPRINT DIRECTORIES. 8vo. 5s. net.

HOFFMAN (W. J.).—THE BEGINNINGS OF WRITING. Cr. 8vo. 6s. net.

M'LENNAN (J. F.).—THE PATRIARCHAL THEORY. Edited and completed by DONALD M'LENNAN, M.A. 8vo. 14s.

—— STUDIES IN ANCIENT HISTORY. Comprising "Primitive Marriage." 8vo. 16s.

MASON (O. T.).—WOMAN'S SHARE IN PRIMITIVE CULTURE. Cr. 8vo. 6s. net.

MONTELIUS—WOODS. —THE CIVILISATION OF SWEDEN IN HEATHEN TIMES. By Prof. OSCAR MONTELIUS. Translated by Rev. F. H. WOODS. Illustr. 8vo. 14s.

ORR (H. B.).—THEORY OF DEVELOPMENT AND HEREDITY. Cr. 8vo. 6s. net.

RATZEL (F.).—HISTORY OF MANKIND. Ed. by E. B. TYLOR. In 30 Monthly Parts. Roy. 8vo. 1s. net each

SEEBOHM (H. E.).—STRUCTURE OF GREEK TRIBAL SOCIETY. 8vo. 5s. net.

TURNER (Rev. Geo.).—SAMOA, A HUNDRED YEARS AGO AND LONG BEFORE. Cr. 8vo. 9s.

TYLOR (E. B.).—ANTHROPOLOGY. With Illustrations. Cr. 8vo. 7s. 6d.

WESTERMARCK (Dr. Edward).—THE HISTORY OF HUMAN MARRIAGE. With Preface by Dr. A. R. WALLACE. 2nd Edit. 8vo. 14s. net.

WILSON (Sir Daniel).—PREHISTORIC ANNALS OF SCOTLAND. Illustrated. 2 vols. 8vo. 36s.

—— PREHISTORIC MAN: Researches into the Origin of Civilisation in the Old and New World. Illustrated. 2 vols. 8vo. 36s.

—— THE RIGHT HAND: LEFT-HANDEDNESS. Cr. 8vo. 4s. 6d.

ANTIQUITIES.

(See also ANTHROPOLOGY.*)*

ATKINSON (Rev. J. C.).—FORTY YEARS IN A MOORLAND PARISH. Ext. cr. 8vo. 8s. 6d. net.—*Illustrated Edition.* 12s. net.

—— MEMORIALS OF OLD WHITBY. Illust. Ex. cr. 8vo. 6s. net.

BURN (Robert).—ROMAN LITERATURE IN RELATION TO ROMAN ART. With Illustrations. Ext. cr. 8vo. 14s.

DILETTANTI SOCIETY'S PUBLICATIONS.
ANTIQUITIES OF IONIA. Vols. I.—III. 2l. 2s. each, or 5l. 5s. the set, net.—Vol. IV. Folio, half morocco, 3l. 13s. 6d. net.
AN INVESTIGATION OF THE PRINCIPLES OF ATHENIAN ARCHITECTURE. By F. C. PENROSE. Illustrated. Folio. 7l. 7s. net.
SPECIMENS OF ANCIENT SCULPTURE: EGYPTIAN, ETRUSCAN, GREEK, AND ROMAN. Vol. II. Folio. 5l. 5s. net.

DYER (Louis).—STUDIES OF THE GODS IN GREECE AT CERTAIN SANCTUARIES RECENTLY EXCAVATED. Ext. cr. 8vo. 8s.6d. net.

ERMAN (A.).—LIFE IN ANCIENT EGYPT. Transl. by H. M. TIRARD. Illust. Super-royal 8vo. 21s. net.

EVANS (Lady). CHAPTERS ON GREEK DRESS. Illustrated. 8vo. 5s. net.

FOWLER (W. W.).—THE CITY-STATE OF THE GREEKS AND ROMANS. Cr. 8vo. 5s.

GARDNER (Ernest).—HANDBOOK OF GREEK SCULPTURE. Illustrated. Ex. cr. 8vo. 5s.

GARDNER (Percy).—SAMOS AND SAMIAN COINS: An Essay. 8vo. 7s. 6d.

GOW (J., Litt.D.).—A COMPANION TO SCHOOL CLASSICS. Illustrated. 3rd Ed. Cr. 8vo. 6s.

HARRISON (Miss Jane) and VERRALL (Mrs.).—MYTHOLOGY AND MONUMENTS OF ANCIENT ATHENS. Illustrated. Cr. 8vo. 16s.

HELLENIC SOCIETY'S PUBLICATIONS
—EXCAVATIONS AT MEGALOPOLIS, 1890—1891. By Messrs. E. A. GARDNER, W. LORING, G. C. RICHARDS, and W. J. WOODHOUSE. With an Architectural Description by R. W. SCHULTZ. 4to. 25s.

—— ECCLESIASTICAL SITES IN ISAURIA (CILICIA TRACHEA). By the Rev. A. C. HEADLAM. Imp. 4to. 5s.

JONES (H. S.).—SELECT PASSAGES FROM ANCIENT WRITERS, ILLUSTRATIVE OF THE HISTORY OF GREEK SCULPTURE. 8vo. 7s. net.

LANCIANI (Prof. R.).—ANCIENT ROME IN THE LIGHT OF RECENT DISCOVERIES. 4to. 24s.

—— PAGAN AND CHRISTIAN ROME. 4to. 24s.

MAHAFFY (Prof. J. P.).—A PRIMER OF GREEK ANTIQUITIES. Pott 8vo. 1s.

—— SOCIAL LIFE IN GREECE FROM HOMER TO MENANDER. 6th Edit. Cr. 8vo. 9s.

—— RAMBLES AND STUDIES IN GREECE. Illustrated. 3rd Edit. Cr. 8vo. 10s. 6d.

(See also HISTORY, p. 13.*)*

NEWTON (Sir C. T.).—ESSAYS ON ART AND ARCHÆOLOGY. 8vo. 12s. 6d.

SCHUCHHARDT (C.).—DR. SCHLIEMANN'S EXCAVATIONS AT TROY, TIRYNS, MYCENAE, ORCHOMENOS, ITHACA, IN THE LIGHT OF RECENT KNOWLEDGE. Trans. by EUGENIE SELLERS. Preface by WALTER LEAF, Litt.D. Illustrated. 8vo. 18s. net.

SCHREIBER (T.).—ATLAS OF CLASSICAL ANTIQUITIES. Edit. by W. C. F. ANDERSON. Oblong 4to. 21s. net.

STRANGFORD. *(See* VOYAGES & TRAVELS.)

WALDSTEIN (C.).—CATALOGUE OF CASTS IN THE MUSEUM OF CLASSICAL ARCHÆOLOGY, CAMBRIDGE. Crown 8vo. 1s. 6d.—Large Paper Edition. Small 4to. 5s.

WHITE (Gilbert). *(See* NATURAL HISTORY.)

WILKINS (Prof. A. S.).—A PRIMER OF ROMAN ANTIQUITIES. Pott 8vo. 1s.

ARCHÆOLOGY. *(See* ANTIQUITIES.)

ARCHITECTURE.

AVERY ARCHITECTURAL CATALOGUE. Imp. 8vo, half mor. 50s. net.

FREEMAN (Prof. E. A.).—HISTORY OF THE CATHEDRAL CHURCH OF WELLS. Cr. 8vo. 3s. 6d.

HULL (E.).—A TREATISE ON ORNAMENTAL AND BUILDING STONES OF GREAT BRITAIN AND FOREIGN COUNTRIES. 8vo. 12s.

LETHABY (W. R.) and SWAINSON (H.). —THE CHURCH OF ST. SOPHIA AT CONSTANTINOPLE. Illust. Med. 8vo. 21s. net.

MOORE (Prof. C. H.).—THE DEVELOPMENT AND CHARACTER OF GOTHIC ARCHITECTURE. Illustrated. Med. 8vo. 18s.

PENROSE (F. C.). *(See* ANTIQUITIES.)

STEVENSON (J. J.).—HOUSE ARCHITECTURE. With Illustrations. 2 vols. Roy. 8vo. 18s. each.—Vol. I. ARCHITECTURE; Vol. II. HOUSE PLANNING.

ART.

(See also MUSIC.)

ANDERSON (L.). LINEAR PERSPECTIVE AND MODEL DRAWING. 8vo. 2s.

ART AT HOME SERIES. Edited by W. J. LOFTIE, B.A. Cr. 8vo.
THE BEDROOM AND BOUDOIR. By Lady BARKER. 2s. 6d.
NEEDLEWORK. By ELIZABETH GLAISTER. Illustrated. 2s. 6d.
MUSIC IN THE HOUSE. By JOHN HULLAH. 4th edit. 2s. 6d.
THE DINING-ROOM. By Mrs. LOFTIE. With Illustrations. 2nd Edit. 2s. 6d.
AMATEUR THEATRICALS. By WALTER H. POLLOCK and LADY POLLOCK. Illustrated by KATE GREENAWAY. 2s. 6d.

ATKINSON (J. B.).—AN ART TOUR TO NORTHERN CAPITALS OF EUROPE. 8vo. 12s.

BENSON (W. A. S.). HANDICRAFT AND DESIGN. Cr. 8vo. 5s. net.

BURN (Robert). *(See* ANTIQUITIES.)

CARR (J. C.)—PAPERS ON ART. Cr. 8vo. 8s. 6d.

COLLIER (Hon. John).—A PRIMER OF ART. Pott 8vo. 1s.

COOK (E. T.).—A POPULAR HANDBOOK TO THE NATIONAL GALLERY. Including Notes collected from the Works of Mr. RUSKIN. 4th Edit. Cr. 8vo, half morocco. 14s.—Large paper Edition, 250 copies. 2 vols. 8vo.

DELAMOTTE (Prof. P. H.).—A BEGINNER'S DRAWING-BOOK. Cr. 8vo. 3s. 6d.

ELLIS (Tristram).—SKETCHING FROM NATURE. Illustr. by H. STACY MARKS, R.A., and the Author. 2nd Edit. Cr. 8vo. 3s. 6d.

FLORY (M. A.).—A BOOK ABOUT FANS. Ex. Cr. 8vo. 10s. 6d.

HAMERTON (P. G.).—THOUGHTS ABOUT ART. New Edit. Cr. 8vo. 8s. 6d.

HOOPER (W. H.) and PHILLIPS (W. C).—A MANUAL OF MARKS ON POTTERY AND PORCELAIN. 2nd Edit. 16mo. 4s. 6d.

HUNT (W.).—TALKS ABOUT ART. With a Letter from Sir J. E. MILLAIS, Bart., R.A. Cr. 8vo. 3s. 6d.

HUTCHINSON (G. W. C.).—SOME HINTS ON LEARNING TO DRAW. Roy. 8vo. 8s. 6d.

LA FARGE (J.)—CONSIDERATIONS ON PAINTING. Cr. 8vo. 6s. net.

LAURIE (A. P.).—FACTS ABOUT PROCESSES, PIGMENTS, AND VEHICLES. Cr. 8vo. 3s. net.

LECTURES ON ART. By REGD. STUART POOLE, Professor W. B. RICHMOND, E. J. POYNTER, R.A., J. T. MICKLETHWAITE, and WILLIAM MORRIS. Cr. 8vo. 4s. 6d.

NEWTON (Sir C. T.).—(See ANTIQUITIES.)

PALGRAVE (Prof. F. T.).—ESSAYS ON ART. Ext. fcp. 8vo. 6s.

PATER (W.).—THE RENAISSANCE: Studies In Art and Poetry. 5th Edit. Cr. 8vo. 10s. 6d.

PENNELL (Joseph).—PEN DRAWING AND PEN DRAUGHTSMEN. New and Enlarged Edit., with 400 Illust. 4to Buckram. 42s. net.

PROPERT (J. Lumsden).—A HISTORY OF MINIATURE ART. Illustrated. Super roy. 4to. 3l. 13s. 6d.—Bound in vellum. 4l. 14s. 6d.

SPANTON (J. H.).—SCIENCE AND ART DRAWING. 8vo. 10s. net.

TAYLOR (E. R.).—DRAWING AND DESIGN. Ob. cr. 8vo. 2s. 6d.

THOMPSON (E.).—ANATOMY FOR ARTISTS. [In the Press.

TURNER'S LIBER STUDIORUM: A DESCRIPTION AND A CATALOGUE. By W. G. RAWLINSON. Med. 8vo. 12s. 6d.

TYRWHITT (Rev. R. St. John).—OUR SKETCHING CLUB. 5th Edit. Cr. 8vo. 7s. 6d.

WARE (W. R.).—MODERN PERSPECTIVE. With Plates. 5th. Edit. 4to. 21s. net.

WYATT (Sir M. Digby).—FINE ART: A Sketch of its History, Theory, Practice, and Application to Industry. 8vo. 5s.

ASTRONOMY.

AIRY (Sir G. B.).—POPULAR ASTRONOMY. Illustrated. 7th Edit. Fcp. 8vo. 4s. 6d.
—— GRAVITATION. An Elementary Explanation of the Principal Perturbations in the Solar System. 2nd Edit. Cr. 8vo. 7s. 6d.

BLAKE (J. F.).—ASTRONOMICAL MYTHS. With Illustrations. Cr. 8vo. 9s.

CHEYNE (C. H. H.).—AN ELEMENTARY TREATISE ON THE PLANETARY THEORY. Cr. 8vo. 7s. 6d.

CLARK (L.) and SADLER (H.).—THE STAR GUIDE. Roy. 8vo. 5s.

CROSSLEY (E.), GLEDHILL (J.), and WILSON (J. M.).—A HANDBOOK OF DOUBLE STARS. 8vo. 21s.
—— CORRECTIONS TO THE HANDBOOK OF DOUBLE STARS. 8vo. 1s.

FORBES (Prof. George).—THE TRANSIT OF VENUS. Illustrated. Cr. 8vo. 3s. 6d.

GODFRAY (Hugh). — AN ELEMENTARY TREATISE ON THE LUNAR THEORY. 2nd Edit. Cr. 8vo. 5s. 6d.
—— A TREATISE ON ASTRONOMY, FOR THE USE OF COLLEGES AND SCHOOLS. 8vo. 12s. 6d.

GREGORY (R. A.).—THE PLANET EARTH. Gl. 8vo. 2s.

LOCKYER (J. Norman, F.R.S.).—A PRIMER OF ASTRONOMY. Illustrated. Pott 8vo. 1s.
—— ELEMENTARY LESSONS IN ASTRONOMY. Illustr. New Edition. Fcp. 8vo. 5s. 6d.
—— QUESTIONS ON THE SAME. By J. FORBES ROBERTSON. Fcp. 8vo. 1s. 6d.
—— THE CHEMISTRY OF THE SUN. Illustrated. 8vo. 14s.
—— THE METEORITIC HYPOTHESIS OF THE ORIGIN OF COSMICAL SYSTEMS. Illustrated. 8vo. 17s. net.
—— THE EVOLUTION OF THE HEAVENS AND THE EARTH. Illustrated. Cr. 8vo. [In the Press.
—— STAR-GAZING PAST AND PRESENT. Expanded from Notes with the assistance of G. M. SEABROKE. Roy. 8vo. 21s.

LODGE (O. J.).—PIONEERS OF SCIENCE. Ex. cr. 8vo. 7s. 6d.

MILLER (R. Kalley).—THE ROMANCE OF ASTRONOMY. 2nd Edit. Cr. 8vo. 4s. 6d.

NEWCOMB (Prof. Simon).—POPULAR ASTRONOMY. Engravings and Maps. 8vo. 18s.

ROSCOE—SCHUSTER. (See CHEMISTRY.)

ATLASES.

(See also GEOGRAPHY).

BARTHOLOMEW (J. G.).—ELEMENTARY SCHOOL ATLAS. 4to. 1s.
—— PHYSICAL AND POLITICAL SCHOOL ATLAS. 80 maps. 4to. 8s. 6d.; half mor. 10s. 6d.
—— LIBRARY REFERENCE ATLAS OF THE WORLD. With Index to 100,000 places. Folio. 52s. 6d. net.—Also in 7 parts, 5s. net each; Geographical Index. 7s. 6d. net.

LABBERTON (R. H.).—NEW HISTORICAL ATLAS AND GENERAL HISTORY. 4to. 15s.

BIBLE. (See under THEOLOGY, p. 38.)

BIBLIOGRAPHY.

A BIBLIOGRAPHICAL CATALOGUE OF MACMILLAN AND CO.'S PUBLICATIONS, 1843—89. Med. 8vo. 10s. net.

MAYOR (Prof. John E. B.).—A BIBLIOGRAPHICAL CLUE TO LATIN LITERATURE. Cr. 8vo. 10s. 6d.

RYLAND (F.).—CHRONOLOGICAL OUTLINES OF ENGLISH LITERATURE. Cr. 8vo. 6s.

SMITH (Adam).—CATALOGUE OF LIBRARY. Ed. by J. BONAR. 8vo. 7s. 6d. net.

WHITCOMB (L. S.).—CHRONOLOGICAL OUTLINES OF AMERICAN LITERATURE. Introduction by BRANDER MATTHEWS. Cr. 8vo. 6s. net.

BIOGRAPHY.

(*See also* HISTORY.)

AGASSIZ (Louis): LIFE AND CORRESPON-
DENCE. Ed. by E. C. AGASSIZ. 2 vols.
Cr. 8vo. 18*s.*
—— LIFE, LETTERS, AND WORKS. By J.
MARCOU. 2 vols. 8vo. 17*s.* net.

ALBEMARLE (Earl of).—FIFTY YEARS OF
MY LIFE. 3rd Edit., revised. Cr. 8vo. 7*s. 6d.*

ALFRED THE GREAT. By THOMAS
HUGHES. Cr. 8vo. 6*s.*

AMIEL(H. F.)–THE JOURNAL INTIME. Trans.
Mrs. HUMPHRY WARD. 2nd Ed. Cr. 8vo. 6*s.*

ANDREWS (Dr. Thomas). (*See* PHYSICS.)

ARNAULD (Angelique). By FRANCES
MARTIN. Cr. 8vo. 4*s. 6d.*

ARTEVELDE. JAMES AND PHILIP VAN
ARTEVELDE. By W. J. ASHLEY. Cr. 8vo. 6*s.*

BACON (Francis): AN ACCOUNT OF HIS LIFE
AND WORKS. By E. A. ABBOTT. 8vo. 14*s.*

BAKER (Sir. S. W.).—A MEMOIR. By T.
DOUGLAS MURRAY and A. SILVA WHITE.
8vo. 21*s.*

BARNES. LIFE OF WILLIAM BARNES, POET
AND PHILOLOGIST. By his Daughter, LUCY
BAXTER ("Leader Scott"). Cr. 8vo. 7*s. 6d.*

BERLIOZ (Hector): AUTOBIOGRAPHY OF.
Trns. by R. & E. HOLMES. 2 vols. Cr. 8vo. 21*s.*

BERNARD (St.). THE LIFE AND TIMES OF
ST. BERNARD, ABBOT OF CLAIRVAUX. By
J. C. MORISON, M.A. Cr. 8vo. 6*s.*

BLACKBURNE. LIFE OF THE RIGHT HON.
FRANCIS BLACKBURNE, late Lord Chancellor
of Ireland, by his Son, EDWARD BLACK-
BURNE. With Portrait. 8vo. 12*s.*

BLAKE. LIFE OF WILLIAM BLAKE. With
Selections from his Poems, etc. Illustr. from
Blake's own Works. By ALEXANDER GIL-
CHRIST. 2 vols. Med. 8vo. 42*s.*

BOLEYN (Anne): A CHAPTER OF ENGLISH
HISTORY, 1527—36. By PAUL FRIEDMANN.
2 vols. 8vo. 28*s.*

BROOKE (Sir Jas.), THE RAJA OF SARA-
WAK (Life of). By GERTRUDE L. JACOB.
2 vols. 8vo. 25*s.*

BURKE. By JOHN MORLEY. Globe 8vo. 5*s.*

CALVIN. (*See* SELECT BIOGRAPHY, p. 6.)

CAMPBELL (Sir G.).—MEMOIRS OF MY IN-
DIAN CAREER. Edited by Sir C. E. BER-
NARD. 2 vols. 8vo. 21*s.* net.

CARLYLE (Thomas). Edited by CHARLES
E. NORTON. Cr. 8vo.
—— REMINISCENCES. 2 vols. 12*s.*
—— EARLY LETTERS, 1814—26. 2 vols. 18*s.*
—— LETTERS, 1826—36. 2 vols. 18*s.*
—— CORRESPONDENCE BETWEEN GOETHE
AND CARLYLE. 9*s.*

CARSTARES (Wm.): A CHARACTER AND
CAREER OF THE REVOLUTIONARY EPOCH
(1649—1715). By R. H. STORY. 8vo. 12*s.*

CAVOUR. (*See* SELECT BIOGRAPHY, p. 6.)

CHATTERTON: A STORY OF THE YEAR
1770. By Prof. DAVID MASSON. Cr. 8vo. 5*s.*
—— A BIOGRAPHICAL STUDY. By Sir DANIEL
WILSON. Cr. 8vo. 6*s. 6d.*

CHURCH (R. W.).—LIFE AND LETTERS.
8vo. 7*s. 6d.*

CLARK. MEMORIALS FROM JOURNALS AND
LETTERS OF SAMUEL CLARK, M.A. Edited
by HIS WIFE. Cr. 8vo. 7*s. 6d.*

CLOUGH (A. H.). (*See* LITERATURE, p. 24.)

COLERIDGE (S. T.): A NARRATIVE OF THE
EVENTS OF HIS LIFE. By J. D. CAMPBELL.
8vo. 10*s. 6d.*

COMBE. LIFE OF GEORGE COMBE. By
CHARLES GIBBON. 2 vols. 8vo. 32*s.*

CROMWELL. (*See* SELECT BIOGRAPHY, p. 6.)

DAMIEN (Father): A JOURNEY FROM CASH-
MERE TO HIS HOME IN HAWAII. By EDWARD
CLIFFORD. Portrait. Cr. 8vo. 2*s. 6d.*

DANTE: AND OTHER ESSAYS. By Dean
CHURCH. Globe 8vo. 5*s.*

DARWIN (Charles): MEMORIAL NOTICES.
By T. H. HUXLEY, G. J. ROMANES, Sir
ARCH. GEIKIE, and W. THISELTON DYER.
With Portrait. Cr. 8vo. 2*s. 6d.*

DEAK (Francis): HUNGARIAN STATESMAN.
A Memoir. 8vo. 12*s. 6d.*

DRUMMOND OF HAWTHORNDEN. By
Prof. D. MASSON. Cr. 8vo. 10*s. 6d.*

EADIE. LIFE OF JOHN EADIE, D.D. By
JAMES BROWN, D.D. Cr. 8vo. 7*s. 6d.*

ELLIOTT. LIFE OF H. V. ELLIOTT, OF
BRIGHTON. By J. BATEMAN. Cr. 8vo. 6*s.*

EMERSON. LIFE OF RALPH WALDO EMER-
SON. By J. L. CABOT. 2 vols. Cr. 8vo. 18*s.*

ENGLISH MEN OF ACTION. Cr. 8vo.
With Portraits. 2*s. 6d.* each.
CAMPBELL (COLIN). By A. FORBES.
CLIVE. By Colonel Sir CHARLES WILSON.
COOK (CAPTAIN). By WALTER BESANT.
DAMPIER. By W. CLARK RUSSELL.
DRAKE. By JULIAN CORBETT.
DUNDONALD. By Hon. J. W. FORTESCUE.
GORDON (GENERAL). By Col. Sir W. BUTLER.
HASTINGS (WARREN). By Sir A. LYALL.
HAVELOCK (SIR HENRY). By A. FORBES.
HENRY V. By Rev. A. J. CHURCH.
LAWRENCE (LORD). By Sir RICH. TEMPLE.
LIVINGSTONE. By THOMAS HUGHES.
MONK. By JULIAN CORBETT.
MONTROSE. By MOWBRAY MORRIS.
NAPIER (SIR CHAS.). By Sir W. BUTLER.
NELSON. By J. K. LAUGHTON.
PETERBOROUGH. By W. STEBBING.
RODNEY. By DAVID HANNAY.
STRAFFORD. By H. D. TRAILL.
WARWICK, THE KING-MAKER. By C. W.
OMAN.
WELLINGTON. By GEORGE HOOPER.
WOLFE. By A. G. BRADLEY.

ENGLISH MEN OF LETTERS. Edited
by JOHN MORLEY. Crown 8vo. 1*s. 6d.*;
sewed, 1*s.*
ADDISON. By W. J. COURTHOPE.
BACON. By Dean CHURCH.
BENTLEY. By Prof. JEBB.
BUNYAN. By J. A. FROUDE.
BURKE. By JOHN MORLEY.
BURNS. By Principal SHAIRP.
BYRON. By JOHN NICHOL.
CARLYLE. By JOHN NICHOL.
CHAUCER. By Prof. A. W. WARD.
COLERIDGE. By H. D. TRAILL.
COWPER. By GOLDWIN SMITH.

BIOGRAPHY. 5

ENGLISH MEN OF LETTERS—*contd.*
DEFOE. By W. MINTO.
DE QUINCEY. By Prof. MASSON.
DICKENS. By A. W. WARD.
DRYDEN. By G. SAINTSBURY.
FIELDING. By AUSTIN DOBSON.
GIBBON. By J. COTTER MORISON.
GOLDSMITH. By WILLIAM BLACK.
GRAY. By EDMUND GOSSE.
HAWTHORNE. By HENRY JAMES.
HUME. By T. H. HUXLEY.
JOHNSON. By LESLIE STEPHEN.
KEATS. By SIDNEY COLVIN.
LAMB. By Rev. ALFRED AINGER.
LANDOR. By SIDNEY COLVIN.
LOCKE. By Prof. FOWLER.
MACAULAY. By J. COTTER MORISON.
MILTON. By MARK PATTISON.
POPE. By LESLIE STEPHEN.
SCOTT. By R. H. HUTTON.
SHELLEY. By J. A. SYMONDS.
SHERIDAN. By Mrs. OLIPHANT.
SIDNEY. By J. A. SYMONDS.
SOUTHEY. By Prof. DOWDEN.
SPENSER. By Dean CHURCH.
STERNE. By H. D. TRAILL.
SWIFT. By LESLIE STEPHEN.
THACKERAY. By ANTHONY TROLLOPE.
WORDSWORTH. By F. W. H. MYERS.

ENGLISH MEN OF LETTERS. Reissue
In 13 vols. Cr. 8vo. 3s. 6d. each.
Vol. I. CHAUCER, SPENSER, DRYDEN.
Vol. II. MILTON, GOLDSMITH, COWPER.
Vol. III. BYRON, SHELLEY, KEATS.
Vol. IV. WORDSWORTH, SOUTHEY, LANDOR.
Vol. V. LAMB, ADDISON, SWIFT.
Vol. VI. SCOTT, BURNS, COLERIDGE.
Vol. VII. HUME, LOCKE, BURKE.
Vol. VIII. DEFOE, STERNE, HAWTHORNE.
Vol. IX. FIELDING, THACKERAY, DICKENS.
Vol. X. GIBBON, CARLYLE, MACAULAY.
Vol. XI. SIDNEY, DE QUINCEY, SHERIDAN.
Vol. XII. POPE, JOHNSON, GRAY.
Vol. XIII. BACON, BUNYAN, BENTLEY.

ENGLISH STATESMEN, TWELVE.
Cr. 8vo. 2s. 6d. each.
WILLIAM THE CONQUEROR. By EDWARD
A. FREEMAN, D.C.L., LL.D.
HENRY II. By Mrs. J. R. GREEN.
EDWARD I. By T. F. TOUT, M.A.
HENRY VII. By JAMES GAIRDNER.
CARDINAL WOLSEY. By Bp. CREIGHTON.
ELIZABETH. By E. S. BEESLY.
OLIVER CROMWELL. By F. HARRISON.
WILLIAM III. By H. D. TRAILL.
WALPOLE. By JOHN MORLEY.
CHATHAM. By JOHN MORLEY. [*In Prep.*
PITT. By LORD ROSEBERY.
PEEL. By J. R. THURSFIELD.

FAIRFAX. LIFE OF ROBERT FAIRFAX OF
STEETON, Vice-Admiral, Alderman, and
Member for York, A.D. 1666-1725. By CLE-
MENTS R. MARKHAM, C.B. 8vo. 12s. 6d.

FITZGERALD (E.). (*See* LITERATURE. p. 25.)

FORBES (Edward): MEMOIR OF. By GEORGE
WILSON, M.P., and Sir ARCHIBALD GEIKIE.
F.R.S., etc. 8vo. 14s.

FORBES-MITCHELL (W.)-REMINISCENCES
OF THE GREAT MUTINY. Cr. 8vo. 3s. 6d.

FOREIGN STATESMEN. Crown 8vo.
2s. 6d. each.
RICHELIEU. By R. LODGE, M.A.
PHILIP AUGUSTUS. By Rev. W. H. HUTTON.

FRANCIS OF ASSISI. By Mrs. OLIPHANT.
Cr. 8vo. 6s.
FRASER. JAMES FRASER, SECOND BISHOP
OF MANCHESTER: A Memoir. By T.
HUGHES. Cr. 8vo. 6s.
FREEMAN (E. A.).—LIFE AND LETTERS.
By W. R. W. STEPHENS. 2 vols. 8vo. 17s. net.
GOETHE: LIFE OF. By Prof. HEINRICH
DÜNTZER. Translated by T. W. LYSTER.
2 vols. Cr. 8vo. 21s.
GORDON (General): A SKETCH. By REGI-
NALD H. BARNES. Cr. 8vo. 1s.
—— LETTERS OF GENERAL C. G. GORDON TO
HIS SISTER, M. A. GORDON. Cr. 8vo. 3s. 6d.
HANDEL: LIFE OF. By W. S. ROCKSTRO.
Cr. 8vo. 10s. 6d.
HAUSER, KASPAR : TRUE STORY OF. By
the DUCHESS OF CLEVELAND. Cr. 8vo. 4s. 6d.
HIGINBOTHAM (Chief Justice).—LIFE OF.
By E. E MORRIS. Ex. cr. 8vo. 9s.
HOBART. (*See* COLLECTED WORKS, p. 26.)
HODGSON. MEMOIR OF REV. FRANCIS
HODGSON, B.D. By his Son, Rev. JAMES T.
HODGSON, M.A. 2 vols. Cr. 8vo. 18s.
JEVONS (W. Stanley).—LETTERS AND JOUR-
NAL. Edited by His WIFE. 8vo. 14s.
KAVANAGH (Rt. Hon. A. McMurrough): A
BIOGRAPHY. From papers chiefly unpub-
lished, compiled by his Cousin, SARAH L.
STEELE. With Portrait. 8vo. 14s. net.
KINGSLEY (Chas.): HIS LETTERS, AND ME-
MORIES OF HIS LIFE. Edit. by His WIFE. 2
vols. Cr. 8vo. 12s.—Cheap Edit. 1 vol. 6s.
LAMB. THE LIFE OF CHARLES LAMB. By
Rev. ALFRED AINGER, M.A. Globe 8vo. 5s.
LETHBRIDGE (Sir R.).—GOLDEN BOOK OF
INDIA. Royal 8vo. 40s.
LIGHTFOOT. BISHOP LIGHTFOOT. Re-
printed from *Quarterly Review*. Cr.8vo. 3s. 6d.
LOUIS (St.). (*See* SELECT BIOGRAPHY, p. 6.)
MACMILLAN (D.). MEMOIR OF DANIEL
MACMILLAN. By THOMAS HUGHES, Q.C.
With Portrait. Cr. 8vo. 4s. 6d.—Cheap
Edition. Cr. 8vo, sewed. 1s.
MALTHUS AND HIS WORK. By JAMES
BONAR. 8vo. 12s. 6d.
MANNING (Cardinal): LIFE OF. By E. S.
PURCELL. 2 vols. 3rd Edit. 8vo. 30s. net.
MAURICE. LIFE OF FREDERICK DENISON
MAURICE. By his Son, F. MAURICE. 2 vols.
8vo. 36s.—Popular Ed. 2 vols. Cr. 8vo. 16s.
MAXWELL. PROFESSOR CLERK MAXWELL,
A LIFE OF. By Prof. L. CAMPBELL, M.A.,
and W. GARNETT, M.A. Cr. 8vo. 7s. 6d.
MAZZINI. (*See* SELECT BIOGRAPHY, p. 6.)
MELBOURNE. MEMOIRS OF VISCOUNT
MELBOURNE. By W. M. TORRENS. With
Portrait. 2nd Edit. 2 vols. 8vo. 32s.
MILTON. THE LIFE OF JOHN MILTON.
By Prof. DAVID MASSON. Vol. I., 21s. ;
Vol. II , 16s. ; Vol. III., 18s. ; Vols. IV.
and V., 32s. ; , Vol. VI., with Portrait,
21s. ; Index to 6 vols. 16s. (*See also* p. 18.)
MILTON : JOHNSON'S LIFE OF. Introduction
and Notes by K. DEIGHTON. Gl. 8vo. 1s. 9d.
NAPOLEON I. : HISTORY OF. By P. LAN-
FREY. 4 vols. Cr. 8vo. 30s.

BIOGRAPHY—*continued*.

NELSON. SOUTHEY'S LIFE OF NELSON. With Introduction and Notes by MICHAEL MACMILLAN, B.A. Globe 8vo. 3*s.* 6*d.*

NEWMAN (Cardinal): THE ANGLICAN CAREER OF. By E. A. ABBOTT. 2 vols. 25*s.* net.

NORTH (M.).—RECOLLECTIONS OF A HAPPY LIFE. Being the Autobiography of MARIANNE NORTH. Ed. by Mrs. J. A. SYMONDS. 2nd Edit. 2 vols. Ex. cr. 8vo. 17*s.* net.
— SOME FURTHER RECOLLECTIONS OF A HAPPY LIFE. Cr. 8vo. 8*s.* 6*d.* net.

OXFORD MOVEMENT, THE, 1833—45 By Dean CHURCH. Gl. 8vo. 5*s.*

PARKER (W. K.)—A BIOGRAPHICAL SKETCH By HIS SON. Cr. 8vo. 4*s.* net.

PARKES (Sir Harry): LIFE OF. Edited by S. LANE-POOLE and F. V. DICKINS. 2 vols. 8vo. 25*s.* net.

PATTESON. LIFE AND LETTERS OF JOHN COLERIDGE PATTESON, D.D., MISSIONARY BISHOP. By C. M. YONGE. 2 vols. Cr. 8vo. 12*s.* (*See also under* AWDRY, p. 48.)

PATTISON (M.).—MEMOIRS. Cr. 8vo. 8*s.* 6*d.*

PITT. (*See* SELECT BIOGRAPHY.)

POLLOCK (Sir Frdk., 2nd Bart.).—PERSONAL REMEMBRANCES. 2 vols. Cr. 8vo. 16*s.*

POOLE, THOS., AND HIS FRIENDS. By Mrs. SANDFORD. 2nd edit. Cr. 8vo. 6*s.*

RAMSAY (Sir A. C.): LIFE OF. By Sir A. GEIKIE, F.R.S. 8vo. 12*s.* 6*d.* net.

RENAN (Ernest): IN MEMORIAM. By Sir M. E. GRANT DUFF. Cr. 8vo. 6*s.*

ROBINSON (Matthew): AUTOBIOGRAPHY OF. Edited by J. E. B. MAYOR. Fcp. 8vo. 5*s.*

ROSSETTI (Dante Gabriel): A RECORD AND A STUDY. By W. SHARP. Cr. 8vo. 10*s.* 6*d.*

RUMFORD. (*See* COLLECTED WORKS, p. 27.)

SCHILLER, LIFE OF. By Prof. H. DÜNTZER. Transl. by P. E. PINKERTON. Cr. 8vo. 10*s.* 6*d.*

SHELBURNE. LIFE OF WILLIAM, EARL OF SHELBURNE. By Lord EDMOND FITZMAURICE. In 3 vols.—Vol. I. 8vo. 12*s.*—Vol. II. 8vo. 12*s.*—Vol. III. 8vo. 16*s.*

SIBSON. (*See* MEDICINE.)

SMETHAM (Jas.).: LETTERS OF. Ed. by SARAH SMETHAM and W. DAVIES. Portrait. Globe 8vo. 5*s.*

SMITH (Adam.): LIFE OF. By J. RAE. 8vo. 12*s.* 6*d.* net.

SPINOZA: A STUDY. By Dr. J. MARTINEAU. Cr. 8vo. 6*s.*

SWIFT: LIFE OF. Edit. by H. CRAIK, C.B. 2 vols. Gl. 8vo. 10*s.*

TAIT. THE LIFE OF ARCHIBALD CAMPBELL TAIT, ARCHBISHOP OF CANTERBURY. By the BISHOP OF WINCHESTER and Rev. W. BENHAM, B.D. 2 vols. Cr. 8vo. 10*s.* net.
— CATHARINE AND CRAWFORD TAIT, WIFE AND SON OF ARCHIBALD CAMPBELL, ARCHBISHOP OF CANTERBURY : A Memoir. Ed. by Rev. W. BENHAM, B.D. Cr. 8vo. 6*s.*
—Popular Edit., abridged. Cr. 8vo. 2*s.* 6*d.*

THRING (Edward): A MEMORY OF. By J. H. SKRINE. Cr. 8vo. 6*s.*

VICTOR EMMANUEL II., FIRST KING OF ITALY. By G. S. GODKIN. Cr. 8vo. 6*s.*

WARD. WILLIAM GEORGE WARD AND THE OXFORD MOVEMENT. By his Son, WILFRID WARD. With Portrait. 8vo. 14*s.*
— WILLIAM GEORGE WARD AND THE CATHOLIC REVIVAL. By the same. 8vo. 14*s.*

WATSON. A RECORD OF ELLEN WATSON. By ANNA BUCKLAND. Cr. 8vo. 6*s.*

WHEWELL. DR. WILLIAM WHEWELL, late Master of Trinity College, Cambridge. An Account of his Writings, with Selections from his Literary and Scientific Correspondence. By I. TODHUNTER, M.A. 2 vols. 8vo. 25*s.*

WILLIAMS (Montagu).—LEAVES OF A LIFE. Cr. 8vo. 3*s.* 6*d.*
— LATER LEAVES. Being further Reminiscences. With Portrait. Cr. 8vo. 3*s.* 6*d.*
— ROUND LONDON, DOWN EAST AND UP WEST. Cr. 8vo. 3*s.* 6*d.*

WILSON. MEMOIR OF PROF. GEORGE WILSON, M.D. By HIS SISTER. With Portrait. 2nd Edit. Cr. 8vo. 6*s.*

WORDSWORTH. DOVE COTTAGE, WORDSWORTH'S HOME 1800—8. Gl. 8vo, swd. 1*s.*

Select Biography.

BIOGRAPHIES OF EMINENT PERSONS. Reprinted from the *Times*. 4 vols. Cr. 8vo. 3*s.* 6*d.* each.

FARRAR (Archdeacon). — SEEKERS AFTER GOD. Cr. 8vo. 3*s.* 6*d.*

FAWCETT (Mrs. H.). — SOME EMINENT WOMEN OF OUR TIMES. Cr. 8vo. 2*s.* 6*d.*

GUIZOT.—GREAT CHRISTIANS OF FRANCE: ST. LOUIS AND CALVIN. Cr. 8vo. 6*s.*

HARRISON (Frederic).—THE NEW CALENDAR OF GREAT MEN. Ex. cr. 8vo. 7*s.* 6*d.* net.

LODGE (O. J.).—PIONEERS OF SCIENCE. Cr. 8vo. 7*s.* 6*d.*

MARRIOTT (J. A. R.).—THE MAKERS OF MODERN ITALY: MAZZINI, CAVOUR, GARIBALDI. Cr. 8vo. 1*s.* 6*d.*

MARTINEAU (Harriet). — BIOGRAPHICAL SKETCHES, 1852—75. Cr. 8vo. 6*s.*

NEW HOUSE OF COMMONS, JULY, 1895. Reprinted from the *Times*. 16mo. 1*s.*

RITCHIE (Mrs.).—RECORDS OF TENNYSON, RUSKIN, AND BROWNING. Globe 8vo. 5*s.*
— CHAPTERS FROM SOME MEMOIRS. Cr. 8vo. 10*s.* 6*d.*

SMALLEY (G. W.).—STUDIES OF MEN. Cr. 8vo. 8*s.* 6*d.* net.

SMITH (Goldwin).—THREE ENGLISH STATESMEN : CROMWELL, PYM, PITT. Cr. 8vo. 5*s.*

STEVENSON (F. S.).—HISTORIC PERSONALITY. Cr. 8vo. 4*s.* 6*d.*

THORPE (T. E.).—ESSAYS IN HISTORICAL CHEMISTRY. Cr. 8vo. 8*s.* 6*d.* net.

WINKWORTH (Catharine). — CHRISTIAN SINGERS OF GERMANY. Cr. 8vo. 4*s.* 6*d.*

YONGE (Charlotte M.).—THE PUPILS OF ST JOHN. Illustrated. Cr. 8vo. 6*s.*
— PIONEERS AND FOUNDERS ; or, Recent Workers in the Mission Field. Cr. 8vo. 6*s.*
— A BOOK OF WORTHIES. Pott 8vo. 2*s.* 6*d.* net.
— A BOOK OF GOLDEN DEEDS. Pott 8vo. 2*s.* 6*d.* net.--*Globe Readings Edition.* Globe 8vo. 2*s.*—*Abridged Edition.* Pott 8vo. 1*s.*

BIOLOGY.

(*See also* BOTANY; NATURAL HISTORY; PHYSIOLOGY; ZOOLOGY.)

BALFOUR (F. M.).—COMPARATIVE EMBRYOLOGY. Illustrated. 2 vols. 8vo. Vol. I. 18s. Vol. II. 21s.

BALL (W. P.).—ARE THE EFFECTS OF USE AND DISUSE INHERITED? Cr. 8vo. 3s. 6d.

BATESON (W.).—MATERIALS FOR THE STUDY OF VARIATION. Illustr. 8vo. 21s. net.

BERNARD (H. M.).—THE APODIDAE. Cr. 8vo. 7s. 6d.

BIRKS (T. R.).—MODERN PHYSICAL FATALISM, AND THE DOCTRINE OF EVOLUTION. Including an Examination of Mr. Herbert Spencer's "First Principles." Cr. 8vo. 6s.

CALDERWOOD (H.). — EVOLUTION AND MAN'S PLACE IN NATURE. 2nd Edit. 8vo. 10s. net.

DE VARIGNY (H.).—EXPERIMENTAL EVOLUTION. Cr. 8vo. 5s.

EIMER (G. H. T.).—ORGANIC EVOLUTION AS THE RESULT OF THE INHERITANCE OF ACQUIRED CHARACTERS ACCORDING TO THE LAWS OF ORGANIC GROWTH. Translated by J. T. CUNNINGHAM, M.A. 8vo. 12s. 6d.

FISKE (John).—OUTLINES OF COSMIC PHILOSOPHY, BASED ON THE DOCTRINE OF EVOLUTION. 2 vols. 8vo. 25s.
—— MAN'S DESTINY VIEWED IN THE LIGHT OF HIS ORIGIN. Cr. 8vo. 3s. 6d.

FOSTER (Prof. M.) and BALFOUR (F. M.).—THE ELEMENTS OF EMBRYOLOGY. Ed. A. SEDGWICK, and WALTER HEAPE. Illust 3rd Edit., revised and enlarged. Cr. 8vo. 10s. 6d.

HUXLEY (T. H.) and MARTIN (H. N.).— (*See under* ZOOLOGY, p. 49.)

KLEIN (Dr. E.).—MICRO-ORGANISMS AND DISEASE. 3rd Edit. Cr. 8vo. 6s.

LANKESTER (Prof. E. Ray).—COMPARATIVE LONGEVITY IN MAN AND THE LOWER ANIMALS. Cr. 8vo. 4s. 6d.

LUBBOCK (Sir John, Bart.).— SCIENTIFIC LECTURES. Illustrated. 2nd Edit. 8vo. 8s. 6d.

MURPHY (J. J.).—NATURAL SELECTION. Gl. 8vo. 5s.

ORR (H. B.).—DEVELOPMENT AND HEREDITY. Cr. 8vo. 6s. net.

OSBORN (H. F.).—FROM THE GREEKS TO DARWIN. 8vo. 9s. net.

PARKER (T. Jeffery).—LESSONS IN ELEMENTARY BIOLOGY. Illustr. Cr. 8vo. 10s. 6d.

ROMANES (G. J.).—SCIENTIFIC EVIDENCES OF ORGANIC EVOLUTION. Cr. 8vo. 2s. 6d.

WALLACE (Alfred R.).—DARWINISM: An Exposition of the Theory of Natural Selection. Illustrated. 3rd Edit. Cr. 8vo. 9s.
—— CONTRIBUTIONS TO THE THEORY OF NATURAL SELECTION, AND TROPICAL NATURE: and other Essays. New Ed. Cr. 8vo. 6s.
—— THE GEOGRAPHICAL DISTRIBUTION OF ANIMALS. Illustrated. 2 vols. 8vo. 42s.
—— ISLAND LIFE. Illustr. Ext. Cr. 8vo. 6s.

WILLEY(A.).—AMPHIOXUS, AND THE ANCESTRY OF THE VERTEBRATES. 8vo. 10s. 6d. net.

BIRDS. (*See* ZOOLOGY; ORNITHOLOGY.)

BOOK-KEEPING.

THORNTON (J.).—FIRST LESSONS IN BOOK-KEEPING. New Edition. Cr. 8vo. 2s. 6d.
—— KEY. Oblong 4to. 10s. 6d.
—— EXERCISE BOOKS TO FIRST LESSONS IN BOOKKEEPING.
No. 1. FOR LESSONS I.—IX. 9d.
No. 2. FOR TEST EXERCISES. 9d.
No. 3. FOR TEST EXERCISES. 1s. 6d.
No. 4. FOR LESSONS XIII. and XIV. 1s. 6d.
Case to contain all the above, 6d. Complete set with case, 5s.
No. 5. CONDENSED EDITION FOR WORKING OUT A SELECTION ON ALL THE LESSONS. 2s.
No. 6. JOURNAL. 6d.
EXAMINATION PAPERS IN BOOKKEEPING. 9d.
KEY TO EXAMINATION PAPERS. 2s.
—— PRIMER OF BOOK-KEEPING. Pott 8vo. 1s.
—— KEY. Demy 8vo. 10s. 6d.
—— EXERCISE BOOKS TO PRIMER OF BOOK-KEEPING.
Part I. LEDGER; Part II. JOURNAL. The Set, 1s.
—— EXERCISES IN BOOK-KEEPING. Pott 8vo. 1s.
—— MANUAL OF BOOK-KEEPING. Gl. 8vo. 7s. 6d.

BOTANY.

(*See also* AGRICULTURE; GARDENING.)

ALLEN (Grant). — ON THE COLOURS OF FLOWERS. Illustrated. Cr. 8vo. 3s. 6d.

ATKINSON (G. F.).—BIOLOGY OF FERNS. 8vo. 8s. 6d. net.

BALFOUR (Prof. J. B.) and WARD (Prof. H. M.). — A GENERAL TEXT-BOOK OF BOTANY. 8vc. [*In preparation.*]

BETTANY (G. T.).—FIRST LESSONS IN PRACTICAL BOTANY. Pott 8vo. 1s.

BOWER (Prof. F. O.).—A COURSE OF PRACTICAL INSTRUCTION IN BOTANY. Cr. 8vo. 10s. 6d.
—— PRACTICAL BOTANY FOR BEGINNERS. Gl. 8vo. 3s. 6d.

CAMPBELL (Prof. D. H.).—STRUCTURE AND DEVELOPMENT OF MOSSES AND FERNS. Illustrated. 8vo. 14s. net.

GRAY (Prof. Asa).—STRUCTURAL BOTANY; or, Organography on the Basis of Morphology. 8vo. 10s. 6d.
—— THE SCIENTIFIC PAPERS OF ASA GRAY. Selected by C. S. SARGENT. 2 vols. 8vo. 21s.

HANBURY (Daniel). — SCIENCE PAPERS, CHIEFLY PHARMACOLOGICAL AND BOTANICAL. Med. 8vo. 14s.

HARTIG (Dr. Robert).—TEXT-BOOK OF THE DISEASES OF TREES. Transl. by Prof. WM. SOMERVILLE, B.Sc. Introduction by Prof. H. MARSHALL WARD. 8vo. 10s. net.

HOOKER (Sir Joseph D.).—THE STUDENT'S FLORA OF THE BRITISH ISLANDS. 3rd Edit. Globe 8vo. 10s. 6d.
—— A PRIMER OF BOTANY. Pott 8vo. 1s.

LASLETT (Thomas).—TIMBER AND TIMBER TREES, NATIVE AND FOREIGN. 2nd Ed. Revised by H. MARSHALL WARD, D.Sc. Cr. 8vo. 8s. 6d.

LUBBOCK (Sir John, Bart.).—ON BRITISH WILD FLOWERS CONSIDERED IN RELATION TO INSECTS. Illustrated. Cr. 8vo. 4s. 6d.
—— FLOWERS, FRUITS, AND LEAVES. With Illustrations. Cr. 8vo. 4s. 6d.

BOTANY—*continued.*

MÜLLER—THOMPSON. — THE FERTILI-
SATION OF FLOWERS. By Prof. H. MÜLLER.
Transl. by D'ARCY W. THOMPSON. Preface
by CHARLES DARWIN, F.R.S. 8vo. 21s.

MURRAY (G.).—INTRODUCTION TO STUDY
OF SEAWEEDS. Cr. 8vo. 7s. 6d.

NISBET (J.).—BRITISH FOREST TREES AND
THEIR SYLVICULTURAL CHARACTERISTICS
AND TREATMENT. Cr. 8vo. 6s. net.

OLIVER (Prof. Daniel).—LESSONS IN ELE-
MENTARY BOTANY. Illustr. Fcp. 8vo. 4s.6d.
—— FIRST BOOK OF INDIAN BOTANY. Illus-
trated. Ext. fcp. 8vo. 6s. 6d.

PETTIGREW (J. Bell).—THE PHYSIOLOGY
OF THE CIRCULATION IN PLANTS, IN THE
LOWER ANIMALS, AND IN MAN. 8vo. 18s.

SMITH (J.).—ECONOMIC PLANTS, DICTION-
ARY OF POPULAR NAMES OF; THEIR HIS-
TORY, PRODUCTS, AND USES. 8vo. 14s.

SMITH (W. G.).—DISEASES OF FIELD AND
GARDEN CROPS, CHIEFLY SUCH AS ARE
CAUSED BY FUNGI. Illust. Fcp. 8vo. 4s. 6d.

VINES (S. H.) and KINCH (E.).—MANUAL
OF VEGETABLE PHYSIOLOGY. Illustrated.
Crown 8vo. [*In preparation.*

WARD (Prof. H. M.).—TIMBER AND SOME OF
ITS DISEASES. Illustrated. Cr. 8vo. 6s.

YONGE (C. M.).—THE HERB OF THE FIELD.
New Edition, revised. Cr. 8vo. 5s.

BREWING AND WINE.

PASTEUR — FAULKNER. — STUDIES ON
FERMENTATION : THE DISEASES OF BEER,
THEIR CAUSES, AND THE MEANS OF PRE-
VENTING THEM. By L. PASTEUR. Trans-
lated by FRANK FAULKNER. 8vo. 21s.

CHEMISTRY.

(*See also* METALLURGY.)

BEHRENS (H.).—MICROCHEMICAL ANALY-
SIS. Cr. 8vo. 6s.

BRODIE(Sir Benjamin).—IDEAL CHEMISTRY.
Cr. 8vo. 2s.

COHEN (J. B.). — THE OWENS COLLEGE
COURSE OF PRACTICAL ORGANIC CHEMIS-
TRY. Fcp. 8vo. 2s. 6d.

COOKE (Prof. J. P., jun.).—PRINCIPLES OF
CHEMICAL PHILOSOPHY. New Ed. 8vo. 19s.

DOBBIN (L.) and WALKER (Jas.).—CHEMI-
CAL THEORY FOR BEGINNERS. Pott 8vo.
2s. 6d.

FLEISCHER (Emil).—A SYSTEM OF VOLU-
METRIC ANALYSIS. Transl. with Additions,
by M. M. P. MUIR, F.R.S.E. Cr.8vo. 7s.6d.

FRANKLAND (Prof. P. F.). (*See* AGRI-
CULTURE.)

GLADSTONE (J. H.) and TRIBE (A.).—
THE CHEMISTRY OF THE SECONDARY BAT-
TERIES OF PLANTÉ AND FAURE. Cr.8vo. 2s.6d.

HARTLEY (Prof. W. N.).—A COURSE OF
QUANTITATIVE ANALYSIS FOR STUDENTS.
Globe 8vo. 5s.

HEMPEL (Dr. W.). — METHODS OF GAS
ANALYSIS. Translated by L. M. DENNIS.
Cr. 8vo. 7s. 6d.

HOFMANN (Prof. A. W.).—THE LIFE WORK
OF LIEBIG IN EXPERIMENTAL AND PHILO-
SOPHIC CHEMISTRY. 8vo. 5s.

JONES (Francis).—THE OWENS COLLEGE
JUNIOR COURSE OF PRACTICAL CHEMISTRY.
Illustrated. Fcp. 8vo. 2s. 6d.
—— QUESTIONS ON CHEMISTRY. Fcp.8vo. 3s.

LANDAUER (J.). — BLOWPIPE ANALYSIS.
Translated by J. TAYLOR. Gl. 8vo. 4s. 6d

LASSAR·COHN. — ORGANIC CHEMISTRY.
Transl. by A. SMITH. Cr. 8vo. 8s. 6d.

LOCKYER (J. Norman, F.R.S.). — THE
CHEMISTRY OF THE SUN. Illustr. 8vo. 14s.

LUPTON (S.). — CHEMICAL ARITHMETIC.
With 1200 Problems. Fcp. 8vo. 4s. 6d.

MANSFIELD (C. B.).—A THEORY OF SALTS.
Cr. 8vo. 14s.

MELDOLA (Prof. R.).—THE CHEMISTRY OF
PHOTOGRAPHY. Illustrated. Cr. 8vo. 6s.

MENSCHUTKIN (A.).—ANALYTICAL CHE-
MISTRY. Trsl. by J. LOCKE. 8vo. 17s. net.

MEYER (E. von).—HISTORY OF CHEMISTRY
FROM EARLIEST TIMES TO THE PRESENT
DAY. Transl. G. McGOWAN. 8vo. 14s. net.

MIXTER (Prof. W. G.).—AN ELEMENTARY
TEXT-BOOK OF CHEMISTRY. Cr.8vo. 7s. 6d.

MUIR (M. M. P.).—PRACTICAL CHEMISTRY
FOR MEDICAL STUDENTS (First M. B. Course).
Fcp. 8vo. 1s. 6d.

MUIR (M. M. P.) and WILSON (D. M.) —
ELEMENTS OF THERMAL CHEMISTRY. 12s.6d.

NERNST (Dr.).—THEORETICAL CHEMISTRY.
Translated by C. S. PALMER. Evo. 15s. net.

OSTWALD (Prof.).—OUTLINES OF GENERAL
CHEMISTRY. Transl. Dr. J. WALKER. 10s.net.
—— MANUAL OF PHYSICO-CHEMICAL MEA-
SUREMENTS. Transl. by Dr. J. WALKER.
8vo. 7s. net.
—— ANALYTICAL CHEMISTRY. Translated by
G. Mc GOWAN. Cr. 8vo. 5s. net.

RAMSAY (Prof. William).—EXPERIMENTAL
PROOFS OF CHEMICAL THEORY FOR BEGIN-
NERS. Pott 8vo. 2s. 6d.

REMSEN (Prof. Ira).—THE ELEMENTS OF
CHEMISTRY. Fcp. 8vo. 2s. 6d.
—— AN INTRODUCTION TO THE STUDY OF
CHEMISTRY (INORGANIC CHEMISTRY). Cr.
8vo. 6s. 6d.
—— A TEXT-BOOK OF INORGANIC CHEMIS-
TRY. 8vo. 16s.
—— COMPOUNDS OF CARBON ; or, An Intro-
duction to the Study of Organic Chemistry.
Cr 8vo. 6s. 6d.

ROSCOE (Sir Henry E., F.R.S.).—A PRIMER
OF CHEMISTRY. Illustrated. Pott 8vo. 1s.
—— LESSONS IN ELEMENTARY CHEMISTRY,
INORGANIC AND ORGANIC. Fcp. 8vo. 4s. 6d.

ROSCOE (Sir H. E.) and HARDEN (A.).—
DALTON'S ATOMIC THEORY. 8vo. 6s. net.

ROSCOE (Sir H. E.) and LUNT (J.).—IN-
ORGANIC CHEMISTRY FOR BEGINNERS. Gl.
8vo. 2s. 6d.

ROSCOE (Sir H. E.) and SCHORLEMMER
(Prof. C.).—A COMPLETE TREATISE ON IN-
ORGANIC AND ORGANIC CHEMISTRY. Illustr.
8vo.—Vols. I. and II. INORGANIC CHEMIS-
TRY: Vol. I. THE NON-METALLIC ELE-
MENTS, New Edit., Revised by Drs. H. G.
COLMAN and A. HARDEN, 21s. Vol. II.
Parts I. and II. METALS, 18s. each.—Vol.
III. ORGANIC CHEMISTRY: THE CHEMISTRY
OF THE HYDRO-CARBONS AND THEIR DERIVA-
TIVES. Parts I. II. IV. and VI. 21s. each ;
Parts III. and V. 18s. each

DICTIONARIES—EDUCATION.

ROSCOE (Sir H. E.) and SCHUSTER (A.). —SPECTRUM ANALYSIS. By Sir HENRY E. ROSCOE. 4th Edit., revised by the Author and A. SCHUSTER, F.R.S. With Coloured Plates. 8vo. 21s.

SCHORLEMMER (C.). — RISE AND DEVELOPMENT OF ORGANIC CHEMISTRY. Trans. by Prof. SMITHELLS. Cr. 8vo. 5s. net.

SCHULTZ (G.) and JULIUS (P.). —ORGANIC COLOURING MATTERS. Transl. by A. G. GREEN. 8vo. 21s. net.

THORPE (Prof. T. E.) and TATE (W.). — A SERIES OF CHEMICAL PROBLEMS. With KEY. Fcp. 8vo. 2s.

THORPE (Prof. T. E.) and RÜCKER (Prof. A. W.). —A TREATISE ON CHEMICAL PHYSICS. Illustrated 8vo. [In preparation.

TURPIN (G. S.). —LESSONS IN ORGANIC CHEMISTRY. Gl. 8vo. 2s. 6d.
—— PRACTICAL INORGANIC CHEMISTRY. Gl. 8vo. 2s. 6d.

WURTZ (Ad.). —A HISTORY OF CHEMICAL THEORY. Transl. by H. WATTS. Cr. 8vo. 6s.

CHRISTIAN CHURCH, History of the.
(See under THEOLOGY, p. 40.)

CHURCH OF ENGLAND, The.
(See under THEOLOGY, p. 40.)

COLLECTED WORKS.
(See under LITERATURE, p. 24.)

COMPARATIVE ANATOMY.
(See under ZOOLOGY, p. 49.)

COOKERY.
(See under DOMESTIC ECONOMY, below.)

DEVOTIONAL BOOKS.
(See under THEOLOGY, p. 41.)

DICTIONARIES AND GLOSSARIES.
AUTENRIETH (Dr. G.). —AN HOMERIC DICTIONARY. Translated from the German, by R. P. KEEP, Ph.D. Cr. 8vo. 6s.

BARTLETT (J.). —FAMILIAR QUOTATIONS. Cr. 8vo. 6s. net.

GROVE (Sir George). —A DICTIONARY OF MUSIC AND MUSICIANS. (See MUSIC.)

HOLE (Rev. C.). —A BRIEF BIOGRAPHICAL DICTIONARY. 2nd Edit. Pott 8vo. 4s. 6d.

MASSON (Gustave). —A COMPENDIOUS DICTIONARY OF THE FRENCH LANGUAGE. Cr. 8vo. 3s. 6d.

PALGRAVE (R. H. I.). —A DICTIONARY OF POLITICAL ECONOMY. (See POLITICAL ECONOMY.)

WHITNEY (Prof. W. D.). —A COMPENDIOUS GERMAN AND ENGLISH DICTIONARY. Cr. 8vo. 5s. —German-English Part separately. 3s. 6d.

WRIGHT (W. Aldis). —THE BIBLE WORD-BOOK. 2nd Edit. Cr. 8vo. 7s. 6d.

YONGE (Charlotte M.). —HISTORY OF CHRISTIAN NAMES. Cr. 8vo. 7s. 6d.

DOMESTIC ECONOMY.
Cookery—Nursing—Needlework.

Cookery.
BARKER (Lady). —FIRST LESSONS IN THE PRINCIPLES OF COOKING. 3rd Edit. Pott 8vo. 1s.

BARNETT (E. A) and O'NEILL (H. C.). —PRIMER OF DOMESTIC ECONOMY. Pott 8vo. 1s.

MIDDLE-CLASS COOKERY BOOK, THE. Compiled for the Manchester School of Cookery. Pott 8vo. 1s. 6d.

TEGETMEIER (W. B.). —HOUSEHOLD MANAGEMENT AND COOKERY. Pott 8vo. 1s.

WRIGHT (Miss Guthrie). — THE SCHOOL COOKERY-BOOK. Pott 8vo. 1s.

Nursing.
CRAVEN (Mrs. Dacre). —A GUIDE TO DISTRICT NURSES. Cr. 8vo. 2s. 6d.

FOTHERGILL (Dr. J. M.). —FOOD FOR THE INVALID, THE CONVALESCENT, THE DYSPEPTIC, AND THE GOUTY. Cr. 8vo. 3s. 6d.

JEX-BLAKE (Dr. Sophia). —THE CARE OF INFANTS. Pott 8vo. 1s.

RATHBONE (Wm.). —THE HISTORY AND PROGRESS OF DISTRICT NURSING, FROM 1859 TO THE PRESENT DATE. Cr. 8vo. 2s. 6d.

RECOLLECTIONS OF A NURSE. By E. D. Cr. 8vo. 2s.

STEPHEN (Caroline E.). —THE SERVICE OF THE POOR. Cr. 8vo. 6s. 6d.

Needlework.
GLAISTER (Elizabeth). —NEEDLEWORK. Cr. 8vo. 2s. 6d.

GRAND'HOMME. — CUTTING OUT AND DRESSMAKING. From the French of Mdlle. E. GRAND'HOMME. Pott 8vo. 1s.

GRENFELL (Mrs.) —DRESSMAKING. Pott 8vo. 1s.

ROSEVEAR (E.). — NEEDLEWORK, KNITTING, AND CUTTING OUT. 3rd Edit. Cr. 8vo. 6s.
—— NEEDLEWORK, KNITTING, AND CUTTING-OUT FOR OLDER GIRLS. Standard IV. 6d.; Standard V. 8d.; Standard VI. VII. and Ex-VII. 1s.
—— NEEDLEWORK, KNITTING, AND CUTTING-OUT FOR EVENING CONTINUATION SCHOOLS. Globe 8vo. 2s.

DRAMA, The.
(See under LITERATURE, p. 17.)

ELECTRICITY.
See under PHYSICS, p. 33.)

EDUCATION.
ARNOLD (Matthew). —HIGHER SCHOOLS AND UNIVERSITIES IN GERMANY. Cr. 8vo. 6s.
—— REPORTS ON ELEMENTARY SCHOOLS, 1852-82. Ed. by Lord SANDFORD. 8vo. 3s. 6d.
—— A FRENCH ETON: OR MIDDLE CLASS EDUCATION AND THE STATE. Cr. 8vo. 6s.

BLAKISTON (J. R.). —THE TEACHER: HINTS ON SCHOOL MANAGEMENT. Cr. 8vo. 2s. 6d.

CALDERWOOD (Prof. H.). —ON TEACHING. 4th Edit. Ext. fcp. 8vo. 2s. 6d.

COMBE (George).—EDUCATION: ITS PRINCIPLES AND PRACTICE AS DEVELOPED BY GEORGE COMBE. Ed. by W. JOLLY. 8vo. 15s.

CRAIK (Henry).—THE STATE IN ITS RELATION TO EDUCATION. Cr. 8vo. 2s. 6d.
—— STATE EDUCATION: A SPEECH. 8vo. Sewed. 6d. net.

FEARON (D. R.).—SCHOOL INSPECTION. 6th Edit. Cr. 8vo. 2s. 6d.

FITCH (J. G.).—NOTES ON AMERICAN SCHOOLS AND TRAINING COLLEGES. Reprinted by permission. Globe 8vo. 2s. 6d.

GLADSTONE (J. H.).—SPELLING REFORM FROM AN EDUCATIONAL POINT OF VIEW. 3rd Edit. Cr. 8vo. 1s. 6d.

HERTEL (Dr.).—OVERPRESSURE IN HIGH SCHOOLS IN DENMARK. With Introduction by Sir J. CRICHTON-BROWNE. Cr. 8vo. 3s. 6d.

KINGSLEY (Charles).—HEALTH AND EDUCATION. Cr. 8vo. 6s.

LUBBOCK (Sir John, Bart.).—POLITICAL AND EDUCATIONAL ADDRESSES. 8vo. 8s. 6d.

MAURICE (F. D.).—LEARNING AND WORKING. Cr. 8vo. 4s. 6d.

PAULSEN (F.).—THE GERMAN UNIVERSITIES. By E. D. PERRY. Cr. 8vo. 7s. net.

RECORD OF TECHNICAL AND SECONDARY EDUCATION. Crown 8vo. Sewed, 2s. 6d. No. I. Nov. 1891.

THRING (Rev. Edward).—EDUCATION AND SCHOOL. 2nd Edit. Cr. 8vo. 6s.

ENGINEERING.

ALEXANDER (T.) and THOMSON (A.W.).—ELEMENTARY APPLIED MECHANICS. Part II. TRANSVERSE STRESS. Cr. 8vo. 10s. 6d.

BERG (L. de C.).—SAFE BUILDING. 4th Ed. 2 vols. 4to. 42s. net.

CHALMERS (J. B.).—GRAPHICAL DETERMINATION OF FORCES IN ENGINEERING STRUCTURES. Illustrated. 8vo. 24s.

CLARK (T. M.).—BUILDING SUPERINTENDENCE. 12th Edit. 4to. 12s. net.

COTTERILL (Prof J. H.).—APPLIED MECHANICS: An Elementary General Introduction to the Theory of Structures and Machines. 4th Edit. 8vo. 18s.

COTTERILL (Prof. J. H.) and SLADE (J. H.).—LESSONS IN APPLIED MECHANICS. Fcp. 8vo. 5s. 6d.

KENNEDY (Prof. A. B. W.).—THE MECHANICS OF MACHINERY. Cr. 8vo. 8s. 6d.

LANGMAID (T.) and GAISFORD (H.).—STEAM MACHINERY. 8vo. 6s. net.

PEABODY (Prof. C. H.).—THERMODYNAMICS OF THE STEAM ENGINE AND OTHER HEAT-ENGINES. 8vo. 21s.

ROBB (R.).—ELECTRIC WIRING. 4to. 10s.

SHANN (G.).—AN ELEMENTARY TREATISE ON HEAT IN RELATION TO STEAM AND THE STEAM-ENGINE. Illustrated. Cr. 8vo. 4s. 6d.

VIOLLET-LE-DUC (E. E.).—RATIONAL BUILDING. Transl. by G. M. HUSS. 8vo. 12s. 6d. net.

WEISBACH (J.) and HERRMANN (G.).—MECHANICS OF HOISTING MACHINERY. Transl. K. P. DAHLSTROM. 8vo. 12s. 6d. net.

WOODWARD (C. M.).—A HISTORY OF THE ST. LOUIS BRIDGE. 4to. 2l. 2s. net.

YOUNG (E. W.).—SIMPLE PRACTICAL METHODS OF CALCULATING STRAINS ON GIRDERS, ARCHES, AND TRUSSES. 8vo. 7s. 6d.

ENGLISH CITIZEN SERIES.
(See POLITICS.)

ENGLISH MEN OF ACTION.
(See BIOGRAPHY.)

ENGLISH MEN OF LETTERS.
(See BIOGRAPHY.)

ENGLISH STATESMEN, Twelve.
(See BIOGRAPHY.)

ENGRAVING. (See ART.)

ESSAYS. (See under LITERATURE, p. 24.)

ETCHING. (See ART.)

ETHICS. (See under PHILOSOPHY, p. 32.)

FATHERS, The.
(See under THEOLOGY, p. 41.)

FICTION, Prose.
(See under LITERATURE, p. 21.)

GARDENING.

(See also AGRICULTURE; BOTANY.)

AUSTIN (Alfred). — THE GARDEN THAT I LOVE. Ex. cr. 8vo. 9s.
—— IN VERONICA'S GARDEN. Ex. cr. 8vo. 9s.

BAILEY (L. H.).—HORTICULTURIST'S RULE BOOK. Fcp. 8vo. 3s. net.
—— PLANT BREEDING. Fcp. 8vo. 4s. net.

BLOMFIELD (R.) and THOMAS (F. I.).—THE FORMAL GARDEN IN ENGLAND. Illustrated. Ex. cr. 8vo. 7s. 6d. net.

BRIGHT (H. A.).—THE ENGLISH FLOWER GARDEN. Cr. 8vo. 3s. 6d.
—— A YEAR IN A LANCASHIRE GARDEN. Cr. 8vo. 3s. 6d.

COLLINS (C.).—GREENHOUSE AND WINDOW PLANTS. Ed. by J. WRIGHT. Pott 8vo. 1s.

DEAN (A.).—VEGETABLE CULTURE. Ed. by J. WRIGHT. Pott 8vo. 1s.

FOSTER-MELLIAR (A.).—THE BOOK OF THE ROSE. Illus. Ex. cr. 8vo. 8s. 6d. net.

HOBDAY (E.). — VILLA GARDENING. A Handbook for Amateur and Practical Gardeners. Ext. cr. 8vo. 6s.

LODEMAN (E. G.).—SPRAYING OF PLANTS. Fcp. 8vo. 4s. net.

WRIGHT (J.).—A PRIMER OF PRACTICAL HORTICULTURE. Pott 8vo. 1s.
—— GARDEN FLOWERS AND PLANTS. Pott 8vo. 1s.

GEOGRAPHY.

(See also ATLASES.)

BLANFORD (H. F.).—ELEMENTARY GEOGRAPHY OF INDIA, BURMA, AND CEYLON. Globe 8vo. 1s. 9d.

CLARKE (C. B.).—A GEOGRAPHICAL READER AND COMPANION TO THE ATLAS. Cr. 8vo. 2s.
—— A GEOGRAPHIC READER. With Maps. Gl. 8vo. 2s. 6d.
—— READER IN GENERAL GEOGRAPHY. Gl. 8vo swd. 1s.
—— A CLASS-BOOK OF GEOGRAPHY. With 18 Coloured Maps. Fcp. 8vo. 2s. 6d.; swd., 2s. Without Maps, 1s. 6d.

DAWSON (G. M.) and SUTHERLAND (A.).
ELEMENTARY GEOGRAPHY OF THE BRITISH
COLONIES. Globe 8vo. 2s.

ELDERTON (W. A.).—MAPS AND MAP-
DRAWING. Pott 8vo. 1s.

GEIKIE (Sir Archibald).—THE TEACHING OF
GEOGRAPHY. A Practical Handbook for the
use of Teachers. Globe 8vo. 2s.

—— GEOGRAPHY OF THE BRITISH ISLES.
Pott 8vo. 1s.

GONNER (E. C. K.).—COMMERCIAL GEO-
GRAPHY. Gl. 8vo. 3s.

GREEN (J. R. and A. S.).—A SHORT GEOGRA-
PHY OF THE BRITISH ISLANDS. Fcp.8vo. 3s.6d.

GROVE (Sir George).—A PRIMER OF GEO-
GRAPHY. Maps. Pott 8vo. 1s.

KIEPERT (H.).—MANUAL OF ANCIENT
GEOGRAPHY. Cr. 8vo. 5s.

MILL (H. R.).—ELEMENTARY CLASS-BOOK
OF GENERAL GEOGRAPHY. Cr. 8vo. 3s. 6d.

SIME (James).—GEOGRAPHY OF EUROPE.
With Illustrations. Globe 8vo. 2s.

STRACHEY (Lieut.-Gen. R.).—LECTURES ON
GEOGRAPHY. Cr. 8vo. 4s. 6d.

SUTHERLAND (A.).—GEOGRAPHY OF VIC-
TORIA. Pott 8vo. 1s.

—— CLASS BOOK OF GEOGRAPHY. With Maps.
Fcp. 8vo. 2s. 6d.

TOZER (H. F.).—A PRIMER OF CLASSICAL
GEOGRAPHY. Pott 8vo. 1s.

GEOLOGY AND MINERALOGY.

BLANFORD (W. T.). — GEOLOGY AND
ZOOLOGY OF ABYSSINIA. 8vo. 21s.

COAL: ITS HISTORY AND ITS USES. By
Profs. GREEN, MIALL, THORPE, RÜCKER,
and MARSHALL. 8vo. 12s. 6d.

DAWSON (Sir J. W.).—THE GEOLOGY OF
NOVA SCOTIA, NEW BRUNSWICK, AND
PRINCE EDWARD ISLAND; or, Acadian Geo-
logy. 4th Edit. 8vo. 21s.

GEIKIE (Sir Archibald).—A PRIMER OF GEO-
LOGY. Illustrated. Pott 8vo. 1s.

—— CLASS-BOOK OF GEOLOGY. Illustrated.
Cr. 8vo. 4s. 6d.

—— GEOLOGICAL SKETCHES AT HOME AND
ABROAD. Illust. 8vo. 10s.6d.

—— OUTLINES OF FIELD GEOLOGY. With
numerous Illustrations. Gl. 8vo. 3s. 6d.

—— TEXT-BOOK OF GEOLOGY. Illustrated.
3rd Edit. Med. 8vo. 28s.

—— THE SCENERY OF SCOTLAND. Viewed in
connection with its Physical Geology. 2nd
Edit. Cr. 8vo. 12s. 6d.

HATCH (F. J.) and CHALMERS (J. A.).—
GOLD MINES OF THE RAND. Sup. roy. 8vo.
17s. net.

HULL (E.).—A TREATISE ON ORNAMENTAL
AND BUILDING STONES OF GREAT BRITAIN
AND FOREIGN COUNTRIES. 8vo. 12s.

KELVIN (Lord) —GEOLOGY AND GENERAL
PHYSICS. Cr. 8vo. 7s. 6d.

LOEWENSON-LESSING (F.)—TABLES FOR
DETERMINATION OF ROCK-FORMING MINE-
RALS. Transl. by J. W. GREGORY. 8vo.
4s. 6d. net.

PENNINGTON (Rooke).—NOTES ON THE
BARROWS AND BONE CAVES OF DERBYSHIRE.
8vo. 6s.

PRESTWICH (J.).—PAPERS ON GEOLOGY.
8vo. 10s. net.

—— CERTAIN PHENOMENA BELONGING TO THE
LAST GEOLOGICAL PERIOD. 8vo. 2s. 6d. net.

RENDU—WILLS.—THE THEORY OF THE
GLACIERS OF SAVOY. By M. LE CHANOINE
RENDU. Trans. by A.WILLS,Q.C. 8vo. 7s.6d.

ROSENBUSCH (H.).—MICROSCOPICAL PHY-
SIOGRAPHY OF THE ROCK-MAKING MINER-
ALS. By H. ROSENBUSCH. Translated by
J. P. IDDINGS. Illust. 8vo. 24s.

TARR (R. S.).—ECONOMIC GEOLOGY OF THE
UNITED STATES. 8vo. 16s. net.

WILLIAMS (G. H.).—ELEMENTS OF CRY-
STALLOGRAPHY. Cr. 8vo. 6s.

GLOBE LIBRARY. (See LITERATURE, p. 25.)

GLOSSARIES. (See DICTIONARIES.)

GOLDEN TREASURY SERIES.
(See LITERATURE, p. 25.)

GRAMMAR. (See PHILOLOGY.)

HEALTH. (See HYGIENE.)

HEAT. (See under PHYSICS, p. 34.)

HISTOLOGY. (See PHYSIOLOGY.)

HISTORY.
(See also BIOGRAPHY.)

ACTON (Lord).—ON THE STUDY OF HISTORY.
Gl. 8vo. 2s. 6d.

AMERICAN HISTORICAL REVIEW.
Quarterly. 8vo. 3s. 6d. net.

ANNALS OF OUR TIME. A Diurnal of
Events, Social and Political, Home and
Foreign. By JOSEPH IRVING. 8vo.—Vol. I.
June 20th, 1837, to Feb. 28th, 1871, 18s.;
Vol. II. Feb. 24th, 1871, to June 24th, 1887,
18s. Also Vol. II. in 3 parts: Part I. Feb.
24th, 1871, to March 19th, 1874, 4s. 6d. ; Part
II. March 20th, 1874, to July 22nd, 1878,
4s. 6d.; Part III. July 23rd, 1878, to June
24th, 1887, 9s. Vol. III. By H. H. FYFE.
Part I. June 25th, 1887, to Dec. 30th, 1890.
4s.6d.; swd.3s.6d. Pt.II. 1891, 11.6d.; swd.1s.

ANDREWS (C. M.).—THE OLD ENGLISH
MANOR: A STUDY IN ECONOMIC HISTORY.
Royal 8vo. 6s. net.

ANNUAL SUMMARIES. Reprinted from
the Times. 2 Vols. Cr. 8vo. 2s. 6d. each.

ARNOLD (T.).—THE SECOND PUNIC WAR.
By THOMAS ARNOLD, D.D. Ed. by W. T.
ARNOLD, M.A. With 8 Maps. Cr. 8vo. 5s.

ARNOLD (W. T.).—A HISTORY OF THE
EARLY ROMAN EMPIRE. Cr. 8vo. [In prep.

BEESLY (Mrs.).—STORIES FROM THE HIS-
TORY OF ROME. Fcp. 8vo. 2s. 6d.

BLACKIE (Prof. John Stuart).—WHAT DOES
HISTORY TEACH? Globe 8vo. 2s. 6d.

BRETT (R. B.).—FOOTPRINTS OF STATES-
MEN DURING THE EIGHTEENTH CENTURY
IN ENGLAND. Cr. 8vo. 6s.

BRYCE (James, M.P.).—THE HOLY ROMAN
EMPIRE. 8th Edit. Cr. 8vo. 7s. 6d.—
Library Edition. 8vo. 14s.

HISTORY—*continued.*

BRUCE (P. A.).—ECONOMIC HISTORY OF VIRGINIA. 2 vols. 8vo. 25*s*. net.

BUCKLEY (Arabella).—HISTORY OF ENG-LAND FOR BEGINNERS. Globe 8vo. 3*s*.
—— PRIMER OF ENGLISH HISTORY. Pott 8vo. 1*s*.

BURKE (Edmund). (*See* POLITICS.)

BURY (J. B.).—A HISTORY OF THE LATER ROMAN EMPIRE FROM ARCADIUS TO IRENE, A.D. 390—800. 2 vols. 8vo. 32*s*.

CASSEL (Dr. D.).— MANUAL OF JEWISH HISTORY AND LITERATURE. Translated by Mrs. HENRY LUCAS. Fcp. 8vo. 2*s*. 6*d*.

CHURCH (Dean).—THE BEGINNING OF THE MIDDLE AGES. Gl. 8vo. 5*s*.

COX (G. V.).—RECOLLECTIONS OF OXFORD 2nd Edit. Cr. 8vo. 6*s*.

DASENT (A. I.). -HISTORY OF ST. JAMES'S SQUARE. 8vo 12*s*. net.

ENGLISH STATESMEN, TWELVE. (*See* BIOGRAPHY, p. 5.)

FISKE (John).—THE CRITICAL PERIOD IN AMERICAN HISTORY, 1783—89. Ext. cr. 8vo. 10*s*. 6*d*.
—— THE BEGINNINGS OF NEW ENGLAND; or, The Puritan Theocracy in its Relations to Civil and Religious Liberty. Cr. 8vo. 7*s*. 6*d*.
—— THE AMERICAN REVOLUTION. 2 vols. Cr. 8vo. 18*s*.
—— THE DISCOVERY OF AMERICA. 2 vols. Cr. 8vo. 18*s*.

FRAMJI (Dosabhai). — HISTORY OF THE PARSIS, INCLUDING THEIR MANNERS, CUS-TOMS, RELIGION, AND PRESENT POSITION. With Illustrations. 2 vols. Med. 8vo. 36*s*

FREEMAN (Prof. E. A.).—HISTORY OF THE CATHEDRAL CHURCH OF WELLS. Cr. 8vo 3*s*. 6*d*.
—— OLD ENGLISH HISTORY. With 3 Coloured Maps. 9th Edit., revised. Ext. fcp. 8vo. 6*s*
—— HISTORICAL ESSAYS. First Series. 5th Edit. 8vo. 10*s*. 6*d*.
—— —— Second Series. 3rd Edit., with Additional Essays. 8vo. 10*s*. 6*d*.
—— —— Third Series. 8vo. 12*s*.
—— —— Fourth Series. 8vo. 12*s*. 6*d*.
—— THE GROWTH OF THE ENGLISH CONSTI-TUTION FROM THE EARLIEST TIMES. 5th Edit. Cr. 8vo. 5*s*.
—— COMPARATIVE POLITICS. Lectures at the Royal Institution. To which is added "The Unity of History." 8vo. 14*s*.
—— SUBJECT AND NEIGHBOUR LANDS OF VENICE. Illustrated. Cr. 8vo. 10*s*. 6*d*.
—— ENGLISH TOWNS AND DISTRICTS. A Series of Addresses and Essays. 8vo. 14*s*.
—— THE OFFICE OF THE HISTORICAL PRO-FESSOR. Cr. 8vo. 2*s*. .
—— DISESTABLISHMENT AND DISENDOW-MENT; WHAT ARE THEY? Cr. 8vo. 2*s*.
—— GREATER GREECE AND GREATER BRI-TAIN: GEORGE WASHINGTON THE EX-PANDER OF ENGLAND. With an Appendix on IMPERIAL FEDERATION. Cr. 8vo. 3*s*. 6*d*.
—— THE METHODS OF HISTORICAL STUDY. Eight Lectures at Oxford. 8vo. 10*s*. 6*d*.
—— THE CHIEF PERIODS OF EUROPEAN HIS-TORY. With Essay on "Greek Cities under Roman Rule." 8vo. 10*s*. 6*d*.
—— FOUR OXFORD LECTURES, 1887; FIFTY YEARS OF EUROPEAN HISTORY; TEUTONIC CONQUEST IN GAUL AND BRITAIN 8vo. 5*s*.

FREEMAN (Prof. E. A.). — HISTORY OF FEDERAL GOVERNMENT IN GREECE AND ITALY. New Edit. by J. B. BURY, M.A. Ex. cr. 8vo. 12*s*. 6*d*.
—— WESTERN EUROPE IN THE FIFTH CEN-TURY. 8vo. [*In the Press.*
—— WESTERN EUROPE IN THE EIGHTH CEN-TURY. 8vo. [*In the Press.*

FRIEDMANN (Paul). (*See* BIOGRAPHY.)

GIBBINS (H. de B.).—HISTORY OF COM MERCE IN EUROPE. Globe 8vo. 3*s*. 6*d*.

GREEN (John Richard).—A SHORT HISTORY OF THE ENGLISH PEOPLE. New Edit., re-vised. 159th Thousand. Cr. 8vo. 8*s*. 6*d*.—Also in Parts, with Analysis. 3*s*. each.—Part I. 607—1265; II. 1204—1553; III. 1540—1689; IV. 1660—1873.—*Illustrated Edition.* Su-per roy. 8vo. 4 vols. 12*s*. each net.
—— HISTORY OF THE ENGLISH PEOPLE. In 4 vols. 8vo. 16*s*. each.—In 8 vols. Gl. 8vo. 5*s*. each.
—— THE MAKING OF ENGLAND. 8vo. 16*s*.
—— THE CONQUEST OF ENGLAND. With Maps and Portrait. 8vo. 18*s*.
—— READINGS IN ENGLISH HISTORY. In 3 Parts. Fcp. 8vo. 1*s*. 6*d*. each.

GREEN (Alice S.).—TOWN LIFE IN THE 15TH CENTURY. 2 vols. 8vo. 32*s*.

GUEST (Dr. E.).—ORIGINES CELTICÆ. Maps. 2 vols. 8vo. 32*s*.

GUEST (M. J.).—LECTURES ON THE HISTORY OF ENGLAND. Cr. 8vo. 6*s*.

HARRISON (F.).—THE MEANING OF HIS-TORY, AND OTHER HISTORICAL PIECES. Ex. cr. 8vo. 8*s*. 6*d*. net.

HASSALL (A.).—HANDBOOK OF EUROPEAN HISTORY. Cr. 8vo. [*In the Press.*

HILL (G. B.).—HARVARD COLLEGE. By AN OXONIAN. Cr. 8vo. 9*s*.

HISTORY PRIMERS. Edited by JOHN RICHARD GREEN. Pott 8vo. 1*s*. each.
EUROPE. By E. A. FREEMAN, M.A.
GREECE. By C. A. FYFFE, M.A.
CATALOGUE OF LANTERN SLIDES TO ILLUS-TRATE ABOVE. By Rev. T. FIELD, M.A. Pott 8vo. 6*d*.
ROME. By Bishop CREIGHTON.
FRANCE. By CHARLOTTE M. YONGE.
ENGLISH HISTORY. By A. B. BUCKLEY.

HISTORICAL COURSE FOR SCHOOLS. Ed. by E. A. FREEMAN, D.C.L. Pott 8vo.
GENERAL SKETCH OF EUROPEAN HISTORY. By E. A. FREEMAN. Maps. 3*s*. 6*d*.
HISTORY OF ENGLAND. By EDITH THOMP-SON. Coloured Maps. 2*s*. 6*d*.
HISTORY OF SCOTLAND. By MARGARET MACARTHUR. 2*s*.
HISTORY OF ITALY. By the Rev. W. HUNT, M.A. With Coloured Maps. 3*s*. 6*d*.
HISTORY OF GERMANY. By J. SIME, M.A. 3*s*.
HISTORY OF AMERICA. By J. A. DOYLE. With Maps. 4*s*. 6*d*.
HISTORY OF EUROPEAN COLONIES. By E. J. PAYNE, M.A. Maps. 4*s*. 6*d*.
HISTORY OF FRANCE. By CHARLOTTE M. YONGE. Maps. 3*s*. 6*d*.

HOLE (Rev. C.).—GENEALOGICAL STEMMA OF THE KINGS OF ENGLAND AND FRANCE. On a Sheet. 1*s*.

HOLM (A.).—History of Greece from its Commencement to the Close of the Independence of the Greek Nation. Translated. 4 vols. Vols. I. and II. Cr. 8vo. 6s. net each. [*Vol. III. in Press.*

INGRAM (T. Dunbar).—A History of the Legislative Union of Great Britain and Ireland. 8vo. 10s. 6d
—— Two Chapters of Irish History: 1. The Irish Parliament of James II.; 2. The Alleged Violation of the Treaty of Limerick. 8vo. 6s.

JEBB (Prof. R. C.).—Modern Greece. Two Lectures. 'Crown 8vo. 5s.

JENNINGS (A. C.).—Chronological Tables of Ancient History. 8vo. 5s.

KEARY (Annie).—The Nations Around Israel. Cr. 8vo. 3s. 6d.

KING (G.).—New Orleans, The Place and the People. Cr. 8vo. 10s. 5d.

KINGSLEY (Charles).—The Roman and the Teuton. Cr. 8vo. 3s. 6d.
—— Historical Lectures and Essays. Cr. 8vo. 3s. 6d.

LABBERTON (R. H.). (*See* Atlases.)

LEE·WARNER (W.).—The Protected Princes of India. 8vo. 10s. 6d.

LEGGE (Alfred O.).—The Growth of the Temporal Power of the Papacy. Cr. 8vo. 8s. 6d.

LETHBRIDGE (Sir Roper).—A Short Manual of the History of India. Cr. 8vo. 5s.
—— The World's History. Cr. 8vo, swd. 1s.
—— History of India. Cr. 8vo. 2s.; sewed, 1s. 6d.
—— History of England. Cr.8vo,swd. 1s.6d.
—— Easy Introduction to the History and Geography of Bengal. Cr.8vo. 1s.6d.

LIGHTFOOT (J. B.).—Historical Essays. Gl. 8vo. 5s.

LYTE (H. C. Maxwell).—A History of Eton College, 1440—1884. Illustrated. 8vo. 21s.
—— A History of the University of Oxford, from the Earliest Times to the Year 1530. 8vo. 16s.

MAHAFFY (Prof. J. P.).—Social Life in Greece, from Homer to Menander. 6th Edit. Cr. 8vo. 9s.
—— Greek Life and Thought, from the Age of Alexander to the Roman Conquest. Cr 8vo. 12s. 6d.
—— The Greek World under Roman Sway, from Polybius to Plutarch. Cr. 8vo. 10s. 6d.
—— Problems in Greek History. Crown 8vo. 7s. 6d.
—— History of the Ptolemies. Cr. 8vo. 12s. 6d.

MARRIOTT (J. A. R.). (*See* Select Biography, p. 6.)

MATHEW (E. J.).—First Sketch of English History. Part II. Gl. 8vo. 2s.

MICHELET (M.).—A Summary of Modern History. Translated by M. C. M. Simpson. Globe 8vo. 4s. 6d.

MULLINGER (J. B.).—Cambridge Characteristics in the Seventeenth Century. Cr. 8vo. 4s. 6d.

NORGATE (Kate).—England under the Angevin Kings. In 2 vols. 8vo. 32s.

OLIPHANT (Mrs. M. O. W.).—The Makers of Florence: Dante, Giotto, Savonarola, and their City. Illustr. Cr. 8vo. 10s. 6d.—*Edition de Luxe.* 8vo. 21s. net.
—— The Makers of Venice: Doges, Conquerors, Painters, and Men of Letters. Illustrated. Cr. 8vo. 10s 6d.
—— Royal Edinburgh: Her Saints, Kings, Prophets, and Poets. Illustrated by Sir G. Reid, R.S.A. Cr. 8vo. 10s. 6d.
—— Jerusalem, its History and Hope. Illust. Cr. 8vo. 10s. 6d.—Large Paper Edit. 50s. net.
—— The Reign of Queen Anne. Illust. Ex. cr. 8vo. 8s. 6d. net.
—— The Makers of Modern Rome. With Illustrations. 8vo. 21s.

OTTE (E. C.).—Scandinavian History. With Maps. Globe 8vo. 6s.

PALGRAVE (Sir F.).—History of Normandy and of England. 4 vols. 8vo. 4l.4s.

PARKIN (G. R.).—The Great Dominion. Crown 8vo. 6s.

PARKMAN (Francis). — Montcalm and Wolfe. Library Edition. Illustrated with Portraits and Maps. 2 vols. 8vo. 12s.6d. each.
—— The Collected Works of Francis Parkman. Popular Edition. In 12 vols. Cr. 8vo. 7s. 6d. each.—Pioneers of France in the New World, 1 vol.; The Jesuits in North America, 1 vol.; La Salle and the Discovery of the Great West, 1 vol.; The Oregon Trail, 1 vol.; The Old Régime in Canada under Louis XIV., 1 vol.; Count Frontenac and New France under Louis XIV., 1 vol.; Montcalm and Wolfe, 2 vols.; The Conspiracy of Pontiac, 2 vols.; A Half Century of Conflict 2 vols.
—— The Oregon Trail. Illustrated. Med. 8vo. 21s.

PERKINS (J. B.).—France under the Regency. Cr. 8vo. 8s. 6d.

PIKE (L. O.).—Constitutional History of the House of Lords. 8vo. 12s. 6d. net.

POOLE (R. L.).—A History of the Huguenots of the Dispersion at the Recall of the Edict of Nantes. Cr. 8vo. 6s.

PROWSE (D. W.).—History of Newfoundland. 8vo. 21s. net.

RHODES (J. F.).—History of the United States from the Compromise of 1850 to 1880. Vols. I. II. 24s. Vol. III. 12s.

ROGERS (Prof. J. E. Thorold).—Historical Gleanings. Cr. 8vo.—1st Series. 4s. 6d.—2nd Series. 6s.

SAYCE (Prof. A. H.).—The Ancient Empires of the East. Cr. 8vo. 6s.

SEELEY (Sir J. R.). — Lectures and Essays. Globe 8vo. 5s.
—— The Expansion of England. Two Courses of Lectures. Globe 8vo. 5s.
—— Our Colonial Expansion. Extracts from the above. Cr. 8vo. 1s.

SEWELL (E. M.) and YONGE (C. M.).—European History: a Series of Historical Selections from the Best Authorities. 2 vols. 3rd Edit. Cr. 8vo. 6s. each.

SHAW (Miss).—Australia. [*In the Press.*

HISTORY—*contd.*

SHUCKBURGH (E. S.).—A HISTORY OF ROME TO THE BATTLE OF ACTIUM. Cr. 8vo. 8s. 6d.

SMITH (Goldwin).—OXFORD AND HER COLLEGES. Pott 8vo. 3s.—Illustrated Edition. 6s. (*See also under* POLITICS, p. 37.)

STEPHEN (Sir J. Fitzjames).—THE STORY OF NUNCOMAR AND THE IMPEACHMENT OF SIR ELIJAH IMPEY. 2 vols. Cr. 8vo. 15s.

TAIT (C. W. A.).—ANALYSIS OF ENGLISH HISTORY, BASED ON GREEN'S "SHORT HISTORY OF THE ENGLISH PEOPLE." Cr. 8vo. 3s. 6d.

TOUT (T. F.).—ANALYSIS OF ENGLISH HISTORY. Pott 8vo. 1s.

TREVELYAN (Sir Geo. Otto).—CAWNPORE. Cr. 8vo. 6s.

TUCKWELL (W.).—THE ANCIENT WAYS; WINCHESTER FIFTY YEARS AGO. Globe 8vo. 4s. 6d.

WHEELER (J. Talboys).—PRIMER OF INDIAN HISTORY, ASIATIC AND EUROPEAN. Pott 8vo. 1s.

—— COLLEGE HISTORY OF INDIA, ASIATIC AND EUROPEAN. Cr. 8vo. 2s. 6d.; swd. 2s.

—— A SHORT HISTORY OF INDIA. With Maps. Cr. 8vo. 12s.

—— INDIA UNDER BRITISH RULE. 8vo. 12s. 6d.

WILLIAMS (H.).—BRITAIN'S NAVAL POWER. Cr. 8vo. 4s. 6d. net.

WOOD (Rev. E. G.).—THE REGAL POWER OF THE CHURCH. 8vo. 4s. 6d.

YONGE (Charlotte).—CAMEOS FROM ENGLISH HISTORY. Ext. fcp. 8vo. 5s. each.—Vol. 1. FROM ROLLO TO EDWARD II.; Vol. 2. THE WARS IN FRANCE; Vol. 3. THE WARS OF THE ROSES; Vol. 4. REFORMATION TIMES; Vol. 5. ENGLAND AND SPAIN; Vol. 6. FORTY YEARS OF STEWART RULE (1603—43); Vol. 7. THE REBELLION AND RESTORATION (1642—1678).

—— THE VICTORIAN HALF-CENTURY. Cr. 8vo. 1s. 6d.; sewed, 1s.

—— THE STORY OF THE CHRISTIANS AND MOORS IN SPAIN. Pott 8vo. 2s. 6d. net.

HORSE BREEDING.

PEASE (A. E.).—HORSE BREEDING FOR FARMERS. Cr. 8vo. 2s. 6d.

HORTICULTURE. (*See* GARDENING.)

HYGIENE.

BERNERS (J.).—FIRST LESSONS ON HEALTH. Pott 8vo. 1s.

BLYTH (A. Wynter).—A MANUAL OF PUBLIC HEALTH. 8vo. 17s. net.

—— LECTURES ON SANITARY LAW. 8vo. 8s. 6d. net.

BROWNE (J. H. Balfour).—WATER SUPPLY. Cr. 8vo. 2s. 6d.

CLIMATES AND BATHS OF GREAT BRITAIN. 8vo. 21s. net.

CORFIELD (Dr. W. H.).—THE TREATMENT AND UTILISATION OF SEWAGE. 3rd Edit. Revised by the Author, and by LOUIS C. PARKES, M.D. 8vo. 16s.

FAYRER (Sir J.).—ON PRESERVATION OF HEALTH IN INDIA. Pott 8vo. 1s.

GOODFELLOW (J.).—THE DIETETIC VALUE OF BREAD. Cr. 8vo. 6s.

KINGSLEY (Charles).—SANITARY AND SOCIAL LECTURES. Cr. 8vo. 3s. 6d.

—— HEALTH AND EDUCATION. Cr. 8vo. 6s.

MIERS (H. A.) and CROSSKEY (R.).—THE SOIL IN RELATION TO HEALTH. Cr. 8vo. 3s. 6d.

REYNOLDS (E. S.).—PRIMER OF HYGIENE. Pott 8vo. 1s.

REYNOLDS (Prof. Osborne).—SEWER GAS, AND HOW TO KEEP IT OUT OF HOUSES. 3rd Edit. Cr. 8vo. 1s. 6d.

RICHARDSON (Dr. Sir B. W.).—HYGEIA: A CITY OF HEALTH. Cr. 8vo. 1s.

—— THE FUTURE OF SANITARY SCIENCE. Cr. 8vo. 1s.

—— ON ALCOHOL. Cr. 8vo. 1s.

WILLOUGHBY (E. F.).—PUBLIC HEALTH AND DEMOGRAPHY. Fcp. 8vo. 4s. 6d.

HYMNOLOGY.

(*See under* THEOLOGY, p. 42.)

ILLUSTRATED BOOKS.

ÆSOP'S FABLES. Selected by J. JACOBS. With 300 Illustrations by R. HEIGHWAY. Cr. 8vo. 6s.—Also with uncut edges, paper label, 6s.

BALCH (Elizabeth). — GLIMPSES OF OLD ENGLISH HOMES. Gl. 4to. 14s.

BARLOW (J.).—THE END OF ELFINTOWN. Illust. by L. HOUSMAN. Cr. 8vo. 5s.

BLAKE. (*See* BIOGRAPHY, p. 4.)

BOUGHTON (G. H.) and ABBEY (E. A.). (*See* VOYAGES AND TRAVELS.)

CHRISTMAS CAROL (A). Printed in Colours, with Illuminated Borders. 4to. 21s.

CORIDON'S SONG, AND OTHER VERSES. Preface by AUSTIN DOBSON. Illustrations by HUGH THOMSON. Cr. 8vo. 6s.—Also with uncut edges, paper label, 6s.

CRAWFORD (F. M.). — CONSTANTINOPLE. Illustrated by E. L. WEEKS. Sm. 4to. 6s. 6d.

DAYS WITH SIR ROGER DE COVERLEY. From the *Spectator*. Illustrated by HUGH THOMSON. Cr. 8vo. 6s.—Also with uncut edges, paper label. 6s.

DELL (E. C.).—PICTURES FROM SHELLEY. Engraved by J. D. COOPER. Folio. 21s. net.

FIELDE (A. M.).—A CORNER OF CATHAY. Illustrated. Fcap. 4to. 8s. 6d. net.

GASKELL (Mrs.).—CRANFORD. Illustrated by HUGH THOMSON. Cr. 8vo. 6s.—Also with uncut edges paper label. 6s.

GOETHE.—REYNARD THE FOX. Edited by J. JACOBS. Illustrated by F. CALDERON. Cr. 8vo. 6s. Also with uncut edges, paper label. 6s.

GOLDSMITH (Oliver). — THE VICAR OF WAKEFIELD. New Edition, with 182 Illustrations by HUGH THOMSON. Preface by AUSTIN DOBSON. Cr. 8vo. 6s.—Also with Uncut Edges, paper label. 6s.

GREEN (John Richard). — ILLUSTRATED EDITION OF THE SHORT HISTORY OF THE ENGLISH PEOPLE. 4 vols. Sup. roy. 8vo. 12s. each net.

GRIMM. (*See* BOOKS FOR THE YOUNG, p. 48.)

HALLWARD (R. F.).—FLOWERS OF PARA-
DISE. Music, Verse, Design, Illustration. 6s.

HAMERTON (P. G.).—MAN IN ART. With
Etchings and Photogravures. 3l. 13s. 6d. net.
—Large Paper Edition. 10l. 10s. net.

HARRISON (F.).—ANNALS OF AN OLD MA-
NOR HOUSE, SUTTON PLACE, GUILDFORD.
4to. 42s. net.

HENLEY (W. E.).—A LONDON GARLAND.
Selected from Five Centuries of English
Verse. Illustrated. 4to. 21s. net.

HOOD (Thomas).—HUMOROUS POEMS. Illustrated by C. E. BROCK. Cr. 8vo. 6s.—Also
with uncut edges, paper label. 6s.

IRVING (Washington).—OLD CHRISTMAS.
From the Sketch Book. Illustr. by RANDOLPH
CALDECOTT. Cr. 8vo. 6s.—Also with uncut
edges, paper label. 6s.—Large Paper Edi-
tion. 30s. net.
—— BRACEBRIDGE HALL. Illustr. by RAN-
DOLPH CALDECOTT. Cr. 8vo. 6s.—Also
with uncut edges, paper label. 6s.
—— OLD CHRISTMAS AND BRACEBRIDGE
HALL. Edition de Luxe. Roy. 8vo. 21s.
—— RIP VAN WINKLE AND THE LEGEND OF
SLEEPY HOLLOW. Illustr. by G. H. BOUGH-
TON. Cr. 8vo. 6s.—Also with uncut edges,
paper label. 6s.—Edition de Luxe. Roy.
8vo. 30s. net.

KINGSLEY (Charles).—THE WATER BABIES.
(See BOOKS FOR THE YOUNG, p. 48.)
—— THE HEROES. (See BOOKS for the YOUNG.)
—— GLAUCUS. (See NATURAL HISTORY.)

KIPLING (Rudyard). (See BOOKS FOR THE
YOUNG.)

LANG (Andrew).—THE LIBRARY. With a
Chapter on Modern English Illustrated
Books, by AUSTIN DOBSON. Cr. 8vo. 4s. 6d.
—Large Paper Edition. 21s. net.

LYTE (H. C. Maxwell). (See HISTORY.)

MAHAFFY (Rev. Prof. J. P.) and ROGERS
(J. E.). (See VOYAGES AND TRAVELS.)

MEREDITH (L. A.).—BUSH FRIENDS IN
TASMANIA. Native Flowers, Fruits, and
Insects, with Prose and Verse Descriptions.
Folio. 52s. 6d. net.

MITFORD (M. R.).—OUR VILLAGE. Illustrated by HUGH THOMSON. Cr. 8vo. 6s.—
Also with uncut edges, paper label. 6s.

OLD SONGS. With Drawings by E. A.
ABBEY and A. PARSONS. 4to, mor. gilt. 31s.6d.

OLIPHANT (Mrs.). (See HISTORY.)

PENNELL (Jos.). (See ART.)

PROPERT (J. L.). (See ART.)

STEEL (F. A.).—TALES OF THE PUNJAB.
Illustr. by J. L. KIPLING. Cr. 8vo. 6s.—
Also with uncut edges, paper label, 6s.

STUART, RELICS OF THE ROYAL
HOUSE OF. Illustrated by 40 Plates in
Colours drawn from Relics of the Stuarts by
WILLIAM GIBB. With an Introduction by
JOHN SKELTON, C.B., LL.D. and Descrip-
tive Notes by W. ST. JOHN HOPE. Folio,
half morocco, gilt edges. 10l. 10s. net.

SWIFT.—GULLIVER'S TRAVELS. Illustrated
by C. E. BROCK. Preface by H. CRAIK, C.B.
Cr. 8vo. 6s.—Also with uncut edges, paper
label, 6s.

TENNYSON (Hallam Lord).—JACK AND THE
BEAN-STALK. English Hexameters. Illustrated by R. CALDECOTT. Fcp. 4to. 3s. 6d.

TRISTRAM (W. O.).—COACHING DAYS AND
COACHING WAYS. Illust. H. RAILTON and
HUGH THOMSON. Cr. 8vo. 6s.—Also with
uncut edges, paper label, 6s.—Large Paper
Edition, 30s. net.

TURNER'S LIBER STUDIORUM: A
DESCRIPTION AND A CATALOGUE. By W. G.
RAWLINSON. Med. 8vo. 12s. 6d.

WALTON and COTTON—LOWELL.—THE
COMPLETE ANGLER. With Introduction by
JAS. RUSSELL LOWELL. 2 vols. Ext. cr. 8vo.
52s. 6d. net.

WHITE (G.).—NATURAL HISTORY OF SEL-
BORNE. Introduction by J. BURROUGHS.
Illustrations by C. JOHNSON. 2 vols. Cr.
8vo. 10s. 6d.

WINTER (W.).—SHAKESPEARE'S ENGLAND.
80 Illustrations. Cr. 8vo. 6s.

LANGUAGE. (See PHILOLOGY.)

LAW.

BALL (W. W. R.).—THE STUDENT'S GUIDE
TO THE BAR. 6th Ed. Cr. 8vo. 2s. 6d. net.

BERNARD (M.).—FOUR LECTURES ON SUB-
JECTS CONNECTED WITH DIPLOMACY. 8vo. 9s.

BIGELOW (M. M.).—HISTORY OF PROCE-
DURE IN ENGLAND FROM THE NORMAN
CONQUEST, 1066-1204. 8vo. 16s.

BORGEAUD (C.). — CONSTITUTIONS IN
EUROPE AND AMERICA. Transl. by C. D.
HAZEN. Cr. 8vo. 8s. 6d. net.

BOUTMY (E.). — STUDIES IN CONSTITU-
TIONAL LAW. Transl. by Mrs. DICEY. Pre-
face by Prof. A. V. DICEY. Cr. 8vo. 6s.
—— THE ENGLISH CONSTITUTION. Transl.
by Mrs. EADEN. Introduction by Sir F.
POLLOCK, Bart. Cr. 8vo. 6s.

CHERRY (R. R.). — LECTURES ON THE
GROWTH OF CRIMINAL LAW IN ANCIENT
COMMUNITIES. 8vo. 5s. net.

DICEY (Prof. A. V.).—INTRODUCTION TO
THE STUDY OF THE LAW OF THE CONSTI-
TUTION. 4th Edit. 8vo. 12s. 6d.

ENGLISH CITIZEN SERIES, THE.
(See POLITICS.)

GOODNOW (F. J.). — MUNICIPAL HOME
RULE. Cr. 8vo. 6s. 6d. net.

HOLLAND (Prof. T. E.).—THE TREATY RE-
LATIONS OF RUSSIA AND TURKEY, FROM
1774 TO 1853. Cr. 8vo. 2s.

HOLMES (O. W., jun.). — THE COMMON
LAW. 8vo. 12s.

HOWELL (G.).—HANDY BOOK OF THE LA-
BOUR LAWS. 3rd Ed. Cr. 8vo. 3s. 6d. net.

LAWRENCE (T. J.).—INTERNATIONAL LAW.
8vo. 12s. 6d. net.

LIGHTWOOD (J. M.).—THE NATURE OF
POSITIVE LAW. 8vo. 12s. 6d.

MAITLAND (F. W.).—PLEAS OF THE CROWN
FOR THE COUNTY OF GLOUCESTER, A.D. 1221.
8vo. 7s. 6d.
—— JUSTICE AND POLICE. Cr. 8vo. 2s. 6d.

MONAHAN (James H.).—THE METHOD OF
LAW. Cr. 8vo. 6s.

MUNRO (J. E. C.).—COMMERCIAL LAW.
Globe 8vo. 3s. 6d.

LAW—continued.

PATERSON (James).—COMMENTARIES ON THE LIBERTY OF THE SUBJECT, AND THE LAWS OF ENGLAND RELATING TO THE SECURITY OF THE PERSON. 2 vols. Cr. 8vo. 21s.
—— THE LIBERTY OF THE PRESS, SPEECH, AND PUBLIC WORSHIP. Cr. 8vo. 12s.

PHILLIMORE (John G.).—PRIVATE LAW AMONG THE ROMANS. 8vo. 6s.

POLLOCK (Sir F., Bart.).—ESSAYS IN JURISPRUDENCE AND ETHICS. 8vo. 10s. 6d.
—— THE LAND LAWS. Cr. 8vo. 2s. 6d.
—— LEADING CASES DONE INTO ENGLISH. Cr. 8vo. 3s. 6d.

RICHEY (Alex. G.).—THE IRISH LAND LAWS. Cr. 8vo. 3s. 6d.

STEPHEN (Sir J. F., Bart.).—A DIGEST OF THE LAW OF EVIDENCE. 6th Ed. Cr. 8vo. 6s.
—— A DIGEST OF THE CRIMINAL LAW; CRIMES AND PUNISHMENTS. 5th Ed. 8vo. 16s.
—— A DIGEST OF THE LAW OF CRIMINAL PROCEDURE IN INDICTABLE OFFENCES. By Sir J. F., Bart., and HERBERT STEPHEN, LL.M. 8vo. 12s. 6d.
—— A HISTORY OF THE CRIMINAL LAW OF ENGLAND. 3 vols. 8vo. 48s.
—— A GENERAL VIEW OF THE CRIMINAL LAW OF ENGLAND. 2nd Edit. 8vo. 14s.

STEPHEN (J. K.).—INTERNATIONAL LAW AND INTERNATIONAL RELATIONS. Cr. 8vo. 6s.

STEVENS (C. E.).—SOURCES OF THE CONSTITUTION OF THE UNITED STATES, CONSIDERED IN RELATION TO COLONIAL AND ENGLISH HISTORY. Cr. 8vo. 6s. 6d. net.

WILLIAMS (S. E.).—FORENSIC FACTS AND FALLACIES. Globe 8vo. 4s. 6d.

LETTERS. (See under LITERATURE, p. 24.)

LIFE-BOAT.

GILMORE (Rev. John).—STORM WARRIORS; or, Life-Boat Work on the Goodwin Sands. Cr. 8vo. 3s. 6d.

LEWIS (Richard).—HISTORY OF THE LIFE-BOAT AND ITS WORK. Cr. 8vo. 5s.

LIGHT. (See under PHYSICS, p. 34.)

LITERATURE.

History and Criticism of—Commentaries, etc.—Poetry and the Drama—Poetical Collections and Selections—Prose Fiction—Collected Works, Essays, Lectures, Letters, isce llaneous

History and Criticism of.
(See also ESSAYS, p. 24.)

ARNOLD (M.). (See ESSAYS. p. 24.)

BROOKE (Stopford A.).—A PRIMER OF ENGLISH LITERATURE. Pott 8vo. 1s.—Large Paper Edition. 8vo. 7s. 6d.
—— A HISTORY OF EARLY ENGLISH LITERATURE. 2 vols. 8vo. 20s. net.

CLASSICAL WRITERS. Edited by JOHN RICHARD GREEN. Fcp. 8vo. 1s. 6d. each.
DEMOSTHENES. By Prof. BUTCHER, M.A.
EURIPIDES. By Prof. MAHAFFY.
LIVY. By the Rev. W. W. CAPES, M.A.
MILTON. By STOPFORD A. BROOKE.
SOPHOCLES. By Prof. L. CAMPBELL, M.A.
TACITUS. By Messrs. CHURCH and BRODRIBB.
VERGIL. By Prof. NETTLESHIP, M.A.

COURTHOPE (W. J.).—HISTORY OF ENGLISH POETRY. Vol. I. 8vo. 10s. net.

ENGLISH MEN OF LETTERS. (See BIOGRAPHY, p. 4.)

HISTORY OF ENGLISH LITERATURE. In 4 vols. Cr. 8vo.
EARLY ENGLISH LITERATURE. By STOPFORD BROOKE, M.A. [In preparation.
ELIZABETHAN LITERATURE (1560—1665). By GEORGE SAINTSBURY. 7s. 6d.
EIGHTEENTH CENTURY LITERATURE (1660—1780). By EDMUND GOSSE, M.A. 7s. 6d.
NINETEENTH CENTURY LITERATURE. By G. SAINTSBURY. 7s. 6d.

JEBB (Prof. R. C.).—A PRIMER OF GREEK LITERATURE. Pott 8vo. 1s.
—— THE ATTIC ORATORS, FROM ANTIPHON TO ISAEOS. 2nd Edit. 2 vols 8vo. 25s.
—— RISE AND DEVELOPMENT OF GREEK POETRY. Cr. 8vo. 7s. net.

JOHNSON'S LIVES OF THE POETS. MILTON, DRYDEN, POPE, ADDISON, SWIFT, AND GRAY With Macaulay's "Life of Johnson" Ed. by M. ARNOLD. Cr. 8vo. 4s. 6d.

JONES (H. A.).—RENASCENCE OF THE ENGLISH DRAMA. Cr. 8vo. 6s.

KINGSLEY (Charles). — LITERARY AND GENERAL LECTURES. Cr. 8vo. 3s. 6d.

MAHAFFY (Prof. J. P.).—A HISTORY OF CLASSICAL GREEK LITERATURE. 2 vols. Cr. 8vo.—Vol. 1. THE POETS. With an Appendix on Homer by Prof. SAYCE. In 2 Parts.—Vol. 2. THE PROSE WRITERS. In 2 Parts. 4s. 6d. each.

MORLEY (John). (See COLLECTED WORKS, p. 27.)

OLIPHANT (Mrs. M. O. W.).—THE LITERARY HISTORY OF ENGLAND IN THE END OF THE 18TH AND BEGINNING OF THE 19TH CENTURY. 3 vols. 8vo. 21s.

PATER (W.).—GREEK STUDIES. Ex. cr. 8vo. 10s. 6d.
—— PLATO AND PLATONISM. Ex. cr. 8vo. 8s. 6d.

RYLAND (F.).—CHRONOLOGICAL OUTLINES OF ENGLISH LITERATURE. Cr. 8vo. 6s.

SAINTSBURY (G.).—A SHORT HISTORY OF ENGLISH LITERATURE. Gl. 8vo. [In prep.

TYRRELL (Prof. R. Y.).—LATIN POETRY. Cr. 8vo. 7s. net

WARD (Prof. A. W.).—A HISTORY OF ENGLISH DRAMATIC LITERATURE, TO THE DEATH OF QUEEN ANNE. 2 vols. 8vo. 32s.

WHITCOMB (L. S.).—CHRONOLOGICAL OUTLINES OF AMERICAN LITERATURE. Cr. 8vo. 6s. net.

WILKINS (Prof. A. S.).—A PRIMER OF ROMAN LITERATURE. Pott 8vo. 1s.

WULKER. — ANGLO SAXON LITERATURE. Transl. by A. W. DEERING and C. F. Mc CLUMPHA. [In the Press.

Commentaries, etc.

BROWNING.
A PRIMER OF BROWNING. By MARY WILSON. Cr. 8vo. 2s. 6d.

CHAUCER.
A PRIMER OF CHAUCER. By A. W. POLLARD. Pott 8vo. 1s.

DANTE.
* READINGS ON THE PURGATORIO OF DANTE. Chiefly based on the Commentary of Benvenuto da Imola. By the Hon. W. W. VERNON, M.A. With an Introduction by Dean CHURCH. 2 vols. Cr. 8vo. 24*.
READINGS ON THE INFERNO OF DANTE. By the Hon. W. W. VERNON, M.A. With an Introduction by Rev. E. MOORE, D.D. 2 vols. Cr. 8vo. 30*.
COMPANION TO DANTE. From G. A. SCARTAZZINI. By A. J. BUTLER. Cr. 8vo. 10*.6d.
HOMER.
HOMERIC DICTIONARY. (See DICTIONARIES.)
THE PROBLEM OF THE HOMERIC POEMS. By Prof. W. D. GEDDES. 8vo. 14*.
HOMERIC SYNCHRONISM. An Inquiry into the Time and Place of Homer. By the Rt. Hon. W. E. GLADSTONE. Cr. 8vo. 6*.
PRIMER OF HOMER. By the Rt. Hon. W. E. GLADSTONE. Pott 8vo. 1*.
LANDMARKS OF HOMERIC STUDY, TOGETHER WITH AN ESSAY ON THE POINTS OF CONTACT BETWEEN THE ASSYRIAN TABLETS AND THE HOMERIC TEXT. By the same. Cr. 8vo. 2*.6d.
COMPANION TO THE ILIAD FOR ENGLISH READERS. By W. LEAF, Litt.D. Crown 8vo. 7*.6d.
HORACE.
STUDIES, LITERARY AND HISTORICAL, IN THE ODES OF HORACE. By A. W. VERRALL, Litt.D. 8vo. 8*.6d.
SHAKESPEARE.
A PRIMER OF SHAKSPERE. By Prof. DOWDEN. Pott 8vo. 1*.
A SHAKESPEARIAN GRAMMAR. By Rev. E. A. ABBOTT. Ext. fcp. 8vo. 6*.
A SHAKESPEARE CONCORDANCE. By J. BARTLETT. 4to. 42*. net. ; half mor., 45*. net.
SHAKESPEAREANA GENEALOGICA. By G. R. FRENCH. 8vo. 15*.
A SELECTION FROM THE LIVES IN NORTH'S PLUTARCH WHICH ILLUSTRATE SHAKESPEARE'S PLAYS. Edited by Rev. W. W. SKEAT, M.A. Cr. 8vo. 6*.
SHORT STUDIES OF SHAKESPEARE'S PLOTS. By Prof. CYRIL RANSOME. Cr. 8vo. 3*.6d. —Also separately: HAMLET, 9d.; MACBETH, 9d.; TEMPEST, 9d.
CALIBAN: A Critique on "The Tempest" and "A Midsummer Night's Dream." By Sir DANIEL WILSON. 8vo. 10*.6d.
TENNYSON.
A COMPANION TO "IN MEMORIAM." By ELIZABETH R. CHAPMAN. Globe 8vo. 2*.
"IN MEMORIAM"-ITS PURPOSE AND STRUCTURE: A STUDY. By J. F. GENUNG. Cr. 8vo. 5*.
ESSAYS ON THE IDYLLS OF THE KING. By H. LITTLEDALE, M.A. Cr. 8vo. 4*.6d.
A STUDY OF THE WORKS OF ALFRED LORD TENNYSON. By E. C. TAINSH. New Ed. Cr. 8vo. 6*.
THACKERAY.
THACKERAY: A Study. By A. A. JACK. Cr. 8vo. 3*.6d.
WORDSWORTH.
WORDSWORTHIANA: A Selection of Papers read to the Wordsworth Society. Edited by W. KNIGHT. Cr. 8vo. 7*.6d.

Poetry and the Drama.

ALDRICH (T. Bailey).—THE SISTERS' TRAGEDY: with other Poems, Lyrical and Dramatic. Fcp. 8vo. 3*.6d. net.

AN ANCIENT CITY: AND OTHER POEMS. Ext. fcp. 8vo. 6*.
ANDERSON (A.).—BALLADS AND SONNETS. Cr. 8vo. 5*.
ARNOLD (Matthew). — THE COMPLETE POETICAL WORKS. New Edition. 3 vols. Cr. 8vo. 7*. 6d. each ; Globe 8vo. 5*. each.
Vol. 1. EARLY POEMS, NARRATIVE POEMS AND SONNETS.
Vol. 2. LYRIC AND ELEGIAC POEMS.
Vol. 3. DRAMATIC AND LATER POEMS.
—— COMPLETE POETICAL WORKS. 1 vol. Cr. 8vo. 7*. 6d.
—— SELECTED POEMS. Pott 8vo. 2*. 6d. net.
AUSTIN (Alfred).—POETICAL WORKS. New Collected Edition. 7 vols. Cr. 8vo. 5*. each.
Vol. 1. THE TOWER OF BABEL.
Vol. 2. SAVONAROLA, etc.
Vol. 3. PRINCE LUCIFER.
Vol. 4. THE HUMAN TRAGEDY.
Vol. 5. LYRICAL POEMS.
Vol. 6. NARRATIVE POEMS.
Vol. 7. FORTUNATUS THE PESSIMIST.
—— SOLILOQUIES IN SONG. Cr. 8vo. 6*.
—— AT THE GATE OF THE CONVENT: and other Poems. Cr. 8vo. 6*.
—— MADONNA'S CHILD. Fcp. 8vo. 2*.6d.net.
—— ROME OR DEATH. Cr. 4to. 9*.
—— THE GOLDEN AGE. Cr. 8vo. 5*.
—— THE SEASON. Cr. 8vo. 5*.
—— LOVE'S WIDOWHOOD. Cr. 8vo. 6*.
—— ENGLISH LYRICS. Cr. 8vo. 3*. 6d.
—— ENGLAND'S DARLING. Cr. 8vo. 6s
BETSY LEE : A FO'C'S'LE YARN. Ext. fcp. 8vo. 3*. 6d.
BLACKIE (J. S.).—MESSIS VITAE: Gleanings of Song from a Happy Life. Cr. 8vo. 4*.6d.
—— THE WISE MEN OF GREECE. In a Series of Dramatic Dialogues. Cr. 8vo. 9*.
—— GOETHE'S FAUST. Translated into English Verse. 2nd Edit. Cr. 8vo. 9*.
BLAKE. (See BIOGRAPHY, p. 4.)
BROOKE (Stopford A.).—RIQUET OF THE TUFT : A Love Drama. Ext. cr. 8vo. 6*.
—— POEMS. Globe 8vo. 6*.
BROWN (T. E.).—THE MANX WITCH : and other Poems. Cr. 8vo. 6*.
—— OLD JOHN, AND OTHER POEMS. Cr 8vo. 6*.
BURGON (Dean).—POEMS. Ex.fcp.8vo. 4*.6d.
BURNS. THE POETICAL WORKS. With a Biographical Memoir by A. SMITH. In 2 vols. Fcp.8vo. 10*. (See also GLOBE LIBRARY,p.25.)
BUTLER (Samuel).—HUDIBRAS. Edit. by ALFRED MILNES. Fcp. 8vo.—Part I. 3*. 6d.; Parts II. and III. 4*. 6d.
BYRON. (See GOLDEN TREASURY SERIES, p. 25)
CALDERON.—SELECT PLAYS. Edited by NORMAN MACCOLL. Cr. 8vo. 14*.
CARR (J. Comyns).—KING ARTHUR. A Drama, as performed at the Lyceum. 8vo 2*. net ; sewed, 1*. net.
CAUTLEY (G. S.).—A CENTURY OF EMBLEMS. With Illustrations by Lady MARION ALFORD. Small 4to. 10*. 6d.
CHAUCER.—CANTERBURY TALES. Edit. by A. W. POLLARD. 2 vols. Gl. 8vo. 10*.
—— THE RICHES OF CHAUCER. With Notes by C. COWDEN CLARKE. Cr. 8vo.
CLOUGH (A. H.).—POEMS. Cr. 8vo. 7*.6d.
—— SELECTIONS FROM THE POEMS. Pott 8vo. 2*. 6d. net.

LITERATURE.

Poetry and the Drama—*continued.*

COLERIDGE: POETICAL AND DRAMATIC WORKS. 4 vols. Fcp. 8vo. 31s. 6d.—Also an Edition on Large Paper, 2l. 12s. 6d.
—— COMPLETE POETICAL WORKS. With Introduction by J. D. CAMPBELL, and Portrait. Cr. 8vo. 7s. 6d.

COLQUHOUN.—RHYMES AND CHIMES. By F. S. COLQUHOUN (*née* F. S. FULLER MAIT-LAND). Ext. fcp. 8vo. 2s. 6d.

COWPER.—THE TASK, BOOK IV. With Introduction and Notes by W. T. WEBB, M.A. Sewed, 1s.—BOOK V. With Notes. Gl. 8vo. 6d. (*See* GLOBE LIBRARY, p. 25; GOLDEN TREASURY SERIES, p. 25.)

CRAIK (Mrs.).—POEMS. Ext. fcp. 8vo. 6s.

DABBS (G. H. R.)—RIGHTON (E.).—DANTE: A DRAMATIC POEM. Fcp. 8vo. 2s. 6d.

DAWSON (W. J.).—POEMS AND LYRICS. Fcp. 8vo. 4s. 6d.

DE VERE (A.).—POETICAL WORKS. 7 vols. Cr. 8vo. 5s. each.
—— SELECTIONS FROM POETICAL WORKS OF. By G. E. WOODBERRY. Globe 8vo. 5s.

DOYLE (Sir F. H.).—THE RETURN OF THE GUARDS: and other Poems. Cr. 8vo. 7s. 6d.

DRYDEN. (*See* COLLECTED WORKS *and* GLOBE LIBRARY, pp. 24, 25.)

EMERSON. (*See* COLLECTED WORKS, p. 24.)

EVANS (Sebastian). — BROTHER FABIAN'S MANUSCRIPT: and other Poems. Fcp. 8vo. 6s.
—— IN THE STUDIO: A Decade of Poems. Ext. fcp. 8vo. 5s.

FITZ GERALD (Caroline).—VENETIA VICTRIX: and other Poems. Ext. fcp. 8vo. 3s. 6d.

FITZGERALD (Edward).—THE RUBÁIYÁT OF OMAR KHÁYYÁM. Ext. cr. 8vo. 10s. 6d.

FO'C'SLE YARNS, including " Betsy Lee," and other Poems. Cr. 8vo. 6s.

FRASER-TYTLER. — SONGS IN MINOR KEYS. By C. C. FRASER-TYTLER (Mrs. EDWARD LIDDELL). 2nd Edit. Pott 8vo. 6s.

FURNIVALL (F. J.).—LE MORTE ARTHUR. Edited from the Harleian MSS. 2252, in the British Museum. Fcp. 8vo. 7s. 6d.

GARNETT (R.).—IDYLLS AND EPIGRAMS. Chiefly from the Greek Anthology. Fcp. 8vo. 2s. 6d.

GOETHE.—FAUST. (*See* BLACKIE.)
—— REYNARD THE FOX. Transl. into English Verse by A. D. AINSLIE. Cr. 8vo. 7s. 6d.

GOLDSMITH.—THE TRAVELLER AND THE DESERTED VILLAGE. With Introduction and Notes, by ARTHUR BARRETT, B.A. 1s. 9d.; sewed, 1s. 6d.; (separately), sewed, 1s. each. —By J. W. HALES. Cr. 8vo. 6d (*See also* GLOBE LIBRARY, p. 25.)

GRAHAM (David).—KING JAMES I. An Historical Tragedy. Globe 8vo. 7s.

GRAY.—POEMS. With Introduction and Notes, by J. BRADSHAW, LL.D. Gl. 8vo. 1s. 9d.; sewed, 1s. 6d. (*See also* COLLECTED WORKS, p. 26.)
—— SELECT ODES. With Notes. Gl. 8vo, sewed. 6d.

HALLWARD. (*See* ILLUSTRATED BOOKS.)

HAYES (A.).—THE MARCH OF MAN: and other Poems. Fcp. 8vo. 3s. 6d. net.

HERRICK. (*See* GOLDEN TREASURY SERIES, p. 25.)

HOPKINS (Ellice).—AUTUMN SWALLOWS: A Book of Lyrics. Ext. fcp. 8vo. 6s.

HOSKEN (J. D.).—PHAON AND SAPPHO, AND NIMROD. Fcp. 8vo. 5s.

JONES (H. A.).—SAINTS AND SINNERS. Ext. fcp. 8vo. 3s. 6d.
—— THE CRUSADERS. Fcp. 8vo. 2s. 6d.
—— JUDAH. Fcp. 8vo. 2s. 6d.

KEATS. (*See* GOLDEN TREASURY SERIES, p. 25.)

KINGSLEY (Charles).—POEMS. Cr. 8vo. 3s. 6d.—*Pocket Edition.* Pott 8vo. 1s. 6d.—*Eversley Edition.* 2 vols. Cr. 8vo. 10s.

LAMB. (*See* COLLECTED WORKS, p. 27.)

LANDOR. (*See* GOLDEN TREASURY SERIES, p. 25.)

LONGFELLOW. (*See* GOLDEN TREASURY SERIES, p. 25.)

LOWELL (Jas. Russell).—COMPLETE POETICAL WORKS. Pott 8vo. 4s. 6d.
—— With Introduction by THOMAS HUGHES, and Portrait. Cr. 8vo. 7s. 6d.
—— HEARTSEASE AND RUE. Cr. 8vo. 5s.
—— OLD ENGLISH DRAMATISTS. Cr. 8vo. 5s. (*See also* COLLECTED WORKS, p. 27.)

LUCAS (F.).—SKETCHES OF RURAL LIFE. Poems. Globe 8vo. 5s.

MEREDITH (George). — A READING OF EARTH. Ext. fcp. 8vo. 5s.
—— POEMS AND LYRICS OF THE JOY OF EARTH. 3rd Edit. Ext. fcp. 8vo. 6s.
—— BALLADS AND POEMS OF TRAGIC LIFE. 2nd Edit. Ext. fcp. 8vo. 6s.
—— MODERN LOVE. Ex. fcap. 8vo. 5s.
—— THE EMPTY PURSE. Fcp. 8vo. 5s.

MILTON.—POETICAL WORKS. Edited, with Introductions and Notes, by Prof. DAVID MASSON, M.A. 3 vols. 8vo. 2l. 2s.—[Uniform with the Cambridge Shakespeare.]
—— Edited by Prof. MASSON. 3 vols. Globe 8vo. 15s.
—— — *Globe Edition.* Edited by Prof. MASSON. Crown 8vo. 3s. 6d.
—— PARADISE LOST, BOOKS 1 and 2. Edited by MICHAEL MACMILLAN, B.A. 1s. 9d.; —BOOKS 1 to 4 (separately), 1s. 3d. each; sewed, 1s. each.
—— L'ALLEGRO, IL PENSEROSO, LYCIDAS, ARCADES, SONNETS, ETC. Edited by WM. BELL, M.A. 1s. 9d.
—— COMUS. By the same. 1s. 3d.; swd. 1s.
—— SAMSON AGONISTES. Edited by H. M. PERCIVAL, M.A. 2s.

MOULTON (Louise Chandler). — IN THE GARDEN OF DREAMS: Lyrics and Sonnets. Cr. 8vo. 6s.
—— SWALLOW FLIGHTS. Cr. 8vo. 6s.

MUDIE (C. E.).—STRAY LEAVES: Poems. 4th Edit. Ext. fcp. 8vo. 3s. 6d.

MYERS (E.).—THE PURITANS: A Poem. Ext. fcp. 8vo. 2s. 6d.
—— POEMS. Ext. fcp. 8vo. 4s. 6d.
—— THE DEFENCE OF ROME: and other Poems. Ext. fcp. 8vo. 5s.
—— THE JUDGMENT OF PROMETHEUS: and other Poems. Ext. fcp. 8vo. 3s. 6d.

MYERS (F. W. H.).—THE RENEWAL OF YOUTH : and other Poems. Cr. 8vo. 7s. 6d.
—— ST. PAUL : A Poem. Ext. fcp. 8vo. 2s.6d.

NORTON (Hon. Mrs.).—THE LADY OF LA GARAYE. 9th Edit. Fcp. 8vo. 4s. 6d.

PALGRAVE (Prof. F.T.).—ORIGINAL HYMNS. 3rd Edit. Pott 8vo. 1s. 6d.
—— LYRICAL POEMS. Ext. fcp. 8vo. 6s.
—— VISIONS OF ENGLAND. Cr. 8vo. 7s. 6d.
—— AMENOPHIS. Pott 8vo. 4s. 6d.

PALGRAVE (W. G.).—A VISION OF LIFE: SEMBLANCE AND REALITY. Cr. 8vo. 7s. net.

PEEL (Edmund).—ECHOES FROM HOREB : and other Poems. Cr. 8vo. 3s. 6d

POPE. (See GLOBE LIBRARY, p. 25.)

RAWNSLEY (H. D.).—POEMS, BALLADS, AND BUCOLICS. Fcp. 8vo. 5s.

ROSCOE (W. C.).—POEMS. Edit. by E. M. ROSCOE. Cr. 8vo. 7s. net.

ROSSETTI (Christina).—POEMS. New Collected Edition. Globe 8vo. 7s. 6d.
—— NEW POEMS. Hitherto unpublished or uncollected. Edited by W. M. ROSSETTI. Gl. 8vo. 7s. 6d.
—— SING-SONG : A Nursery Rhyme Book. Small 4to. Illustrated. 4s. 6d.
—— GOBLIN MARKET. Illust. Fcp. 8vo. 5s.

SCOTT.—THE LAY OF THE LAST MINSTREL, and THE LADY OF THE LAKE. Edited by Prof. F. T. PALGRAVE. 1s.
—— THE LAY OF THE LAST MINSTREL. By G. H. STUART, M.A., and E. H. ELLIOT, B.A. Globe 8vo. 2s.—Canto I. 9d.—Cantos I.—III. and IV.—VI. 1s. 3d. each ; sewed, 1s. each.
—— MARMION. Edited by MICHAEL MACMILLAN, B A. 3s. ; sewed, 2s. 6d.
—— MARMION, and THE LORD OF THE ISLES. By Prof. F. T. PALGRAVE. 1s.
—— THE LADY OF THE LAKE. By G. H. STUART, M.A. Gl. 8vo. 2s. 6d. ; swd. 2s.—Canto I., sewed, 9d.
—— ROKEBY. By MICHAEL MACMILLAN, B.A. 3s. ; sewed, 2s. 6d.
(See also GLOBE LIBRARY, p. 25.)

SHAIRP (John Campbell).—GLEN DESSERAY: and other Poems, Lyrical and Elegiac. Ed. by F. T. PALGRAVE. Cr. 8vo. 6s.

SHAKESPEARE.—THE WORKS OF WILLIAM SHAKESPEARE. Cambridge Edition. New and Revised Edition, by W. ALDIS WRIGHT, M.A. 9 vols. 8vo. 10s. 6d. each.—Edition de Luxe. 40 vols. Sup. roy. 8vo. 6s. each net.
—— Victoria Edition. In 3 vols.—COMEDIES; HISTORIES; TRAGEDIES. Cr. 8vo. 6s. each.
—— THE TEMPEST. With Introduction and Notes, by K. DEIGHTON. Gl. 8vo. 1s. 9d.
—— MUCH ADO ABOUT NOTHING. 2s.
—— A MIDSUMMER NIGHT'S DREAM. 1s. 9d.
—— THE MERCHANT OF VENICE. 1s. 9d.
—— AS YOU LIKE IT. 1s. 9d.
—— TWELFTH NIGHT. 1s. 9d.
—— THE WINTER'S TALE. 2s.
—— KING JOHN. 1s. 9d.
—— RICHARD II. 1s. 9d.
—— HENRY IV. Part I. 2s. 6d. ; sewed, 2s.
—— HENRY IV. Part II. 2s. 6d. ; sewed, 2s.
—— HENRY V. 1s. 9d.

SHAKESPEARE. — CORIOLANUS. By K. DEIGHTON. 2s. 6d ; sewed, 2s.
—— RICHARD III. By C. H. TAWNEY, M.A. 2s. 6d. ; sewed, 2s.
—— HENRY VIII. By K. DRIGHTON. 1s. 9d.
—— ROMEO AND JULIET. 2s. 6d. ; sewed 2s.
—— JULIUS CÆSAR. 1s. 9d.
—— MACBETH. 1s. 9d.
—— HAMLET. 2s. 6d. ; sewed, 2s.
—— KING LEAR. 1s. 9d.
—— OTHELLO. 2s.
—— ANTONY AND CLEOPATRA. 2s.6d.; swd. 2s.
—— CYMBELINE. 2s. 6d. ; sewed, 2s.
(See also GLOBE LIBRARY, p. 25 ; GOLDEN TREASURY SERIES, p. 26.)

SHELLEY.—COMPLETE POETICAL WORKS. Edited by Prof. DOWDEN. Portrait. Cr. 8vo. 7s.6d. (See GOLDEN TREASURY SERIES, p. 26.)

SKRINE (J. H.).—JOAN THE MAID. Ex. cr. 8vo. 6s. 6d.

SMITH (C. Barnard).—POEMS. Fcp. 8vo. 5s.

SMITH (Horace).—POEMS. Globe 8vo. 5s.
—— INTERLUDES. Cr. 8vo. 5s.
—— INTERLUDES. Second Series. Cr. 8vo. 5s.

SPENSER.—FAIRIE QUEENE. Book I. By H. M. PERCIVAL, M.A. Gl. 8vo. 3s. ; swd., 2s. 6d.
—— SHEPHEARD'S CALENDAR. By C. H. HERFORD, Litt.D. Gl. 8vo. 2s. 6d.
(See also GLOBE LIBRARY, p. 25.)

STEPHENS (J. B.).—CONVICT ONCE : and other Poems. Cr. 8vo. 7s. 6d.

STRETTELL (Alma).—SPANISH AND ITALIAN FOLK SONGS. Illustr. Roy.16mo. 12s.6d.

SYMONS (Arthur). — DAYS AND NIGHTS. Globe 8vo. 6s.

TENNYSON (Lord).—COMPLETE WORKS. New and Enlarged Edition, with Portrait. Cr. 8vo. 7s. 6d.—School Edition. In Four Parts. Cr. 8vo. 2s. 6d. each.
—— POETICAL WORKS. Pocket Edition. Pott 8vo, morocco, gilt edges. 7s. 6d. net.
—— WORKS. Library Edition. In 9 vols. Globe 8vo. 5s. each. [Each volume may be had separately.]—POEMS, 2 vols.—IDYLLS OF THE KING.—THE PRINCESS, and MAUD.—ENOCH ARDEN, and IN MEMORIAM.—BALLADS, and other Poems.—QUEEN MARY, and HAROLD.—BECKET, and other Plays.—DEMETER, and other Poems.
—— WORKS. Ext. fcp. 8vo. Edition, on Hand-made Paper. In 10 vols. (supplied in sets only). 5l. 5s. 0d.—EARLY POEMS.—LUCRETIUS, and other Poems.—IDYLLS OF THE KING.—THE PRINCESS, and MAUD.—ENOCH ARDEN, and IN MEMORIAM.—QUEEN MARY, and HAROLD.—BALLADS, and other Poems.—BECKET, THE CUP.—THE FORESTERS, THE FALCON, THE PROMISE OF MAY.—TIRESIAS, and other Poems.
—— WORKS. Miniature Edition, in 16 vols., viz. THE POETICAL WORKS. 12 vols. In a box. 25s.—THE DRAMATIC WORKS. 4 vols. in a box. 10s. 6d.
—— The Original Editions. Fcp. 8vo. POEMS. 6s.
MAUD : and other Poems. 3s. 6d.
THE PRINCESS. 3s. 6d.
THE HOLY GRAIL and other Poems. 4s.6d.
BALLADS : and other Poems. 5s.
HAROLD : A Drama. 6s.
QUEEN MARY : A Drama. 6s.

LITERATURE.

Poetry and the Drama—*continued.*

TENNYSON (Lord)—*continued.*
The Original Editions. Fcp. 8vo.
THE CUP, and THE FALCON. 5*s.*
BECKET. 6*s.*
TIRESIAS : and other Poems. 6*s.*
LOCKSLEY HALL SIXTY YEARS AFTER, etc. 6*s.*
DEMETER : and other Poems. 6*s.*
THE FORESTERS : ROBIN HOOD AND MAID MARIAN. 6*s.*
THE DEATH OF ŒNONE, AKBAR'S DREAM, AND OTHER POEMS. 6*s.*
—— *The People's Edition.* In 23 volumes, demy 16mo., cloth, 1*s.* net ; leather, 1*s.* 6*d.* net per volume. Two volumes monthly from November, 1895.—JUVENILIA.—THE LADY OF SHALOTT, and other Poems.—A DREAM OF FAIR WOMEN, and other Poems —LOCKSLEY HALL, and other Poems.—WILL WATERPROOF, and other Poems.—THE PRINCESS, I.—III.—THE PRINCESS IV. to end.—ENOCH ARDEN, AYLMER'S FIELD, and LUCRETIUS.—IN MEMORIAM.—MAUD, THE WINDOW, and other Poems.—THE BROOK, and other Poems.—IDYLLS OF THE KING : THE COMING OF ARTHUR, GARETH AND LYNETTE.—IDYLLS OF THE KING : THE MARRIAGE OF GERAINT, GERAINT AND ENID.—IDYLLS OF THE KING : BALIN AND BALAN, MERLIN AND VIVIEN.—IDYLLS OF THE KING : LANCELOT AND ELAINE, THE HOLY GRAIL.-IDYLLS OF THE KING : : PELLEAS AND ETTARRE, THE LAST TOURNAMENT.—IDYLLS OF THE KING : GUINEVERE, THE PASSING OF ARTHUR, TO THE QUEEN.—THE LOVER'S TALE, and other Poems.—RIZPAH, and other Poems.—THE VOYAGE OF MAELDUNE, and other Poems.—THE SPINSTER'S SWEET ARTS, and other Poems.—DEMETER, and other Poems.—THE DEATH OF ŒNONE, and other Poems.
—— POEMS BY TWO BROTHERS. Fcp. 8vo. 6*s.*
—— MAUD. *Kelmscott Edition.* Small 4to, vellum. 42*s.* net.
—— POEMS. Reprint of 1857 Edition. Original Illustrations. 4to. 21*s.*—*Edition de Luxe.* Roy. 8vo. 42*s.* net.
—— *The Royal Edition.* 1 vol. 8vo. 16*s.*
—— THE TENNYSON BIRTHDAY BOOK. Edit. by EMILY SHAKESPEAR. Pott 8vo. 2*s.* 6*d.*
—— SONGS FROM TENNYSON'S WRITINGS. Square 8vo. 2*s.* 6*d.*
—— SELECTIONS FROM TENNYSON. With Introduction and Notes, by F. J. ROWE, M.A., and W. T. WEBB, M.A. Globe 8vo. 3*s.* 6*d.* Or Part I. 2*s.* 6*d.* ; Part II. 2*s.* 6*d.*
—— MORTE D'ARTHUR. By F. J. ROWE, M.A., and W. T. WEBB, M.A. Swd., 1*s.*
—— GERAINT AND ENID : AND THE MARRIAGE OF GERAINT. By G. C. MACAULAY, M.A. Globe 8vo. 2*s.* 6*d.*
—— ENOCH ARDEN. By W. T. WEBB, M.A. Globe 8vo. 2*s.* 6*d.*
—— AYLMER'S FIELD. By W. T. WEBB, M.A. Globe 8vo. 2*s.* 6*d.*
—— THE COMING OF ARTHUR, and THE PASSING OF ARTHUR. By F. J. ROWE. Gl.8vo. 2*s.*6*d.*
—— THE PRINCESS. By P. M. WALLACE, M.A. Globe 8vo. 3*s.* 6*d.*
—— GARETH AND LYNETTE. By G. C. MACAULAY, M.A. Globe 8vo. 2*s.* 6*d.*
—— THE HOLY GRAIL. By G. C. MACAULAY, M.A. Globe 8vo. 2*s.* 6*d.*

TENNYSON (Lord).—GUINEVERE. By G. C. MACAULAY, M.A. 2*s.* 6*d.*
—— LANCELOT AND ELAINE. By F. J. ROWE, M.A. 2*s.* 6*d.*
—— TENNYSON FOR THE YOUNG. By Canon AINGER. Pott 8vo. 1*s.* net.—Large Paper, uncut, 3*s.* 6*d.* ; gilt edges, 4*s.* 6*d.*
—— BECKET. As arranged for the Stage by H. IRVING. 8vo. swd. 2*s.* net
—— THE BROOK. With 20 Illustrations by A. WOODRUFF. 32mo. 2*s.* 6*d.*
TENNYSON (Frederick).—THE ISLES OF GREECE : SAPPHO AND ALCAEUS. Cr. 8vo. 7*s.* 6*d.*
—— DAPHNE : and other Poems. Cr.8vo. 7*s.*6*d.*
TENNYSON (Hallam, Lord). (*See* ILLUSTRATED BOOKS.)
TREVOR (G. H.).—RHYMES OF RAJPUTANA. Cr. 8vo. 7*s.* 6*d.*
TRUMAN (Jos.).—AFTER-THOUGHTS : Poems. Cr. 8vo. 3*s.* 6*d.*
TURNER (Charles Tennyson).—COLLECTED SONNETS, OLD AND NEW. Ext.fcp.8vo. 7*s.*6*d.*
TYRWHITT (R. St. John).—FREE FIELD. • Lyrics, chiefly Descriptive. Gl. 8vo. 3*s.* 6*d.*
—— BATTLE AND AFTER, CONCERNING SERGEANT THOMAS ATKINS, GRENADIER GUARDS : and other Verses. Gl. 8vo. 3*s.*6*d.*
WARD (Samuel).—LYRICAL RECREATIONS. Fcp. 8vo. 6*s.*
WATSON (W.). —POEMS. Fcap. 8vo. 5*s.*
—— LACHRYMAE MUSARUM. Fcp.8vo. 4*s.*6*d.*
(*See also* GOLDEN TREASURY SERIES, p. 25.)
WEBSTER (A.).—PORTRAITS. Fcp. 8vo. 5*s.*
—— SELECTIONS FROM VERSE. Fp. 8vo. 4*s.* 6*d.*
—— DISGUISES : A Drama. Fcp. 8vo. 5*s.*
—— IN A DAY : A Drama. Fcp. 8vo. 2*s.* 6*d.*
—— THE SENTENCE. Fcp. 8vo. 3*s.* 6*d.*
—— SONNETS. Fcp. 8vo. 2*s.* 6*d.* net.
—— MOTHER AND DAUGHTER. Fcp. 8vo. 2*s.* 6*d.* net.
WHITTIER.—COMPLETE POETICAL WORKS OF JOHN GREENLEAF WHITTIER. With Portrait. Pott 8vo. 4*s.* 6*d.* (*See also* GOLDEN TREASURY SERIES, p. 26 ; COLLECTED WORKS, p. 28.)
WILLS (W. G.).—MELCHIOR. Cr. 8vo. 9*s.*
WOOD (Andrew Goldie).—THE ISLES OF THE BLEST : and other Poems. Globe 8vo. 5*s.*
WOOLNER (Thomas). — MY BEAUTIFUL LADY. 3rd Edit. Fcp. 8vo. 5*s.*
—— PYGMALION. Cr. 8vo. 7*s.* 6*d.*
—— SILENUS. Cr. 8vo. 6*s.*
WORDSWORTH. — COMPLETE POETICAL WORKS. Copyright Edition. With an Introduction by JOHN MORLEY, and Portrait. Cr. 8vo. 7*s.* 6*d.*
—— THE RECLUSE. Fcp. 8vo. 2*s.* 6*d.*—Large Paper Edition. 8vo. 10*s.* 6*d.*
(*See also* GOLDEN TREASURY SERIES, p. 26 ; COLLECTED WORKS, p. 28.)

Poetical Collections and Selections.

(*See also* GOLDEN TREASURY SERIES, p. 25 ; BOOKS FOR THE YOUNG, p. 48.)

ELLIS (A.).—CHOSEN ENGLISH. Selections from Wordsworth, Byron, Shelley, Lamb, Scott. Globe 8vo. 2*s.* 6*d.*
GEORGE (H. B.)—SIDGWICK (A.)—POEMS OF ENGLAND. With Notes. Gl. 8vo. 2*s.*6*d.*

HALES (Prof. J. W.).—LONGER ENGLISH POEMS. With Notes, Philological and Explanatory, and an Introduction on the Teaching of English. Ext. fcp. 8vo. 4s. 6d.

MACDONALD (George).—ENGLAND'S ANTIPHON. Cr. 8vo. 4s. 6d.

MARTIN (F.). (See BOOKS FOR THE YOUNG, p. 48.)

MASSON (R. O. and D.).—THREE CENTURIES OF ENGLISH POETRY. Being Selections from Chaucer to Herrick. Globe 8vo. 3s. 6d.

PALGRAVE (Prof. F. T.).—THE GOLDEN TREASURY OF THE BEST SONGS AND LYRICAL POEMS IN THE ENGLISH LANGUAGE. Large Type. Cr. 8vo. 10s. 6d. (See also GOLDEN TREASURY SERIES, p. 25; BOOKS FOR THE YOUNG, p. 49.)

SMITH (Goldwin).—BAY LEAVES. Translations from Latin Poets. Globe 8vo. 5s.

WARD (T. H.).—ENGLISH POETS. Selections, with Critical Introductions by various Writers, and a General Introduction by MATTHEW ARNOLD. Edited by T. H. WARD, M.A. 4 vols. 2nd Edit. Cr. 8vo.- Vol. I. CHAUCER TO DONNE, 7s. 6d.; II. BEN JONSON TO DRYDEN, 7s. 6d.; III. ADDISON TO BLAKE, 7s. 6d. IV. WORDSWORTH TO TENNYSON, 8s. 6d.

—— Appendix to Vol. IV. containing BROWNING, ARNOLD, and TENNYSON. Cr. 8vo. 2s.

WOODS (M. A.).—A FIRST POETRY BOOK. Fcp. 8vo. 2s. 6d.

—— A SECOND POETRY BOOK. 2 Parts. Fcp. 8vo. 2s. 6d. each.—Complete, 4s. 6d.

—— A THIRD POETRY BOOK. Fcp.8vo. 4s. 6d.

WORDS FROM THE POETS. With a Vignette and Frontispiece. 12th Edit. Pott8vo. 1s.

Prose Fiction.

AUSTEN (Jane). — PRIDE AND PREJUDICE. Illustrated. Cr. 8vo. 3s. 6d.

BIKELAS (D.).—LOUKIS LARAS; or, The Reminiscences of a Chiote Merchant during the Greek War of Independence. Translated by J. GENNADIUS. Cr. 8vo. 7s. 6d.

BJÖRNSON (B.).—SYNNÖVÉ SOLBAKKEN. Translated by JULIE SUTTER. Cr. 8vo. 6s.

BOLDREWOOD (Rolf).—Uniform Edition. Cr. 8vo. 3s. 6d. each.
ROBBERY UNDER ARMS.
THE MINER'S RIGHT.
THE SQUATTER'S DREAM.
A SYDNEY-SIDE SAXON.
A COLONIAL REFORMER.
NEVERMORE.
A MODERN BUCCANEER.
—— THE CROOKED STICK. Cr. 8vo. 6s.
—— OLD MELBOURNE MEMORIES. Cr. 8vo. 6s.
—— THE SPHINX OF EAGLEHAWK. Fcp.8vo. 2s.

BORROW (G.). — LAVENGRO. Illustrated. Cr. 8vo. 3s. 6d.

BURNETT (F. H.).–HAWORTH'S. Gl. 8vo. 2s.
—— LOUISIANA, and THAT LASS O' LOWRIE'S. Illustrated. Cr.8vo. 3s. 6d.

CALMIRE. 2 vols. Cr. 8vo. 21s.

CARMARTHEN (Marchioness of). — A LOVER OF THE BEAUTIFUL. Cr. 8vo. 6s.

CONWAY (Hugh). — A FAMILY AFFAIR. Cr. 8vo. 3s. 6d.
—— LIVING OR DEAD. Cr. 8vo. 3s. 6d.

COOPER (E. H.).—RICHARD ESCOTT. Cr. 8vo. 6s.

CORBETT (Julian).—THE FALL OF ASGARD: A Tale of St. Olaf's Day. 2 vols. Gl. 8vo. 12s.
—— FOR GOD AND GOLD. Cr. 8vo. 6s.
—— KOPHETUA THE THIRTEENTH. 2 vols. Globe 8vo. 12s.

COTES (E.).—THE STORY OF SONNY SAHIB. Fcp. 8vo. 2s.

CRAIK (Mrs.).—Uniform Edition. Cr. 8vo. 3s. 6d. each.
OLIVE.
THE OGILVIES. Also Globe 8vo, 2s.
AGATHA'S HUSBAND. Also Globe 8vo, 2s.
THE HEAD OF THE FAMILY.
TWO MARRIAGES. Also Globe 8vo, 2s.
THE LAUREL BUSH.
MY MOTHER AND I.
MISS TOMMY: A Mediæval Romance.
KING ARTHUR: Not a Love Story.

CRAWFORD (F. Marion).—Uniform Edition. Cr. 8vo. 3s. 6d. each.
MR. ISAACS: A Tale of Modern India.
DR. CLAUDIUS.
A ROMAN SINGER. | ZOROASTER.
A TALE OF A LONELY PARISH.
MARZIO'S CRUCIFIX. | PAUL PATOFF.
WITH THE IMMORTALS.
GREIFENSTEIN. | SANT' ILARIO.
A CIGARETTE MAKER'S ROMANCE.
KHALED: A Tale of Arabia.
THE WITCH OF PRAGUE.
THE THREE FATES. | DON ORSINO.
CHILDREN OF THE KING.
PIETRO GHISLERI. | MARION DARCHE.
KATHARINE LAUDERDALE.
—— THE RALSTONS. Cr. 8vo. 6s.
—— CASA BRACCIO. 2 vols. Gl. 8vo. 12s.
—— LOVE IN IDLENESS. Fcp. 8vo. 2s.

CUNNINGHAM (Sir H. S.).—THE CŒRULEANS: A Vacation Idyll. Cr. 8vo. 3s. 6d.
—— THE HERIOTS. Cr. 8vo. 3s. 6d.
—— WHEAT AND TARES. Cr. 8vo. 3s. 6d.
—— SIBYLLA. 2 vols. Gl. 8vo. 12s.

CURTIN (J.).—HERO TALES OF IRELAND. Ex. cr. 8vo. 8s. 6d. net.

DAHN (Felix).—FELICITAS. Translated by M. A. C. E. Cr. 8vo. 4s. 6d.

DAVIS (R. H.). — THE PRINCESS ALINE. Fcp. 8vo. 1s. 6d.

DAY (Rev. Lal Behari).—BENGAL PEASANT LIFE. Cr. 8vo. 6s.
—— FOLK TALES OF BENGAL. Cr 8vo. 4s.6d

DEFOE (D.). (See GLOBE LIBRARY, p. 25; GOLDEN TREASURY SERIES, p. 25.)

DEMOCRACY: AN AMERICAN NOVEL. Cr. 8vo. 4s. 6d.

DICKENS (Charles). — Uniform Edition. Cr. 8vo. 2s. 6d. each.
THE PICKWICK PAPERS.
OLIVER TWIST. | NICHOLAS NICKLEBY.
MARTIN CHUZZLEWIT.
THE OLD CURIOSITY SHOP.
BARNABY RUDGE. | DOMBEY AND SON.
CHRISTMAS BOOKS. | SKETCHES BY BOZ.
DAVID COPPERFIELD.
AMERICAN NOTES, AND PICTURES FROM ITALY.
BLEAK HOUSE.
—— THE POSTHUMOUS PAPERS OF THE PICKWICK CLUB. Illust. Edit. by C. DICKENS, Jun. 2 vols. Ext. cr. 8vo. 21s.

LITERATURE.
Prose Fiction—*continued.*

DICKENS M. A.).—A MERE CYPHER. Cr. 8vo. 3*s.* 6*d.*
—— A VALIANT IGNORANCE. Cr. 8vo. 3*s.* 6*d.*

DILLWYN (E. A.).—JILL. Cr. 8vo. 6*s.*
—— JILL AND JACK. 2 vols. Globe 8vo. 12*s.*

DISRAELI (B.).—SYBIL. Illustrated. Cr. 8vo. 3*s.* 6*d.*

DUNSMUIR (Amy).—VIDA: Study of a Girl. 3rd Edit. Cr. 8vo. 6*s.*

DURAND (Sir M.).—HELEN TREVERYAN. Cr. 8vo. 3*s.* 6*d.*

EBERS (Dr. George).—THE BURGOMASTER'S WIFE. Transl. by C. BELL. Cr. 8vo. 4*s.* 6*d.*
—— ONLY A WORD. Translated by CLARA BELL. Cr. 8vo. 4*s.* 6*d.*

EDGEWORTH (M.).—CASTLE RACKRENT. Illustrated. Cr. 8vo. 3*s.* 6*d.*
—— ORMOND. Illustrated. Cr. 8vo. 3*s.* 6*d.*
—— POPULAR TALES. Illust. Cr. 8vo. 3*s.* 6*d.*

"ESTELLE RUSSELL" (The Author of).—HARMONIA. 3 vols. Cr. 8vo. 31*s.* 6*d.*

FALCONER (Lanoe).—CECILIA DE NOEL. Cr. 8vo. 3*s.* 6*d.*

FLEMING (G.).—A NILE NOVEL. Gl. 8vo. 2*s.*
—— MIRAGE: A Novel. Globe 8vo. 2*s.*
—— THE HEAD OF MEDUSA. Globe 8vo. 2*s.*
—— VESTIGIA. Globe 8vo. 2*s.*

FRANCIS (Francis)—WILD ROSE. Cr. 8vo. 6*s.*

FRATERNITY: A Romance. 2 vols. Cr. 8vo. 21*s.*

"FRIENDS IN COUNCIL" (The Author of).—REALMAH. Cr. 8vo. 6*s.*

GALT (J.).—ANNALS OF THE PARISH AND THE AYRSHIRE LEGATEES. Illustrated. Cr. 8vo. 3*s.* 6*d.*

GRAHAM (John W.).—NEÆRA: A Tale of Ancient Rome. Cr. 8vo. 6*s.*

GRANT (C.).—TALES OF NAPLES AND THE CAMORRA.   [*In the Press.*

HARBOUR BAR, THE. Cr. 8vo. 6*s.*

HARDY (Arthur Sherburne).—BUT YET A WOMAN: A Novel. Cr. 8vo. 4*s.* 6*d.*
—— THE WIND OF DESTINY. 2 vols. Gl. 8vo. 12*s.*

HARTE (Bret).—CRESSY. Cr. 8vo. 3*s.* 6*d.*
—— THE HERITAGE OF DEDLOW MARSH and other Tales. Cr. 8vo. 3*s.* 6*d.*
—— A FIRST FAMILY OF TASAJARA. Cr. 8vo. 3*s.* 6*d.*

"HOGAN, M.P." (The Author of).—HOGAN, M.P. Cr. 8vo. 3*s.* 6*d.*
—— THE HON. MISS FERRARD. Gl. 8vo. 2*s.*
—— FLITTERS, TATTERS, AND THE COUN-SELLOR, ETC. Cr. 8vo. 3*s.* 6*d.*
—— CHRISTY CAREW. Globe 8vo. 2*s.*
—— ISMAY'S CHILDREN. Globe 8vo. 2*s.*

HOPPUS (Mary).—A GREAT TREASON: A Story of the War of Independence. 2 vols. Cr. 8vo. 9*s.*

HUGHES (Thomas).—TOM BROWN'S SCHOOL DAYS. By AN OLD BOY.—Golden Treasury Edition. 2*s.* 6*d.* net.—Uniform Edit. 3*s.* 6*d.*—People's Edition. 2*s.*—People's Sixpenny Edition. Illustr. Med. 4to. 6*d.*—Uniform with Sixpenny Kingsley. Med. 8vo. 6*d.*
—— TOM BROWN AT OXFORD. Cr. 8vo. 3*s.* 6*d.*
—— THE SCOURING OF THE WHITE HORSE, and THE ASHEN FAGGOT. Cr. 8vo. 3*s.* 6*d.*

IRVING (Washington). (*See* ILLUSTRATED BOOKS, p. 15.)

JACKSON (Helen).—RAMONA. Gl. 8vo. 2*s.*

JAMES (Henry).—THE EUROPEANS: A Novel. Cr. 8vo. 6*s.*; Pott 8vo, 2*s.*
—— DAISY MILLER; and other Stories. Cr. 8vo. 6*s.*; Globe 8vo, 2*s.*
—— THE AMERICAN. Cr. 8vo. 6*s.*—Pott 8vo. 2 vols. 4*s.*
—— RODERICK HUDSON. Cr. 8vo. 6*s.*; Gl. 8vo, 2*s.*; Pott 8vo, 2 vols. 4*s.*
—— THE MADONNA OF THE FUTURE: and other Tales. Cr. 8vo. 6*s.*; Globe 8vo, 2*s.*
—— WASHINGTON SQUARE, THE PENSION BEAUREPAS. Globe 8vo. 2*s.*
—— THE PORTRAIT OF A LADY. Cr. 8vo. 6*s.* Pott 8vo, 3 vols. 6*s.*
—— STORIES REVIVED. In Two Series. Cr. 8vo. 6*s.* each.
—— THE BOSTONIANS. Cr. 8vo. 6*s.*
—— NOVELS AND TALES. Pocket Edition. Pott 8vo. 2*s.* each volume.
    CONFIDENCE. 1 vol.
    THE SIEGE OF LONDON; MADAME DE MAUVES. 1 vol.
    AN INTERNATIONAL EPISODE; THE PEN-SION BEAUREPAS; THE POINT OF VIEW. 1 vol.
    DAISY MILLER, a Study; FOUR MEET-INGS; LONGSTAFF'S MARRIAGE; BEN-VOLIO. 1 vol.
    THE MADONNA OF THE FUTURE; A BUNDLE OF LETTERS; THE DIARY OF A MAN OF FIFTY; EUGENE PICKERING. 1 vol.
—— TALES OF THREE CITIES. Cr. 8vo. 4*s.* 6*d.*
—— THE PRINCESS CASAMASSIMA. Cr. 8vo. 6*s.*; Globe 8vo, 2*s.*
—— THE REVERBERATOR. Cr. 8vo. 6*s.*
—— THE ASPERN PAPERS; LOUISA PALLANT; THE MODERN WARNING. Cr. 8vo. 3*s.* 6*d.*
—— A LONDON LIFE. Cr. 8vo. 3*s.* 6*d.*
—— THE TRAGIC MUSE. Cr. 8vo. 3*s.* 6*d.*
—— THE LESSON OF THE MASTER, AND OTHER STORIES. Cr. 8vo. 6*s.*
—— THE REAL THING, AND OTHER TALES. Cr. 8vo. 6*s.*

KEARY (Annie).—JANET'S HOME. Cr. 8vo. 3*s.* 6*d.*
—— CLEMENCY FRANKLYN. Globe 8vo. 2*s.*
—— OLDBURY. Cr. 8vo. 3*s.* 6*d.*
—— A YORK AND A LANCASTER ROSE. Cr. 8vo. 3*s.* 6*d.*
—— CASTLE DALY. Cr. 8vo. 3*s.* 6*d.*
—— A DOUBTING HEART. Cr. 8vo. 3*s.* 6*d.*

KENNEDY (P.).—LEGENDARY FICTIONS OF THE IRISH CELTS. Cr. 8vo. 3*s.* 6*d.*

KINGSLEY (Charles).—*Eversley Edition.* 13 vols. Globe 8vo. 5*s.* each.—WESTWARD HO! 2 vols.—TWO YEARS AGO. 2 vols.—HYPATIA. 2 vols.—YEAST. 1 vol.—ALTON LOCKE. 2 vols.—HEREWARD THE WAKE. 2 vols.
—— *Sixpenny Edition.* Med. 8vo. 6*d.* each. — WESTWARD HO! — HYPATIA. — YEAST.—ALTON LOCKE.—TWO YEARS AGO.—HEREWARD THE WAKE.
—— *Pocket Edition.* Pott 8vo. 1*s.* 6*d.* each. HYPATIA. — ALTON LOCKE. — WESTWARD HO! 2 vols.—HEREWARD THE WAKE.—TWO YEARS AGO. 2 vols.—YEAST.

KINGSLEY (C.).—*Complete Edition.* Cr. 8vo. 3s. 6d. each —WESTWARD HO! With a Portrait. – HYPATIA. — YEAST. — ALTON LOCKE. — TWO YEARS AGO. — HEREWARD THE WAKE.

KIPLING (Rudyard).—PLAIN TALES FROM THE HILLS. Cr. 8vo. 6s.
—— THE LIGHT THAT FAILED. Cr. 8vo. 6s.
—— LIFE'S HANDICAP : Being Stories of mine own People. Cr. 8vo. 6s.
—— MANY INVENTIONS. Cr. 8vo. 6s.
—— SOLDIERS THREE, ETC. Cr. 8vo. 6s.
—— WEE WILLIE WINKIE, ETC. Cr. 8vo. 6s.

LAFARGUE (Philip).—THE NEW JUDGMENT OF PARIS. 2 vols. Globe 8vo. 12s.

LEE (Margaret).—FAITHFUL AND UNFAITH-FUL. Cr. 8vo 3s. 6d.

LEVY (A.).—REUBEN SACHS. Cr. 8vo. 3s.6d.

LITTLE PILGRIM IN THE UNSEEN, A. 24th Thousand. Cr. 8vo. 2s. 6d.

"LITTLE PILGRIM IN THE UNSEEN, A" (Author of).—THE LAND OF DARKNESS. Cr. 8vo. 5s.

LYSAGHT (S. R.).—THE MARPLOT. Cr. 8vo. 3s. 6d.

LYTTON (Earl of).—THE RING OF AMASIS ! A Romance. Cr. 8vo. 3s. 6d.

McLENNAN (Malcolm).—MUCKLE JOCK ! and other Stories of Peasant Life in the North. Cr. 8vo. 3s. 6d.

MACMILLAN (M. K.). — DAGONET THE JESTER. Cr. 8vo. 3s. 6d.

MACQUOID (K. S.).—PATTY. Gl. 8vo. 2s.

MADOC (Fayr).—THE STORY OF MELICENT. Cr. 8vo. 4s. 6d.

MALET (Lucas).—MRS. LORIMER : A Sketch in Black and White. Cr. 8vo. 3s. 6d.

MALORY (Sir Thos.). (*See* GLOBE LIBRARY, p. 25.)

MARRYAT (Capt.).—JAPHET IN SEARCH OF A FATHER. Illustrated. Cr. 8vo. 3s. 6d.
—— JACOB FAITHFUL. Illust. Cr. 8vo. 3s. 6d.
—— PETER SIMPLE. Illust. Cr. 8vo. 3s. 6d.
—— MIDSHIPMAN EASY. Illust. Cr. 8vo.
[*In the Press.*
—— THE PHANTOM SHIP. Illust. Cr. 8vo.
[*In the Press.*
—— THE KING'S OWN. Illust. Cr. 8vo.
[*In the Press.*
—— POOR JACK. Illust. Cr. 8vo. [*In Press.*
—— THE DOG-FIEND. Illust. Cr.8vo.[*In Press.*

MASON (A. E. W.).—THE COURTSHIP OF MORRICE BUCKLER. Cr. 8vo. 6s.

MINTO (W.).—THE MEDIATION OF RALPH HARDELOT. 3 vols. Cr. 8vo. 31s. 6d.

MITFORD (A. B.).—TALES OF OLD JAPAN. With Illustrations. Cr. 8vo. 3s. 6d.

MIZ MAZE, THE ; OR, THE WINKWORTH PUZZLE. A Story in Letters by Nine Authors. Cr. 8vo. 4s. 6d.

MORIER (J.).—HAJJI BABA OF ISPAHAN. Illustrated. Cr. 8vo. 3s. 6d.

MURRAY (D. Christie). — AUNT RACHEL. Cr. 8vo. 3s. 6d.
—— SCHWARTZ. Cr. 8vo. 3s 6d.
—— THE WEAKER VESSEL. Cr. 8vo. 3s. 6d.
—— JOHN VALE'S GUARDIAN. Cr. 8vo. 3s. 6d.

MURRAY (D. Christie) and HERMAN (H.). —HE FELL AMONG THIEVES. Cr.8vo. 3s.6d.

NEW ANTIGONE, THE: A ROMANCE. Cr. 8vo. 3s. 6d.

NOEL (Lady Augusta).—HITHERSEA MERE. 3 vols. Cr. 8vo. 31s. 6d.

NORRIS (W. E.).—MY FRIEND JIM. Globe 8vo. 2s.
—— CHRIS. Globe 8vo. 2s.

NORTON (Hon. Mrs.).—OLD SIR DOUG-LAS. Cr. 8vo. 6s.

OLIPHANT (Mrs. M. O. W.).—*Uniform Edition.* Cr. 8vo. 3s. 6d. each.
A SON OF THE SOIL.
THE CURATE IN CHARGE.
YOUNG MUSGRAVE. | SIR TOM.
HE THAT WILL NOT WHEN HE MAY.
THE WIZARD'S SON. | HESTER.
A COUNTRY GENTLEMAN AND HIS FAMILY.
THE SECOND SON.
THE MARRIAGE OF ELINOR.
NEIGHBOURS ON THE GREEN. | JOYCE.
A BELEAGUERED CITY. | KIRSTEEN.
THE RAILWAY MAN AND HIS CHILDREN.
THE HEIR-PRESUMPTIVE AND THE HEIR-APPARENT.
LADY WILLIAM.

PALMER (Lady Sophia).—MRS. PENICOTT'S LODGER ; and other Stories. Cr. 8vo. 2s. 6d.

PARRY (Gambier).—THE STORY OF DICK. Cr. 8vo. 3s. 6d.

PATER (Walter).—MARIUS THE EPICUREAN ! His SENSATIONS AND IDEAS. 3rd Edit. 2 vols. 8vo. 15s.

PATERSON (A.).—A SON OF THE PLAINS. Cr. 8vo. 6s.

PEACOCK (T. L.).—MAID MARIAN, ETC. Illustrated. Cr. 8vo. 3s. 6d.
—— HEADLONG HALL AND NIGHTMARE AB-BEY. Illust. Cr. 8vo. 3s. 6d.
—— GRYLL GRANGE. Illust. Cr. 8vo. 3s. 6d.

PHILLIPS (F. E.). — THE EDUCATION OF ANTONIA. Cr. 8vo. 6s.

PRICE (E. C.).—IN THE LION'S MOUTH. Cr. 8vo. 3s. 6d.

RHOADES (J.).—THE STORY OF JOHN TRE-VENNICK. Cr. 8vo. 3s. 6d.

ROSS (Percy).—A MISGUIDIT LASSIE. Cr. 8vo. 4s. 6d.

ROY (Neil).—THE HORSEMAN'S WORD. Cr. 8vo. 6s.

RUSSELL (W. Clark).—MAROONED. Cr. 8vo. 3s. 6d.
—— A STRANGE ELOPEMENT. Cr. 8vo. 3s.6d.

ST. JOHNSTON (A.). — A SOUTH SEA LOVER: A Romance. Cr. 8vo. 6s.

SCOTT (M.).—TOM CRINGLE'S LOG. Illus-trated. Cr. 8vo. 3s. 6d.

SHIPTON (Helen). — THE HERONS. Cr. 8vo. 6s.

SHORTHOUSE (J. Henry).—*Uniform Edi-tion.* Cr. 8vo. 3s. 6d. each.
JOHN INGLESANT: A Romance.
SIR PERCIVAL : A Story of the Past and of the Present.
THE LITTLE SCHOOLMASTER MARK : A Spiritual Romance.
THE COUNTESS EVE.
A TEACHER OF THE VIOLIN : and other Tales.
BLANCHE, LADY FALAISE.

LITERATURE.
Prose Fiction—continued.

SLIP IN THE FENS, A. Globe 8vo. 2s.

SMITH (Garnet).—THE MELANCHOLY OF STEPHEN ALLARD. Cr. 8vo. 7s. 6d. net.

SMITH (L. P.).—THE YOUTH OF PARNASSUS. Cr. 8vo. 6s.

STEEL (Mrs. F. A.).—MISS STUART'S LEGACY. Cr. 8vo. 3s. 6d.

—— THE FLOWER OF FORGIVENESS. Crown 8vo. 3s. 6d.

—— RED ROWANS. Cr. 8vo. 6s.

—— TALES OF THE PUNJAB. Illust. Cr. 8vo. 6s.

THEODOLI (Marchesa)—UNDER PRESSURE. Cr. 8vo. 3s. 6d.

TIM. Cr. 8vo. 3s. 6d.

TOURGÉNIEF.—VIRGIN SOIL. Translated by ASHTON W. DILKE. Cr. 8vo. 6s.

VELEY (Margaret).—A GARDEN OF MEMORIES ; MRS. AUSTIN ; LIZZIE'S BARGAIN. Three Stories. 2 vols. Globe 8vo. 12s.

VICTOR (H.).—MARIAM : OR TWENTY-ONE DAYS. Cr. 8vo. 6s.

VOICES CRYING IN THE WILDERNESS : A NOVEL. Cr. 8vo. 7s. 6d.

WARD (Mrs. T. Humphry).—MISS BRETHERTON. Cr. 8vo. 3s. 6d.

WEST (M.).—A BORN PLAYER. Cr. 8vo. 6s

WORTHEY (Mrs.).—THE NEW CONTINENT ! A Novel. 2 vols. Globe 8vo. 12s.

YONGE (C. M.).—THE LONG VACATION. Cr. 8vo. 6s.

—— THE RELEASE. Cr. 8vo. 6s.

—— THE RUBIES OF ST. LO. Fcp. 8vo. 2s. (See also p. 28.)

YONGE (C. M.) and COLERIDGE (C. R.). —STROLLING PLAYERS. Cr. 8vo. 6s.

Collected Works; Essays; Lectures; Letters; Miscellaneous Works.

ADDISON.—SELECTIONS FROM THE "SPECTATOR." With Introduction and Notes by K. DEIGHTON. Globe 8vo. 2s. 6d.

AN AUTHOR'S LOVE. Being the Unpublished Letters of PROSPER MÉRIMÉE'S "Inconnue." 2 vols. Extr. cr. 8vo. 12s.

ARNOLD (Matthew).—LETTERS. Edited by G. W. E. RUSSELL, M.P. 2 vols. Cr. 8vo. 15s. net.

—— ESSAYS IN CRITICISM. 6th Ed. Cr. 8vo 9s. Gl. 8vo. 5s.

—— ESSAYS IN CRITICISM. Second Series. Cr. 8vo. 7s. 6d. Gl. 8vo. 5s.

—— DISCOURSES IN AMERICA. Cr. 8vo. 4s. 6d Gl. 8vo. 5s.

ASPECTS OF MODERN STUDY. Cr. 8vo. 2s. 6d. net.

AUSTIN (A.)—THE GARDEN THAT I LOVE. 3rd Edit. Ex. cr. 8vo. 9s.

—— IN VERONICA'S GARDEN. Ex. cr. 8vo. 9s.

BACON.—ESSAYS. Introduction and Notes, by F. G. SELBY, M.A. Gl. 8vo. 3s swd., 2s. 6d.

—— ADVANCEMENT OF LEARNING. By the same. Gl. 8vo. Book I. 2s. Book II. 4s. 6d. (See also GOLDEN TREASURY SERIES, p. 25)

BATES (K. L.).—ENGLISH RELIGIOUS DRAMA. Cr. 8vo. 6s. 6d. net.

BLACKIE (J. S.).—LAY SERMONS. Cr. 8vo. 6s

BRADFORD (G.).—TYPES OF AMERICAN CHARACTER. Pott 8vo. 3s.

BRIDGES (John A.).—IDYLLS OF A LOST VILLAGE. Cr. 8vo. 7s. 6d.

BRIMLEY (George).—ESSAYS. Globe 8vo. 5s.

BUNYAN (John).—THE PILGRIM'S PROGRESS FROM THIS WORLD TO THAT WHICH IS TO COME. Pott 8vo. 2s. 6d. net.

BUTCHER (Prof. S. H.)—SOME ASPECTS OF THE GREEK GENIUS. Cr. 8vo. 7s. net.

CARLYLE (Thomas). (See BIOGRAPHY.)

CHURCH (Dean).—MISCELLANEOUS WRITINGS. Collected Edition. 7 vols. Globe 8vo. 5s. each.—Vol. I. MISCELLANEOUS ESSAYS.—II. DANTE : AND OTHER ESSAYS. —III. ST. ANSELM.—IV. SPENSER.—V. BACON.—VI. THE OXFORD MOVEMENT, 1833—45.—VII. THE BEGINNING OF THE MIDDLE AGES.

CLIFFORD (Prof. W. K.). LECTURES AND ESSAYS. Edited by LESLIE STEPHEN and Sir F. POLLOCK. Cr. 8vo. 8s. 6d.

CLOUGH (A. H.).—PROSE REMAINS. With a Selection from his Letters, and a Memoir by HIS WIFE. Cr. 8vo. 7s. 6d.

COLLINS (J. Churton).—THE STUDY OF ENGLISH LITERATURE. Cr. 8vo. 4s. 6d.

—— ESSAYS AND STUDIES. 8vo. 9s. net.

CORSON (Hiram).—THE AIMS OF LITERARY STUDY. Pott 8vo. 3s.

COWPER.—LETTERS. Ed. by W. T. WEBB, M.A. Globe 8vo. 2s. 6d.

CRAIK (H.).—ENGLISH PROSE SELECTIONS. With Critical Introductions by various writers, and General Introductions to each Period. Edited by H. CRAIK, C.B. Vols. I. II. III. and IV. Cr. 8vo. 7s. 6d. each. [V. in Press.

CRAIK (Mrs.). — CONCERNING MEN : and other Papers. Cr. 8vo. 3s. 6d.

—— ABOUT MONEY : and other Things. Cr. 8vo. 3s. 6d.

—— SERMONS OUT OF CHURCH. Cr. 8vo. 3s. 6d.

CRAWFORD (F. M.).—THE NOVEL : WHAT IT IS. Pott 8vo. 3s.

CUNLIFFE (J. W.).—THE INFLUENCE OF SENECA ON ELIZABETHAN TRAGEDY. 4s. net.

DE VERE (Aubrey).—ESSAYS CHIEFLY ON POETRY. 2 vols. Globe 8vo. 12s.

—— ESSAYS, CHIEFLY LITERARY AND ETHICAL. Globe 8vo. 6s.

DICKENS.—LETTERS OF CHARLES DICKENS. Edited by his Sister-in-Law and MARY DICKENS. Cr. 8vo. 3s. 6d.

DRYDEN, ESSAYS OF. Edited by Prof. C. D. YONGE. Fcp. 8vo. 2s. 6d. (See also GLOBE LIBRARY, p. 25.)

—— THE SATIRES. Edited by J. CHURTON COLLINS. Gl. 8vo. 1s. 9d.

DUFF (Rt. Hon. Sir M. E. Grant).—MISCELLANIES, Political and Literary. 8vo. 10s. 6d.

ELLIS (A.).—CHOSEN ENGLISH. Selections from Wordsworth, Byron, Shelley, Lamb, Scott. Globe 8vo. 2s. 6d.

EMERSON (Ralph Waldo).—THE COLLECTED WORKS. 6 vols. Globe 8vo 5s. each.— I. MISCELLANIES. With an Introductory Essay by JOHN MORLEY.—II. ESSAYS.— III. POEMS.—IV. ENGLISH TRAITS; REPRESENTATIVE MEN.—V. CONDUCT OF LIFE; SOCIETY AND SOLITUDE.—VI. LETTERS; SOCIAL AIMS ETC.

FASNACHT (G. E.).—Select Specimens of the Great French Writers in the Seventeenth, Eighteenth, and Nineteenth Centuries. With Literary Appreciations by the most eminent French Critics, and a Historical Sketch of French Literature. Edit. by G. E. Fasnacht. Cr. 8vo. 7s. 6d.

FITZGERALD (Edward): Letters and Literary Remains of. Ed. by W. Aldis Wright, M.A. 3 vols. Cr. 8vo. 31s. 6d.
— Letters. Edited by W. A. Wright. 2 vols. Globe 8vo. 10s.

FOWLER (W. W.).—Summer Studies of Birds and Books. Ex. cr. 8vo. 6s.

GLOBE LIBRARY. Cr. 8vo. 3s. 6d. each:
Boswell's Life of Johnson. Introduction by Mowbray Morris.
Burns.—Complete Poetical Works and Letters. Edited, with Life and Glossarial Index, by Alexander Smith.
Cowper.—Poetical Works. Edited by the Rev. W. Benham, B.D.
Defoe.—The Adventures of Robinson Crusoe. Introduction by H. Kingsley.
Dryden.—Poetical Works. A Revised Text and Notes. By W. D. Christie, M.A.
Froissart's Chronicles. Transl. by Lord Berners. Ed. by G. C. Macaulay, M.A.
Goldsmith. — Miscellaneous Works. Edited by Prof. Masson.
Horace.—Works. Rendered into English Prose by James Lonsdale and S. Lee.
Malory.—Le Morte d'Arthur. Sir Thos. Malory's Book of King Arthur and of his Noble Knights of the Round Table. The Edition of Caxton, revised for modern use. By Sir E. Strachey, Bart.
Milton.—Poetical Works. Edited, with Introductions, by Prof. Masson.
Pope.—Poetical Works. Edited, with Memoir and Notes, by Prof. Ward.
Scott.—Poetical Works. With Essay by Prof. Palgrave.
Shakespeare.—Complete Works. Edit. by W. G. Clark and W. Aldis Wright. India Paper Edition. Cr. 8vo, cloth extra, gilt edges. 10s. 6d. net.
Spenser.—Complete Works Edited by R. Morris. Memoir by J. W. Hales. M.A.
Virgil.—Works. Rendered into English Prose by James Lonsdale and S. Lee.

GOETHE. — Maxims and Reflections. Trans. by T. B. Saunders. Gl. 8vo. 5s.
— Nature Aphorisms. Transl. by T. B. Saunders. Pott 8vo 6d. net.

GOLDEN TREASURY SERIES.—Uniformly printed in Pott 8vo, with Vignette Titles by Sir J. E. Millais, Sir Noel Paton, T. Woolner W. Holman Hunt, Arthur Hughes, etc. 2s. 6d. net each.
Golden Treasury of the Best Songs and Lyrical Poems in the English Language, The. Selected and arranged, with Notes, by Prof. F T. Palgrave.—Large Type. Cr. 8vo. 10s. 6d.—Large Paper Edition. 8vo. 10s. 6d. net
Lyric Love: An Anthology. Edited by W. Watson.
Children's Garland from the Best Poets The. Selected by Coventry Patmore.
Children's Treasury of Lyrical Poetry. By F. T. Palgrave.
The Jest Book. The Choicest Anecdotes and Sayings. Arranged by Mark Lemon.

GOLDEN TREASURY SERIES—contd.
Fairy Book, The: the Best Popular Fairy Stories. Selected by Mrs. Craik, Author of "John Halifax, Gentleman."
Book of Golden Thoughts, A. By Sir Henry Attwell.
Sunday Book of Poetry for the Young, The. Selected by C. F. Alexander.
Golden Treasury Psalter. By Four Friends.
Book of Praise, The. From the Best English Hymn Writers. Selected by Roundell, Earl of Selborne.
Theologia Germanica. By S. Winkworth.
The Ballad Book. A Selection of the Choicest British Ballads. Edited by William Allingham.
Song Book, The. Words and Tunes selected and arranged by John Hullah.
Scottish Song. Compiled by Mary Carlyle Aitken.
La Lyre Française Selected and arranged, with Notes, by G. Masson.
Balladen und Romanzen. Being a Selection of the best German Ballads and Romances. Edited, with Introduction and Notes, by Dr. Buchheim.
Deutsche Lyrik. The Golden Treasury of the best German Lyrical Poems. Selected by Dr. Buchheim.
Matthew Arnold.—Selected Poems.
Addison.—Essays. Chosen and Edited by John Richard Green.
Bacon.—Essays, and Colours of Good and Evil. With Notes and Glossarial Index by W. Aldis Wright, M.A.—Large Paper Edition. 8vo. 10s. 6d net.
Browne, Sir Thomas.—Religio Medici, Letter to a Friend, &c., and Christian Morals. Ed. by W. A. Greenhill.
— Hydriotaphia and the Garden of Cyrus. Ed. by W. A. Greenhill.
Bunyan.—The Pilgrim's Progress from this World to that which is to Come. —Large Paper Edition 8vo. 10s. 6d. net.
Byron.—Poetry. Chosen and arranged by M. Arnold.—Large Paper Edit. 9s.
Clough.—Selections from the Poems.
Cowper.—Letters. Edited, with Introduction, by Rev. W. Benham.
— Selections from Poems. With an Introduction by Mrs. Oliphant.
Defoe.—The Adventures of Robinson Crusoe. Edited by J. W. Clark, M.A.
Gracian (Balthasar).—Art of Worldly Wisdom. Translated by J. Jacobs.
Herrick.—Chrysomela. Edited by Prof. F. T. Palgrave.
Hughes.—Tom Brown s School Days.
Keats.—The Poetical Works. Edited by Prof. F. T. Palgrave.
Keble.—The Christian Year. Edit. by C. M. Yonge.
Lamb.—Tales from Shakspeare. Edited by Rev. Alfred Ainger, M.A.
Landor.—Selections. Ed. by S. Colvin.
Longfellow. — Ballads, Lyrics, and Sonnets.
Mohammad.—Speeches and Table-Talk. Translated by Stanley Lane-Poole.
Newcastle.—The Cavalier and his Lady. Selections from the Works of the First Duke and Duchess of Newcastle. With Introductory Essay by E. Jenkins.

LITERATURE.

Collected Works; Essays; Lectures; Letters; Miscellaneous Works—*contd.*

GOLDEN TREASURY SERIES—*contd.*

PLATO.—THE REPUBLIC. Translated by J. LL. DAVIES, M.A., and D. J. VAUGHAN. —Large Paper Edition. 8vo. 10s. 6d. net.
— THE TRIAL AND DEATH OF SOCRATES. Being the Euthyphron, Apology, Crito and Phaedo of Plato. Trans. by F. J. CHURCH.
— THE PHAEDRUS, LYSIS, AND PROTAGORAS. Translated by J. WRIGHT.

SHAKESPEARE.—SONGS AND SONNETS. Ed. with Notes, by Prof. F. T. PALGRAVE.

SHELLEY.—POEMS. Edited by STOPFORD A. BROOKE.—Large Paper Edit. 12s. 6d.

SOUTHEY.—POEMS. Chosen and Arranged by E. DOWDEN.

THEOCRITUS, BION, AND MOSCHUS. Rendered into English Prose by ANDREW LANG.—Large Paper Edition. 9s.

WHITTIER.—POEMS, RELIGIOUS AND DEVOTIONAL.

WORDSWORTH.—POEMS. Chosen and Edited by M. ARNOLD.—Large Paper Edition. 10s. 6d net.

YONGE.—A BOOK OF GOLDEN DEEDS.
— A BOOK OF WORTHIES.
— THE STORY OF THE CHRISTIANS AND MOORS IN SPAIN.

HARE.—GUESSES AT TRUTH. By Two Brothers. 4s. 6d.

LONGFELLOW.—POEMS OF PLACES: ENGLAND AND WALES. Edited by H. W. LONGFELLOW. 2 vols. 9s.

TENNYSON.—LYRICAL POEMS. Selected and Annotated by Prof. F. T. PALGRAVE. 4s.6d.
—Large Paper Edition. 9s.
— IN MEMORIAM. 4s. 6d.—Large Paper Edition. 9s.

GOLDSMITH, ESSAYS OF. Edited by C. D. YONGE, M.A. Fcp. 8vo. 2s. 6d. (*See also* GLOBE LIBRARY, p. 25: ILLUSTRATED BOOKS, p. 14.)

GRAY (Asa).—LETTERS. Edited by J. L. GRAY. 2 vols. Cr. 8vo. 15s. net.

GRAY (Thomas).—WORKS. Edited by EDMUND GOSSE. In 4 vols. Gl. 8vo. 5s. each.— Vol. I. POEMS, JOURNALS, AND ESSAYS.— II. LETTERS.—III. LETTERS.—IV. NOTES ON ARISTOPHANES AND PLATO.

GREEN (J. R.).—STRAY STUDIES FROM ENGLAND AND ITALY. Globe 8vo. 5s.

GREENWOOD (F.).—THE LOVER'S LEXICON. Cr. 8vo. 6s.

HAMERTON (P. G.).—THE INTELLECTUAL LIFE. Cr. 8vo. 10s. 6d.
— HUMAN INTERCOURSE. Cr. 8vo. 8s. 6d.
— FRENCH AND ENGLISH : A Comparison. Cr. 8vo. 10s. 6d.

HARRISON (Frederic).—THE CHOICE OF BOOKS. Gl. 8vo. 6s.—Large Paper Ed. 15s.

HELPS (Sir Arthur).—ESSAYS WRITTEN IN THE INTERVALS OF BUSINESS. With Introduction and Notes, by F. J. ROWE, M.A., and W. T. WEBB, M.A. 1s. 9d.; swd. 1s. 6d.

HOBART (Lord).—ESSAYS AND MISCELLANEOUS WRITINGS. With Biographical Sketch. Ed. Lady HOBART. 2 vols. 8vo. 25s.

HUTTON (R. H.).—ESSAYS ON SOME OF THE MODERN GUIDES OF ENGLISH THOUGHT IN MATTERS OF FAITH. Globe 8vo. 5s.
— ESSAYS. 2 vols. Gl. 8vo 5s. each.—Vol I. LITERARY; II. THEOLOGICAL.
— CRITICISMS ON CONTEMPORARY THOUGHT AND THINKERS. 2 vols. Gl. 8vo. 10s.

HUXLEY (Prof. T. H.).—COLLECTED ESSAYS. Gl. 8vo. 5s. each.—I. METHOD AND RESULTS.—II. DARWINIANA.—III. SCIENCE AND EDUCATION.—IV. SCIENCE AND HEBREW TRADITION.—V. SCIENCE AND CHRISTIAN TRADITION.—VI. HUME.—VII. MAN'S PLACE IN NATURE.—VIII. DISCOURSES, BIOLOGICAL AND GEOLOGICAL.—IX. EVOLUTION AND ETHICS, ETC.
— LAY SERMONS, ADDRESSES, AND REVIEWS. 8vo. 7s. 6d.
— CRITIQUES AND ADDRESSES. 8vo. 10s. 6d.
— AMERICAN ADDRESSES, WITH A LECTURE ON THE STUDY OF BIOLOGY. 8vo. 6s. 6d.
— SCIENCE AND CULTURE, AND OTHER ESSAYS. 8vo. 10s. 6d.
— INTRODUCTORY SCIENCE PRIMER. Pott 8vo. 1s.
— ESSAYS UPON SOME CONTROVERTED QUESTIONS. 8vo. 14s.

IRELAND (A.).—THE BOOK-LOVER'S ENCHIRIDION. Fcp. 8vo. 7s.; vellum, 10s. 6d.

JAMES (Henry).—FRENCH POETS AND NOVELISTS. New Edition. Gl. 8vo. 5s.
— PORTRAITS OF PLACES. Cr. 8vo. 7s. 6d.
— PARTIAL PORTRAITS. Gl. 8vo. 5s

JEBB (R. C.).—GROWTH AND INFLUENCE OF CLASSICAL GREEK POETRY. Cr. 8vo. 7s. net.

JOCELINE (E.). THE MOTHER'S LEGACIE TO HER UNBORN CHILD. Cr. 16mo. 4s.6d.

JONES (H. A.).—THE RENASCENCE OF THE ENGLISH DRAMA. Cr. 8vo. 6s.

KEATS.—LETTERS. Edited by SID EY COLVIN. Globe 8vo. 5s.

KINGSLEY (Charles).—COMPLETE EDITION OF THE WORKS OF CHARLES KINGS EY. Cr. 8vo. 3s. 6d. each.
WESTWARD HO With a Portrait.
HYPATIA. | YEAST.
ALTON LOCKE. | TWO YEARS AGO.
HEREWARD THE WAKE.
POEMS.
THE HEROES; or, Greek Fairy Tales for my Children.
THE WATER BABIES: A Fairy Tale for a Land Baby.
MADAM HOW AND LADY WHY; or, First Lesson in Earth-Lore for Children.
AT LAST: A Christmas in the West Indies.
PROSE IDYLLS.
PLAYS AND PURITANS.
THE ROMAN AND THE TEUTON. With Preface by Professor MAX MÜLLER.
SANITARY AND SOCIAL LECTURES.
HISTORICAL LECTURES AND ESSAYS.
SCIENTIFIC LECTURES AND ESSAYS.
LITERARY AND GENERAL LECTURES.
THE HERMITS.
GLAUCUS: or, The Wonders of the Seashore. With Coloured Illustrations.
VILLAGE AND TOWN AND COUNTRY SERMONS.
THE WATER OF LIFE, AND OTHER SERMONS.
SERMONS ON NATIONAL SUBJECTS: AND THE KING OF THE EARTH.

KINGSLEY (C.).—COMPLETE EDITION—*continued.*
SERMONS FOR THE TIMES.
GOOD NEWS OF GOD.
THE GOSPEL OF THE PENTATEUCH: AND DAVID.
DISCIPLINE, AND OTHER SERMONS.
WESTMINSTER SERMONS.
ALL SAINTS' DAY, AND OTHER SERMONS.
—— *Pocket Edition.* Pott 8vo. 1s. 6d. each.
—HYPATIA.—ALTON LOCKE.—WESTWARD HO! 2 vols.—HEREWARD THE WAKE.—TWO YEARS AGO. 2 vols.—YEAST.—WATER BABIES.—HEROES.

LAMB (Charles).—COLLECTED WORKS. Ed., with Introduction and Notes, by the Rev. ALFRED AINGER, M.A. Globe 8vo. 5s. each volume.—I. ESSAYS OF ELIA.—II. PLAYS, POEMS, AND MISCELLANEOUS ESSAYS.—III. MRS. LEICESTER'S SCHOOL; THE ADVENTURES OF ULYSSES; AND OTHER ESSAYS.—IV. TALES FROM SHAKESPEARE.—V. and VI. LETTERS. Newly arranged, with additions.
—— TALES FROM SHAKESPEARE. Pott 8vo. 2s. 6d. net.
—— ESSAYS OF ELIA. Edit. by N. L. HALLWARD, M.A. and S. C. HILL, B.A. Gl. 8vo. 3s. ; sewed, 2s. 6d.

LANKESTER(Prof. E. Ray).—THE ADVANCEMENT OF SCIENCE. Occasional Essays and Addresses. 8vo. 10s. 6d.

LESLIE (G. D.).—LETTERS TO MARCO. Ex. cr. 8vo. 7s. 6d.

LETTERS FROM SOUTH AFRICA. Reprinted from the *Times.* Cr. 8vo. 2s. 6d.

LETTERS FROM QUEENSLAND. Reprinted from the *Times.* Cr. 8vo. 2s. 6d.

LODGE (Prof. Oliver).—THE PIONEERS OF SCIENCE. Illustrated. Ext. cr. 8vo. 7s. 6d.

LOWELL (Jas. Russell).—COMPLETE WORKS. 10 vols. Cr. 8vo. 6s. each.—Vols. I.—IV. LITERARY ESSAYS.—V. POLITICAL ESSAYS. —VI. LITERARY AND POLITICAL ADDRESSES. VII.—X. POETICAL WORKS.
—— POLITICAL ESSAYS. Ext. cr. 8vo. 7s. 6d.
—— LATEST LITERARY ESSAYS. Cr. 8vo. 6s.

LUBBOCK (Rt. Hon. Sir John, Bart.).—SCIENTIFIC LECTURES. Illustrated. 2nd Edit. revised. 8vo. 8s. 6d.
—— POLITICAL AND EDUCATIONAL ADDRESSES. 8vo. 8s. 6d.
—— FIFTY YEARS OF SCIENCE: Address to the British Association, 1881. Cr. 8vo. 2s. 6d.
—— THE PLEASURES OF LIFE. New Edit. Gl. 8vo. Part I. 1s.6d.; swd. 1s.— Part II. 1s. 6d.; sewed, 1s.—Complete in 1 vol. 2s. 6d.
—— THE BEAUTIES OF NATURE. Cr. 8vo. 6s. —— —— Without Illustrations. Cr. 8vo. 1s.6d. ; sewed, 1s.
—— THE USE OF LIFE. Globe 8vo. 3s. 6d. ; Cheap Edition, 1s. 6d. ; sewed, 1s.

LYTTELTON (E.).—MOTHERS AND SONS. Cr. 8vo. 3s. 6d.

MACAULAY.—ESSAY ON WARREN HASTINGS. Ed. by K. DEIGHTON. Gl 8vo. 2s.6d.
—— ESSAY ON LORD CLIVE. By the same. 2s.
—— ESSAY ON ADDISON. Edited by J. W. HALES. Globe 8vo. [*In the Press.*]
—— BOSWELL'S LIFE OF JOHNSON. Edit. by R. F. WINCH. Gl 8vo. 2s. 6d.

MACMILLAN (Rev. Hugh).—ROMAN MOSAICS, or, Studies in Rome and its Neighbourhood. Globe 8vo. 6s.

MAHAFFY (Prof. J. P.).—THE PRINCIPLES OF THE ART OF CONVERSATION. Cr.8vo. 4s.6d.

MAURICE (F. D.).—THE FRIENDSHIP OF BOOKS: and other Lectures. Cr. 8vo. 3s. 6d.

MILTON.—TRACTATE OF EDUCATION. Ed. by E. E. MORRIS. Gl. 8vo. 1s. 9d.

MORLEY (John).—WORKS. Collected Edit. In 11 vols. Globe 8vo. 5s. each.—VOLTAIRE. 1 vol.—ROUSSEAU. 2 vols.—DIDEROT AND THE ENCYLOPÆDISTS. 2 vols.—ON COMPROMISE. 1 vol.—MISCELLANIES. 3 vols.—BURKE. 1 vol.—STUDIES IN LITERATURE. 1 vol.

MYERS (F. W. H.).—ESSAYS. 2 vols. Cr. 8vo. 4s. 6d. each.—I. CLASSICAL; II. MODERN.
—— SCIENCE AND A FUTURE LIFE. Gl. 8vo. 5s.

NADAL (E. S.).—ESSAYS AT HOME AND ELSEWHERE. Cr. 8vo. 6s.

OLIPHANT(T.L. Kington).—THE DUKE AND THE SCHOLAR: and other Essays. 8vo. 7s.6d.

OWENS COLLEGE ESSAYS AND ADDRESSES. By Professors and Lecturers of the College. 8vo. 14s.

PATER (W.).—THE RENAISSANCE; Studies in Art and Poetry. 4th Ed. Cr. 8vo. 10s. 6d.
—— IMAGINARY PORTRAITS. Cr. 8vo. 6s.
—— APPRECIATIONS. With an Essay on "Style." 2nd Edit. Cr. 8vo. 8s. 6d.
—— MARIUS THE EPICUREAN. 2 vols. Cr. 8vo. 15s.
—— PLATO AND PLATONISM. Ex.cr.8vo. 8s.6d.
—— GREEK STUDIES. Ex. cr. 8vo. 10s. 6d.
—— MISCELLANEOUS STUDIES. Ex. cr. 8vo. 9s.

PICTON (J. A.).—THE MYSTERY OF MATTER: and other Essays. Cr. 8vo. 6s.

POLLOCK (Sir F., Bart.).—OXFORD LECTURES: and other Discourses. 8vo. 9s.

POOLE (M. E.).—PICTURES OF COTTAGE LIFE IN THE WEST OF ENGLAND. 2nd Ed. Cr. 8vo. 3s. 6d.

POPE.—ESSAY ON MAN, I.—IV. Edited by E. E. MORRIS, M.A. 1s. 9d.
—— ESSAY ON MAN. Epistle I. Gl 8vo. 6d.

POTTER (Louisa).—LANCASHIRE MEMORIES. Cr. 8vo. 6s.

POTTS (W.). — FROM A NEW ENGLAND HILLSIDE. Pott 8vo. 3s.

PRICKARD (A. O.).—ARISTOTLE ON THE ART OF POETRY. Cr. 8vo. 3s. 6d.

RUMFORD.—COMPLETE WORKS OF COUNT RUMFORD. Memoir by G. ELLIS. Portrait. 5 vols. 8vo. 4l. 14s. 6d.

SCAIFE (W. B.).—FLORENTINE LIFE DURING THE RENAISSANCE. 8vo. 6s. net.

SCIENCE LECTURES AT SOUTH KENSINGTON. Illustr. 2 vols. Cr. 8vo. 6s. each.

SMALLEY (George W.).—LONDON LETTERS AND SOME OTHERS. 2 vols. 8vo. 32s.
—— STUDIES OF MEN. Cr. 8vo. 8s. 6d. net.

SMITH (Goldwin).—ESSAYS ON QUESTIONS OF THE DAY. 2nd Ed. revised. Ex.cr.8vo. 9s.

STEPHEN (Sir James F., Bart.).—HORAE SABBATICAE. Three Series. Gl. 8vo. 5s. each.

LITERATURE.

Collected Works; Essays: Lectures; Letters; Miscellaneous Works—*contd.*

THOREAU.—Selections from Writings. Edited by H. S. Salt. Gl. 8vo. 5s.

THRING (Edward).—Thoughts on Life Science. 2nd Edit. Cr. 8vo. 7s. 6d.

TREVELYAN (G. O.).—The Competition Wallah. Cr. 8vo. 6s.

TYRRELL (R. Y.).—Latin Poetry. Cr. 8vo. 7s net.

VAUGHAN (D. J.).—Questions of the Day. Cr. 8vo. 5s.

WARD (W.).—Witnesses to the Unseen. 8vo. 10s. 6d.

WESTCOTT (Bishop). (*See* Theology, p. 45)

WHITE (Andrew).—The Warfare of Science. [*In the Press.*

WHITTIER (John Greenleaf). The Complete Works. 7 vols. Cr. 8vo. 6s. each.—Vol. I. Narrative and Legendary Poems.—II. Poems of Nature; Poems Subjective and Reminiscent; Religious Poems.—III. Anti-Slavery Poems; Songs of Labour and Reform.—IV. Personal Poems; Occasional Poems; The Tent on the Beach; with the Poems of Elizabeth H. Whittier, and an Appendix containing Early and Uncollected Verses.—V. Margaret Smith's Journal; Tales and Sketches.—VI. Old Portraits and Modern Sketches; Personal Sketches and Tributes; Historical Papers.—VII. The Conflict with Slavery, Politics, and Reform; The Inner Life, Criticism.

WILSON (Dr. George).—Religio Chemici. Cr. 8vo. 8s. 6d.
—— The Five Gateways of Knowledge. 9th Edit. Ext. fcp. 8vo. 2s. 6d.
—— The Works of William and Dorothy Wordsworth. Edited by W. Knight. 16 vols. [*Monthly from April,* 1896

WRIGHT (M. O.).—The Friendship of Nature. 16mo. 3s.

YONGE (Charlotte M.).—*Uniform Edition.* Cr. 8vo. 3s. 6d. each.
The Heir of Redclyffe.
Heartsease.
Hopes and Fears.
Dynevor Terrace.
The Daisy Chain.
The Trial: More Links of the Daisy Chain.
Pillars of the House. 2 vols.
The Young Stepmother.
Clever Woman of the Family.
The Three Brides.
My Young Alcides.
The Caged Lion.
The Dove in the Eagle's Nest.
The Chaplet of Pearls.
Lady Hester, and The Danvers Papers.
Magnum Bonum.
Love and Life.
Unknown to History.
Stray Pearls.
The Armourer's Prentices.
The Two Sides of the Shield.
Nuttie's Father.
Scenes and Characters.
Chantry House.

YONGE (C. M.)—*continued.*
A Modern Telemachus.
Bye Words.
Beechcroft at Rockstone.
More Bywords.
A Reputed Changeling.
The Little Duke, Richard the Fearless.
The Lances of Lynwood.
The Prince and the Page.
P's and Q's: Little Lucy's Wonderful Globe.
The Two Penniless Princesses.
That Stick.
An Old Woman's Outlook.
Grisly Grisell.

LOGIC. (*See under* Philosophy, p. 32.)

MAGAZINES. (*See* Periodicals, p. 31.)

MAGNETISM. (*See under* Physics, p. 33.)

MATHEMATICS, History of.

BALL (W. W. R.).—A Short Account of the History of Mathematics. 2nd Ed. Cr. 8vo. 10s. net.
—— Mathematical Recreations and Problems. Cr. 8vo. 7s. net.
—— Primer of History of Mathematics. Gl. 8vo. 2s. net.
—— An Essay on Newton's Principia. Cr. 8vo. 6s. net.

CAJORI (F.).—History of Mathematics. Ext. cr. 8vo. 14s. net.

KLEIN (F.)—Lectures on Mathematics 8vo. 6s. 6d. net.

MATHEMATICAL GAZETTE, THE. Ed. by E. M. Langley, M.A. Nos. i.—iii. 4to, swd. 6d. net. each. Nos. 4—6. 1s. net each.

MEDICINE.

(*See also* Domestic Economy; Nursing; Hygiene; Physiology.)

ALLBUTT (Dr. T. Clifford).—On the Use of the Ophthalmoscope. 8vo. 15s.

ANDERSON (Dr. McCall).—Lectures on Clinical Medicine. Illustr. 8vo. 10s. 6d.

BALLANCE (C.A.) and EDMUNDS (Dr.W.). Ligation in Continuity. Illustr. Roy.8vo. 10s. net.

BARWELL (Richard, F.R.C.S.). — The Causes and Treatment of Lateral Curvature of the Spine. Cr. 8vo. 6s.
—— On Aneurism, especially of the Thorax and Root of the Neck. 3s. 6d.

BICKERTON (T. H.).—On Colour Blindness. Cr. 8vo.

BRAIN: A Journal of Neurology. Edited for the Neurological Society of London, by A. De Watteville, Quarterly. 8vo. 3s. 6d. (Part I. in Jan. 1878.) Vols. 15s. each. [Cloth covers for binding, 1s. each.]

BRUNTON (Dr. T. Lauder). — A Text-Book of Pharmacology, Therapeutics, and Materia Medica. 3rd Edit. Med. 8vo. 21s.—Or in 2 vols. 22s. 6d.—Supplement, 1s.
—— Disorders of Digestion: their Consequences and Treatment. 8vo. 10s. 6d.
—— Pharmacology and Therapeutics; or, Medicine Past and Present. Cr. 8vo. 6s.

BRUNTON (Dr. T. L.).—TABLES OF MATERIA MEDICA : A Con panion to the Materia Medica Museum 8vo. 5*.
— AN INTRODUCTION TO MODERN THERAPEUTICS Croonian Lectures on the Relationship between Chemical Structure and Physiological Action. 8vo. 3*. 6d. net.
— MODERN DEVELOPMENTS OF HARVEY'S WORK. 8vo. 2*.

BUCKNILL (Dr.).—THE CARE OF THE INSANE. Cr. 8vo. 3*. 6d.

CARTER (R. Brudenell, F.C.S.).—A PRACTICAL TREATISE ON DISEASES OF THE EYE. 8vo. 16*.
— EYESIGHT, GOOD AND BAD. Cr. 8vo. 6*.
— MODERN OPERATIONS FOR CATARACT. 8vo. 6*.

COWELL (George).—LECTURES ON CATARACT : ITS CAUSES, VARIETIES, AND TREATMENT. Cr. 8vo. 4*. 6d.

ECCLES (A. S.).—SCIATICA. 8vo. 3*. 6d.
— PRACTICE OF MASSAGE. Ex. cr. 8vo. 7*. 6d. net.

FLÜCKIGER (F. A.) and HANBURY (D.).—PHARMACOGRAPHIA. A History of the Principal Drugs of Vegetable Origin met with in Great Britain and India. 8vo. 21*.

FOTHERGILL (Dr. J. Milner).—THE PRACTITIONER'S HANDBOOK OF TREATMENT; or, The Principles of Therapeutics. 8vo. 16*.
— THE ANTAGONISM OF THERAPEUTIC AGENTS, AND WHAT IT TEACHES. Cr. 8vo. 6*.
— FOOD FOR THE INVALID, THE CONVALESCENT, THE DYSPEPTIC, AND THE GOUTY. 2nd Edit. Cr. 8vo. 3*. 6d.

FOX (Dr. Wilson). — ON THE ARTIFICIAL PRODUCTION OF TUBERCLE IN THE LOWER ANIMALS. With Plates. 4to. 5*. 6d.
— ON THE TREATMENT OF HYPERPYREXIA, AS ILLUSTRATED IN ACUTE ARTICULAR RHEUMATISM BY MEANS OF THE EXTERNAL APPLICATION OF COLD. 8vo. 2*. 6d.

GILLIES (H. C.).—COUNTER-IRRITATION. 8vo. 6*. net.

GRIFFITHS (W. H.).—LESSONS ON PRESCRIPTIONS AND THE ART OF PRESCRIBING. New Edition. Pott 8vo. 3*. 6d.

HAMILTON (Prof. D. J.).—ON THE PATHOLOGY OF BRONCHITIS, CATARRHAL PNEUMONIA, TUBERCLE, AND ALLIED LESIONS OF THE HUMAN LUNG. 8vo. 8*. 6d.
— A TEXT-BOOK OF PATHOLOGY, SYSTEMATIC AND PRACTICAL. Illustrated. 8vo. Vol. I. 21*. net. Vol. II. in 2 parts. 15*. each net.

HANBURY (Daniel). — SCIENCE PAPERS, CHIEFLY PHARMACOLOGICAL AND BOTANICAL. Med. 8vo. 14*.

HAWKINS(H. P.).—DISEASES OF THE VERMIFORM APPENDIX. 8vo. 7*. net.

KAHLDEN (C.).—METHODS OF PATHOLOGICAL HISTOLOGY. Transl. by H. M. FLETCHER. 8vo. 6*.

KANTHACK (A. A.) and DRYSDALE (J. H.).—ELEMENTARY PRACTICAL BACTERIOLOGY. Cr. 8vo. 4*. 6d.

KLEIN (Dr. E.).—MICRO-ORGANISMS AND DISEASE. An Introduction into the Study of Specific Micro-Organisms. Cr. 8vo. 6*.
— THE BACTERIA IN ASIATIC CHOLERA. Cr. 8vo. 5*.

LEPROSY INVESTIGATION COMMITTEE, JOURNAL OF THE. Edited by P. S. ABRAHAM, M.A. Nos. 2—4. 8vo. 2*. 6d each net.
— PRIZE ESSAYS. By E. S. EHLERS and S. P. IMPEY. 8vo. 3*. 6d. net.

LINDSAY (Dr. J. A.). — THE CLIMATIC TREATMENT OF CONSUMPTION. Cr. 8vo. 5*.

MACDONALD(G.)—DISEASES OF THE NOSE. 2nd Edit. Cr. 8vo. 10*. 6d. net.

MACLAGAN (Dr. T.).—THE GERM THEORY. 8vo. 10*. 6d.

MACLEAN (Surgeon-General W. C.).—DISEASES OF TROPICAL CLIMATES. Cr. 8vo. 10*. 6d.

MERCIER (Dr. C.).—THE NERVOUS SYSTEM AND THE MIND. 8vo. 12*. 6d.

NEWMAN(G.).—DECLINE AND EXTINCTION OF LEPROSY. 8vo. 3*. 6d. net.

PIFFARD (H. G.).—AN ELEMENTARY TREATISE ON DISEASES OF THE SKIN. 8vo. 16*.

PRACTITIONER, THE : INDEX TO VOLS. I.-L. 8vo. 10*. 6d.

REYNOLDS(Sir J. R.)—A SYSTEM OF MEDICINE. Edited by Sir J. RUSSELL REYNOLDS, Bart., M.D., In 5 vols. Vols. I.—III. and V. 8vo. 25*. each.—Vol. IV. 21*.

RICHARDSON (Dr. B. W.).—DISEASES OF MODERN LIFE. Cr. 8vo.
— THE FIELD OF DISEASE. A Book of Preventive Medicine. 8vo. 25*.

SEATON (Dr. Edward C.).—A HANDBOOK OF VACCINATION. Ext. fcp. 8vo. 8*. 6d.

SEILER (Dr. Carl). — MICRO-PHOTOGRAPHS IN HISTOLOGY, NORMAL AND PATHOLOGICAL. 4to. 31*. 6d.

SIBSON (Dr. Francis).—COLLECTED WORKS. Edited by W. M. ORD, M.D. Illustrated. 4 vols. 8vo. 3*l*. 3*.

SPENDER (J. Kent).—THERAPEUTIC MEANS FOR THE RELIEF OF PAIN. 8vo. 8*. 6d.

SURGERY (THE INTERNATIONAL ENCYCLOPAEDIA OF). A Systematic Treatise on the Theory and Practice of Surgery by Authors of various Nations. Edited by JOHN ASHHURST, jun., M.D. 7 vols. Roy. 8vo. 31*. 6d. each.

THORNE (Dr. Thorne).—DIPHTHERIA. Cr. 8vo. 8*. 6d.

WHITE (Dr. W. Hale).—A TEXT-BOOK OF GENERAL THERAPEUTICS. Cr. 8vo. 8*. 6d.

WILLIAMS (C. T.).—AERO-THERAPEUTICS. 8vo. 6*. net.

ZIEGLER (Ernst).—A TEXT-BOOK OF PATHOLOGICAL ANATOMY AND PATHOGENESIS. Translated and Edited by DONALD MACALISTER, M.A., M.D. Illustrated. 8vo.— Part I. GENERAL PATHOLOGICAL ANATOMY. 12*. 6d.—Part II. SPECIAL PATHOLOGICAL ANATOMY. Sections I.—VIII. and IX.—XII. 8vo. 12*. 6d. each.

METALLURGY.
(*See also* CHEMISTRY.)

HIORNS (Arthur H.).—A TEXT-BOOK OF ELEMENTARY METALLURGY. 2nd Edition. Gl. 8vo. 3*.
— PRACTICAL METALLURGY AND ASSAYING. Illustrated. 2nd Edit. Globe 8vo. 6*.

METALLURGY—*continued.*

HIORNS (A. H.).—MIXED METALS OR ME-
TALLIC ALLOYS. Globe 8vo. 6s.
—— IRON AND STEEL MANUFACTURE. Illus-
trated. Globe 8vo. 3s. 6d.
—— METAL COLOURING AND BRONZING.
Globe 8vo. 5s.
—— PRINCIPLES OF METALLURGY. Gl. 8vo. 6s.
—— QUESTIONS ON METALLURGY. Gl. 8vo,
sewed. 1s.

PHILLIPS (J. A.).—A TREATISE ON ORE
DEPOSITS. Illustrated.
[*New edition in preparation.*

METAPHYSICS.

(*See under* PHILOSOPHY, p. 32.)

MILITARY ART AND HISTORY.

AITKEN (Sir W.).—THE GROWTH OF THE
RECRUIT AND YOUNG SOLDIER. Cr. 8vo. 8s. 6d.

CUNYNGHAME (Gen. Sir A. T.).—MY
COMMAND IN SOUTH AFRICA, 1874—78.
8vo. 12s. 6d.

DILKE (Sir C.) and WILKINSON (S.).—IM-
PERIAL DEFENCE. Cr. 8vo. 3s. 6d.

FORTESCUE (J. W.).—HISTORY OF THE
17TH LANCERS. Roy. 8vo. 25s. net.

HOZIER (Lieut.-Col. H. M.).—THE SEVEN
WEEKS' WAR. 2nd Edit. Cr. 8vo. 6s.
—— THE INVASIONS OF ENGLAND. 2 vols.
8vo. 28s.

MARTEL (Chas.).—MILITARY ITALY. With
Map. 8vo. 12s. 6d.

MAURICE (Maj.-Gen.).—WAR. 8vo. 5s. net.
—— THE NATIONAL DEFENCES. Cr. 8vo.

MERCUR (Prof. J.).—ELEMENTS OF THE
ART OF WAR. 8vo. 17s.

MOLYNEUX (W. C. F.).—CAMPAIGNING IN
SOUTH AFRICA AND EGYPT. 8vo. 10s. net.

SCRATCHLEY — KINLOCH COOKE. —
AUSTRALIAN DEFENCES AND NEW GUINEA.
Compiled from the Papers of the late Major-
General Sir PETER SCRATCHLEY, R.E., by
C. KINLOCH COOKE. 8vo. 14s.

THROUGH THE RANKS TO A COM-
MISSION. New Edition. Cr. 8vo. 2s. 6d.

WINGATE (Major F. R.).—MAHDIISM AND
THE EGYPTIAN SUDAN. An Account of the
Rise and Progress of Mahdiism, and of Sub-
sequent Events in the Sudan to the Present
Time. With 17 Maps. 8vo. 30s. net.

WOLSELEY (General Viscount).—THE SOL-
DIER'S POCKET-BOOK FOR FIELD SERVICE.
5th Edit. 16mo, roan. 5s.
—— FIELD POCKET-BOOK FOR THE AUXILIARY
FORCES. 16mo. 1s. 6d.

YOUNGHUSBAND (G. J. and F. E.).—
RELIEF OF CHITRAL. 8vo. 8s. 6d. net.

MINERALOGY. (*See* GEOLOGY.)

MISCELLANEOUS WORKS.

(*See under* LITERATURE, p. 24.)

MUSIC.

CHAPPELL (W.).—OLD ENGLISH POPULAR
MUSIC. 2 vols. 4to. 42s. net.—*Edition de
Luxe.* 4to. 84s. net.

FAY (Amy).—MUSIC-STUDY IN GERMANY.
Preface by Sir GEO. GROVE. Cr. 8vo. 4s. 6d.

GROVE (Sir George).—A DICTIONARY OF
MUSIC AND MUSICIANS, A.D. 1450—1889.
Edited by Sir GEORGE GROVE, D.C.L. In
4 vols. 8vo. 21s. each. With Illustrations in
Music Type and Woodcut.—Also published
in Parts. Parts I.—XIV., XIX.—XXII
3s. 6d. each; XV. XVI. 7s.; XVII. XVIII.
7s.; XXIII.—XXV. Appendix, Edited by
J. A. FULLER MAITLAND, M.A. 9s. [Cloth
cases for binding the volumes, 1s. each.]
—— A COMPLETE INDEX TO THE ABOVE. By
Mrs. E. WODEHOUSE. 8vo. 7s. 6d.

HULLAH (John).—MUSIC IN THE HOUSE.
4th Edit. Cr. 8vo. 2s. 6d.

TAYLOR (Franklin).—A PRIMER OF PIANO-
FORTE PLAYING. Pott 8vo. 1s.

TAYLOR (Sedley).—SOUND AND MUSIC. 3rd
Edit. Ext. cr. 8vo. 8s. 6d.
—— A SYSTEM OF SIGHT-SINGING FROM THE
ESTABLISHED MUSICAL NOTATION. 8vo.
5s. net.
—— RECORD OF THE CAMBRIDGE CENTENARY
OF W. A. MOZART. Cr. 8vo. 2s. 6d. net.

NATURAL HISTORY.

ATKINSON (J. C.) (*See* ANTIQUITIES, p. 1.)

BADENOCH (L. N.).—ROMANCE OF INSECT
WORLD. Cr. 8vo. 6s.

BAKER (Sir Samuel W.). (*See* SPORT, p. 37.)

BLANFORD (W. T.). — GEOLOGY AND
ZOOLOGY OF ABYSSINIA. 8vo. 21s.

CAMBRIDGE NATURAL HISTORY,
THE. Edit. by J. W. CLARK, S. F. HAR-
MER, and A. E. SHIPLEY. 8vo. Vol. III.
MOLLUSCS AND BRACHIOPODS. By Rev.
A. H. COOKE. 17s. net. Vol. V. PERIPATUS,
MYRIAPODS, INSECTS. By A. SEDGWICK,
F. G. SINCLAIR, and D. SHARP. 17s. net.

FOWLER (W. W.).—TALES OF THE BIRDS.
Illustrated. Cr. 8vo. 3s. 6d.
—— A YEAR WITH THE BIRDS. Illustrated.
Cr. 8vo. 3s. 6d.
—— SUMMER STUDIES OF BIRDS AND BOOKS.
Cr. 8vo. 6s.

HEADLEY (F. W.) —STRUCTURE AND LIFE
OF BIRDS. Cr. 8vo. 7s. 6d.

KINGSLEY (Charles).—MADAM HOW AND
LADY WHY; or, First Lessons in Earth-Lore
for Children. Cr. 8vo. 3s. 6d.
—— GLAUCUS; or, The Wonders of the Sea-
Shore. With Coloured Illustrations. Cr.
8vo. 3s. 6d.—*Presentation Edition.* Cr.
8vo, extra cloth. 7s. 6d.

KLEIN (E.).—ETIOLOGY AND PATHOLOGY
OF GROUSE DISEASE. 8vo. 7s. net.

MEYRICK (E.). — HANDBOOK OF BRITISH
LEPIDOPTERA. Ex. cr. 8vo. 10s. 6d. net.

MIALL (L. C.).—NATURAL HISTORY OF
AQUATIC INSECTS. Cr. 8vo. 6s.

WALLACE (Alfred Russel).—THE MALAY
ARCHIPELAGO: The Land of the Orang
Utang and the Bird of Paradise. Maps and
Illustr. Ext. cr. 8vo. 6s. (*See also* BIOLOGY.)

WATERTON (Charles).—WANDERINGS IN
SOUTH AMERICA, THE NORTH-WEST OF
THE UNITED STATES, AND THE ANTILLES.
Edited by Rev. J. G. WOOD. Illustrated.
Cr. 8vo. 6s.—*People's Edition.* 4to. 6d.

WHITE (Gilbert).—NATURAL HISTORY AND ANTIQUITIES OF SELBORNE. Ed. by FRANK BUCKLAND. With a Chapter on Antiquities by the EARL OF SELBORNE. Cr. 8vo. 6s. —— Edited by J. BURROUGHS. 2 vols. Cr. 8vo. 10s. 6d

WRIGHT (M. O.).—BIRDCRAFT. Ex. cr. 8vo. 12s. 6d. net.

NATURAL PHILOSOPHY. (See PHYSICS.)

NAVAL SCIENCE AND HISTORY.

DELBOS (L.).—LECTURES MARITIMES. Cr. 8vo. 2s. net. —— SEA STORIES FOR FRENCH COMPOSITION. Fcp. 8vo. 2s. net.

FLAGG (A. T.).—PRIMER OF NAVIGATION. Pott 8vo. 1s.

GOW (W.).—MARINE INSURANCE. Globe 8vo. 4s. 6d.

KELVIN (Lord).—POPULAR LECTURES AND ADDRESSES.—Vol. III. NAVIGATION. Cr. 8vo. 7s. 6d.

NORWAY (A. H.).—HISTORY OF THE POST OFFICE PACKET SERVICE, 1793—1815. Illustrated. Cr. 8vo. 8s. 6d. net.

ROBINSON (Rev. J. L.).—ELEMENTS OF MARINE SURVEYING. For Junior Naval Officers. Illustrated. 2nd Edit. Cr. 8vo. 7s. 6d.

SHORTLAND (Admiral).—NAUTICAL SURVEYING. 8vo. 21s.

WILLIAMS (H.)—BRITAIN'S NAVAL POWER. Cr. 8vo. 4s. 6d. net.

NOVELS. (See PROSE FICTION, p. 21.)

NURSING.

(See under DOMESTIC ECONOMY, p. 9.)

OPTICS (or LIGHT). (See PHYSICS, p. 34.)

PAINTING. (See ART, p. 2.)

PATHOLOGY. (See MEDICINE, p. 28.)

PERIODICALS.

AMERICAN HISTORICAL REVIEW. (See HISTORY.)

AMERICAN JOURNAL OF PHILOLOGY, THE. (See PHILOLOGY.)

BRAIN. (See MEDICINE.)

CANTERBURY DIOCESAN GAZETTE. Monthly. 8vo. 2d.

CENTURY MAGAZINE. Monthly. 8vo. 1s. 4d

ECONOMIC JOURNAL, THE. (See Po-LITICAL ECONOMY.)

ECONOMICS, THE QUARTERLY JOURNAL OF. (See POLITICAL ECONOMY.)

HELLENIC STUDIES, THE JOURNAL OF. Published Half-Yearly from 1880. 8vo. 30s.; or Quarterly Parts, 15s. net. The Journal will be sold at a reduced price to Libraries wishing to subscribe, but official application must in each case be made to the Council. Information on this point, and upon the conditions of Membership, may be obtained on application to the Hon. Sec., Mr. George Macmillan, 29, Bedford Street, Covent Garden.

JEWISH QUARTERLY REVIEW. Edited by I. ABRAHAMS and C. G. MONTEFIORE. 8vo. 3s. 6d.

LEPROSY INVESTIGATION COMMIT-TEE, JOURNAL OF. (See MEDICINE.)

MACMILLAN'S MAGAZINE. Published Monthly. 1s.—Half-Yearly Vols. 7s. 6d, each. [Cloth covers for binding, 1s. each.]

MATHEMATICAL GAZETTE, THE. (See MATHEMATICS.)

NATURE: A WEEKLY ILLUSTRATED JOUR-NAL OF SCIENCE. Published every Thursday. Price 6d. Monthly Parts, 2s. and 2s. 6d.; Current Half-yearly vols., 15s. each. [Cases for binding vols. 1s. 6d. each.]

PHILOLOGY, THE JOURNAL OF. (See PHILOLOGY.)

PHYSICAL REVIEW, THE. (See PHYSICS.)

PSYCHOLOGICAL REVIEW, THE. (See PSYCHOLOGY.)

RECORD OF TECHNICAL AND SE-CONDARY EDUCATION. (See EDU-CATION, p. 10.)

ST. NICHOLAS MAGAZINE. Monthly. 8vo. 1s.

PHILOLOGY.

AMERICAN JOURNAL OF PHILOLOGY, THE. Edited by Prof. BASIL L. GILDER-SLEEVE. 4s. 6d. each No. (quarterly).

CORNELL UNIVERSITY STUDIES IN CLASSICAL PHILOLOGY. Edited by I. FLAGG, W. G. HALE, and B. I. WHEELER. I. THE C U M-CONSTRUCTIONS: their His-tory and Functions. Part I. Critical. 1s.8d. net Part II. Constructive By W. G. HALE. 2s. 4d. net.—II. ANALOGY AND THE SCOPE OF ITS APPLICATION IN LANGUAGE. By B. I. WHEELER 1s.3d. net.

EMERSON (O. F.).—HISTORY OF THE ENG-LISH LANGUAGE. Cr. 8vo. 6s. net.

GILES (P.).—A MANUAL OF COMPARATIVE PHILOLOGY FOR CLASSICAL STUDENTS. Cr. 8vo. 10s. 6d.

JOURNAL OF SACRED AND CLASSI-CAL PHILOLOGY. 4 vols. 8vo. 12s.6d.each.

JOURNAL OF PHILOLOGY. New Series. Edited by W. A. WRIGHT M.A., I. BY-WATER, M.A., and H. JACKSON, M.A. 4s. 6d. each No. (half-yearly).

KELLNER (Dr. L.). — HISTORICAL OUT-LINES IN ENGLISH SYNTAX. Revised by L. KELLNER and H. BRADLEY. Globe 8vo. 6s.

MACLEAN (G. E.).—AN OLD AND MIDDLE-ENGLISH READER. Cr. 8vo. 8s. net.

MORRIS (Rev. Richard, LL.D.).—PRIMER OF ENGLISH GRAMMAR. Pott 8vo. 1s. —— ELEMENTARY LESSONS IN HISTORICAL ENGLISH GRAMMAR. Pott 8vo. 2s. 6d. —— HISTORICAL OUTLINES OF ENGLISH AC-CIDENCE. Revised by L. KELLNER and H. BRADLEY. Gl 8vo. 6s.

MORRIS (R.) and BOWEN (H. C.).—ENG-LISH GRAMMAR EXERCISES. Pott 8vo. 1s.

OLIPHANT (T. L. Kington). — THE OLD AND MIDDLE ENGLISH. Globe 8vo. 9s. —— THE NEW ENGLISH. 2 vols. Cr. 8vo. 21s.

PEILE (John).—A PRIMER OF PHILOLOGY. Pott 8vo. 1s.

PHILOSOPHY.

32

PELLISSIER (E.).—French Roots and
their Families. Globe 8vo. 6s.

TAYLOR (Isaac).—Words and Places.
9th Edit. Maps. Globe 8vo. 6s.
—— Etruscan Researches. 8vo. 14s.
—— Greeks and Goths: A Study of the
Runes. 8vo. 9s.

WETHERELL (J.).—Exercises on Morris's Primer of English Grammar.
Pott 8vo. 1s.

YONGE (C. M.).—History of Christian
Names. New Edit., revised. Cr. 8vo. 7s. 6d.

PHILOSOPHY.

Ethics and Metaphysics—Logic—Psychology.

Ethics and Metaphysics.

BIRKS(Thomas Rawson).—First Principles
of Moral Science. Cr. 8vo. 8s. 6d.
—— Modern Utilitarianism; or, The Sys-
tems of Paley, Bentham, and Mill Examined
and Compared. Cr. 8vo. 6s. 6d.
—— Modern Physical Fatalism, and the
Doctrine of Evolution. Including an
Examination of Mr. Herbert Spencer's
"First Principles." Cr. 8vo. 6s.

CALDERWOOD (Prof. H.).—A Handbook
of Moral Philosophy. Cr. 8vo. 6s.

D'ARCY (C. F.).—Short Study of Ethics.
Cr. 8vo. 5s. net.

DEUSSEN (P.)—Elements of Metaphysics. Cr. 8vo. 6s.

FISKE (John).—Outlines of Cosmic Philo
sophy, based on the Doctrine of Evolution. 2 vols. 8vo. 25s.

FOWLER (Rev. Thomas). — Progressive
Morality: An Essay in Ethics. 2nd Edit.
Cr. 8vo. 3s net.

HILL (D. J.).—Genetic Philosophy. Cr.
8vo. 7s. net.

HUXLEY (Prof. T. H.).—Evolution and
Ethics. 8vo. 2s. net.

KANT.—Kant's Critical Philosophy for
English Readers. By J. P. Mahaffy,
D.D., and J. H. Bernard, B.D. 2 vols.
Cr. 8vo.—Vol. I. The Kritik of Pure
Reason Explained and Defended. 7s.6d.
—Vol. II. The Prolegomena. Translated,
with Notes and Appendices. 6s.
—— Kritik of Judgment. Translated by
J. H. Bernard, D.D. 8vo. 10s. net.

KANT—MAX MÜLLER. — Critique of
Pure Reason by Immanuel Kant. Translated by F. Max Müller. With Introduction by Ludwig Noiré. 2 vols. 8vo.
16s. each (sold separately).—Vol. I. Historical Introduction, by Ludwig Noiré,
etc.—Vol. II. Critique of Pure Reason.

KNIGHT (W. A.).—Aspects of Theism.
8vo. 8s. 6d.

MARSHALL (H. R.).— Pain, Pleasure,
and Aesthetics. 8vo. 8s. 6d. net.
—— Aesthetic Principles. Cr. 8vo. 5s. net.

MAURICE (F. D.).—Moral and Meta-
physical Philosophy. 2 vols. 8vo. 16s.

McCOSH (Rev. Dr. James).—The Method
of the Divine Government, Physical
and Moral. 8vo. 10s. 6d.
—— The Supernatural in Relation to
the Natural. Cr. 8vo. 7s. 6d.
—— Intuitions of the Mind. 8vo. 10s. 6d.
—— An Examination of Mr. J. S. Mill's
Philosophy. 8vo. 10s. 6d.
—— Christianity and Positivism. Lec-
tures on Natural Theology and Apologetics.
Cr 8vo. 7s. 6d.
—— The Scottish Philosophy from Hut-
cheson to Hamilton, Biographical, Ex-
pository, Critical. Roy. 8vo. 16s.
—— Realistic Philosophy Defended in a
Philosophic Series. 2 vols. — Vol. I.
Expository. Vol. II. Historical and
Critical. Cr. 8vo. 14s.
—— First and Fundamental Truths.
Being a Treatise on Metaphysics. 8vo. 9s.
—— The Prevailing Types of Philosophy:
Can they Logically reach Reality?
8vo. 3s. 6d.
—— Our Moral Nature. Cr. 8vo. 2s. 6d.

MASSON (Prof. David).—Recent British
Philosophy. 3rd Edit. Cr. 8vo. 6s.

SIDGWICK (Prof. Henry).—The Methods
of Ethics. 5th Edit., revised. 8vo. 14s.
—— A Supplement to the Second Edition.
Containing all the important Additions and
Alterations in the Fourth Edition. 8vo. 6s.
—— Outlines of the History of Ethics
for English Readers. Cr. 8vo. 3s. 6d.

THORNTON (W. T.). — Old-Fashioned
Ethics and Common-Sense Metaphysics.
8vo. 10s. 6d.

WILLIAMS (C. M.).—A Review of the Systems of Ethics founded on the Theory
of Evolution. Cr. 8vo. 12s. net.

WINDELBAND (W.).—History of Philosophy. Transl. by J.H. Tufts. 8vo. 21s. net.

Logic.

BOOLE (George). — The Mathematical
Analysis of Logic. 8vo. sewed. 5s.

BOSANQUET (B.).—Essentials of Logic.
Cr. 8vo. 3s. net.

CARROLL (Lewis).—The Game of Logic.
Cr. 8vo. 3s. net.
—— Symbolic Logic. I. Elementary. Gl.
8vo. 2s. net.

JEVONS (W. Stanley).—A Primer of Logic.
Pott 8vo. 1s.
—— Elementary Lessons in Logic, De-
ductive and Inductive. Pott 8vo. 3s. 6d.
—— Studies in Deductive Logic. 2nd
Edit. Cr. 8vo. 6s.
—— The Principles of Science: Treatise on
Logic and Scientific Method. Cr. 8vo. 12s. 6d.
—— Pure Logic: and other Minor Works.
Edited by R. Adamson, M.A., and Har-
riet A. Jevons. 8vo. 10s. 6d.

KEYNES (J. N.).—Studies and Exercises
in Formal Logic. 3rd Edit. 8vo. 12s.

McCOSH (Rev. Dr.).—The Laws of Dis-
cursive Thought. A Text-Book of Formal
Logic. Cr. 8vo. 5s.

RAY (Prof. P. K.).—A Text-Book of Deductive Logic. 4th Edit. Globe 8vo. 4s. 6d.

VENN (Rev. John).—THE LOGIC OF CHANCE. 2nd Edit. Cr. 8vo. 10s. 6d.
— SYMBOLIC LOGIC. 2nd Ed. Cr. 8vo. 10s.6d.
— THE PRINCIPLES OF EMPIRICAL OR INDUCTIVE LOGIC. 8vo. 18s.

Psychology.

BALDWIN (Prof. J. M.).—HANDBOOK OF PSYCHOLOGY: Senses and Intellect. 8vo. 8s. 6d. net.
— FEELING AND WILL. 8vo. 8s. 6d. net.
— ELEMENTS OF PSYCHOLOGY. Cr.8vo. 7s.6d.
— MENTAL DEVELOPMENT IN THE CHILD AND THE RACE. 8vo. 10s. net.
CALDERWOOD (Prof. H.). — THE RELATIONS OF MIND AND BRAIN. 3rd Ed. 8vo. 8s.
CATTELL (J. McK.). — EXPERIMENTAL PSYCHOLOGY. [In the Press.
CLIFFORD (W. K.).—SEEING AND THINKING. Cr. 8vo. 3s. 6d.
HÖFFDING (Prof. H.).—OUTLINES OF PSYCHOLOGY. Translated by M. E. LOWNDES. Cr. 8vo. 6s.
JAMES (Prof. William).—THE PRINCIPLES OF PSYCHOLOGY. 2 vols. Demy 8vo. 25s. net.
— TEXT-BOOK OF PSYCHOLOGY. Cr. 8vo. 7s. net.
JARDINE (Rev. Robert).—THE ELEMENTS OF THE PSYCHOLOGY OF COGNITION. 3rd Edit. Cr. 8vo. 6s. 6d.
McCOSH (Rev. Dr.).—PSYCHOLOGY. Cr. 8vo. I. THE COGNITIVE POWERS. 6s. 6d.—II. THE MOTIVE POWERS. 6s. 6d.
— THE EMOTIONS. 8vo. 9s.
MAUDSLEY (Dr. Henry).—THE PHYSIOLOGY OF MIND. Cr. 8vo. 10s. 6d.
— THE PATHOLOGY OF MIND. 8vo. 15s. net.
— BODY AND MIND. Cr. 8vo. 6s. 6d.
MURPHY (J. J.).—HABIT AND INTELLIGENCE. 2nd Edit. Illustrated. 8vo. 16s.
PSYCHOLOGICAL REVIEW, THE. Ed. by J. M. CATTELL and J. M. BALDWIN. 8vo. 3s. net. Annual Subscription, 16s.6d. net.

PHOTOGRAPHY.

MELDOLA (Prof. R.).—THE CHEMISTRY OF PHOTOGRAPHY. Cr. 8vo. 6s.

PHYSICS OR NATURAL PHILOSOPHY.

General—Electricity and Magnetism—Heat, Light, and Sound.

General.

ANDREWS (Dr. Thomas): THE SCIENTIFIC PAPERS OF THE LATE. With a Memoir by Profs. TAIT and CRUM BROWN. 8vo. 18s.
BARKER (G. F.). — PHYSICS: ADVANCED COURSE. 8vo. 21s.
DANIELL (A.).—A TEXT-BOOK OF THE PRINCIPLES OF PHYSICS. Illustrated. 3rd Edit. Med. 8vo. 21s.
EARL (A).—PRACTICAL LESSONS IN PHYSICAL MEASUREMENT. Cr. 8vo. 5s.

EVERETT (Prof. J. D.).—THE C. G. S. SYSTEM OF UNITS, WITH TABLES OF PHYSICAL CONSTANTS. New Edit. Globe 8vo. 5s.
FESSENDEN (C.).—ELEMENTS OF PHYSICS. Fcp. 8vo. 3s.
FISHER (Rev. Osmond).—PHYSICS OF THE EARTH'S CRUST. 2nd Edit. 8vo. 12s.
GEE (W.). — SHORT STUDIES IN NATURE KNOWLEDGE. Globe 8vo. 3s. 6d.
GORDON (H.)—PRACTICAL SCIENCE. Part I. Pott 8vo. 1s. [Part II. in the Press.
GREGORY (R. A.).—ELEMENTARY PRACTICAL PHYSICS. 4to. 2s. 6d.
GUILLEMIN (Amédée).—THE FORCES OF NATURE. A Popular Introduction to the Study of Physical Phenomena. 455 Woodcuts. Rcy. 8vo. 21s.
HUXLEY (T. H.).—INTRODUCTORY PRIMER OF SCIENCE. Pott 8vo. 1s.
KELVIN (Lord).—POPULAR LECTURES AND ADDRESSES.—Vol. I. CONSTITUTION OF MATTER. Cr. 8vo. 7s. 6d.
KEMPE (A. B.).—HOW TO DRAW A STRAIGHT LINE. Cr. 8vo. 1s. 6d.
LOEWY (B.).—QUESTIONS AND EXAMPLES IN EXPERIMENTAL PHYSICS, SOUND, LIGHT, HEAT, ELECTRICITY, AND MAGNETISM. Fcp. 8vo. 2s.
— A GRADUATED COURSE OF NATURAL SCIENCE. Part I. Gl. 8vo. 2s.—Part II. 2s.6d.
LOUDOUN (W. J.) and Mc LENNAN (J. C.).—LABORATORY COURSE IN EXPERIMENTAL PHYSICS. 8vo. 8s. 6d. net.
MOLLOY (Rev. G.).—GLEANINGS IN SCIENCE: A Series of Popular Lectures on Scientific Subjects. 8vo. 7s. 6d.
NICHOLS (E. L.).—LABORATORY MANUAL OF PHYSICS AND APPLIED ELECTRICITY. Vol. I. JUNIOR COURSE IN GENERAL PHYSICS. With Tables. 8vo. 12s. 6d. net.—Vol. II. SENIOR COURSES. 12s. 6d. net.
PHYSICAL REVIEW, THE. Edited by E. L. NICHOLS and E. MERRITT. Bi-Monthly. 8vo. 3s. net.
STEWART (Prof. Balfour). — A PRIMER OF PHYSICS. Illustrated. Pott 8vo. 1s.
— LESSONS IN ELEMENTARY PHYSICS. Illustrated. Fcp. 8vo. 4s. 6d.
— QUESTIONS ON THE SAME. By T. H. CORE. Pott 8vo. 2s.
STEWART (Prof. Balfour) and GEE (W. W. Haldane).—LESSONS IN ELEMENTARY PRACTICAL PHYSICS. Illustrated.—GENERAL PHYSICAL PROCESSES. Cr. 8vo. 6s.
TAIT (Prof. P. G.).—LECTURES ON SOME RECENT ADVANCES IN PHYSICAL SCIENCE. 3rd Edit. Cr. 8vo. 9s.

Electricity and Magnetism.

CUMMING (Linnæus).—AN INTRODUCTION TO ELECTRICITY. 4th Ed. Cr. 8vo. 8s. 6d.
DAY (R. E.).—ELECTRIC LIGHT ARITHMETIC. Pott 8vo. 2s.

PHYSICS—PHYSIOLOGY.

34

Electricity—continued.

GRAY (Prof. Andrew).—THE THEORY AND PRACTICE OF ABSOLUTE MEASUREMENTS IN ELECTRICITY AND MAGNETISM. 2 vols. Cr. 8vo. Vol. I. 12s. 6d.—Vol. II. 2 parts. 25s.
—— ABSOLUTE MEASUREMENTS IN ELECTRICITY AND MAGNETISM. Fcp. 8vo. 5s. 6d.
—— MAGNETISM AND ELECTRICITY. 8vo. [In the Press.

GUILLEMIN (A.).—ELECTRICITY AND MAGNETISM. A Popular Treatise. Translated and Edited by Prof. SILVANUS P. THOMPSON. Super Roy. 8vo. 31s. 6d.

HEAVISIDE (O.) — ELECTRICAL PAPERS. 2 vols. 8vo. 30s. net.

HERTZ (H.).—ELECTRIC WAVES. Transl. by D. E. JONES, B.Sc. 8vo. 10s. net.

JACKSON (D. C.).—TEXT-BOOK ON ELECTRO-MAGNETISM. Vol. I. Cr. 8vo. 9s. net.

KELVIN (Lord). — PAPERS ON ELECTRO-STATICS AND MAGNETISM. 8vo. 18s.

LODGE (Prof. Oliver).—MODERN VIEWS OF ELECTRICITY. Illust. Cr. 8vo. 6s. 6d.

MENDENHALL (T. C.).—A CENTURY OF ELECTRICITY. Cr. 8vo. 4s. 6d.

STEWART (Prof. Balfour) and GEE (W. W. Haldane).—LESSONS IN ELEMENTARY PRACTICAL PHYSICS. Cr. 8vo. Illustrated.—ELECTRICITY AND MAGNETISM. 7s. 6d.
—— PRACTICAL PHYSICS FOR SCHOOLS. Gl. 8vo.—ELECTRICITY AND MAGNETISM. 2s.6d.

THOMPSON (Prof. Silvanus P.). — ELEMENTARY LESSONS IN ELECTRICITY AND MAGNETISM. New Edition. Illustrated. Fcp. 8vo. 4s. 6d.

TURNER (H. H.).—EXAMPLES ON HEAT AND ELECTRICITY. Cr. 8vo. 2s. 6d.

Heat, Light, and Sound.

AIRY (Sir G. B.).—ON SOUND AND ATMOSPHERIC VIBRATIONS. Cr. 8vo. 9s.

CARNOT-THURSTON.--REFLECTIONS ON THE MOTIVE POWER OF HEAT, AND ON MACHINES FITTED TO DEVELOP THAT POWER. From the French of N. L. S. CARNOT. Edited by R. H. THURSTON, LL.D. Cr. 8vo. 7s. 6d.

JOHNSON(A.).—SUNSHINE. Illust. Cr.8vo.6s.

JONES (Prof. D. E.).—HEAT, LIGHT, AND SOUND. Globe 8vo. 2s. 6d.
—— LESSONS IN HEAT AND LIGHT. Globe 8vo. 3s. 6d.

MARTINEAU (C. A.).—EASY LESSONS IN HEAT. Gl. 8vo. 2s. 6d.

MAYER (Prof. A. M.).—SOUND. A Series of Simple Experiments. Illustr. Cr.8vo. 3s.6d.

MAYER (Prof. A. M.) and BARNARD (C.)— LIGHT. A Series of Simple Experiments. Illustrated. Cr. 8vo. 2s. 6d.

PARKINSON (S.).—A TREATISE ON OPTICS. 4th Edit., revised. Cr. 8vo. 10s. 6d.

PEABODY(Prof. C. H.).—THERMODYNAMICS OF THE STEAM ENGINE AND OTHER HEAT-ENGINES. 8vo. 21s.

PRESTON (T.).—THE THEORY OF LIGHT. Illustrated. 8vo. 15s. net.
—— THE THEORY OF HEAT. 8vo. 17s. net.

RAYLEIGH (Lord).—THEORY OF SOUND. Vol. I. 8vo. 12s. net.

SHANN (G.).—AN ELEMENTARY TREATISE ON HEAT IN RELATION TO STEAM AND THE STEAM-ENGINE. Illustr. Cr. 8vo. 4s. 6d.

SPOTTISWOODE (W.).—POLARISATION OF LIGHT. Illustrated. Cr. 8vo. 3s. 6d.

STEWART (Prof. Balfour) and GEE (W. W. Haldane).—LESSONS IN ELEMENTARY PRACTICAL PHYSICS. Cr. 8vo. Illustrated.— OPTICS, HEAT, AND SOUND. [In the Press.
—— PRACTICAL PHYSICS FOR SCHOOLS. Gl. 8vo.—HEAT, LIGHT, AND SOUND.

STOKES (Sir George G.).—ON LIGHT. The Burnett Lectures. Cr. 8vo. 7s. 6d.

STONE (W. H.).—ELEMENTARY LESSONS ON SOUND. Illustrated. Fcp. 8vo. 3s. 6d.

TAIT (Prof. P. G.).—HEAT. With Illustrations. Cr. 8vo. 6s.

TAYLOR (Sedley).—SOUND AND MUSIC. 2nd Edit. Ext. cr. 8vo. 8s. 6d.

TURNER (H. H.). (See ELECTRICITY.)

WRIGHT (Lewis).—LIGHT. A Course of Experimental Optics. Illust. Cr.8vo. 7s. 6d.

YEO (J.).—STEAM AND THE MARINE STEAM ENGINE. 8vo. 7s. 6d. net.

PHYSIOGRAPHY and METEOROLOGY.

ARATUS.—THE SKIES AND WEATHER FORECASTS OF ARATUS. Translated by E. POSTE, M.A. Cr. 8vo. 3s. 6d.

BLANFORD (H. F.).—THE RUDIMENTS OF PHYSICAL GEOGRAPHY FOR THE USE OF INDIAN SCHOOLS. Illustr. Cr.8vo. 2s. 6d.
—— A PRACTICAL GUIDE TO THE CLIMATES AND WEATHER OF INDIA, CEYLON AND BURMAH, AND THE STORMS OF INDIAN SEAS. 8vo. 12s. 6d.

FERREL (Prof. W.).—A POPULAR TREATISE ON THE WINDS. 2nd Ed. 8vo. 17s. net.

GEIKIE (Sir Archibald).—A PRIMER OF PHYSICAL GEOGRAPHY. Illustr. Pott 8vo. 1s.
—— ELEMENTARY LESSONS IN PHYSICAL GEOGRAPHY. Illustrated. Fcp. 8vo. 4s. 6d.
—— QUESTIONS ON THE SAME. 1s. 6d.

HUXLEY (Prof. T. H.).—PHYSIOGRAPHY. Illustrated. Cr. 8vo. 6s.

LOCKYER (J. Norman).—OUTLINES OF PHYSIOGRAPHY: THE MOVEMENTS OF THE EARTH. Illustrated. Cr. 8vo, swd. 1s. 6d.

MARR (J. E.) and HARKER (A.).—PHYSIOGRAPHY FOR BEGINNERS. Gl. 8vo. In Press.

MELDOLA (Prof. R.) and WHITE (Wm.).— REPORT ON THE EAST ANGLIAN EARTHQUAKE OF APRIL 22ND, 1884. 8vo. 3s. 6d.

RUSSELL(T.)—METEOROLOGY. 8vo. 16s.net.

TARR (R. S.). — ELEMENTARY PHYSICAL GEOGRAPHY. Cr. 8vo. 7s. 6d. net.

PHYSIOLOGY.

FEARNLEY (W.).—A MANUAL OF ELEMENTARY PRACTICAL HISTOLOGY. Cr.8vo. 7s.6d.

FOSTER (Prof. M.) and LANGLEY (J. N.). —A COURSE OF ELEMENTARY PRACTICAL PHYSIOLOGY AND HISTOLOGY. Cr. 8vo. 7s. 6d.

FOSTER (Prof. M.) and SHORE (L. E.).— PHYSIOLOGY FOR BEGINNERS. Gl. 8vo. 2s.6d.

FOSTER (Prof. Michael).—A TEXT-BOOK OF PHYSIOLOGY. Illustrated. 6th Edit. 8vo.—Part I. Book I. BLOOD: THE TISSUES OF MOVEMENT, THE VASCULAR MECHANISM. 10s. 6d.—Part II. Book II. THE TISSUES OF CHEMICAL ACTION, WITH THEIR RESPECTIVE MECHANISMS: NUTRITION. 10s. 6d.—Part III. Book III. THE CENTRAL NERVOUS SYSTEM. 7s. 6d.—Part IV. Book III. THE SENSES, AND SOME SPECIAL MUSCULAR MECHANISMS.—BOOK IV. THE TISSUES AND MECHANISMS OF REPRODUCTION. 10s. 6d. —Appendix, by A. S. LEA. 7s. 6d.
—— A PRIMER OF PHYSIOLOGY. Pott 8vo. 1s.

GAMGEE (Arthur).—A TEXT-BOOK OF THE PHYSIOLOGICAL CHEMISTRY OF THE ANIMAL BODY. 8vo. Vol. I. 18s. Vol. II. 18s.

HUMPHRY (Prof. Sir G. M.).—THE HUMAN FOOT AND THE HUMAN HAND. Illustrated. Fcp. 8vo. 4s. 6d.

HUXLEY (Prof. Thos. H.).—LESSONS IN ELEMENTARY PHYSIOLOGY. Fcp. 8vo. 4s. 6d.
—— QUESTIONS. By T. ALCOCK. Pott 8vo. 1s. 6d.

KIMBER (D. C.).—ANATOMY AND PHYSIOLOGY FOR NURSES. 8vo. 10s. net.

MIVART (St. George).—LESSONS IN ELEMENTARY ANATOMY. Fcp. 8vo. 6s. 6d.

PETTIGREW (J. Bell).—THE PHYSIOLOGY OF THE CIRCULATION IN PLANTS IN THE LOWER ANIMALS AND IN MAN. 8vo. 12s.

SEILER (Dr. Carl).—MICRO-PHOTOGRAPHS IN HISTOLOGY, NORMAL AND PATHOLOGICAL. 4to. 31s. 6d.

WIEDERSHEIM (R.).—THE STRUCTURE OF MAN. Translated by H. M. BERNARD. Revised by G. B. HOWES. 8vo. 8s. net.

POETRY. (See under LITERATURE, p. 17.)

POLITICAL ECONOMY.
BASTABLE (Prof. C. F.).—PUBLIC FINANCE. 2nd Ed. 8vo. 12s. 6d. net.

BÖHM-BAWERK (Prof.).—CAPITAL AND INTEREST. Transl. by W. SMART. 8vo. 12s. net.
—— THE POSITIVE THEORY OF CAPITAL. By the same Translator. 8vo. 12s. net.

BONAR (James).—MALTHUS AND HIS WORK. 8vo. 12s. 6d.
—— CATALOGUE OF THE LIBRARY OF ADAM SMITH. 8vo. 7s. 6d. net.

BRUCE (P. A.).. (See under HISTORY.)

CAIRNES (J. E.).—SOME LEADING PRINCIPLES OF POLITICAL ECONOMY NEWLY EXPOUNDED. 8vo. 14s.
—— THE CHARACTER AND LOGICAL METHOD OF POLITICAL ECONOMY. Cr. 8vo. 6s.

CANTILLON.—ESSAI SUR LE COMMERCE. 12mo. 7s. net.

CLARE (G.).—A B C OF THE FOREIGN EXCHANGES. Cr. 8vo. 3s. net.

CLARKE (C. B.). — SPECULATIONS FROM POLITICAL ECONOMY. Cr. 8vo. 3s. 6d.

COLUMBIA COLLEGE. STUDIES IN HISTORY, ECONOMICS, AND PUBLIC LAWS. 4 vols. 8vo. 18s. net. each.

COMMONS (J. R.)—DISTRIBUTION OF WEALTH. Cr. 8vo. 7s. net.

COSSA (L.).—INTRODUCTION TO THE STUDY OF POLITICAL ECONOMY. Translated by L. DYER. Cr. 8vo. 8s. 6d. net.

DICTIONARY OF POLITICAL ECONOMY, A. By various Writers. Ed. R. H. I. PALGRAVE. Parts I. to VI. 3s. 6d. each net. —Vol. I. Med. 8vo. 21s. net.

ECONOMIC CLASSICS. Edited by W. J. ASHLEY Globe 8vo. 3s. net. each.
SELECT CHAPTERS FROM THE "WEALTH OF NATIONS" OF ADAM SMITH.
FIRST SIX CHAPTERS OF "PRINCIPLES OF POLITICAL ECONOMY" OF DAVID RICARDO.
PARALLEL CHAPTERS FROM FIRST AND SECOND EDITIONS OF "PRINCIPLE OF POPULATION." By T. R. MALTHUS.
ENGLAND'S TREASURE BY FORRAIGN TRADE. By T. MUN.
PEASANT RENTS. By RICHARD JONES.
MERCANTILE SYSTEM. By G. SCHMOLLER.

ECONOMIC JOURNAL, THE. — THE JOURNAL OF THE BRITISH ECONOMIC ASSOCIATION. Edit. by Prof. F. Y. EDGEWORTH. Published Quarterly. 5s. net. (Part I. April, 1891.) Vols. I.-IV. 21s. net each. [Cloth Covers for binding Volumes, 1s. 6d. net each.]

ECONOMICS: THE QUARTERLY JOURNAL OF. Vol. II. Parts II. III. IV. 2s. 6d. net each. —Vol. III. 4 parts. 2s. 6d. net each.—Vol. IV. 4 parts. 2s. 6d. net each.—Vol. V. 4 parts. 2s. 6d. net each.—Vol. VI. 4 parts. 2s. 6d. net each.—Vol. VII. 4 parts. 2s. 6d. net each.—Vol. VIII. 4 parts. 2s. 6d. net each.—Vol. IX. 4 parts. 2s. 6d. net each.—Vol. X. Part I. 2s. 6d. net.

FAWCETT (Henry).—MANUAL OF POLITICAL ECONOMY. 7th Edit. Cr. 8vo. 12s.
—— AN EXPLANATORY DIGEST OF THE ABOVE. By C. A. WATERS. Cr. 8vo. 2s. 6d.
—— FREE TRADE AND PROTECTION. 6th Edit. Cr. 8vo. 3s. 6d.

FAWCETT (Mrs. H.).—POLITICAL ECONOMY FOR BEGINNERS, WITH QUESTIONS. 7th Edit. Pott 8vo. 2s. 6d.

FIRST LESSONS IN BUSINESS MATTERS. By A BANKER'S DAUGHTER. 2nd Edit. Pott 8vo. 1s.

FONDA (A. J.).—HONEST MONEY. Cr. 8vo. 3s. 6d. net.

GILMAN (N. P.). — PROFIT-SHARING BETWEEN EMPLOYER AND EMPLOYEE. Cr. 8vo. 7s. 6d.

GOSCHEN (Rt. Hon. George J.).—REPORTS AND SPEECHES ON LOCAL TAXATION. 8vo. 5s.

GUIDE TO THE UNPROTECTED: IN EVERY-DAY MATTERS RELATING TO PROPERTY AND INCOME. Ext. fcp. 8vo. 3s. 6d.

GUNTON (George).—WEALTH AND PROGRESS. Cr. 8vo. 6s.

HALLE (E. von).—TRUSTS OR INDUSTRIAL COMBINATIONS AND COALITIONS IN THE UNITED STATES. Cr. 8vo. 5s. net.

HELM (E.).—THE JOINT STANDARD. Cr. 8vo. 3s. 6d. net.

HORTON (Hon. S. Dana).—THE SILVER POUND AND ENGLAND'S MONETARY POLICY SINCE THE RESTORATION. 8vo. 14s.

HOWELL (George).—THE CONFLICTS OF CAPITAL AND LABOUR. Cr. 8vo. 7s. 6d.
—— A HANDY BOOK OF THE LABOUR LAWS. 3rd Edit. Cr. 8vo. 3s. 6d. net.

JEVONS (W. Stanley).—A PRIMER OF POLITICAL ECONOMY. Pott 8vo. 1s.

POLITICAL ECONOMY—*continued.*
JEVONS (W. S.).—THE THEORY OF POLITI-
CAL ECONOMY, 3rd Ed. 8vo. 10s. 6d.
—— INVESTIGATIONS IN CURRENCY AND FI-
NANCE. Edit. by H. S. FOXWELL. 8vo. 21s

KEYNES (J. N.).—THE SCOPE AND METHOD
OF POLITICAL ECONOMY. Cr. 8vo. 7s. net.

LEIBNITZ.—NOUVEAUX ESSAIS. Transl. by
A. G. LANGLEY. [*In the Press.*

MARSHALL (Prof. Alfred).—PRINCIPLES OF
ECONOMICS. 3rd Ed. 8vo. Vol. I. 12s.6d. net.
—— ELEMENTS OF ECONOMICS OF INDUSTRY.
Crown 8vo. 3s. 6d.

MARTIN (Frederick).—THE HISTORY OF
LLOYDS, AND OF MARINE INSURANCE IN
GREAT BRITAIN. 8vo. 14s.

MENGER (C.).—THE RIGHT TO THE WHOLE
PRODUCE OF LABOUR. Transl. by M. E.
TANNER. [*In the Press.*

PRICE (L. L. F. R).—INDUSTRIAL PEACE :
ITS ADVANTAGES, METHODS, AND DIFFI-
CULTIES. Med. 8vo. 6s.

QUESNAY (F.).—TABLEAU OECONOMIQUE.
4to. 2s. 6d. net.

RABBENO (U.).—AMERICAN COMMERCIAL
POLICY. 8vo. 12s. net.

RAE (J.).—EIGHT HOURS FOR WORK. Cr.
8vo. 4s. 6d. net.

RICARDO.—CHAPTERS I.—VI. OF "THE
PRINCIPLES OF POLITICAL ECONOMY AND
TAXATION." Globe 8vo. 3s. net.

SELIGMAN (E. R. A.).—ESSAYS IN TAXA-
TION. 8vo. 12s. 6d. net.

SIDGWICK (Prof. Henry).—THE PRINCIPLES
OF POLITICAL ECONOMY. [*New Ed. in Press.*

SMART (W.).—AN INTRODUCTION TO THE
THEORY OF VALUE. Cr. 8vo. 3s. net.
—— STUDIES IN ECONOMICS. Ex. cr. 8vo.
8s. 6d. net.

SMITH (Adam).—SELECT CHAPTERS FROM
"THE WEALTH OF NATIONS." Gl.8vo. 3s.net.

THOMPSON (H. M.).—THE THEORY OF
WAGES AND ITS APPLICATION TO THE EIGHT
HOURS QUESTION. Cr. 8vo. 3s. 6d.

WALKER (Francis A.).—FIRST LESSONS IN
POLITICAL ECONOMY. Cr. 8vo. 5s.
—— A BRIEF TEXT-BOOK OF POLITICAL
ECONOMY. Cr. 8vo. 6s. 6d.
—— POLITICAL ECONOMY. 8vo. 12s. 6d.
—— THE WAGES QUESTION. Ext. cr. 8vo.
8s. 6d. net.
—— MONEY. New Edit. Ext.cr.8vo. 8s.6d.net.
—— MONEY IN ITS RELATION TO TRADE AND
INDUSTRY. Cr. 8vo. 7s. 6d.
—— LAND AND ITS RENT. Fcp. 8vo. 3s. 6d

WALLACE (A. R.).—BAD TIMES : An Essay.
Cr. 8vo. 2s. 6d.

WICKSTEED (Ph. H.).—THE ALPHABET OF
ECONOMIC SCIENCE.—I. ELEMENTS OF THE
THEORY OF VALUE OR WORTH. Gl.8vo. 2s.6d.

WIESER (F. von).—NATURAL VALUE. Edit.
by W. SMART, M.A. 8vo. 10s. net.

POLITICS.

(*See also* HISTORY, p. 11.)

ADAMS (Sir F. O.) and CUNNINGHAM
(C.).—THE SWISS CONFEDERATION. 8vo. 14s.

BAKER (Sir Samuel W.).—THE EGYPTIAN
QUESTION. 8vo, sewed. 2s.

BATH (Marquis of).—OBSERVATIONS ON
BULGARIAN AFFAIRS. Cr. 8vo. 3s. 6d.

BRIGHT (John).—SPEECHES ON QUESTIONS
OF PUBLIC POLICY. Edit. by J. E. THOROLD
ROGERS. With Portrait. 2 vols. 8vo. 25s.
—*Popular Edition.* Ext. fcp. 8vo. 3s. 6d.
—— PUBLIC ADDRESSES. Edited by J. E. T.
ROGERS. 8vo. 14s.

BRYCE (Jas., M.P.).—THE AMERICAN COM-
MONWEALTH. 3rd Edit. Ext. cr. 8vo.
2 vols. 12s. 6d. each.

BUCKLAND (Anna).—OUR NATIONAL IN-
STITUTIONS. Pott 8vo. 1s.

BURKE (Edmund).—LETTERS, TRACTS, AND
SPEECHES ON IRISH AFFAIRS. Edited by
MATTHEW ARNOLD,with Preface. Cr.8vo. 6s.
—— REFLECTIONS ON THE FRENCH REVOLU-
TION. Ed. by F. G. SELBY. Globe 8vo. 5s.
—— SPEECH ON AMERICAN TAXATION, SPEECH
ON CONCILIATION WITH AMERICA, LETTER
TO THE SHERIFFS OF BRISTOL. Edited by
F. G. SELBY. Globe 8vo. 3s. 6d.

CAIRNES (J. E.).—POLITICAL ESSAYS. 8vo.
10s. 6d.
—— THE SLAVE POWER. 8vo. 10s. 6d

CHIROL (V.).—THE FAR EASTERN QUES-
TION. 8vo. 8s. 6d. net.

COBDEN (Richard).—SPEECHES ON QUES-
TIONS OF PUBLIC POLICY. Ed. by J. BRIGHT
and J. E. THOROLD ROGERS. Gl. 8vo. 3s. 6d.

DICEY (Prof. A. V.).—LETTERS ON UNIONIST
DELUSIONS. Cr. 8vo. 2s. 6d.

DILKE (Rt. Hon. Sir Charles W.).—GREATER
BRITAIN. 9th Edit. Cr. 8vo. 6s.
—— PROBLEMS OF GREATER BRITAIN. Maps.
3rd Edit. Ext. cr. 8vo. 12s. 6d.

DONISTHORPE (Wordsworth).—INDIVID-
UALISM : A System of Politics. 8vo. 14s.
—— LAW IN A FREE STATE. Cr. 8vo. 5s. net.

DUFF (Rt. Hon. Sir M. E.Grant).—MISCELLA-
NIES, POLITICAL AND LITERARY. 8vo. 10s.6d.

ENGLISH CITIZEN, THE.—His Rights
and Responsibilities. Ed. by HENRY CRAIK,
C.B. New Edit. Cr. 8vo. 2s. 6d. each.
CENTRAL GOVERNMENT. By H. D. TRAILL.
THE ELECTORATE AND THE LEGISLATURE.
By SPENCER WALPOLE.
THE LAND LAWS. By Sir F. POLLOCK,
Bart. 2nd Edit.
THE PUNISHMENT AND PREVENTION OF
CRIME. By Col. Sir EDMUND DU CANE.
LOCAL GOVERNMENT. By M. D. CHALMERS.
COLONIES AND DEPENDENCIES : Part I. IN-
DIA. By J. S COTTON, M.A.—II. THE
COLONIES. By E. J. PAYNE.
THE STATE IN ITS RELATION TO EDUCA-
TION. By HENRY CRAIK, C.B.
THE STATE AND THE CHURCH. By Hon.
ARTHUR ELLIOTT, M.P.
THE STATE IN ITS RELATION TO TRADE.
By Sir T. H. FARRER, Bart.
THE POOR LAW. By the Rev. T. W. FOWLE.
THE STATE IN RELATION TO LABOUR. By
W. STANLEY JEVONS. 3rd. Edit. By M.
CABABÉ.
JUSTICE AND POLICE. By F. W. MAITLAND.
THE NATIONAL DEFENCES. By Major-Gen.
MAURICE, R.A. \   [*In the Press.*
FOREIGN RELATIONS. By S. WALPOLE.
THE NATIONAL BUDGET ; NATIONAL DEBT ;
TAXES AND RATES. By A. J. WILSON.

FAWCETT (Henry). — Speeches on some Current Political Questions. 8vo. 10s. 6d.
—— Free Trade and Protection. 6th Edit. Cr. 8vo. 3s. 6d.

FAWCETT (Henry and Mrs. H.).—Essays and Lectures on Political and Social Subjects. 8vo. 10s. 6d.

FISKE (John).—American Political Ideas Viewed from the Stand-point of Universal History. Cr. 8vo. 4s.
—— Civil Government in the United States considered with some Reference to its Origin. Cr. 8vo. 6s. 6d.

FREEMAN (E. A.). — Disestablishment and Disendowment. What are They? 4th Edit. Cr. 8vo. 1s.
—— The Growth of the English Constitution. 5th Edit. Cr. 8vo. 5s.

HILL (Florence D.).—Children of the State. Edited by Fanny Fowke. Crown 8vo. 3s. 6d.

HILL (Octavia).—Our Common Land, and other Essays. Ext. fcp. 8vo. 3s. 6d.

HOLLAND (Prof. T. E.).—The Treaty Relations of Russia and Turkey, from 1774 to 1853. Cr. 8vo. 2s.

JENKS (Prof. Edward).—The Government of Victoria (Australia). 8vo. 14s.

JEPHSON (H.).—The Platform: its Rise and Progress. 2 vols. 8vo. 21s.

LOWELL (J. R.). (See Collected Works.)

LUBBOCK (Sir J.). (See Collected Works.)

MACKNIGHT (J.).—Ulster as it is. 2 vols. 8vo. 21s. net.

MATHEW (E. J.)-Representative Government. Gl. 8vo. 1s. 6d.

PALGRAVE (W. Gifford). — Essays on Eastern Questions. 8vo. · 10s. 6d.

PARKIN (G. R.).—Imperial Federation. Cr. 8vo. 4s. 6d.
—— The Great Dominion, Studies in Canada. Cr. 8vo. 6s.

POLLOCK (Sir F., Bart.).—Introduction to the History of the Science of Politics. Cr. 8vo. 2s. 6d.
—— Leading Cases done into English. Crown 8vo 3s. 6d.

PRACTICAL POLITICS. 8vo. 6s.

ROGERS (Prof. J. E. T.).—Cobden and Political Opinion. 8vo. 10s. 6d.

ROUTLEDGE (Jas.).—Popular Progress in England. 8vo. 16s.

RUSSELL (Sir Charles).—New Views on Ireland. Cr. 8vo. 2s. 6d.
—— The Parnell Commission : The Opening Speech for the Defence. 8vo. 10s. 6d. —Popular Edition. Sewed. 2s.

SEELEY (Sir J. R.).—Introduction to Political Science. Gl. 8vo. 5s.

SIDGWICK (Prof. Henry).—The Elements of Politics. 8vo. 14s. net.

SMITH (Goldwin).—Canada and the Canadian Question. 8vo. 8s. net.
—— The United States, 1492—1871. Cr. 8vo. 8s. 6d.

STATESMAN'S YEAR-BOOK, THE. (See under Statistics.)

STATHAM (R.). — Blacks, Boers, and British. Cr. 8vo. 6s.

STRACHEY (J. St. L.).—The Empire. Gl. 8vo. 1s. 6d.

THORNTON (W. T.).···A Plea for Peasant Proprietors. New Edit. Cr. 8vo. 7s. 6d.
—— Indian Public Works, and Cognate Indian Topics. Cr. 8vo. 8s. 6d.

TRENCH (Capt. F.).—The Russo-Indian Question. Cr. 8vo. 7s. 6d.

WALLACE (Sir Donald M.).—Egypt and the Egyptian Question. 8vo. 14s.

PSYCHOLOGY.
(See under Philosophy, p. 33.)

SCULPTURE. *(See Art.)*

SOCIAL ECONOMY.

BARNETT (E. A.).—Training of Girls for Work. Gl. 8vo. 2s. 6d.

BOOTH (C.).—A Picture of Pauperism. Cr. 8vo. 5s.—Cheap Edit 8vo. Swd., 6d.
—— Life and Labour of the People of London. Vols. I.-IV. Cr. 8vo. 3s. 6d. each. — Vols. V. VII., and VII., 7s. 6d. net each vol. — Maps to illustrate the above. 5s.
—— The Aged Poor in England and Wales—Condition. Ext. crown 8vo. 8s. 6d. net.

BOSANQUET (B.).—Aspects of the Social Problem. By Various Writers. Ed. by B. Bosanquet. Cr. 8vo. 2s. 6d. net.

DRAGE (G.).—The Unemployed. Cr. 8vo. 3s. 6d. net.

DYER (H.).—The Evolution of Industry. 8vo. 10s. net.

FAWCETT (H. and Mrs. H.). (See Politics.)

GILMAN (N. P.). — Socialism and the American Spirit. Cr. 8vo. 6s. 6d.

GOLDIE (J.).—The Poor and their Happiness Cr. 8vo. 3s. 6d. net.

HILL (Octavia).—Homes of the London Poor. Cr. 8vo, sewed. 1s.

HUXLEY (Prof. T. H.).—Social Diseases and Worse Remedies : Letters to the "Times." Cr. 8vo. sewed. 1s. net.

JEVONS (W. Stanley).—Methods of Social Reform. 8vo. 10s. 6d.

KIDD (B.).—Social Evolution. Cr. 8vo. 5s. net.

MAYO-SMITH (R.). — Statistics and Sociology. 8vo. 12s. 6d. net.

PEARSON (C. H.).—National Life and Character: A Forecast. Cr. 8vo. 5s. net.

STANLEY (Hon. Maude). — Clubs for Working Girls. Cr. 8vo. 3s. 6d.

SOUND. *(See under Physics, p. 34.)*

SPORT.

BAKER (Sir Samuel W.).—Wild Beasts and their Ways: Reminiscences of Europe, Asia, Africa, America, from 1845—88. Illustrated. Cr. 8vo. 12s. 6d.

CHASSERESSE (D.).—Sporting Sketches. Illustrated. Cr. 8vo. 3s. 6d.

CLARK (R.).—Golf : A Royal and Ancient Game. Small 4to. 8s. 6d. net.

EDWARDS-MOSS (Sir J. E., Bart). — A
SEASON IN SUTHERLAND. Cr. 8vo. 1s. 6d.
KINGSLEY (G.).—SKETCHES IN SPORT AND
NATURAL HISTORY. Ex. cr. 8vo. [In Press.

STATISTICS.

STATESMAN'S YEAR-BOOK, THE. Sta-
tistical and Historical Annual of the States
of the World for the Year 1896. Revised after
Official Returns. Ed. by J. SCOTT KELTIE
and I. P. A. RENWICK. Cr. 8vo. 10s. 6d.

SURGERY. (See MEDICINE.)

SWIMMING.

LEAHY (Sergeant).—THE ART OF SWIMMING
IN THE ETON STYLE. Cr. 8vo. 2s.

TECHNOLOGY.

BENEDIKT (R.) and LEWKOWITSCH (J.)
—CHEMICAL ANALYSIS OF OILS, FATS,
WAXES, AND THEIR COMMERCIAL PRODUCTS
8vo. 21s. net.
BENSON (W. A. S.).—HANDICRAFT AND
DESIGN. Cr. 8vo. 5s. net.
BURDETT (C. W. B.).—BOOT AND SHOE
MANUFACTURE. Cr. 8vo. [In the Press.
DEGERDON (W. E.).—THE GRAMMAR OF
WOODWORK. 4to. 3s. ; sewed, 2s.
FOX (T. W.).—THE MECHANISM OF WEAV-
ING. Cr. 8vo. 7s. 6d. net.
LETHABY (W. R.).—LEAD WORK. Cr. 8vo.
4s. 6d. net.
LOUIS (H.).—HANDBOOK OF GOLD-MILLING.
Cr. 8vo. 10s. net.
TAGGART (W. S.).—COTTON SPINNING.
Cr. 8vo. 4s. net.
VICKERMAN (C.).—WOOLLEN SPINNING.
Cr. 8vo. 6s. net.
WALKER (Louisa).—VARIED OCCUPATIONS
IN WEAVING AND CANE AND STRAW WORK.
Globe 8vo. 3s. 6d.
—— VARIED OCCUPATIONS IN STRING WORK.
By the same. Gl. 8vo. 3s. 6d.

THEOLOGY.

*The Bible—History of the Christian Church—
The Church of England—Devotional Books
—The Fathers—Hymnology—Sermons, Lec-
tures, Addresses, and Theological Essays.*

The Bible.

History of the Bible—
THE ENGLISH BIBLE; An External and
Critical History of the various English
Translations of Scripture. By Prof. JOHN
EADIE. 2 vols. 8vo. 28s.
THE BIBLE IN THE CHURCH. By Right Rev.
Bp. WESTCOTT. 10th edit. Pott 8vo. 4s. 6d.
Biblical History—
THE MODERN READER'S BIBLE. A Series
of Books from the Sacred Scriptures pre-
sented in Modern Literary Form. Ed. by
R. G. MOULTON, M.A.
PROVERBS. A Miscellany of Sayings and
Poems embodying isolated Observations of
Life. 2s. 6d.
ECCLESIASTICUS. A Miscellany including
longer compositions, still embodying only
isolated Observations of Life. 2s. 6d.

Biblical History—
ECCLESIASTES—WISDOM OF SOLOMON. Each
is a Series of Connected Writings embody-
ing, from different standpoints, a Solution
of the whole Mystery of Life. [In Press.
THE BOOK OF JOB. A Dramatic Poem in
which are embodied Varying Solutions of
the Mystery of Life. [In the Press.
BIBLE LESSONS. By Rev. E. A. ABBOTT.
Cr. 8vo. 4s. 6d.
SIDE-LIGHTS UPON BIBLE HISTORY. By
Mrs. SYDNEY BUXTON. Cr. 8vo. 5s.
STORIES FROM THE BIBLE. By Rev. A. J.
CHURCH. Illust. Cr. 8vo. 2 parts. 3s. 6d. each.
BIBLE READINGS SELECTED FROM THE PEN-
TATEUCH AND THE BOOK OF JOSHUA.
By Rev. J. A. CROSS. Gl. 8vo. 2s. 6d.
A CLASS-BOOK OF OLD TESTAMENT HIS-
TORY. By Rev. Dr. MACLEAR. Pott 8vo.
4s. 6d.
A CLASS-BOOK OF NEW TESTAMENT HIS-
TORY. By the same. Pott 8vo. 5s. 6d.
A SHILLING BOOK OF OLD TESTAMENT
HISTORY. By the same. Pott 8vo. 1s.
A SHILLING BOOK OF NEW TESTAMENT
HISTORY. By the same. Pott 8vo. 1s.
THE CHILDREN'S TREASURY OF BIBLE
STORIES. By Mrs. H. GASKOIN. Pott 8vo.
1s. each.—Part I. Old Testament ; II.
New Testament ; III. Three Apostles.
THE NATIONS AROUND ISRAEL. By A.
KEARY. Cr. 8vo. 3s. 6d.
The Old Testament—
SCRIPTURE READINGS FOR SCHOOLS AND
FAMILIES. By C. M. YONGE. Globe 8vo.
1s. 6d. each : also with comments, 3s. 6d.
each. — GENESIS TO DEUTERONOMY. —
JOSHUA TO SOLOMON.—KINGS AND THE
PROPHETS.—THE GOSPELTIMES.—APOS-
TOLIC TIMES.
THE DIVINE LIBRARY OF THE OLD TESTA-
MENT. By Prof. KIRKPATRICK. Cr. 8vo.
3s. net.
DOCTRINE OF THE PROPHETS. By Prof.
KIRKPATRICK. Cr. 8vo. 6s.
THE PATRIARCHS AND LAWGIVERS OF THE
OLD TESTAMENT. By F. D. MAURICE.
Cr. 8vo. 3s. 6d.
THE PROPHETS AND KINGS OF THE OLD
TESTAMENT. By same. Cr. 8vo. 3s. 6d.
THE CANON OF THE OLD TESTAMENT. By
Prof. H. E. RYLE. 2nd Ed. Cr. 8vo. 6s.
PHILO AND HOLY SCRIPTURE. By Prof.
H. E. RYLE. Cr. 8vo. 10s. net.
The Pentateuch—
AN HISTORICO-CRITICAL INQUIRY INTO THE
ORIGIN AND COMPOSITION OF THE HEXA-
TEUCH (PENTATEUCH AND BOOK OF
JOSHUA). By Prof. A. KUENEN. Trans.
by P. H. WICKSTEED, M.A. 8vo. 14s.
The Psalms—
THE PSALMS CHRONOLOGICALLY ARRANGED.
By FOUR FRIENDS. Cr. 8vo. 5s. net.
GOLDEN TREASURY PSALTER. Student's
Edition of the above. Pott 8vo. 2s. 6d. net.
THE PSALMS. With Introduction and Notes.
By A. C. JENNINGS, M.A., and W. H.
LOWE, M.A. 2 vols. Cr. 8vo. 10s. 6d. each.
INTRODUCTION TO THE STUDY AND USE OF
THE PSALMS. By Rev. J. F. THRUPP.
2nd Edit. 2 vols. 8vo. 21s.
Isaiah—
ISAIAH XL.—LXVI. With the Shorter Pro-
phecies allied to it. Edited by MATTHEW
ARNOLD. Cr. 8vo. 5s.

Isaiah—
ISAIAH OF JERUSALEM. In the Authorised English Version, with Introduction and Notes. By M. ARNOLD. Cr. 8vo. 4s. 6d.
A BIBLE-READING FOR SCHOOLS. The Great Prophecy of Israel's Restoration (Isaiah xl.—lxvi.). Arranged and Edited for Young Learners. By the same. Pott 8vo. 1s.
COMMENTARY ON THE BOOK OF ISAIAH: Critical, Historical, and Prophetical; including a Revised English Translation. By T. R. BIRKS. 2nd Edit. 8vo. 12s. 6d.
THE BOOK OF ISAIAH CHRONOLOGICALLY ARRANGED. By T. K. CHEYNE. Cr. 8vo. 7s. 6d.

Zechariah—
THE HEBREW STUDENT'S COMMENTARY ON ZECHARIAH, Hebrew and LXX. By W. H. LOWE, M.A. 8vo. 10s. 6d.

The New Testament—
THE NEW TESTAMENT. Essay on the Right Estimation of MS. Evidence in the Text of the New Testament. By T. R. BIRKS. Cr. 8vo. 3s. 6d.
THE MESSAGES OF THE BOOKS. Discourses and Notes on the Books of the New Testament. By Archd. FARRAR. 8vo. 14s.
THE CLASSICAL ELEMENT IN THE NEW TESTAMENT. Considered as a Proof of its Genuineness, with an Appendix on the Oldest Authorities used in the Formation of the Canon. By C.H. HOOLE. 8vo. 10s. 6d.
ON A FRESH REVISION OF THE ENGLISH NEW TESTAMENT. With an Appendix on the last Petition of the Lord's Prayer. By Bishop LIGHTFOOT. Cr. 8vo. 7s. 6d.
THE UNITY OF THE NEW TESTAMENT. By F. D. MAURICE. 2 vols. Cr. 8vo. 12s.
THE SYNOPTIC PROBLEM FOR ENGLISH READERS. By A. J. JOLLEY. Cr. 8vo. 3s. net.
TRANSLATION OF THE FOUR GOSPELS FROM THE SYRIAC OF THE SINAITIC PALIMPSEST. By AGNES S. LEWIS. Cr. 8vo. 6s. net.
A GENERAL SURVEY OF THE HISTORY OF THE CANON OF THE NEW TESTAMENT DURING THE FIRST FOUR CENTURIES. By Bishop WESTCOTT. Cr. 8vo. 10s. 6d
GREEK-ENGLISH LEXICON TO THE NEW TESTAMENT. By W. J. HICKIE, M.A. Pott 8vo. 3s.
THE NEW TESTAMENT IN THE ORIGINAL GREEK. The Text revised by Bishop WESTCOTT, D.D., and Prof. F. J. A. HORT, D.D. 2 vols. Cr. 8vo. 10s. 6d. each.—Vol. I. Text.—Vol. II. Introduction and Appendix.
SCHOOL EDITION OF THE ABOVE. Pott 8vo. 4s. 6d.; Pott 8vo, roan, 5s. 6d.; morocco, gilt edges, 6s. 6d.—Library Edition. 8vo. 10s. net.
ESSENTIALS OF NEW TESTAMENT GREEK. By J. H. HUDDILSTON. Pott 8vo. 3s. net.

The Gospels—
THE COMMON TRADITION OF THE SYNOPTIC GOSPELS. In the Text of the Revised Version. By Rev. E. A. ABBOTT and W. G. RUSHBROOKE. Cr. 8vo. 3s. 6d.
SYNOPTICON: An Exposition of the Common Matter of the Synoptic Gospels. By W. G. RUSHBROOKE. Printed in Colours. 4to. 35s.
INTRODUCTION TO THE STUDY OF THE FOUR GOSPELS. By Bp. WESTCOTT. Cr. 8vo. 10s. 6d.
THE COMPOSITION OF THE FOUR GOSPELS. By Rev. ARTHUR WRIGHT. Cr. 8vo. 5s.

The Gospels—
SYNOPSIS OF THE GOSPELS IN GREEK. With Introduction and Index. By Rev. A. WRIGHT. 4to. [In the Press.
SYRO-LATIN TEXT OF THE GOSPELS. By F. H. CHASE. 7s. 6d. net.
THE AKHMIM FRAGMENT OF THE APOCRYPHAL GOSPEL OF ST. PETER. By H. B. SWETE. 8vo. 5s. net.

Gospel of St. Matthew—
THE GREEK TEXT, with Introduction and Notes by Rev. A. SLOMAN. Fcp. 8vo. 2s. 6d.
CHOICE NOTES ON ST. MATTHEW. Drawn from Old and New Sources. Cr. 8vo. 4s. 6d. (St. Matthew and St. Mark in 1 vol. 9s.)

Gospel of St. Mark—
SCHOOL READINGS IN THE GREEK TESTAMENT. Being the Outlines of the Life of our Lord as given by St. Mark, with additions from the Text of the other Evangelists. Edited, with Notes and Vocabulary, by Rev. A. CALVERT, M.A. Fcp. 8vo. 2s. 6d.
CHOICE NOTES ON ST. MARK. Drawn from Old and New Sources. Cr. 8vo. 4s. 6d. (St. Matthew and St. Mark in 1 vol. 9s.)

Gospel of St. Luke—
GREEK TEXT, with Introduction and Notes by Rev. J. BOND, M.A. Fcp. 8vo. 2s. 6d.
CHOICE NOTES ON ST. LUKE. Drawn from Old and New Sources. Cr. 8vo. 4s. 6d.
THE GOSPEL OF THE KINGDOM OF HEAVEN. A Course of Lectures on the Gospel of St. Luke. By F. D. MAURICE. Cr. 8vo. 3s. 6d.

Gospel of St. John—
THE GOSPEL OF ST. JOHN. By F. D. MAURICE. Cr. 8vo. 3s. 6d.
CHOICE NOTES ON ST. JOHN. Drawn from Old and New Sources. Cr. 8vo. 4s. 6d.

The Acts of the Apostles—
THE OLD SYRIAC ELEMENT IN THE TEXT OF THE CODEX BEZÆ. By F. H. CHASE. 8vo. 7s. 6d. net.
THE ACTS OF THE APOSTLES. By F. D. MAURICE. Cr. 8vo. 3s. 6d.
ENGLISH VERSION. By T. E. PAGE, M.A., and Rev. A. S. WALPOLE, M.A. Pott 8vo 2s. 6d.
GREEK TEXT, with Notes by T. E. PAGE, M.A. Fcp. 8vo. 3s. 6d.
THE CHURCH OF THE FIRST DAYS: THE CHURCH OF JERUSALEM, THE CHURCH OF THE GENTILES, THE CHURCH OF THE WORLD. Lectures on the Acts of the Apostles. By Very Rev. C. J. VAUGHAN. Cr. 8vo. 10s. 6d.

The Epistles of St. Paul—
NOTES ON EPISTLES OF ST. PAUL FROM UNPUBLISHED COMMENTARIES. By Bishop LIGHTFOOT. 8vo. 12s.
THE EPISTLE TO THE ROMANS. The Greek Text, with English Notes. By the Very Rev. C. J. VAUGHAN. 7th Edit. Cr. 8vo. 7s. 6d.
PROLEGOMENA TO THE ROMANS AND THE EPHESIANS. By F. J. A. HORT, D.D. Cr. 8vo. 6s.
THE EPISTLES TO THE CORINTHIANS. Greek Text, with Commentary. By Rev. W. KAY. 8vo. 9s.
THE EPISTLE TO THE GALATIANS. A Revised Text, with Introduction, Notes, and Dissertations. By Bishop LIGHTFOOT. 10th Edit. 8vo. 12s.

THEOLOGY.

The Bible—*continued.*

The Epistles of St. Paul:—

THE EPISTLE TO THE PHILIPPIANS. A Revised Text, with Introduction, Notes, and Dissertations. By Bishop LIGHTFOOT. 8vo. 12s.

THE EPISTLE TO THE PHILIPPIANS. With Translation, Paraphrase, and Notes for English Readers. By the Very Rev. C. J. VAUGHAN. Cr. 8vo. 5s.

THE EPISTLES TO THE COLOSSIANS AND TO PHILEMON. A Revised Text, with Introductions, etc. By Bishop LIGHTFOOT. 9th Edit. 8vo. 12s.

THE EPISTLES TO THE EPHESIANS, THE COLOSSIANS, AND PHILEMON. With Introduction and Notes. By Rev. J. Ll. DAVIES. 2nd Edit. 8vo. 7s. 6d.

THE FIRST EPISTLE TO THE THESSALONIANS. By Very Rev. C. J. VAUGHAN 8vo, sewed. 1s. 6d.

THE EPISTLES TO THE THESSALONIANS Commentary on the Greek Text. By Prof JOHN EADIE. 8vo. 12s.

The Epistle of St. James—

THE GREEK TEXT, with Introduction and Notes. By Rev. JOSEPH B. MAYOR. 8vo. 14s.

The Epistles of St. John—

THE EPISTLES OF ST. JOHN. By F. D. MAURICE. Cr. 8vo. 3s. 6d.

— The Greek Text, with Notes, by Bishop WESTCOTT. 3rd Edit. 8vo. 12s. 6d.

The Epistle to the Hebrews—

GREEK AND ENGLISH. Edited by Rev. FREDERIC RENDALL. Cr. 8vo. 6s.

ENGLISH TEXT, with Commentary. By the same. Cr. 8vo. 7s. 6d.

THE GREEK TEXT, with Notes, by Very Rev C. J. VAUGHAN. Cr. 8vo. 7s. 6d.

THE GREEK TEXT, with Notes and Essays, by Bishop WESTCOTT. 8vo. 14s.

Revelation—

LECTURES ON THE APOCALYPSE. By F. D. MAURICE. Cr. 8vo. 3s. 6d.

THE REVELATION OF ST. JOHN. By Rev. Prof. W. MILLIGAN. Cr. 8vo. 7s. 6d.

LECTURES ON THE APOCALYPSE. By the same. Crown 8vo. 5s.

DISCUSSIONS ON THE APOCALYPSE. By the same. Cr. 8vo. 5s.

LECTURES ON THE REVELATION OF ST. JOHN. By Very Rev. C. J. VAUGHAN. 5th Edit. Cr. 8vo. 10s. 6d.

THE BIBLE WORD-BOOK. By W. ALDIS WRIGHT. 2nd Edit. Cr. 8vo. 7s. 6d.

History of the Christian Church.

CHEETHAM (Archdeacon).—HISTORY OF THE CHRISTIAN CHURCH DURING THE FIRST SIX CENTURIES. Cr. 8vo. 10s. 6d.

CUNNINGHAM (Rev. John).—THE GROWTH OF THE CHURCH IN ITS ORGANISATION AND INSTITUTIONS. 8vo. 9s.

CUNNINGHAM (Rev. William). — THE CHURCHES OF ASIA : A Methodical Sketch of the Second Century. Cr. 8vo. 6s.

DALE (A. W. W.).—THE SYNOD OF ELVIRA, AND CHRISTIAN LIFE IN THE FOURTH CENTURY. Cr. 8vo. 10s. 6d.

GEE (H.) and HARDY (W. J.).—DOCUMENTS ILLUSTRATIVE OF THE HISTORY OF THE ENGLISH CHURCH. Cr. 8vo. [*In the Press.*

GWATKIN (H. M.).—SELECTIONS FROM EARLY WRITERS ILLUSTRATIVE OF CHURCH HISTORY TO THE TIME OF CONSTANTINE. Cr. 8vo. 4s. net.

HARDWICK (Archdeacon).—A H . ,RY OF THE CHRISTIAN CHURCH: MIDDLE AGES. Edited by Bp. STUBBS. Cr. 8vo. 10s. 6d.

— A HISTORY OF THE CHRISTIAN CHURCH DURING THE REFORMATION. 9th Edit., revised by Bishop STUBBS. Cr. 8vo. 10s. 6d.

HORT (Dr. F. J. A.).—TWO DISSERTATIONS. I. ON MONOΓENHΣ ΘEOΣ IN SCRIPTURE AND TRADITION. II. ON THE "CONSTANTINOPOLITAN" CREED AND OTHER EASTERN CREEDS OF THE FOURTH CENTURY. 8vo. 7s. 6d.

— JUDAISTIC CHRISTIANITY. Cr. 8vo. 6s.

SIMPSON (Rev. W.).—AN EPITOME OF THE HISTORY OF THE CHRISTIAN CHURCH. 7th Edit. Fcp. 8vo 3s. 6d.

SOHM (R.).—OUTLINES OF CHURCH HISTORY. Transl. by Miss SINCLAIR. Ed. by Prof. GWATKIN. Cr. 8vo. 3s. 6d.

VAUGHAN (Very Rev. C. J.).—THE CHURCH OF THE FIRST DAYS: THE CHURCH OF JERUSALEM, THE CHURCH OF THE GENTILES, THE CHURCH OF THE WORLD. Cr. 8vo. 10s. 6d.

The Church of England.

Catechism of—

CATECHISM AND CONFIRMATION. By Rev. J. C. P. ALDOUS. Pott 8vo. 1s. net.

A CLASS-BOOK OF THE CATECHISM OF THE CHURCH OF ENGLAND. By Rev. Canon MACLEAR. Pott 8vo. 1s. 6d.

A FIRST CLASS-BOOK OF THE CATECHISM OF THE CHURCH OF ENGLAND. By the same. Pott 8vo. 6d.

THE ORDER OF CONFIRMATION. With Prayers and Devotions. By the same. 32mo. 6d.

Collects—

COLLECTS OF THE CHURCH OF ENGLAND. With a Coloured Floral Design to each Collect. Cr. 8vo. 12s.

Disestablishment—

DISESTABLISHMENT AND DISENDOWMENT. WHAT ARE THEY? By Prof. E. A. FREEMAN. 4th Edit. Cr. 8vo. 1s.

HAND BOOK ON WELSH CHURCH DEFENCE. By the BISHOP OF ST. ASAPH Fcap. 8vo, sewed. 6d.

A DEFENCE OF THE CHURCH OF ENGLAND AGAINST DISESTABLISHMENT. By ROUNDELL, EARL OF SELBORNE. Cr. 8vo. 2s. 6d.

ANCIENT FACTS AND FICTIONS CONCERNING CHURCHES AND TITHES By the same. 2nd Edit. Cr. 8vo. 7s. 6d.

Dissent in its Relation to—

DISSENT IN ITS RELATION TO THE CHURCH OF ENGLAND. By Rev. G. H. CURTEIS. Bampton Lectures for 1871. Cr. 8vo. 7s. 6d.

Holy Communion—

THOSE HOLY MYSTERIES. By Rev. J. C. P. ALDOUS. 16mo. 1s. net.
THE COMMUNION SERVICE FROM THE BOOK OF COMMON PRAYER. With Select Readings from the Writings of the Rev. F. D. MAURICE. Edited by Bishop COLENSO. 6th Edit. 16mo. 2s. 6d.
BEFORE THE TABLE: An Inquiry, Historical and Theological, into the Meaning of the Consecration Rubric in the Communion Service of the Church of England. By Very Rev. J. S. HOWSON. 8vo. 7s. 6d.
FIRST COMMUNION. With Prayers and Devotions for the newly Confirmed. By Rev. Canon MACLEAR. 32mo. 6d.
A MANUAL OF INSTRUCTION FOR CONFIRMATION AND FIRST COMMUNION. With Prayers and Devotions. By the same. 32mo. 2s.

Liturgy—

AN INTRODUCTION TO THE CREEDS. By Rev. Canon MACLEAR. Pott 8vo. 3s. 6d.
AN INTRODUCTION TO THE ARTICLES OF THE CHURCH OF ENGLAND. By Rev. G. F. MACLEAR and Rev. W. W. WILLIAMS. Cr. 8vo. 10s. 6d.
A HISTORY OF THE BOOK OF COMMON PRAYER. By Rev F. PROCTER. 18th Edit. Cr. 8vo. 10s. 6d.
AN ELEMENTAY INTRODUCTION TO THE BOOK OF COMMON PRAYER. By Rev. F. PROCTER and Rev. Canon MACLEAR. Pott 8vo. 2s. 6d.
TWELVE DISCOURSES ON SUBJECTS CONNECTED WITH THE LITURGY AND WORSHIP OF THE CHURCH OF ENGLAND. By Very Rev. C. J. VAUGHAN. Fcp. 8vo. 6s.
A COMPANION TO THE LECTIONARY. By Rev. W. BENHAM, B.D. Cr. 8vo. 4s. 6d.
READ AND OTHERS v. THE LORD BISHOP OF LINCOLN. JUDGMENT, Nov. 21, 1890. 2nd Edit. 8vo. 2s. net.

Historical and Biographical—

THE OXFORD MOVEMENT, 1833—45. By DEAN CHURCH. Gl. 8vo. 5s.
THE LIFE AND LETTERS OF R. W. CHURCH, late Dean of St. Paul's. 8vo. 7s. 6d.
JAMES FRASER, Second Bishop of Manchester. A Memoir. 1818—1885. By THOMAS HUGHES, Q.C. 2nd Edit. Cr. 8vo. 6s.
THE LIFE OF FREDERICK DENISON MAURICE. Chiefly told in his own letters. Ed. by his Son, FREDERICK MAURICE. With Portraits. In 2 vols. 2nd Edit. 8vo. 36s. Cheap Edit. 2 vols. Cr. 8vo. 16s.
LIFE OF ARCHIBALD CAMPBELL TAIT, Archbishop of Canterbury. By the BISHOP OF WINCHESTER and W. BENHAM, B.D. With Portraits. 3rd Ed. 2 vols. Cr. 8vo. 10s. net.
WILLIAM GEORGE WARD AND THE OXFORD MOVEMENT. By W. WARD. Portrait. 8vo. 14s.
WILLIAM GEORGE WARD AND THE CATHOLIC REVIVAL. By the Same. 8vo. 14s.

CANTERBURY DIOCESAN GAZETTE. Monthly. 8vo. 2d.
JEWISH QUARTERLY REVIEW. Edited by I. ABRAHAMS and C. G. MONTEFIORE. Demy 8vo. 3s. 6d.

Devotional Books.

EASTLAKE (Lady).—FELLOWSHIP: LETTERS ADDRESSED TO MY SISTER-MOURNERS. Cr. 8vo. 2s. 6d.
IMITATIO CHRISTI. Libri IV. Printed in Borders after Holbein, Dürer, and other old Masters, containing Dances of Death, Acts of Mercy, Emblems, etc. Cr.8vo. 7s.6d.
KINGSLEY (Charles).—OUT OF THE DEEP: WORDS FOR THE SORROWFUL. From the Writings of CHARLES KINGSLEY. Ext. fcp. 8vo. 3s. 6d.
—— DAILY THOUGHTS. Selected from the Writings of CHARLES KINGSLEY. By His WIFE. Cr. 8vo. 6s.
—— FROM DEATH TO LIFE. Fragments of Teaching to a Village Congregation. Edit. by His WIFE. Fcp. 8vo. 2s. 6d.
MACLEAR (Rev. Canon).—A MANUAL OF INSTRUCTION FOR CONFIRMATION AND FIRST COMMUNION, WITH PRAYERS AND DEVOTIONS. 32mo. 2s.
—— THE HOUR OF SORROW; or, The Office for the Burial of the Dead. 32mo. 2s.
MAURICE (F. D.).—LESSONS OF HOPE. Readings from the Works of F. D. MAURICE. Selected by Rev. J. LL. DAVIES, M.A. Cr. 8vo. 5s.
RAYS OF SUNLIGHT FOR DARK DAYS. With a Preface by Very Rev. C. J. VAUGHAN, D.D. New Edition. Pott 8vo. 3s. 6d.
SERVICE (Rev. J.).—PRAYERS FOR PUBLIC WORSHIP. Cr. 8vo. 4s. 6d.
THE WORSHIP OF GOD, AND FELLOWSHIP AMONG MEN. By Prof. MAURICE and others. Fcp. 8vo. 3s. 6d.
WELBY-GREGORY (Hon. Lady).—LINKS AND CLUES. 2nd Edit. Cr. 8vo. 6s.
WESTCOTT (Rt. Rev. Bishop).—THOUGHTS ON REVELATION AND LIFE. Selections from the Writings of Bishop WESTCOTT. Edited by Rev. S. PHILLIPS. Cr. 8vo. 6s.
WILBRAHAM (Francis M.).—IN THE SERE AND YELLOW LEAF: THOUGHTS AND RECOLLECTIONS FOR OLD AND YOUNG. Globe 8vo. 3s. 6d.

The Fathers.

DONALDSON (Prof. James).—THE APOSTOLIC FATHERS. A Critical Account of their Genuine Writings, and of their Doctrines. 2nd Edit. Cr. 8vo. 7s. 6d.
Works of the Greek and Latin Fathers:
THE APOSTOLIC FATHERS. Revised Texts, with Introductions, Notes, Dissertations, and Translations. By Bishop LIGHTFOOT. —Part I. ST. CLEMENT OF ROME. 2 vols. 8vo. 32s.—Part II. ST. IGNATIUS to ST. POLYCARP. 3 vols. 2nd Edit. 8vo. 48s.
THE APOSTOLIC FATHERS. Abridged Edit. With Short Introductions, Greek Text, and English Translation. By same. 8vo. 16s.
INDEX OF NOTEWORTHY WORDS AND PHRASES FOUND IN THE CLEMENTINE WRITINGS. 8vo. 5s.
SIX LECTURES ON THE ANTE-NICENE FATHERS. By F. J. A. HORT. Cr. 8vo. 3s. 6d.
THE EPISTLE OF ST. BARNABAS. Its Date and Authorship. With Greek Text, Latin Version, Translation and Commentary. By Rev. W. CUNNINGHAM. Cr. 8vo. 7s. 6d.

THEOLOGY.

Hymnology.

BROOKE (S. A.).—CHRISTIAN HYMNS. Gl. 8vo. 2s.6d.net.--CHRISTIAN HYMNS AND SERVICE BOOK OF BEDFORD CHAPEL, BLOOMSBURY. Gl. 8vo. 3s. 6d. net.—SERVICE BOOK. Gl. 8vo. 1s. net.

PALGRAVE (Prof. F. T.). — ORIGINAL HYMNS. 3rd Edit. Pott 8vo. 1s. 6d.

SELBORNE (Roundell, Earl of).—THE BOOK OF PRAISE. Pott 8vo. 2s. 6d. net. — A HYMNAL. Chiefly from " The Book of Praise."—A. Royal 32mo, limp. 6d.—B. Pott 8vo, larger type. 1s.—C. Fine paper. 1s.6d.—With Music, Selected, Harmonised, and Composed by JOHN HULLAH. Pott 8vo. 3s. 6d.

WOODS (Miss M. A.).—HYMNS FOR SCHOOL WORSHIP. Pott 8vo. 1s. 6d.

Sermons, Lectures, Addresses, and Theological Essays.

ABBOT (F. E.).—SCIENTIFIC THEISM. Cr 8vo. 7s. 6d. — THE WAY OUT OF AGNOSTICISM ; or, The Philosophy of Free Religion. Cr. 8vo. 4s. 6d

ABBOTT (Rev. E. A.).—CAMBRIDGE SERMONS. 8vo. 6s. — OXFORD SERMONS. 8vo. 7s. 6d. — PHILOMYTHUS. A discussion of Cardinal Newman's Essay on Ecclesiastical Miracles. Cr. 8vo. 3s. 6d. — NEWMANIANISM. Cr. 8vo. 1s. net.

ABRAHAMS(I.)and MONTEFIORE(C. G.) —ASPECTS OF JUDAISM. 2nd Edit. Fcp. 8vo. 3s. 6d. net.

AINGER (Canon).—SERMONS PREACHED IN THE TEMPLE CHURCH. Ext. fcp. 8vo. 6s.

ALEXANDER (Archbishop).—THE LEADING IDEAS OF THE GOSPELS. New Edit. Cr. 8vo. 6s.

BAINES (Rev. Edward).—SERMONS. Preface and Memoir by Bishop BARRY. Cr. 8vo. 6s.

BARRY (A.).—ECCLESIASTICAL EXPANSION OF ENGLAND. Cr. 8vo. 6s.

BATHER (Archdeacon).—ON SOME MINISTERIAL DUTIES, CATECHISING, PREACHING, Etc. Edited, with a Preface, by Very Rev. C. J. VAUGHAN, D.D. Fcp. 8vo. 4s. 6d.

BERNARD(Canon).—THE CENTRAL TEACHING OF CHRIST. Cr. 8vo. 7s. 6d. — SONGS OF THE HOLY NATIVITY. Cr. 8vo. 5s.

BINNIE (Rev. W.).—SERMONS. Cr. 8vo. 6s.

BIRKS (Thomas Rawson).—THE DIFFICULTIES OF BELIEF IN CONNECTION WITH THE CREATION AND THE FALL, REDEMPTION. AND JUDGMENT. 2nd Edit. Cr. 8vo. 5s. — JUSTIFICATION AND IMPUTED RIGHTEOUSNESS. A Review. Cr. 8vo. 6s. — SUPERNATURAL REVELATION ; or, First Principles of Moral Theology. 8vo. 8s.

BRADFORD (A. H.).—HEREDITY AND CHRISTIAN PROBLEMS. Cr. 8vo. 5s. net.

BROOKE (S. A.).—SHORT SERMONS. Crown 8vo. 6s.

BROOKS (Bishop Phillips).— THE CANDLE OF THE LORD : and other Sermons. Cr. 8vo. 6s. — SERMONS PREACHED IN ENGLISH CHURCHES. Cr. 8vo. 6s. — TWENTY SERMONS. Cr. 8vo. 6s. — TOLERANCE. Cr. 8vo. 2s. 6d. — THE LIGHT OF THE WORLD. Cr.8vo. 3s.6d. — THE MYSTERY OF INIQUITY. Cr. 8vo. 6s. — ESSAYS AND ADDRESSES. Cr.8vo. 8s.6d.net.

BRUNTON (T. Lauder).—THE BIBLE AND SCIENCE. Illustrated. Cr. 8vo. 10s. 6d.

BUTLER (Archer).—SERMONS, DOCTRINAL AND PRACTICAL. 11th Edit. 8vo. 8s. — SECOND SERIES OF SERMONS. 8vo. 7s. — LETTERS ON ROMANISM. 8vo. 10s. 6d.

BUTLER (Rev. Geo.).—SERMONS PREACHED IN CHELTENHAM COLLEGE CHAPEL. 8vo. 7s. 6d.

CAMPBELL (Dr. John M'Leod).—THE NATURE OF THE ATONEMENT. Cr. 8vo. 6s. — REMINISCENCES AND REFLECTIONS. Edited by his Son, DONALD CAMPBELL, M.A. Cr. 8vo. 7s. 6d. — THOUGHTS ON REVELATION. Cr. 8vo. 5s. — RESPONSIBILITY FOR THE GIFT OF ETERNAL LIFE. Compiled from Sermons preached 1829—31. Cr. 8vo. 5s.

CANTERBURY (Edward White, Archbishop of).—BOY-LIFE : ITS TRIAL, ITS STRENGTH, ITS FULNESS. Sundays in Wellington College, 1859—73. Cr. 8vo. 6s. — THE SEVEN GIFTS. Primary Visitation Address. Cr. 8vo. 6s. — CHRIST AND HIS TIMES. Second Visitation Address. Cr. 8vo. 6s. — A PASTORAL LETTER TO THE DIOCESE OF CANTERBURY, 1890. 8vo, sewed. 1d. — FISHERS OF MEN. Third Visitation Address. Cr. 8vo. 6s.

CARPENTER(W. Boyd, Bishop of Ripon).— TRUTH IN TALE. Addresses, chiefly to Children. Cr. 8vo. 4s. 6d. — TWILIGHT DREAMS. Cr. 8vo. 4s. 6d. — THE PERMANENT ELEMENTS OF RELIGION. 2nd Edit. Cr. 8vo. 6s. — LECTURES ON PREACHING. Cr. 8vo. 3s. 6d. net. — THOUGHTS ON CHRISTIAN REUNION. Cr. 8vo. 3s. 6d. net.

CAZENOVE (J. Gibson).—CONCERNING THE BEING AND ATTRIBUTES OF GOD. 8vo. 5s.

CHURCH (Dean).—HUMAN LIFE AND ITS CONDITIONS. Cr. 8vo. 6s. — THE GIFTS OF CIVILISATION : and other Sermons and Letters. Cr. 8vo. 7s. 6d. — DISCIPLINE OF THE CHRISTIAN CHARACTER ; and other Sermons. Cr. 8vo. 4s. 6d. — ADVENT SERMONS,1885. Cr. 8vo. 4s. 6d. — VILLAGE SERMONS. Cr. 8vo. 6s. — VILLAGE SERMONS. 2nd Series. Cr.8vo. 6s. — CATHEDRAL AND UNIVERSITY SERMONS. Cr. 8vo. 6s. — PASCAL, AND OTHER SERMONS. Cr.8vo. 6s.

CLERGYMAN'S SELF-EXAMINATION CONCERNING THE APOSTLES' CREED. Ext. fcp. 8vo. 1s. 6d.

CONFESSION OF FAITH (A). Fcp. 8vo. 3s. 6d.

CONGREVE (Rev. John). — HIGH HOPES AND PLEADINGS FOR A REASONABLE FAITH, NOBLER THOUGHTS, AND LARGER CHARITY. Cr. 8vo. 5s.

SERMONS, LECTURES, ETC. 43

COOKE (Josiah P., jun.).—RELIGION AND CHEMISTRY. Cr. 8vo. 7s. 6d.
—— THE CREDENTIALS OF SCIENCE, THE WARRANT OF FAITH. 8vo. 8s. 6d. net.
CORNISH (F.).—WEEK BY WEEK. Fcap. 8vo. 3s. 6d.
COTTON (Bishop).—SERMONS PREACHED TO ENGLISH CONGREGATIONS IN INDIA. Cr. 8vo. 7s. 6d.
CUNNINGHAM (Rev. W.).—CHRISTIAN CIVILISATION, WITH SPECIAL REFERENCE TO INDIA. Cr. 8vo. 5s.
CURTEIS (Rev. G. H.).—THE SCIENTIFIC OBSTACLES TO CHRISTIAN BELIEF. The Boyle Lectures, 1884. Cr. 8vo. 6s.
DAVIES (Rev. J. Llewelyn).—THE GOSPEL AND MODERN LIFE. Ext. fcp. 8vo. 6s.
—— SOCIAL QUESTIONS FROM THE POINT OF VIEW OF CHRISTIAN THEOLOGY. Cr.8vo. 6s.
—— WARNINGS AGAINST SUPERSTITION. Ext. fcp. 8vo. 2s. 6d.
—— THE CHRISTIAN CALLING. Ext.fp.8vo. 6s.
—— ORDER AND GROWTH AS INVOLVED IN THE SPIRITUAL CONSTITUTION OF HUMAN SOCIETY. Cr. 8vo. 3s. 6d.
—— BAPTISM, CONFIRMATION, AND THE LORD'S SUPPER. Addresses. Pott 8vo. 1s.
DAVIDSON (Bp.).—CHARGE DELIVERED TO THE CLERGY OF THE DIOCESE OF ROCHESTER, 1894. 8vo, sewed. 2s. net.
DAVIES (W.).—THE PILGRIM OF THE INFINITE. Fcp. 8vo. 3s. 6d.
DIGGLE (Rev. J. W.).—GODLINESS AND MANLINESS. Cr. 8vo. 6s.
DRUMMOND (Prof. Jas.).—INTRODUCTION TO THE STUDY OF THEOLOGY. Cr. 8vo. 5s.
DU BOSE (W. P.).—THE SOTERIOLOGY OF THE NEW TESTAMENT. Cr. 8vo. 7s. 6d.
ELLERTON (Rev. John).—THE HOLIEST MANHOOD, AND ITS LESSONS FOR BUSY LIVES. Cr. 8vo. 6s.
FAITH AND CONDUCT: AN ESSAY ON VERIFIABLE RELIGION. Cr. 8vo. 7s. 6d.
FARRAR (Ven. Archdeacon).—WORKS. Uniform Edition. Cr. 8vo. 3s. 6d. each.
SEEKERS AFTER GOD.
ETERNAL HOPE. Westminster Abbey Sermons.
THE FALL OF MAN: and other Sermons.
THE WITNESS OF HISTORY TO CHRIST Hulsean Lectures, 1870.
THE SILENCE AND VOICES OF GOD. Sermons.
IN THE DAYS OF THY YOUTH. Marlborough College Sermons
SAINTLY WORKERS. Five Lenten Lectures.
EPHPHATHA; or, The Amelioration of the MERCY AND JUDGMENT. [World.
SERMONS AND ADDRESSES DELIVERED IN AMERICA.
—— THE HISTORY OF INTERPRETATION. Bampton Lectures, 1885. 8vo. 16s.
FISKE (John).—MAN'S DESTINY VIEWED IN THE LIGHT OF HIS ORIGIN. Cr. 8vo. 3s. 6d.
FORBES (Rev. Granville).—THE VOICE OF GOD IN THE PSALMS. Cr. 8vo. 6s. 6d.
FOWLE (Rev. T. W.).—A NEW ANALOGY BETWEEN REVEALED RELIGION AND THE COURSE AND CONSTITUTION OF NATURE. Cr 8vo. 6s.
FRASER (Bishop).—SERMONS. Edited by JOHN W. DIGGLE. 2 vols. Cr. 8vo. 6s. each.

GLOVER (E.).—MEMORIALS OF. By G. GLOVER. Cr. 8vo. 3s. net.
GRANE (W. L.).—THE WORD AND THE WAY. Cr. 8vo. 6s.
HARE (Julius Charles).—THE MISSION OF THE COMFORTER. New Edition. Edited by Dean PLUMPTRE. Cr. 8vo. 7s. 6d.
HAMILTON (John).—ON TRUTH AND ERROR. Cr. 8vo. 5s.
—— ARTHUR'S SEAT; or, The Church of the Banned. Cr. 8vo. 6s.
—— ABOVE AND AROUND: Thoughts on God and Man. 12mo. 2s. 6d.
HARDWICK (Archdeacon).—CHRIST AND OTHER MASTERS. 6th Edit. Cr. 8vo. 10s.6d.
HARRIS (Rev. G. C.).—SERMONS. With a Memoir by C. M. YONGE. Ext. fcp. 8vo. 6s.
HORT (F. J. A.).—THE WAY, THE TRUTH, THE LIFE. Cr. 8vo. 6s.
—— JUDAISTIC CHRISTIANITY. Cr. 8vo. 6s.
HUGHES (T.).—MANLINESS OF CHRIST. 2nd Edit. Fcp. 8vo. 3s. 6d.
HUTTON (R. H.). (See p. 26.)
HYDE (W. de W.).—OUTLINES OF SOCIAL THEOLOGY. Cr. 8vo. 6s.
ILLINGWORTH (Rev. J. R.).—SERMONS PREACHED IN A COLLEGE CHAPEL. Cr.8vo. 5s.
—— UNIVERSITY AND CATHEDRAL SERMONS. Crown 8vo. 5s.
—— PERSONALITY, HUMAN, AND DIVINE. Crown 8vo. 6s.
JACOB (Rev. J. A.).—BUILDING IN SILENCE: and other Sermons. Ext. fcp. 8vo. 6s.
JAMES (Rev. Herbert).—THE COUNTRY CLERGYMAN AND HIS WORK. Cr. 8vo. 6s.
JEANS (Rev. G. E.).—HAILEYBURY CHAPEL: and other Sermons. Fcp. 8vo. 3s. 6d.
JELLETT (Rev. Dr.).—THE ELDER SON: and other Sermons. Cr. 8vo. 6s.
—— THE EFFICACY OF PRAYER. Cr. 8vo. 5s.
KELLOGG (Rev. S. H.).—THE LIGHT OF ASIA AND THE LIGHT OF THE WORLD. Cr. 8vo. 7s. 6d.
—— GENESIS AND GROWTH OF RELIGION. Cr. 8vo. 6s.
KELLY (E.).—EVOLUTION AND EFFORT. Cr. 8vo. 4s. 6d. net.
KINGSLEY (Charles). (See COLLECTED WORKS, p. 26.)
KIRKPATRICK (Prof.).—THE DIVINE LIBRARY OF THE OLD TESTAMENT. Cr. 8vo. 3s. net.
—— DOCTRINE OF THE PROPHETS. Cr. 8vo. 6s.
KYNASTON (Rev. Herbert, D.D.).—CHELTENHAM COLLEGE SERMONS. Cr. 8vo. 6s.
LEGGE (A. O.).—THE GROWTH OF THE TEMPORAL POWER OF THE PAPACY. Cr.8vo. 8s.6d.
LIGHTFOOT (Bishop).—LEADERS IN THE NORTHERN CHURCH: Sermons. Cr. 8vo. 6s.
—— ORDINATION ADDRESSES AND COUNSELS TO CLERGY. Cr. 8vo. 6s.
—— CAMBRIDGE SERMONS. Cr. 8vo. 6s.
—— SERMONS PREACHED IN ST. PAUL'S CATHEDRAL. Cr. 8vo. 6s.
—— SERMONS ON SPECIAL OCCASIONS. 8vo. 6s.
—— A CHARGE DELIVERED TO THE CLERGY OF THE DIOCESE OF DURHAM, 1886. 8vo. 2s.

THEOLOGY.
Sermons, Lectures, Addresses, and Theological Essays—*continued*.

LIGHTFOOT (Bp.). -ESSAYS ON THE WORK ENTITLED "SUPERNATURAL RELIGION." 2nd Edit. 8vo. 10s. 6d.
—— ON A FRESH REVISION OF THE ENGLISH NEW TESTAMENT. Cr. 8vo. 7s. 6d.
—— DISSERTATIONS ON THE APOSTOLIC AGE. 8vo. 14s.
—— BIBLICAL ESSAYS. 8vo. 12s.
—— HISTORICAL ESSAYS. Gl. 8vo. 5s.

LYTTELTON(A.T.). SERMONS. Cr.8vo. 6s.

MACLAREN(Rev. A.).—SERMONS PREACHED AT MANCHESTER. 11th Ed. Fcp. 8vo. 4s. 6d.
—— SECOND SERIES 7th Ed. Fcp. 8vo 4s. 6d.
—— THIRD SERIES. 6th Ed. Fcp. 8vo. 4s.6d.
—— WEEK-DAY EVENING ADDRESSES. 4th Edit. Fcp. 8vo. 2s. 6d.
—— THE SECRET OF POWER : and other Sermons. Fcp. 8vo. 4s. 6d.

MACMILLAN (Rev. Hugh).—BIBLE TEACHINGS IN NATURE. 15th Edit. Globe 8vo. 6s.
—— THE TRUE VINE; or, The Analogies of our Lord's Allegory. 5th Edit. Gl. 8vo. 6s.
—— THE MINISTRY OF NATURE. 8th Edit. Globe 8vo. 6s.
—— THE SABBATH OF THE FIELDS. 6th Edit. Globe 8vo. 6s.
—— THE MARRIAGE IN CANA. Gl. 8vo. 6s.
—— TWO WORLDS ARE OURS. Gl. 8vo. 6s.
—— THE OLIVE LEAF. Globe 8vo. 6s.
—— THE GATE BEAUTIFUL : and other Bible Teachings for the Young. Cr. 8vo. 3s. 6d.

MAHAFFY (Prof. J. P.).—THE DECAY OF MODERN PREACHING. Cr. 8vo. 3s. 6d.

MATURIN (Rev. W.).—THE BLESSEDNESS OF THE DEAD IN CHRIST. Cr. 8vo. 7s. 6d.

MAURICE (Frederick Denison).—THE KINGDOM OF CHRIST. 3rd Ed. 2 vols. Cr. 8vo 12s.
—— DIALOGUES ON FAMILY WORSHIP. Cr. 8vo. 4s. 6d.
—— EXPOSITORY SERMONS ON THE PRAYER-BOOK, AND THE LORD'S PRAYER. Cr.8vo. 6s.
—— SERMONS PREACHED IN COUNTRY CHURCHES. 2nd Edit. Cr. 8vo. 6s.
—— THE CONSCIENCE : Lectures on Casuistry. 3rd Edit. Cr. 8vo. 4s. 6d.
—— THE DOCTRINE OF SACRIFICE DEDUCED FROM THE SCRIPTURES. 2nd Edit. Cr.8vo. 6s.
—— THE RELIGIONS OF THE WORLD. 6th Edit. Cr. 8vo. 4s. 6d.
—— ON THE SABBATH DAY; THE CHARACTER OF THE WARRIOR; AND ON THE INTERPRETATION OF HISTORY. Fcp. 8vo. 2s. 6d.
—— LEARNING AND WORKING. Cr. 8vo. 4s.6d.
—— THE LORD'S PRAYER, THE CREED, AND THE COMMANDMENTS. Pott 8vo. 1s.
—— SERMONS PREACHED IN LINCOLN'S INN CHAPEL. 6 vols. Cr. 8vo. 3s. 6d. each.
—— COLLECTED WORKS. Cr. 8vo. 3s. 6d. each.
CHRISTMAS DAY AND OTHER SERMONS.
THEOLOGICAL ESSAYS.
PROPHETS AND KINGS.
PATRIARCHS AND LAWGIVERS.
THE GOSPEL OF THE KINGDOM OF HEAVEN.
GOSPEL OF ST. JOHN.
EPISTLE OF ST. JOHN.
LECTURES ON THE APOCALYPSE.
FRIENDSHIP OF BOOKS.
SOCIAL MORALITY.
PRAYER BOOK AND LORD'S PRAYER.
THE DOCTRINE OF SACRIFICE.
THE ACTS OF THE APOSTLES.

McCURDY(J. F.)—HISTORY, PROPHECY, AND THE MONUMENTS. 2 vols. Vol. I., 14s. net

MILLIGAN (Rev. Prof. W.).—THE RESURRECTION OF OUR LORD. 4th Edit. Cr.8vo. 5s.
—— THE ASCENSION AND HEAVENLY PRIESTHOOD OF OUR LORD. Cr. 8vo. 7s. 6d.

MOORHOUSE (J., Bishop of Manchester).—JACOB : Three Sermons. Ext fcp. 8vo. 3s 6d.
—— THE TEACHING OF CHRIST : its Conditions, Secret, and Results. Cr. 8vo. 3s. net.
—— CHURCH WORK : ITS MEANS AND METHODS. Cr. 8vo. 3s. net.

MURPHY(J. J.).—NATURAL SELECTION AND SPIRITUAL FREEDOM. Gl. 8vo. 5s.

MYLNE (L. G., Bishop of Bombay).—SERMONS PREACHED IN ST. THOMAS'S CATHEDRAL, BOMBAY. Cr. 8vo. 6s.

PATTISON (Mark).—SERMONS. Cr. 8vo. 6s.

PAUL OF TARSUS. 8vo. 10s. 6d.

PHILOCHRISTUS : MEMOIRS OF A DISCIPLE OF THE LORD. 3rd. Edit. 8vo. 12s.

PLUMPTRE (Dean).—MOVEMENTS IN RELIGIOUS THOUGHT. Fcp. 8vo. 3s. 6d.

POTTER (R.).—THE RELATION OF ETHICS TO RELIGION. Cr. 8vo. 2s. 6d.

REASONABLE FAITH : A SHORT ESSAY By "Three Friends." Cr. 8vo. 1s.

REICHEL (C. P., Bishop of Meath).—THE LORD'S PRAYER. Cr. 8vo. 7s. 6d.
—— CATHEDRAL AND UNIVERSITY SERMONS. Cr. 8vo. 6s.

RENDALL (Rev. F.).—THE THEOLOGY OF THE HEBREW CHRISTIANS. Cr. 8vo. 5s.

REYNOLDS (H. R.).—NOTES OF THE CHRISTIAN LIFE. Cr. 8vo. 7s. 6d.

ROBINSON (Prebendary H. G.).—MAN IN THE IMAGE OF GOD : and other Sermons. Cr. 8vo. 7s. 6d.

RUSSELL(Dean).—THE LIGHT THAT LIGHTETH EVERY MAN : Sermons. With an Introduction by Dean PLUMPTRE, D. D. Cr.8vo. 6s.

RYLE(Rev. Prof. H.).—THE EARLY NARRATIVES OF GENESIS. Cr. 8vo. 3s. net.

SALMON (Rev. George, D.D.).—NON-MIRACULOUS CHRISTIANITY : and other Sermons. 2nd Edit. Cr. 8vo. 6s.
—— GNOSTICISM AND AGNOSTICISM : and other Sermons. Cr. 8vo. 7s. 6d.

SANDFORD (Rt. Rev. C. W., Bishop of Gibraltar).—COUNSEL TO ENGLISH CHURCHMEN ABROAD. Cr. 8vo. 6s.

SCOTCH SERMONS, 1880. By Principal CAIRD and others. 3rd Edit. 8vo. 10s. 6d.

SEELEY (J. R.).—ECCE HOMO. Gl. 8vo. 5s.
—— NATURAL RELIGION. Gl. 8vo. 5s.

SERVICE (Rev. J.).—SERMONS. Cr. 8vo. 6s.

SHIRLEY (W. N.).—ELIJAH : Four University Sermons. Fcp. 8vo. 2s. 6d.

SMITH (Rev. Travers).—MAN'S KNOWLEDGE OF MAN AND OF GOD. Cr. 8vo. 6s.

STANLEY (Dean). ··THE NATIONAL THANKSGIVING. Sermons Preached in Westminster Abbey. 2nd Edit. Cr. 8vo. 2s. 6d.
—— ADDRESSES AND SERMONS delivered In America, 1878. Cr. 8vo. 6s.

STEWART (Prof. Balfour) and TAIT (Prof. P. G.).—THE UNSEEN UNIVERSE, OR PHYSICAL SPECULATIONS ON A FUTURE STATE. 15th Edit. Cr. 8vo. 6s.
—— PARADOXICAL PHILOSOPHY: A Sequel to the above. Cr. 8vo. 7s. 6d.

STUBBS (Dean).—FOR CHRIST AND CITY. Sermons and Addresses. Cr. 8vo. 6s.
—— "CHRISTUS IMPERATOR!" A Series of Lecture-Sermons. Cr. 8vo. 6s.

TAIT (Archbp.).—THE PRESENT CONDITION OF THE CHURCH OF ENGLAND. Primary Visitation Charge. 3rd Edit. 8vo. 3s. 6d.
—— DUTIES OF THE CHURCH OF ENGLAND. Second Visitation Addresses. 8vo. 4s. 6d.
—— THE CHURCH OF THE FUTURE. Quadrennial Visitation Charges. Cr. 8vo. 3s. 6d.

TAYLOR (Isaac).—THE RESTORATION OF BELIEF. Cr. 8vo. 8s. 6d.

TEMPLE (Frederick, Bishop of London).—SERMONS PREACHED IN THE CHAPEL OF RUGBY SCHOOL. Second Series. Ex. fcp. 8vo. 6s. Third Series 4th Edit. Ext. fcp. 8vo. 6s.
—— THE RELATIONS BETWEEN RELIGION AND SCIENCE. Bampton Lectures, 1884. 7th and Cheaper Edition. Cr. 8vo. 6s.

TRENCH (Archbishop).—THE HULSEAN LECTURES FOR 1845—6. 8vo. 7s. 6d.

TULLOCH (Principal).—THE CHRIST OF THE GOSPELS AND THE CHRIST OF MODERN CRITICISM. Ext. fcp. 8vo. 4s. 6d.

VAUGHAN (C. J., Dean of Landaff).—MEMORIALS OF HARROW SUNDAYS. 8vo. 10s.6d.
—— EPIPHANY, LENT, AND EASTER. 8vo. 10s.6d.
—— HEROES OF FAITH. 2nd Edit. Cr. 8vo. 6s.
—— LIFE'S WORK AND GOD'S DISCIPLINE. Ext. fcp. 8vo. 2s. 6d.
—— THE WHOLESOME WORDS OF JESUS CHRIST. 2nd Edit. Fcp. 8vo. 3s. 6d.
—— FOES OF FAITH. 2nd Edit. Fcp.8vo. 3s.6d.
—— CHRIST SATISFYING THE INSTINCTS OF HUMANITY. 2nd Edit. Ext. fcp. 8vo. 3s.6d.
—— COUNSELS FOR YOUNG STUDENTS. Fcp. 8vo. 2s. 6d.
—— THE TWO GREAT TEMPTATIONS. 2nd Edit. Fcp. 8vo. 3s. 6d.
—— ADDRESSES FOR YOUNG CLERGYMEN. Ext. fcp. 8vo. 4s. 6d.
—— "MY SON GIVE ME THINE HEART." Ext. fcp. 8vo. 5s.
—— REST AWHILE. Addresses to Toilers in the Ministry. Ext. fcp. 8vo. 5s.
—— TEMPLE SERMONS. Cr. 8vo. 10s. 6d.
—— AUTHORISED OR REVISED? Sermons. Cr. 8vo. 7s. 6d.
—— LESSONS OF THE CROSS AND PASSION; WORDS FROM THE CROSS; THE REIGN OF SIN; THE LORD'S PRAYER. Four Courses of Lent Lectures. Cr. 8vo. 10s. 6d.
—— UNIVERSITY SERMONS, NEW AND OLD. Cr. 8vo. 10s. 6d.
—— THE PRAYERS OF JESUS CHRIST. Globe 8vo. 3s. 6d.
—— DONCASTER SERMONS; LESSONS OF LIFE AND GODLINESS; WORDS FROM THE GOSPELS. Cr. 8vo. 10s. 6d.
—— NOTES FOR LECTURES ON CONFIRMATION. 14th Edit. Fcp. 8vo. 1s. 6d.
—— RESTFUL THOUGHTS IN RESTLESS TIMES. Crown 8vo. 5s.
— LAST WORDS IN THE TEMPLE CHURCH Gl. 8vo. 5s.

VAUGHAN (Rev. D. J.).—THE PRESENT TRIAL OF FAITH. Cr. 8vo. 5s. (See p. 26.)

VAUGHAN (Rev. E. T.)—SOME REASONS OF OUR CHRISTIAN HOPE. Hulsean Lectures for 1875. Cr. 8vo. 6s. 6d.

VAUGHAN (Rev. Robert).—STONES FROM THE QUARRY. Sermons. Cr. 8vo. 5s.

VENN (Rev. John).—ON SOME CHARACTERISTICS OF BELIEF, SCIENTIFIC, AND RELIGIOUS. Hulsean Lectures, 1869. 8vo. 6s.6d.

WELLDON (Rev. J. E. C.).—THE SPIRITUAL LIFE: and other Sermons. Cr. 8vo. 6s.

WESTCOTT (Rt. Rev. B. F., Bishop of Durham).—ON THE RELIGIOUS OFFICE OF THE UNIVERSITIES. Sermons. Cr. 8vo. 4s. 6d.
—— GIFTS FOR MINISTRY. Addresses to Candidates for Ordination. Cr. 8vo. 1s. 6d.
—— THE VICTORY OF THE CROSS. Sermons Preached in 1888. Cr. 8vo. 3s. 6d.
—— FROM STRENGTH TO STRENGTH. Three Sermons (In Memoriam J. B. D.). Cr. 8vo. 2s.
—— THE REVELATION OF THE RISEN LORD. 4th Edit. Cr. 8vo. 6s.
—— THE HISTORIC FAITH. Cr. 8vo. 6s.
—— THE GOSPEL OF THE RESURRECTION. 6th Edit. Cr. 8vo. 6s.
—— THE REVELATION OF THE FATHER. Cr. 8vo. 6s.
—— CHRISTUS CONSUMMATOR. Cr. 8vo. 6s.
—— SOME THOUGHTS FROM THE ORDINAL. Cr. 8vo. 1s. 6d.
—— SOCIAL ASPECTS OF CHRISTIANITY. Cr. 8vo. 6s.
—— THE GOSPEL OF LIFE. Cr. 8vo. 6s.
—— ESSAYS IN THE HISTORY OF RELIGIOUS THOUGHT IN THE WEST. Globe 8vo. 5s.
—— INCARNATION AND COMMON LIFE. Cr. 8vo. 9s.

WHITTUCK (C. A.).—CHURCH OF ENGLAND AND RECENT RELIGIOUS THOUGHT. Cr. 8vo. 7s. 6d.

WICKHAM (Rev. E. C.).—WELLINGTON COLLEGE SERMONS. Cr. 8vo. 6s.

WILKINS (Prof. A. S.).—THE LIGHT OF THE WORLD: An Essay. 2nd Ed. Cr. 8vo. 3s. 6d.

WILLIAMSON (M. B.).—TRUTH AND THE WITNESS. Cr. 8vo. 4s. 6d.

WILLINK (A.).—THE WORLD OF THE UNSEEN. Cr. 8vo. 3s. 6d.

WILSON (J. M., Archdeacon of Manchester).—SERMONS PREACHED IN CLIFTON COLLEGE CHAPEL. 2nd Series, 1888—90. Cr. 8vo. 6s.
—— ESSAYS AND ADDRESSES. Crown 8vo. 2s. 6d. net.
—— SOME CONTRIBUTIONS TO THE RELIGIOUS THOUGHT OF OUR TIME. Cr. 8vo. 6s.

WOOD(C. J.).—SURVIVALS IN CHRISTIANITY. Crown 8vo. 6s.

WOOD (Rev. E. G.).—THE REGAL POWER OF THE CHURCH. 8vo. 4s. 6d.

THERAPEUTICS. (See MEDICINE, p. 28.)

TRANSLATIONS.

From the Greek—From the Italian—From the Latin—Into Latin and Greek Verse.

From the Greek.

SPECIMENS OF GREEK TRAGEDY. Transl. by GOLDWIN SMITH, D.C.L. 2 vols. Gl. 8vo. 10s.

TRANSLATIONS—*continued.*

AESCHYLUS.—THE SUPPLICES. With Translation, by T. G. TUCKER, Litt.D. 8vo. 10*s.*6*d.*
—— THE SEVEN AGAINST THEBES. With Translation, by A. W. VERRALL, Litt.D. 8vo. 7*s.* 6*d.*
—— THE CHOEPHORI. With Translation. By the same. 8vo. 12*s.*
—— EUMENIDES. With Verse Translation, by BERNARD DRAKE, M.A. 8vo. 5*s.*

ARATUS. (*See* PHYSIOGRAPHY, p. 34.)

ARISTOPHANES.—THE BIRDS. Trans. Into English Verse, by B. H. KENNEDY. 8vo. 6*s.*
—— SCHOLIA ARISTOPHANICA. Transl. by W. G. RUTHERFORD, LL.D. Vols. I. and II. 8vo. 50*s.* net.

ARISTOTLE ON FALLACIES; OR, THE SOPHISTICI ELENCHI. With Translation, by E. POSTE M.A. 8vo. 8*s.* 6*d.*

ARISTOTLE.—THE FIRST BOOK OF THE METAPHYSICS OF ARISTOTLE. By a Cambridge Graduate. 8vo. 5*s.*
—— THE POLITICS. By J. E. C. WELLDON, M.A. Cr. 8vo. 10*s.* 6*d.*
—— THE RHETORIC. By same. Cr.8vo. 7*s.*6*d.*
—— THE NICOMACHEAN ETHICS. By same. Cr. 8vo. 7*s.* 6*d.*
—— ON THE CONSTITUTION OF ATHENS. By E. POSTE. 2nd Edit. Cr. 8vo. 3*s.* 6*d.*
—— THE POETICS. By S. H. BUTCHER, Litt.D. 8vo. 10*s.* net.—Text and Translation. 3*s.*net.

BION. (*See* THEOCRITUS.)

EURIPIDES.—THE TRAGEDIES IN ENGLISH VERSE. By A. S. WAY, M.A. 3 vols. Cr. 8vo. 6*s.* net each.
—— ALCESTIS, HECUBA, MEDEA. Separately, ewed. 1*s.* 6*d.* each.

HERODOTUS.—THE HISTORY. By G. C. MACAULAY, M.A. 2 vols. Cr. 8vo. 18*s.*

HOMER.—THE ODYSSEY DONE INTO ENGLISH PROSE, by S. H. BUTCHER, M.A., and A. LANG, M.A. Cr. 8vo. 6*s.*
—— THE ODYSSEY. Books I.–XII. Transl. into English Verse by EARL OF CARNARVON. Cr. 8vo. 7*s.* 6*d.*
—— THE ILIAD DONE INTO ENGLISH PROSE, by ANDREW LANG, WALTER LEAF, and ERNEST MYERS. Cr. 8vo. 12*s.* 6*d.*
—— THE ILIAD DONE INTO ENGLISH VERSE. By A. S. WAY, M.A. 2 vols. 4to. 10*s.*6*d.* net.

MOSCHUS. (*See* THEOCRITUS).

PINDAR.—THE EXTANT ODES. By ERNEST MYERS. Cr. 8vo. 5*s.*

PLATO.—TIMÆUS. With Translation, by R. D. ARCHER-HIND, M.A. 8vo. 16*s.* (*See also* GOLDEN TREASURY SERIES, p. 26.)

POLYBIUS.—THE HISTORIES. By E. S. SHUCKBURGH. Cr. 8vo. 24*s.*

SOPHOCLES.—ŒDIPUS THE KING. Translated into English Verse by E. D. A. MORSHEAD, M.A. Fcp. 8vo. 3*s.* 6*d.*

THEOCRITUS, BION, AND MOSCHUS. By A. LANG, M.A. Pott 8vo. 2*s* 6*d.* net.—Large Paper Edition. 8vo. 9*s.*

XENOPHON.— THE COMPLETE WORKS. By H. G. DAKYNS, M.A. Cr. 8vo.—Vols. I. and II. 10*s.* 6*d.* each.

From the Italian.

DANTE.—THE PURGATORY. With Transl. and Notes, by A. J. BUTLER. Cr. 8vo. 12*s.*6*d.*

DANTE.—THE PARADISE. By A. J. BUTLER. 2nd Edit Cr. 8vo. 12*s.* 6*d.*
—— THE HELL. By the same. Cr. 8vo. 12*s.*6*d.*
—— DE MONARCHIA. By F. J. CHURCH 8vo. 4*s.* 6*d.*
—— THE DIVINE COMEDY. By C. E. NORTON. I. HELL. II. PURGATORY. III. PARADISE. Cr. 8vo. 6*s.* each.
—— NEW LIFE OF DANTE. Transl. by C E. NORTON. 5*s.*
—— THE PURGATORY. Transl. by C. L SHADWELL. Ext. cr. 8vo. 10*s.* net.

From the Latin.

CICERO.—THE LIFE AND LETTERS OF MARCUS TULLIUS CICERO. By the Rev. G. E. JEANS, M.A. 2nd Edit. Cr. 8vo. 10*s.* 6*d.*
—— THE ACADEMICS. By J. S. REID. 8vo. 5*s.*6*d.*
—— IN DEFENCE OF CLUENTIUS. By W. PETERSON, M.A. Cr. 8vo. 5*s.*

HORACE.—THE WORKS OF. By J. LONSDALE, M.A., and S. LEE, M.A. Gl. 8vo. 3*s.* 6*d.*
—— THE ODES IN A METRICAL PARAPHRASE. By R. M. HOVENDEN, B.A. Ext.fcp.8vo. 4*s.*6*d.*
—— LIFE AND CHARACTER: AN EPITOME OF HIS SATIRES AND EPISTLES. By R. M. HOVENDEN, B.A. Ext. fcp. 8vo. 4*s.* 6*d.*
—— WORD FOR WORD FROM HORACE: The Odes Literally Versified. By W. T. THORNTON, C.B. Cr. 8vo. 7*s.* 6*d.*

JUVENAL.—THIRTEEN SATIRES. By ALEX. LEEPER, LL.D. New Ed. Cr. 8vo. 3*s.* 6*d.*

LIVY.—BOOKS XXI.—XXV. THE SECOND PUNIC WAR. By A. J. CHURCH, M.A., and W. J. BRODRIBB, M.A. Cr. 8vo. 7*s.* 6*d.*—BOOK XXI separately, 2*s.*

MARCUS AURELIUS ANTONINUS.—BOOK IV. OF THE MEDITATIONS. With Translation and Commentary, by H. CROSSLEY, M.A. 8vo. 6*s.*

SALLUST.—THE CONSPIRACY OF CATILINE AND THE JUGURTHINE WAR. By A. W. POLLARD. Cr. 8vo. 6*s.*—CATILINE. 3*s.*

TACITUS, THE WORKS OF. By A. J. CHURCH, M.A., and W. J BRODRIBB, M.A. THE HISTORY. 4th Edit. Cr. 8vo. 6*s.* THE AGRICOLA AND GERMANIA. With the Dialogue on Oratory. Cr. 8vo. 4*s.* 6*d.* THE ANNALS. 5th Edit. Cr. 8vo. 7*s.* 6*d.*

VIRGIL: THE WORKS OF. By J. LONSDALE, M.A., and S. LEE, M.A. Globe 8vo. 3*s.* 6*d.*
—— THE ÆNEID. By J. W. MACKAIL, M.A. Cr. 8vo. 7*s.* 6*d.*

Into Latin and Greek Verse.

CHURCH (Rev. A. J.).—LATIN VERSION OF SELECTIONS FROM TENNYSON. By Prof. CONINGTON, Prof SEELEY, Dr. HESSEY, T. E. KEBBEL, &c. Edited by A. J. CHURCH, M.A. Ext. fcp. 8vo. 6*s.*

GEDDES (Prof. W. D.).—FLOSCULI GRÆCI BOREALES. Cr. 8vo. 6*s.*

KYNASTON (Herbert D.D.).—EXEMPLARIA CHELTONIENSIA. Ext. fcp. 8vo. 5*s.*

VOYAGES AND TRAVELS.

(*See also* HISTORY, p. 11; SPORT, p. 37.)

APPLETON (T. G.).—A NILE JOURNAL. Illustrated by EUGENE BENSON. Cr. 8vo. 6*s.*

"BACCHANTE." THE CRUISE OF H.M.S. "BACCHANTE," 1879—1882. Compiled from the Private Journals, Letters and Note-books of PRINCE ALBERT VICTOR and PRINCE GEORGE OF WALES. By the Rev. Canon DALTON. 2 vols. Med. 8vo. 52*s.* 6*d.*

BAKER (Sir Samuel W.).—Ismailia. A Narrative of the Expedition to Central Africa for the Suppression of the Slave Trade, organised by Ismail, Khedive of Egypt. Cr. 8vo. 6s.
—— The Nile Tributaries of Abyssinia, and the Sword Hunters of the Hamran Arabs. Cr. 8vo. 6s.
—— The Albert N'yanza Great Basin of the Nile and Exploration of the Nile Sources. Cr. 8vo. 6s.
—— Cyprus as I saw it in 1879. 8vo. 12s. 6d.
BARKER (Lady).—A Year's Housekeeping in South Africa. Illustr. Cr. 8vo. 3s. 6d.
—— Station Life in New Zealand. Cr. 8vo. 3s. 6d.
—— Letters to Guy. Cr. 8vo. 5s.
BLENNERHASSETT (R.) and SLEEMAN (L.)—Adventures in Mashonaland. Cr. 8vo. 3s. 6d.
BOUGHTON (G. H.) and ABBEY (E. A.).— Sketching Rambles in Holland. With Illustrations. Fcp. 4to. 21s.
BROOKS (Bishop P.).—Letters of Travel. Ext. cr. 8vo. 8s. 6d. net.
CAMERON (V. L.).—Our Future Highway to India. 2 vols. Cr. 8vo. 21s.
CAMPBELL (J. F.).—My Circular Notes. Cr. 8vo. 6s.
CARLES(W. R.).—Life in Corea. 8vo.12s.6d.
CAUCASUS: Notes on the. By "Wanderer." 8vo. 9s.
COLE (G. A. G.).—The Gypsy Road: A Journey from Krakow to Coblentz. Cr. 8vo. 6s.
CRAIK (Mrs.).—An Unknown Country. Illustr. by F. Noel Paton. Roy. 8vo. 7s 6d.
—— An Unsentimental Journey through Cornwall. Illustrated. 4to. 12s. 6d.
DILKE (Sir Charles). (See pp. 30, 36.)
DORR (J. C. R.).—The Flower of England's Face. Pott 8vo. 3s.
DUFF (Right Hon. Sir M. E. Grant).—Notes of an Indian Journey. 8vo. 10s. 6d
FORBES (Archibald).—Souvenirs of some Continents. Cr. 8vo. 3s. 6d.
—— Barracks, Bivouacs, and Battles. Cr. 8vo. 3s. 6d
FORBES-MITCHELL(W.)-Reminiscences of the Great Mutiny. Cr. 8vo. 3s. 6d.
FULLERTON (W. M.).—In Cairo. Fcp. 8vo. 3s. 6d.
GONE TO TEXAS: Letters from Our Boys. Ed. by Thos. Hughes. Cr.8vo. 4s.6d.
GORDON (Lady Duff). — Last Letters from Egypt, to which are added Letters from the Cape. 2nd Edit. Cr. 8vo. 9s.
GREEN (W. S.).—Among the Selkirk Glaciers. Cr. 8vo. 7s. 6d.
HOOKER (Sir Joseph D.) and BALL (J.).— Journal of a Tour in Marocco and the Great Atlas. 8vo. 21s.
HÜBNER (Baron von).—A Ramble Round the World. Cr. 8vo. 6s.
HUGHES (Thos.).—Rugby, Tennessee. Cr. 8vo. 4s. 6d.
—— Vacation Rambles. Cr. 8vo. 6s.

JACKSON (F. G.).—The Great Frozen Land. Ed. by A. Montefiore. 8vo. 15s. net.
KALM (P.).—Account of his Visit to England. Trans. J. Lucas. Illns. 8vo. 12s. net.
KINGSLEY (Charles).—At Last : A Christmas in the West Indies. Cr. 8vo. 3s. 6d.
KINGSLEY (Henry). — Tales of Old Travel. Cr. 8vo. 3s. 6d.
KIPLING (J. L.).—Beast and Man in India. Illustrated. Ext. cr. 8vo. 7s. 6d.
MAHAFFY (Prof. J. P.).—Rambles and Studies in Greece. Illust. Cr.8vo. 10s.6d.
MAHAFFY (Prof. J. P.) and ROGERS (J. E.).—Sketches from a Tour through Holland and Germany. Illustrated by J. E. Rogers. Ext. cr. 8vo. 10s. 6d.
NORDENSKIÖLD. — Voyage of the "Vega" round Asia and Europe. By Baron A. E. Von Nordenskiöld. Trans. by Alex. Leslie. 400 Illustrations, Maps, etc. 2 vols. 8vo. 45s.—Popular Edit. Cr. 8vo. 6s.
OLIPHANT (Mrs.). (See History, p. 13.)
OLIVER (Capt. S. P.).—Madagascar : An Historical and Descriptive Account of the Island. 2 vols. Med. 8vo. 52s. 6d.
PALGRAVE (W. Gifford).—A Narrative of a Year's Journey through Central and Eastern Arabia, 1862-63. Cr. 8vo. 6s.
—— Dutch Guiana. 8vo. 9s.
—— Ulysses; or, Scenes and Studies in many Lands. 8vo. 12s. 6d.
PARKMAN (F.). — The Oregon Trail. Illustrated. Med. 8vo. 21s.
PERSIA, EASTERN. An Account of the Journeys of the Persian Boundary Commission, 1870-71-72. 2 vols. 8vo. 42s.
PIKE(W.)—The Barren Ground of Northern Canada. 8vo. 10s. 6d.
ST. JOHNSTON (A.).—Camping among Cannibals. Cr. 8vo. 4s. 6d.
SANDYS (J. E.).—An Easter Vacation in Greece. Cr. 8vo. 3s. 6d.
SMITH (Goldwin)—A Trip to England. Pott 8vo. 3s.
—— Oxford and her Colleges. Pott 8vo. 3s. Illustrated Edition. 6s.
STRANGFORD (Viscountess). —Egyptian Sepulchres and Syrian Shrines. New Edition. Cr. 8vo. 7s. 6d.
TAVERNIER (Baron) : Travels in India of Jean Baptiste Tavernier. Transl. by V. Ball, LL.D. 2 vols. 8vo. 42s.
TRISTRAM (O.). (See Illustrated Books.)
TURNER (Rev. G.). (See Anthropology.)
WALLACE (A. R.). (See Natural History.)
WATERTON (Charles).—Wanderings in South America, the North-West of the United States, and the Antilles. Edited by Rev. J. G. Wood. Illustr. Cr. 8vo. 6s.—People's Edition. 4to. 6d.
WATSON (R. Spence).—A Visit to Wazan, the Sacred City of Morocco. 8vo. 10s.6d.
YOE (Shway).—The Burman. 2nd Edition. 8vo. 12s. 6d.

YOUNG, Books for the.

(*See also* BIBLICAL HISTORY, p. 38.)

ÆSOP—CALDECOTT —SOME OF ÆSOP'S FABLES, with Modern Instances, shown in Designs by RANDOLPH CALDECOTT. 4to. 5s.
—— ÆSOP'S FABLES. Selected by J. JACOBS. Illustrated by R. HEIGHWAY. Gilt or uncut. Cr. 8vo. 6s.

ARIOSTO.—PALADIN AND SARACEN. Stories from Ariosto. By H. C. HOLLWAY-CAL-THROP. Illustrated. Cr. 8vo. 6s.

ATKINSON (Rev. J. C.).—THE LAST OF THE GIANT KILLERS. Globe 8vo. 3s. 6d.
—— WALKS, TALKS, TRAVELS, AND EXPLOITS OF TWO SCHOOLBOYS. Cr. 8vo. 3s. 6d.
—— PLAYHOURS AND HALF-HOLIDAYS, OR FURTHER EXPERIENCES OF TWO SCHOOL-BOYS. Cr. 8vo. 3s. 6d.
—— SCENES IN FAIRYLAND. Cr. 8vo. 4s. 6d.

AWDRY (Frances).—THE STORY OF A FEL LOW SOLDIER. (A Life of Bishop Patteson for the Young.) Globe 8vo. 2s. 6d.

BAKER (Sir S. W.).—TRUE TALES FOR MY GRANDSONS. Illustrated. Cr. 8vo. 3s. 6d.
—— CAST UP BY THE SEA: OR, THE ADVEN-TURES OF NED GRAY. Illust. Cr. 8vo. 6s.

BARKER (Lady).—THE WHITE RAT. Gl. 8vo. 2s. 6d.

BARLOW (Jane).—THE END OF ELFINTOWN. Illust. by L. HOUSMAN. Cr. 8vo. 5s.— *Edition de Luxe.* Roy. 8vo. 21s. net.

CARROLL (Lewis).—ALICE'S ADVENTURES IN WONDERLAND. With 42 Illustrations by TENNIEL. Cr. 8vo. 6s. net. *People's Edition.* With all the original Illustrations. Cr. 8vo. 2s. 6d. net.
A GERMAN TRANSLATION OF THE SAME. Cr. 8vo. 6s. net. —A FRENCH TRANSLA-TION OF THE SAME. Cr. 8vo. 6s. net. AN ITALIAN TRANSLATION OF THE SAME. Cr. 8vo. 6s. net.
—— ALICE'S ADVENTURES UNDER-GROUND. Being a Fascimile of the Original MS. Book, afterwards developed in to " Alice's Adven-tures in Wonderland." With 27 Illustra-tions by the Author. Cr. 8vo. 4s net.
—— THROUGH THE LOOKING-GLASS AND WHAT ALICE FOUND THERE. With 50 Illus-trations by TENNIEL. Cr. 8vo. 6s. net. *People's Edition.* With all the original Illustrations. Cr. 8vo. 2s. 6d. net. People's Edition of " Alice's Adventures in Wonderland," and "Through the Looking-Glass." 1 vol. Cr 8vo. 4s. 6d. net.
—— RHYME? AND REASON With 65 Illus-trations by ARTHUR B. FROST, and 9 by HENRY HOLIDAY. Cr. 8vo. 6s. net.
—— A TANGLED TALE. With 6 Illustrations by ARTHUR B. FROST. Cr. 8vo. 4s. 6d. net.
—— SYLVIE AND BRUNO. With 46 Illustra-tions by HARRY FURNISS. Cr. 8vo. 7s. 6d. net.
—— —— CONCLUDED. With Illustrations by HARRY FURNISS. Cr. 8vo. 7s. 6d. net.
—— THE NURSERY " ALICE." Twenty Coloured Enlargements from TENNIEL'S Illustrations to "Alice's Adventures in Wonderland," with Text adapted to Nursery Readers. 4to. 4s. net.
—— THE HUNTING OF THE SNARK, AN AGONY IN EIGHT FITS. With 9 Illustrations by HENRY HOLIDAY. Cr. 8vo. · 4s. 6d. net.

CLIFFORD (Mrs. W. K.).—ANYHOW STORIES. With Illustrations by DOROTHY TENNANT. Cr. 8vo. 1s. 6d. ; paper covers, 1s.

CORBETT (Julian).—FOR GOD AND GOLD. Cr. 8vo. 6s.

CRAIK (Mrs.).—ALICE LEARMONT : A FAIRY TALE. Illustrated. Globe 8vo. 2s. 6d.
—— THE ADVENTURES OF A BROWNIE. Illus-trated by Mrs. ALLINGHAM. Gl. 8vo. 2s. 6d.
—— THE LITTLE LAME PRINCE AND HIS TRAVELLING CLOAK. Illustrated by J. McL. RALSTON. Globe 8vo 2s. 6d.
—— OUR YEAR : A CHILD'S BOOK IN PROSE AND VERSE. Illustrated. Gl. 8vo. 2s. 6d.
—— LITTLE SUNSHINE'S HOLIDAY. Globe 8vo. 2s. 6d.
—— THE FAIRY BOOK : THE BEST POPULAR FAIRY STORIES. Pott 8vo. 2s. 6d. net.
—— CHILDREN S POETRY. Ex. fcp. 8vo. 4s. 6d.
—— SONGS OF OUR YOUTH. Small 4to. 6s.

DE MORGAN (Mary).—THE NECKLACE OF PRINCESS FIORIMONDE, AND OTHER STORIES. Illustrated by WALTER CRANE. Ext. fcp. 8vo. 3s. 6d.—Large Paper Ed., with Illus-trations on India Paper. 100 copies printed.

FOWLER (W. W.). (*See* NATURAL HISTORY.)

FRASER (Mrs.).—THE BROWN AMBASSADOR. Cr. 8vo. 3s. 6d.

GRIMM'S FAIRY TALES. Translated by LUCY CRANE, and Illustrated by WALTER CRANE. Cr. 8vo. 6s.

GREENWOOD (Jessy E.). — THE MOON MAIDEN: AND OTHER STORIES. Cr. 8vo. 3s. 6d.

JERSEY (Countess of).—MAURICE : OR, THE RED JAR. Illustrated by ROSIE M. M. PITMAN. Gl. 8vo. 2s. 6d.
—— ERIC, PRINCE OF LORLONIA. Illustrated by A. R. WOODWARD. Cr. 8vo. 6s.

KEARY (A. and E.). — THE HEROES OF ASGARD. Tales from Scandinavian My-thology. Globe 8vo. 2s. 6d

KEARY (E.).—THE MAGIC VALLEY. Illustr. by " E.V.B." Globe 8vo. 2s. 6d.

KINGSLEY (Charles).—THE HEROES ; or, Greek Fairy Tales for my Children. Cr. 8vo. 3s. 6d.—*Presentation Ed.*, gilt edges. 7s. 6d.
—— MADAM HOW AND LADY WHY ; or, First Lessons in Earth-Lore. Cr. 8vo. 3s. 6d.
—— THE WATER-BABIES : A Fairy Tale for a Land Baby. Cr. 8vo. 3s. 6d.—New Edit. Illus. by L. SAMBOURNE. Fcp. 4to. 12s. 6d.

KIPLING (Rudyard).—THE JUNGLE BOOK. Illustrated. Cr. 8vo. 6s.
—— THE SECOND JUNGLE BOOK. Illustrated. Cr. 8vo. 6s.

MACLAREN (Arch.).—THE FAIRY FAMILY. A Series of Ballads and Metrical Tales. Cr. 8vo. 5s.

MACMILLAN (Rev. Hugh). (*See* p. 44.)

MADAME TABBY'S ESTABLISHMENT. By KARI. Illust. by L. WAIN. Cr. 8vo. 4s. 6d.

MAGUIRE (J. F.).—YOUNG PRINCE MARI-GOLD. Illustrated. Globe 8vo. 4s. 6d.

MARTIN (Frances).—THE POET'S HOUR. Poetry selected for Children. Pott 8vo. 2s. 6d.
—— SPRING-TIME WITH THE POETS. Pott 8vo. 3s. 6d.

MAZINI (Linda).—IN THE GOLDEN SHELL.
With Illustrations. Globe 8vo. 4s. 6d.
MOLESWORTH (Mrs.).—WORKS. Illustr.
Globe 8vo. 2s. 6d. each.
"CARROTS," JUST A LITTLE BOY.
A CHRISTMAS CHILD.
CHRISTMAS-TREE LAND.
THE CUCKOO CLOCK.
FOUR WINDS FARM.
GRANDMOTHER DEAR.
HERR BABY.
LITTLE MISS PEGGY.
THE RECTORY CHILDREN.
ROSY.
THE TAPESTRY ROOM.
TELL ME A STORY.
TWO LITTLE WAIFS.
"US": An Old-Fashioned Story.
CHILDREN OF THE CASTLE.
A CHRISTMAS POSY.
NURSE HEATHERDALE'S STORY.
THE GIRLS AND I.
MY NEW HOME.
MARY.
—— FOUR GHOST STORIES. Cr. 8vo. 6s.
—— SHEILA'S MYSTERY. Illustrated. Cr.
8vo. 3s. 6d.
—— THE CARVED LIONS. Illust. Cr. 8vo. 3s.6d.
OLIPHANT (Mrs.). — AGNES HOPETOUN'S
SCHOOLS AND HOLIDAYS. Illust. Gl.8vo. 2s.6d.
PALGRAVE (Francis Turner).—THE FIVE
DAYS' ENTERTAINMENTS AT WENTWORTH
GRANGE. Small 4to. 6s.
—— THE CHILDREN'S TREASURY OF LYRICAL
POETRY. Pott 8vo. 2s. 6d.—Or in 2 parts,
1s. each.
PATMORE (C.).—THE CHILDREN'S GAR-
LAND FROM THE BEST POETS. Pott 8vo.
2s. 6d. net.
ROSSETTI (Christina). —SPEAKING LIKE-
NESSES. Illust. by A. HUGHES. Cr.8vo. 4s.6d.
—— SING-SONG: A Nursery Rhyme-Book.
Small 4to. 4s. 6d.
RUTH AND HER FRIENDS: A STORY
FOR GIRLS. Illustrated. Globe 8vo. 2s. 6d.
ST. JOHNSTON (A.). — CAMPING AMONG
CANNIBALS. Cr. 8vo. 4s. 6d.
—— CHARLIE ASGARDE: THE STORY OF A
FRIENDSHIP. Illustrated by HUGH THOM-
SON. Cr. 8vo. 5s.
"ST. OLAVE'S" (Author of). Illustrated.
Globe 8vo.
WHEN I WAS A LITTLE GIRL. 2s. 6d.
NINE YEARS OLD. 2s. 6d.
WHEN PAPA COMES HOME. 4s. 6d.
FANSIE'S FLOUR BIN. 2s. 6d.
STEEL (F. A.).—TALES OF THE PUNJAB.
(See under ILLUSTRATED BOOKS, p. 15.)
STEWART (Aubrey).—THE TALE OF TROY.
Done into English. Globe 8vo. 3s. 6d.
SWIFT.—GULLIVER'S TRAVELS. (See under
ILLUSTRATED BOOKS, p. 15.)
TENNYSON (Lord H.).—JACK AND THE
BEAN-STALK. English Hexameters. Illust.
by R. CALDECOTT. Fcp. 4to. 3s. 6d.
"WANDERING WILLIE" (Author of).—
CONRAD THE SQUIRREL. Globe 8vo. 2s. 6d.
WARD (Mrs. T. Humphry).—MILLY AND
OLLY. With Illustrations by Mrs. ALMA
TADEMA. Globe 8vo. 2s. 6d.

WEBSTER (Augusta).—DAFFODIL AND THE
CROÄXAXICANS. Cr. 8vo. 6s.
WILLOUGHBY (F.).—FAIRY GUARDIANS.
Illustr. by TOWNLEY GREEN. Cr. 8vo. 5s.
WOODS (M. A.). (See COLLECTIONS, p. 21.)
YONGE (Charlotte M.).—THE PRINCE AND
THE PAGE. Cr. 8vo. 2s. 6d.
—— A BOOK OF GOLDEN DEEDS. Pott 8vo.
2s. 6d. net. Globe 8vo. 2s.—Abridged Edi-
tion. 1s.
—— LANCES OF LYNWOOD. Cr. 8vo. 3s. 6d.
—Abridged Edition. 1s. 6d.
—— P's AND Q's; and LITTLE LUCY'S WON-
DERFUL GLOBE. Illustrated. Cr. 8vo. 3s. 6d.
—— A STOREHOUSE OF STORIES. 2 vols.
Globe 8vo. 2s. 6d. each.
—— THE POPULATION OF AN OLD PEAR-
TREE; or, Stories of Insect Life. From E.
VAN BRUYSSEL. Illustr. Gl. 8vo. 2s. 6d.

ZOOLOGY.

Comparative Anatomy—Practical Zoology—
Entomology—Ornithology.

(See also BIOLOGY; NATURAL HISTORY;
PHYSIOLOGY.)

Comparative Anatomy.

FLOWER (Sir W. H.).—AN INTRODUCTION
TO THE OSTEOLOGY OF THE MAMMALIA.
Illustrated. 3rd Edit., revised with the assist-
ance of HANS GADOW, Ph.D. Cr. 8vo. 10s.6d.
HUMPHRY (Prof. Sir G. M.).—OBSERVA-
TIONS IN MYOLOGY. 8vo. 6s.
LANG (Prof. Arnold).—TEXT-BOOK OF COM-
PARATIVE ANATOMY. Transl. by H. M. and
M. BERNARD. Preface by Prof. E. HAEC-
KEL. Illustr. 2 vols. 8vo. Part I. 17s. net.
[Part II. in the Press.
PARKER (T. Jeffery).—A COURSE OF IN-
STRUCTION IN ZOOTOMY (VERTEBRATA).
Illustrated. Cr. 8vo. 8s. 6d.
PETTIGREW (J. Bell).—THE PHYSIOLOGY
OF THE CIRCULATION IN PLANTS, IN THE
LOWER ANIMALS, AND IN MAN. 8vo. 12s.
SHUFELDT (R. W.).—THE MYOLOGY OF
THE RAVEN (Corvus corax Sinuatus). A
Guide to the Study of the Muscular System
in Birds. Illustrated. 8vo. 13s. net.
WIEDERSHEIM (Prof. R.).—ELEMENTS OF
THE COMPARATIVE ANATOMY OF VERTE-
BRATES. Adapted by W. NEWTON PARKER.
With Additions. Illustrated. 8vo. 12s. 6d.

Practical Zoology.

CALDERWOOD (W. L.)—MUSSEL CULTURE
AND THE BAIT SUPPLY. Cr. 8vo. 2s. 6d.
DEAN (B.).—FISHES, LIVING AND FOSSIL.
8vo. 10s. 6d. net.
HOWES (Prof. G. B.).—AN ATLAS OF PRAC-
TICAL ELEMENTARY BIOLOGY. With a Pre-
face by Prof. HUXLEY. 4to. 14s.
HUXLEY (T. H.) and MARTIN (H. N.).—
A COURSE OF ELEMENTARY INSTRUCTION
IN PRACTICAL BIOLOGY. Revised and ex-
tended by Prof. G. B. HOWES and D. H.
SCOTT, Ph.D. Cr. 8vo. 10s. 6d.

ZOOLOGY.

50
THOMSON (Sir C. Wyville).—THE VOYAGE
OF THE "CHALLENGER": THE ATLANTIC.
With Illustrations, Coloured Maps, Charts,
etc 2 vols. 8vo. 45s.
—— THE DEPTHS OF THE SEA. An Account
of the Results of the Dredging Cruises of
H.M.SS. "Lightning" and "Porcupine,"
1868-69-70. With Illustrations, Maps, and
Plans. 8vo. 31s. 6d.

WILSON (E. B.). and LEAMING (E.).—
ATLAS OF THE KARYOKINESIS OF THE OVUM.
4to. 17s. net.

Entomology.

BADENOCH (L. N.).—ROMANCE OF THE
INSECT WORLD. Cr. 8vo. 6s.

BUCKTON (G. B.).—MONOGRAPH OF THE
BRITISH CICADÆ, OR TETTIGIDÆ. 2 vols.
42s.net ; or in 8 Parts. 8s. each net.
—— NATURAL HISTORY OF ERISTALIS TENAX.
8vo. 8s. net.

LUBBOCK (Sir John).—THE ORIGIN AND
METAMORPHOSES OF INSECTS Illustrated.
Cr. 8vo. 3s. 6d.

MEYRICK (E.). — HANDBOOK OF BRITISH
LEPIDOPTERA. Ex. cr. 8vo. 10s. 6d. net.

MIALL (L. C.). — NATURAL HISTORY OF
AQUATIC INSECTS. Cr. 8vo. 6s.

SCUDDER (S. H.).—FOSSIL INSECTS OF
NORTH AMERICA. Map and Plates. 2
vols. 4to. 90s. net.

Ornithology.

COUES (Elliott).—KEY TO NORTH AMERICAN
BIRDS. Illustrated. 8vo. 2l. 2s.
—— HANDBOOK OF FIELD AND GENERAL OR-
NITHOLOGY. Illustrated. 8vo. 10s. net.

FOWLER(W. W.). (See NATURAL HISTORY.)

HEADLEY (F. W.).—STRUCTURE AND LIFE
OF BIRDS. Cr. 8vo. 7s. 6d.

WHITE (Gilbert). (See NATURAL HISTORY.)

WRIGHT (M. O.). (See NATURAL HISTORY.)

INDEX.

	PAGE
ABRAHAMS (I.)	42
ABBEY (E. A.)	15, 47
ABBOT (F. E.)	42
ABBOTT (E. A.)	6, 17, 38, 39, 42
ACTON (Lord)	11
ADAMS (Sir F. O.)	36
ADDISON	4, 24, 25
ÆSOP	14, 48
AGASSIZ (L.)	4
AINGER (Rev. A.)	5, 20, 27, 42
AINSLIE (A. D.)	18
AIRY (Sir G. B.)	3, 34
AITKEN (Mary C.)	25
AITKEN (Sir W.)	30
ALBEMARLE (Earl of)	4
ALDOUS (J. C. P.)	40, 41
ALDRICH (T. B.)	17
ALEXANDER (C. F.)	25
ALEXANDER (T.)	10
ALEXANDER (Bishop)	42
ALLBUTT (T. C.)	28
ALLEN (G.)	7
ALLINGHAM (W.)	25
AMIEL (H. F.)	4
ANDERSON (A.)	17
ANDERSON (L.)	2
ANDERSON (Dr. McCall)	28
ANDREWS (C. M.)	11
ANDREWS (Dr. Thomas)	33
APPLETON (T. G.)	46
ARCHER-HIND (R. D.)	46
ARNOLD (M.)	9, 17, 24, 25, 38, 39
ARNOLD (Dr. T.)	11
ARNOLD (W. T.)	11
ASHLEY (W. J.)	4, 35
ATKINSON (G. F.)	7
ATKINSON (J. B.)	2
ATKINSON (Rev. J. C.)	2, 48
ATTWELL (H.)	25
AUSTEN (Jane)	21
AUSTIN (Alfred)	10, 17, 24
AUTENRIETH (Georg)	9
AWDRY (F.)	48
BACON (Francis)	4, 24, 25
BADENOCH (L. N.)	30, 50
BAILEY (L. H.)	10
BAINES (Rev. E.)	42
BAKER (Sir S. W.)	4, 36, 37, 47, 48
BALCH (Elizabeth)	14
BALDWIN (Prof. J. M.)	33
BALFOUR (F. M.)	7
BALFOUR (J. B.)	7
BALL (J.)	47
BALL (W. Platt)	7
BALL (W. W. R.)	15, 28
BALLANCE (C. A.)	28
BARKER (G. F.)	33
BARKER (Lady)	2, 9, 47, 48
BARLOW (J.)	14, 48
BARNARD (C.)	34
BARNES (R. H.)	5
BARNES (W.)	4
BARNETT (E. A.)	9, 37
BARRY (A.)	42
BARTHOLOMEW (J. G.)	3
BARTLETT (J.)	9, 17
BARWELL (R.)	28

	PAGE
BASTABLE (Prof. C. F.)	35
BATEMAN (J.)	4
BATES (K. L.)	24
BATESON (W.)	7
BATH (Marquis of)	36
BATHER (Archdeacon)	42
BAXTER (L.)	4
BEESLY (Mrs.)	5, 11
BEHRENS (H.)	8
BENEDIKT (R.)	38
BENHAM (Rev. W.)	6, 25, 41
BENSON (Archbishop)	42
BENSON (W. A. S.)	2, 38
BENTLEY	4
BERG (L.)	10
BERLIOZ (H.)	4
BERNARD (C. E.)	4
BERNARD (J. H.)	32
BERNARD (H. M.)	7, 35
BERNARD (M.)	15
BERNARD (T. D.)	42
BERNERS (J.)	14
BESANT (Sir W.)	4
BETTANY (G. T.)	7
BICKERTON (T. H.)	28
BIGELOW (M. M.)	15
BIKÉLAS (D.)	21
BINNIE (Rev. W.)	42
BIRKS (T. R.)	7, 32, 39, 42
BJÖRNSON (B).	21
BLACK (W.)	5
BLACKBURNE (E.)	4
BLACKIE (J. S.)	11, 17, 24
BLAKE (J. F.)	3
BLAKE (W.)	4
BLAKISTON (J. R.)	9
BLANFORD (H. F.)	10, 24
BLANFORD (W. T.)	11, 30
BLENNERHASSETT (R.)	47
BLOMFIELD (R.)	10
BLYTH (A. W.)	14
BÖHM-BAWERK (Prof.)	35
BOLDREWOOD (Rolf)	4
BONAR (J.)	3, 5, 35
BOND (Rev. J.)	39
BOOLE (G.)	32
BOOTH (C.)	37
BORGEAUD (C.)	15
BORROW (G.)	4
BOSANQUET (B.)	32, 37
BOSE (W. P. du)	43
BOUGHTON (G. H.)	47
BOUTMY (E.)	15
BOWEN (H. C.)	31
BOWER (F. O.)	7
BRADFORD (A. H.)	42
BRADFORD (G.)	24
BRADLEY (A. G.)	4
BRETT (R. B)	11
BRIDGES (J. A.)	24
BRIGHT (H. A.)	10
BRIGHT (John)	36
BRIMLEY (G.)	24
BRODIE (Sir B.)	8
BRODRIBB (W. J.)	16, 46
BROOKE (Sir J.)	4
BROOKE (S. A.)	16, 17, 26, 42

	PAGE
BROOKS (Bishop)	42, 47
BROWN (Prof. C.)	33
BROWN (J. A.)	1
BROWN (Dr. James)	4
BROWN (T. E.)	17
BROWNE (J. H. B.)	14
BROWNE (Sir T.)	25
BRUCE (P. A.)	12, 35
BRUNTON (Dr. T. L.)	28, 29, 42
BRYCE (James)	11, 36
BUCHHEIM (C. A.)	25
BUCKLAND (A.)	6, 36
BUCKLEY (A. B.)	12
BUCKNILL (Dr. J. C)	29
BUCKTON (G. B.)	50
BUNYAN	4, 24, 25
BURDETT (C. W. B.)	38
BURGON (J. W.)	17
BURKE (E.)	36
BURN (R.)	2
BURNETT (F. Hodgson)	21
BURNS	17, 25
BURY (J. B.)	12
BUTCHER (Prof. S. H.)	16, 24, 46
BUTLER (A. J.)	17, 46
BUTLER (Rev. G.)	42
BUTLER (Samuel)	17
BUTLER (Archer)	42
BUTLER (Sir W. F.)	4
BUXTON (Mrs. S.)	38
BYRON	25
CAIRNES (J. E.)	35, 36
CAJORI (F.)	28
CALDECOTT (R.)	15, 48
CALDERON	17
CALDERWOOD (H.)	7, 9, 32, 33
CALDERWOOD (W. L.)	49
CALVERT (Rev. A.)	39
CAMERON (V. L.)	47
CAMPBELL (D. H)	7
CAMPBELL (Sir G.)	4
CAMPBELL (J. D.)	4, 18
CAMPBELL (J. F.)	47
CAMPBELL (Dr. J. M.)	42
CAMPBELL (Prof. Lewis)	5, 16
CANTILLON	35
CAPES (W. W.)	16
CARLES (W. R.)	47
CARLYLE (T.)	4
CARMARTHEN (Lady)	21
CARNARVON (Earl of)	46
CARNOT (N. L. G.)	34
CARPENTER (Bishop)	42
CARR (J. C.)	2, 17
CARROLL (Lewis)	32, 48
CARTER (R. Brudenell)	29
CASSEL (Dr. D.)	12
CATTEL (J. McK.)	33
CAUTLEY (G. S.)	17
CAZENOVE (J. G.)	42
CHALMERS (J. A.)	11
CHALMERS (J. B.)	10
CHALMERS (M. D.)	36
CHAPMAN (Elizabeth R.)	17
CHAPPELL (W.)	30
CHASE (Rev. F. H.)	39

	PAGE
CHASSERESSE (Diana)	. 37
CHAUCER . . .	16, 17
CHEETHAM (Archdeacon).	40
CHERRY (R. R.) . .	15
CHEYNE (C. H. H.) .	3
CHEYNE (T. K.) .	39
CHIROL (V.) . .	36
CHRISTIE (W. D.) .	25
CHURCH (Rev. A. J.).4,16,38,46	
CHURCH (F. J.).	26, 46
CHURCH (R. W.).	
4, 5, 6, 12, 17, 24, 41, 42	
CLARE (G.) . .	. 35
CLARK (J. W.) . .	25
CLARK (L.) . .	3
CLARK (R.) . .	37
CLARK (S.) . .	4
CLARK (T. M.). .	10
CLARKE (C. B.). .	10, 35
CLEVELAND (Duchess)	5
CLIFFORD (Ed.) .	4
CLIFFORD (W. K.) .	24, 33
CLIFFORD (Mrs. W. K.) .	48
CLOUGH (A. H.) .18, 24, 25	
COBDEN (R.) . .	36
COHEN (J. B.) .	8
COLE (G. A. G.) .	47
COLENSO (J. W.) .	41
COLERIDGE (C. R.) .	24
COLERIDGE (S. T.) .	4, 18
COLLIER (Hon. John)	2
COLLINS (C) .	10
COLLINS (J. Churton)	24
COLQUHOUN (F. S.) .	18
COLVIN (Sidney) .	5, 26
COMBE (G.) .	4, 10
COMMONS (J. R.) .	35
CONGREVE (Rev. J.) .	42
CONWAY (Hugh) .	21
COOK (E. T.) .	2
COOKE (A. H.) . .	30
COOKE (C. Kinloch) .	30
COOKE (J. P.) .	8, 43
COOPER (E. H.) .	21
CORBETT (J.) . . 4, 21, 48	
CORFIELD (W. H.) .	14
CORNISH (F.) .	43
CORSON (H) . .	24
COSSA (L.) . .	35
COTES (E.). .	21
COTTERILL (J. H.) .	10
COTTON (Bishop) .	43
COTTON (C.) . .	15
COTTON (J. S.) . .	36
COUES (E.) . .	50
COURTHOPE (W. J.) .	4, 16
COWELL (G.) . .	29
COWPER . . .18, 24, 25	
COX (G. V.) .	12
CRAIK (Mrs.) 18,21,24,25,47,48	
CRAIK (H.) . 6, 10, 24, 36	
CRANE (Lucy) . .	47
CRANE (Walter) .	47
CRAVEN (Mrs. D.) .	9
CRAWFORD (F. M.) .14, 21, 24	
CREIGHTON (Bishop M.) 5, 12	
CRICHTON-BROWNE(Sir J.)	10
CROSS (J. A.) . .	38
CROSSKEY (R.) . .	14
CROSSLEY (J.) . .	3
CROSSLEY (H.) . .	46
CUMMING (L.) . .	33
CUNLIFFE (J. W.) .	24
CUNNINGHAM (C.) .	36

	PAGE
CUNNINGHAM (Sir H. S.).	21
CUNNINGHAM (Rev. J.) .	40
CUNNINGHAM(Rev. W)40,41,43	
CUNVNGHAME (Sir A. T.).	30
CURTEIS (Rev. G. H.)	40, 43
CURTIN (J.) . .	21
D'ARCY (C. F.). .	32
DABBS (G. H. R.) .	18
DAHLSTROM (K. P.).	10
DAHN (F.) . .	21
DAKYNS (H. G.) .	46
DALE (A. W. W.) .	40
DALTON (Rev. J. N.)	46
DANIELL (Alfred). .	33
DANTE . . 4, 17, 46	
DASENT (A. I.). .	12
DAVIDSON (Bishop) .	43
DAVIES (Rev. J. Ll.)	40, 43
DAVIES (W.) . 6, 43	
DAVIS (R. H.). .	21
DAWKINS (W. B.) .	1
DAWSON (G. M.) .	11
DAWSON (Sir J. W.) .	11
DAWSON (W. J.) .	18
DAY (L. B.) . .	21
DAY (R. E.) . .	33
DEAN (A.). .	10
DEAN (B.). .	49
DEFOE (D.) . . 5, 25	
DEGERDON (W. E.) .	38
DEIGHTON (K.). 5, 19, 24, 27	
DELAMOTTE (P. H.).	3
DELBOS (L.) . .	31
DELL (E. C.) . .	14
DE MORGAN (M.) .	48
DEUSSEN (P.) . .	32
DE QUATREFAGES (A.) .	1
DE VARIGNY (H.) .	7
DE VERE (A.) . . 18, 24	
D'ISRAELI (B.). .	22
DICEY (A. V.) . . 15, 36	
DICKENS (C.) . .	21, 24
DICKENS (M. A.) .	22, 24
DIGGLE (Rev. J. W.).	43
DILKE (Ashton W.) .	24
DILKE (Sir Charles W.) 30, 36	
DILLWYN (E. A.) .	22
DOBBIN (L.) . .	8
DOBSON (A.) . . 5, 14	
DONALDSON (J.) .	41
DONISTHORPE (W.) .	36
DORR (J. C. R.) .	47
DOWDEN (E.) . 5, 17, 19, 26	
DOYLE (Sir F. H.) .	18
DOYLE (J. A.) .	12
DRAGE (G.) . .	37
DRAKE (B.) . .	46
DRUMMOND (Prof. J.)	43
DRYDEN . . 24, 25	
DU CANE (E. F.) .	36
DUFF (Sir M. E. G.) 6,24,36,47	
DUNSMUIR (A.). .	22
DÜNTZER (H.) . . 5, 6	
DURAND (Sir M.) .	22
DYER (L.) . . 2, 35	
DYER (H.). .	37
EADIE (J.) . . 4, 38, 40	
EARL (A.). .	33
EASTLAKE (Lady) .	41
EBERS (G.) . .	22
ECCLES (A. S.) . .	29
EDGEWORTH (Prof. F. Y.)	35
EDGEWORTH (M.) .	22
EDMUNDS (Dr. W.) .	28

	PAGE
EDWARDS-MOSS (Sir J. E.)	38
EHLERS (E. S.). .	29
EIMER (G. H. T.) .	7
ELDERTON (W. A.) .	11
ELLERTON (Rev. J.).	43
ELLIOTT (Hon. A.) .	36
ELLIS (A.). . 20, 24	
ELLIS (T.). .	3
EMERSON (R. W.) .	4, 24
EMERSON (O. F.) .	31
ERMAN (A.) . .	2
EVANS (Lady) . .	2
EVANS (S.) . .	18
EVERETT (J. D.) .	33
FALCONER (Lance) .	22
FARRAR (Archd.) 6, 39, 43	
FARRER (Sir T. H.) .	36
FASNACHT (G. E.) .	25.
FAULKNER (F.). .	8
FAWCETT (Prof. H.).	35, 37
FAWCETT (Mrs. H.). 6, 35, 37	
FAY (Amy) . .	30
FAVRER (Sir J.) .	14.
FEARNLEY (W.) .	34
FEARON (D. R.) .	10
FERREL (W.) . .	34
FESSENDEN (C.) .	33
FIELD (Rev. T.) .	12
FIELDE (A. M.). .	14
FINCK (H. T.) . .	1
FISHER (Rev. O.) .	33
FISKE (J.). . 7, 12, 32, 37, 43	
FISON (L.). .	7
FITCH (J. G.) . .	10.
FITZ GERALD (Caroline) .	18.
FITZGERALD (Edward) 18, 25.	
FITZMAURICE (Lord E.)	6
FLAGG (A. T.) . .	31
FLEISCHER (E). .	8
FLEMING (G.) . .	22
FLORY (M. A.) . .	3
FLOWER (Sir W. H.) .	49
FLÜCKIGER (F. A.) .	29
FONDA (A. J.) . .	35.
FORBES (A.) . .	4, 41
FORBES (Prof. G.) .	3
FORBES (Rev. G.) .	43
FORBES-MITCHELL (W.) 5, 47	
FORTESCUE (Hon. J. W.). 4,30	
FOSTER (Prof. M.) . 7, 34, 35.	
FOSTER-MELLIAR (A.) .	10
FOTHERGILL (Dr. J. M.) 9, 10	
FOWLE (Rev. T. W.). 36, 43	
FOWLER (Rev. T.) . 5, 32	
FOWLER (W. W.) . 2, 25, 30	
FOX (T. W.) . .	38
FOX (Dr. Wilson) .	29
FOXWELL (Prof. H. S)	36
FRAMJI (D.) . .	12
FRANCIS (F.) . .	22
FRANKLAND (P. F.).	1
FRASER (Mrs) . .	48
FRASER (Bishop) .	43
FRASER-TYTLER (C. C.) .	18
FRAZER (J. G.) . .	1
FREEMAN (Prof. E. A.)	
2, 5, 12, 37, 40	
FRENCH (G. R.) .	17
FRIEDMANN (P.) .	2
FROISSART . .	25
FROST (A. B.) . .	48
FROUDE (J. A.). .	4
FULLERTON (W. M.) .	47
FURNIVALL (F. J.) .	18.

	PAGE
FYFFE (C. A.)	12
FYFE (H. H.)	11
GAIRDNER (J.)	5
GAISFORD (H.)	10
GALT (J.)	22
GALTON (F.)	1
GAMGEE (Arthur)	35
GARDNER (E.)	2
GARDNER (Percy)	2
GARNETT (R.)	18
GARNETT (W.)	5
GASKELL (Mrs.)	14
GASKOIN (Mrs. H.)	38
GEDDES (W. D.)	17, 46
GEE (H.)	40
GEE (W. W. H.)	33, 34
GEIKIE (Sir A.)	4, 5, 6, 11, 34
GENNADIUS (J.)	21
GENUNG (J. F.)	17
GEORGE (H. B.)	20
GIBBINS (H. de B.)	12
GIBBON (Charles)	4
GILLIES (H. C.)	29
GILCHRIST (A.)	4
GILES (P.)	31
GILMAN (N. P.)	35, 37
GILMORE (Rev. J.)	16
GLADSTONE (Dr. J. H.)	8, 10
GLADSTONE (W. E.)	17
GLAISTER (E.)	2, 9
GLOVER (E.)	43
GODFRAY (H.)	3
GODKIN (G. S.)	6
GOETHE	5, 14, 18, 25
GOLDIE (J.)	37
GOLDSMITH	5, 14, 18, 25, 26
GONNER (E. C. K.)	11
GOODFELLOW (J.)	14
GOODNOW (F. J.)	15
GORDON (General C. G.)	5
GORDON (Lady Duff)	47
GORDON (H.)	33
GOSCHEN (Rt. Hon. G. J.)	35
GOSSE (Edmund)	5, 16
GOW (J.)	2
GOW (W.)	31
GRACIAN (Balthasar)	25
GRAHAM (D.)	18
GRAHAM (J. W.)	22
GRAND'HOMME (E.)	9
GRANE (W. L.)	43
GRANT (C.)	22
GRAY (Prof. Andrew)	34
GRAY (Asa)	7, 26
GRAY	5, 18, 26
GRAY (J. L.)	26
GREGORY (R. A.)	3, 33
GREEN (J. R.)	11, 12, 14, 25, 26
GREEN (Mrs. J. R.)	5, 11, 12
GREEN (W. S.)	47
GREENHILL (W. A.)	25
GREENWOOD (F.)	26
GREENWOOD (J. E.)	48
GRENFELL (Mrs.)	9
GRIFFITHS (W. H.)	29
GRIMM	48
GROVE (Sir G.)	11, 30
GUEST (E.)	12
GUEST (M. J.)	12
GUILLEMIN (A.)	33, 34
GUIZOT (F. P. G.)	6
GUNTON (G.)	35
GWATKIN (H. M.)	40
HALLE (E. von)	35
	PAGE
HALES (J. W.)	18, 21, 25, 26
HALLWARD (R. F.)	15
HAMERTON (P. G.)	3, 15, 26
HAMILTON (Prof. D. J.)	29
HAMILTON (J.)	43
HANBURY (D.)	7, 29
HANNAY (David)	4
HARDEN (A.)	8
HARDWICK (Archd. C.)	40, 43
HARDY (A. S.)	22
HARDY (W. J.)	40
HARE (A. W.)	26
HARE (J. C.)	43
HARKER (A.)	34
HARRIS (Rev. G. C.)	43
HARRISON (F.)	5, 6, 12, 15, 26
HARRISON (Miss J.)	2
HARTE (Bret)	22
HARTIG (Dr. R.)	7
HARTLEY (Prof. W. N.)	8
HASSALL (A.)	12
HATCH (F. J.)	11
HAUSER (K.)	5
HAWKINS (H. P.)	29
HAVES (A.)	18
HEADLAM (A. C.)	2
HEADLEY (F. W.)	30, 50
HEAVISIDE (O.)	34
HELM (E.)	35
HELPS (Sir A.)	26
HEMPEL (Dr. W.)	8
HENLEY (W. E.)	15
HERMAN (H.)	23
HERODOTUS	46
HERRICK	25
HERRMANN (G.)	10
HERTEL (Dr.)	10
HERTZ (H.)	34
HICKIE (W. J.)	39
HIGINBOTHAM (C. J.)	5
HILL (D. J.)	32
HILL (F. Davenport)	37
HILL (O.)	37
HILL (G. B.)	12
HIORNS (A. H.)	29, 30
HOBART (Lord)	26
HOBDAY (E.)	10
HODGSON (Rev. J. T.)	5
HOFFDING (Prof. H.)	33
HOFFMAN (W. J.)	1
HOFMANN (A. W.)	8
HOLE (Rev. C.)	9, 12
HOLIDAY (Henry)	48
HOLLAND (T. E.)	15, 37
HOLLWAY-CALTHROP (H.)	48
HOLM (A.)	13
HOLMES (O. W., junr.)	15
HOMER	17, 46
HOOD (T.)	15
HOOKER (Sir J. D.)	7, 47
HOOLE (C. H.)	39
HOOPER (E.)	4
HOOPER (W. H.)	3
HOPKINS (E.)	18
HOPPUS (M. A. M.)	2
HORACE	17, 25, 46
HORT (F. J. A.)	39, 40, 41, 43
HORTON (Hon. S. D.)	35
HOSKEN (J. D.)	18
HOVENDEN (R. M.)	46
HOWELL (George)	15, 35
HOWES (G. B.)	35, 49
HOWITT (A. W.)	1
HOWSON (Very Rev. J. S.)	41
	PAGE
HOZIER (Col. H. M.)	30
HÜBNER (Baron)	47
HUGHES (T.)	4, 5, 18, 22, 25, 41, 43, 47
HUDDILSTON (J. H.)	39
HULL (E.)	2, 11
HULLAH (J.)	2, 25, 30
HUMPHRY (Prof. Sir G. M.)	35, 49
HUNT (Rev. W.)	12
HUNT (W.)	3
HUTCHINSON (G. W. C.)	3
HUTTON (R. H.)	5, 26
HUTTON (Rev. W. H.)	5
HUXLEY (T)	5, 26, 32, 33, 34, 35, 37, 49
HYDE (W. de W.)	43
ILLINGWORTH (Rev. J. R.)	43
IMPEY (S. P.)	29
INGRAM (T. D.)	13
IRELAND (A.)	26
IRVING (H.)	20
IRVING (J.)	11
IRVING (Washington)	15
JACK (A. A.)	17
JACKSON (D. C.)	34
JACKSON (F. G.)	47
JACKSON (Helen)	22
JACOB (Rev. J. A.)	43
JACOBS (J.)	14, 25, 47
JAMES (Henry)	5, 22, 26
JAMES (Rev. H.)	43
JAMES (Prof. W.)	33
JARDINE (Rev. R.)	33
JEANS (Rev. G E.)	43, 46
JEBB (Prof. R. C.)	4, 13, 16, 26
JELLETT (Rev. J. H.)	43
JENKS (Prof. Ed.)	37
JENNINGS (A. C.)	13, 38
JERSEY (Countess of)	48
JEPHSON (H.)	37
JEVONS (W. S.)	5, 32, 35, 36, 37
JEX-BLAKE (Sophia)	9
JOCELINE (E.)	26
JOHNSON (Amy)	34
JOHNSON (Samuel)	5, 16, 25
JOLLEY (A. J.)	39
JONES (Prof. D. E.)	34
JONES (F.)	8
JONES (H. Arthur)	16, 18, 26
JONES (H. S.)	2
JULIUS (Dr. P.)	9
KAHLDEN (C.)	29
KALM (P.)	47
KANT	32
KANTHACK (A. A.)	29
KARI	48
KAVANAGH (Rt. Hn. A. M.)	5
KAY (Rev. W.)	39
KEARY (Annie)	13, 22, 38, 48
KEARY (Eliza)	48
KEATS	5, 25, 26
KELLIE (J.)	25
KELLNER (Dr. L.)	31
KELLOGG (Rev. S. H.)	43
KELLY (E.)	43
KELTIE (J. S.)	38
KELVIN (Lord)	11, 31, 33, 34
KEMPE (A. B.)	33
KENNEDY (Prof. A. B. W.)	10
KENNEDY (B. H.)	46
KENNEDY (P.)	22
KEYNES (J. N.)	32, 36
KIDD (B.)	37
KIEPERT (H.)	11

	PAGE
KIMBER (D. C.)	35
KING (F. H.)	1
KING (G.)	13
KINGSLEY (Charles) 5, 10, 13, 14, 16, 18, 22, 23, 26, 27, 30, 41, 47, 48	
KINGSLEY (G.)	38
KINGSLEY (Henry)	25, 47
KIPLING (J. L.)	47
KIPLING (Rudyard)	23, 48
KIRKPATRICK (Prof.)	38, 43
KLEIN (Dr. E.)	7, 29, 30
KLEIN (F.)	28
KNIGHT (W.)	17, 28, 32
KUENEN (Prof. A.)	38
KYNASTON (Rev. H.)	43, 46
LABBERTON (R. H.)	3
LA FARGE (J.)	3
LAFARGUE (P.)	23
LAMB	5, 25, 27
LANCIANI (Prof. R.)	2
LANDAUER (J.)	8
LANDOR	5, 25
LANE-POOLE (S.)	6, 25
LANFREY (P.)	5
LANG (Andrew)	15, 26, 46
LANG (Prof. Arnold)	49
LANGLEY (J. N.)	34
LANGMAID (T.)	10
LANKESTER (Prof. Ray)	7, 27
LASSAR-COHN (Dr.)	8
LASLETT (T.)	7
LAUGHTON (J. K.)	4
LAURIE (A. P.)	1, 3
LAWRENCE (T. J.)	15
LEA (A. S.)	35
LEAF (W.)	17, 46
LEAHY (Sergeant)	38
LEE (M.)	23
LEE (S.)	25, 46
LEE-WARNER (W.)	13
LEEPER (A.)	46
LEGGE (A. O.)	13, 43
LEIBNITZ	36
LESLIE (G. D.)	27
LETHABY (W. R.)	2, 38
LETHBRIDGE (Sir Roper)	5, 13
LEVY (Amy)	23
LEWIS (Mrs. A. S.)	39
LEWIS (R.)	16
LEWKOWITSCH (J.)	38
LIGHTFOOT (Bishop) 5, 13, 39, 40, 41, 43, 44	
LIGHTWOOD (J. M.)	15
LINDSAY (Dr. J. A.)	29
LITTLEDALE (H.)	17
LOCKYER (J. N.)	3, 8, 34
LODEMAN (E. G.)	10
LODGE (Prof. O. J.)	3, 27, 34
LODGE (R.)	5
LOWENSON-LESSING (F.)	11
LOEWY (B.)	33
LOFTIE (Mrs. W. J.)	2
LONGFELLOW (H. W.)	25, 26
LONSDALE (J.)	25, 46
LOWE (W. H.)	38, 39
LOWELL (J. R.)	15, 18, 27
LOUDOUN (W. J.)	33
LOUIS (H.)	38
LUBBOCK (Sir J.)	7, 10, 27, 50
LUCAS (F.)	18
LUCAS (Joseph)	47
LUNT (J.)	8
LUPTON (S.)	8
LYALL (Sir Alfred)	4

	PAGE
LYSAGHT (S. R.)	23
LYTE (H. C. M.)	13
LYTTELTON (A. T.)	44
LYTTELTON (E.)	27
LYTTON (Earl of)	23
MACALISTER (D.)	29
MACARTHUR (M.)	12
MACAULAY (G. C.)	20, 25, 46
MACAULAY (Lord)	27
MACCOLL (Norman)	17
McCURDY (J. F.)	44
M'COSH (Dr. J.)	32, 33
MACDONALD (George)	21
MACDONALD (G.)	29
MACKAIL (J. W.)	46
MACKNIGHT (J.)	37
MACLAGAN (Dr. T.)	29
MACLAREN (Rev. Alex.)	44
MACLAREN (Archibald)	48
MACLEAN (G. E.)	31
MACLEAN (W. C.)	29
MACLEAR (Rev. Dr.)	38, 40, 41
McLENNAN (J. C.)	33
M'LENNAN (J. F.)	1
M'LENNAN (Malcolm)	23
MACMILLAN (Rev. H.)	27, 44
MACMILLAN (Michael)	6, 19
MACMILLAN (M. K.)	23
MACQUOID (K. S.)	23
MADOC (F.)	23
MAGUIRE (J. F.)	48
MAHAFFY (Prof. J. P.) 2, 13, 16, 27, 32, 44, 47	
MAITLAND (F. W.)	15, 36
MALET (L.)	23
MALORY (Sir T.)	25
MALTHUS (T. R.)	35
MANSFIELD (C. B.)	8
MARCOU (J.)	4
MARKHAM (C. R.)	5
MARR (J. E.)	34
MARRIOTT (J. A. R.)	6
MARRYAT (Capt.)	23
MARSHALL (Prof. A.)	36
MARSHALL (H. R.)	32
MARTEL (C.)	30
MARTIN (Frances)	4, 48
MARTIN (Frederick)	36
MARTIN (H. N.)	49
MARTINEAU (C. A.)	34
MARTINEAU (H.)	6
MARTINEAU (Dr. J.)	6
MASON (A. E. W.)	23
MASON (O. T.)	1
MASSON (D.)	5, 18, 21, 25, 32
MASSON (G.)	9, 25
MASSON (R. O.)	21
MATHEW (E. J.)	13, 37
MATURIN (Rev. W.)	44
MAUDSLEY (Dr. H.)	33
MAURICE (F. D.) 10, 27, 32, 38-40, 41, 44	
MAURICE (Gen. F.)	5, 30, 36
MAX MÜLLER (F.)	32
MAYER (A. M.)	34
MAYO-SMITH (R.)	37
MAYOR (J. B.)	44
MAYOR (Prof. J. E. B.)	3, 6
MAZINI (L.)	49
MELDOLA (Prof. R.)	8, 33, 34
MENDENHALL (T. C.)	34
MENGER (C.)	36
MENSCHUTKIN (A.)	8
MERCIER (Dr. C.)	29

	PAGE
MERCUR (Prof. J.)	30
MEREDITH (G.)	18
MEREDITH (L. A.)	15
MEYER (E. von)	8
MEYRICK (E.)	30
MIALL (L. C.)	30, 50
MICHELET (M.)	13
MIERS (H. A.)	14
MILL (H. R.)	11
MILLER (R. K.)	3
MILLIGAN (Rev. W.)	40, 44
MILTON	5, 16, 18, 25, 27
MINTO (Prof. W.)	5, 23
MITFORD (A. B.)	23
MITFORD (M. R.)	15
MIVART (St. George)	35
MIXTER (W. G.)	8
MOLESWORTH (Mrs.)	49
MOLLOY (G.)	33
MOLYNEUX (W. C. F.)	30
MONAHAN (J. H.)	15
MONTEFIORE (C. G.)	42
MONTELIUS (O.)	1
MOORE (C. H.)	4
MOORHOUSE (Bishop)	44
MORIER (J.)	23
MORISON (J. C.)	5
MORLEY (John)	4, 5, 20, 27
MORRIS (E. E.)	5
MORRIS (Mowbray)	4, 25
MORRIS (R.)	25, 31
MORSHEAD (E. D. A.)	46
MOULTON (L. C.)	18
MOULTON (R. G.)	38
MUDIE (C. E.)	18
MUIR (J.)	1
MUIR (M. M. P.)	8
MÜLLER (H.)	8
MULLINGER (J. B.)	13
MUN (T.)	35
MUNRO (J. E. C.)	15
MURPHY (J. J.)	7, 33, 44
MURRAY (D. Christie)	23
MURRAY (G.)	8
MYERS (E.)	18, 46
MYERS (F. W. H.)	5, 19, 27
MYLNE (Bishop)	44
NADAL (E. S.)	27
NERNST (Dr.)	8
NETTLESHIP (H.)	16
NEWCOMB (S.)	3
NEWCASTLE (Duke and Duchess)	25
NEWMAN (G.)	29
NEWTON (Sir C. T.)	2
NICHOL (J.)	4
NICHOLS (E. L.)	33
NICHOLLS (H. A. A.)	1
NISBET (J.)	8
NOEL (Lady A.)	23
NORDENSKIÖLD (A. E.)	47
NORGATE (Kate)	13
NORRIS (W. E.)	23
NORTON (Charles Eliot)	4, 45
NORTON (Hon. Mrs.)	19, 23
NORWAY (A. H.)	31
OLIPHANT (T. L. K.)	27, 31
OLIPHANT (Mrs. M. O. W.) 5, 13, 16, 23, 25, 49	
OLIVER (Prof. D.)	8
OLIVER (Capt. S. P.)	47
OMAN (C. W.)	4
ORR (H. B.)	1
OSBORN (H. F.)	7

	PAGE
OSTWALD (Prof.)	8
OTTÉ (E. C.)	13
PAGE (T. E.)	39
PALGRAVE (Sir F.)	13
PATERSON (J.)	16
PATMORE (Coventry)	25, 49
PATTESON (J. C.)	6
PATTISON (Mark)	5, 6, 44
PAULSEN (F.)	10
PAYNE (E. J.)	12, 36
PEABODY (C. H.)	10, 34
PEACOCK (T. L.)	23
PEARSON (C. H.)	37
PEASE (A. E.)	14
PEEL (F.)	19
PEILE (J.)	31
PELLISSIER (E.)	32
PENNELL (J.)	3
PENNINGTON (R.)	11
PENROSE (F. C.)	2
PERCIVAL (H. M.)	18, 19
PERKINS (J. B.)	13
PETERSON (W.)	46
PETTIGREW (J. B.)	8, 35, 49
PHILLIMORE (J. G.)	16
PHILLIPS (F. E.)	23
PHILLIPS (J. A.)	30
PHILLIPS (W. C.)	3
PICTON (J. A.)	27
PIFFARD (H. G.)	29
PIKE (L. O.)	13
PIKE (W.)	47
PLATO	26, 46
PLUMPTRE (Dean)	44
POLLARD (A. W.)	16, 17, 46
POLLOCK (Sir F., Bart.)	6, 16, 27, 36, 37
POLLOCK (Lady)	2
POOLE (M. E.)	27
POOLE (R. L.)	13
POPE	5, 25, 27
POSTE (E.)	34, 46
POTTER (L.)	27
POTTER (R.)	44
POTTS (W.)	27
PRESTON (T.)	34
PRESTWICH (J.)	11
PRICE (E. C.)	23
PRICE (L. L. F. R.)	36
PRICKARD (A. O.)	27
PRINCE ALBERT VICTOR	46
PRINCE GEORGE	46
PROCTER (F.)	41
PROPERT (J. L.)	3
PROWSE (D. W.)	13
PURCELL (E. S.)	5
QUESNAY (F.)	36
RABBENO (U.)	36
RAE (J.)	6, 36
RAMSAY (Sir A. C.)	6
RAMSAY (W.)	8
RANSOME (C.)	17
RATHBONE (W.)	9
RATZEL (F.)	1
RAWLINSON (W. G.)	15
RAWNSLEY (H. D.)	19
RAY (P. K.)	32
RAYLEIGH (Lord)	34
REICHEL (Bishop)	44
REID (J. S.)	46
REMSEN (I.)	8
RENAN (E.)	6
RENDALL (Rev. F.)	40, 44
RENDU (M. le C.)	11

	PAGE
REYNOLDS (E. S.)	14
REYNOLDS (H. R.)	44
PALGRAVE (F. T.)	3, 19, 21, 25, 26, 42, 49
PALGRAVE (R. H. Inglis)	35
PALGRAVE (W. G.)	19, 37, 47
PALMER (Lady S.)	23
PARKER (T. J.)	7, 49
PARKER (W. K.)	6
PARKER (W. N.)	49
PARKES (Sir H.)	6
PARKIN (G. R.)	13, 37
PARKINSON (S.)	34
PARKMAN (F.)	13, 47
PARRY (G.)	23
PARSONS (Alfred)	15
PASTEUR (L.)	8
PATER (W.)	3, 16, 23, 27
PATERSON (A.)	23
REYNOLDS (Sir J. R.)	29
REYNOLDS (O.)	14
RHOADES (J.)	23
RHODES (J. F.)	13
RICARDO	35, 36
RICHARDSON (B. W.)	14, 29
RICHEY (A. G.)	16
RIGHTON (E.)	18
RITCHIE (A.)	6
ROBB (R.)	10
ROBINSON (Preb. H. G.)	44
ROBINSON (J. L.)	31
ROBINSON (Matthew)	6
ROCKSTRO (W. S.)	5
ROGERS (J. E. T.)	13, 37
ROMANES (G. J.)	7
ROSCOE (Sir H. E.)	8, 9
ROSCOE (W. C.)	19
ROSEBERY (Earl of)	5
ROSENBUSCH (H.)	11
ROSEVEAR (E.)	9
ROSS (P.)	23
ROSSETTI (C. G.)	19, 49
ROUTLEDGE (J.)	37
ROWE (F. J.)	20
ROY (Neil)	23
RÜCKER (Prof. A. W.)	9
RUMFORD (Count)	27
RUSHBROOKE (W. G.)	39
RUSSELL (Dean)	44
RUSSELL (Sir Charles)	37
RUSSELL (W. Clark)	4, 23
RUSSELL (T.)	34
RUTHERFORD (W. G.)	46
RYLAND (F.)	16
RYLE (Prof. H. E.)	38, 44
SADLER (H.)	3
SAINTSBURY (G.)	5, 16
SALMON (Rev. G.)	44
SALT (H. S.)	28
SANDFORD (Bishop)	44
SANDFORD (M. E.)	6
SANDYS (J. E.)	47
SAYCE (A. H.)	13
SCAIFE (W. B.)	27
SCARTAZZINI (G. A.)	17
SCHLIEMANN (Dr.)	2
SCHMOLLER (G.)	35
SCHORLEMMER (C.)	8, 9
SCHREIBER (T.)	2
SCHUCHHARDT (C.)	2
SCHULTZ (Dr. G.)	9
SCOTT (M.)	23
SCOTT (Sir W.)	19, 25
SCRATCHLEY (Sir Peter)	30

	PAGE
SCUDDER (S. H.)	50
SEATON (Dr. E. C.)	29
SEEBOHM (H. E.)	1
SEELEY (Sir J. R.)	13, 37, 44
SEILER (Dr. Carl)	29, 35
SELBORNE (Earl of)	25, 40, 42
SELIGMAN (E.)	36
SELLERS (E.)	2
SERVICE (J.)	41, 44
SEWELL (E. M.)	13
SHADWELL (C. L.)	46
SHAIRP (J. C.)	4, 19
SHAKESPEARE	17, 19, 25, 26
SHANN (G.)	10, 34
SHARP (W.)	6
SHAW (Miss)	13
SHELLEY	19, 26
SHIPTON (Helen)	23
SHIRLEY (W. N.)	44
SHORE (L. E.)	34
SHORTHOUSE (J. H.)	23
SHORTLAND (Admiral)	31
SHUCKBURGH (E. S.)	14, 46
SHUFELDT (R. W.)	49
SIBSON (Dr. F.)	29
SIDGWICK (A.)	20
SIDGWICK (Prof. H.)	32, 36, 37
SIME (J.)	11, 12
SIMPSON (Rev. W.)	40
SKEAT (W. W.)	17
SKRINE (J. H.)	6, 19
SLADE (J. H.)	10
SLEEMAN (L.)	47
SLOMAN (Rev. A.)	39
SMART (W.)	36
SMALLEY (G. W.)	6, 27
SMETHAM (J. and S.)	6
SMITH (Adam)	3, 6, 35, 36
SMITH (Alexander)	17, 25
SMITH (C. B.)	19
SMITH (Garnet)	24
SMITH (Goldwin)	4, 6, 14, 21, 27, 37, 45, 47
SMITH (H.)	19
SMITH (J.)	8
SMITH (Rev. T.)	44
SMITH (W. G.)	8
SMITH (L. Pearsall)	24
SOHM (R.)	40
SOMERVILLE (Prof. W.)	7
SOUTHEY	6, 26
SPANTON (J.)	3
SPENDER (J. K.)	29
SPENSER	19, 25
SPOTTISWOODE (W.)	34
ST. ASAPH (Bishop of)	40
ST. JOHNSTON (A.)	23, 47, 49
STANLEY (Dean)	44
STANLEY (Hon. Maude)	37
STATHAM (R.)	37
STEBBING (W.)	4
STEEL (F. A.)	15, 24
STEPHEN (C. E.)	9
STEPHEN (H.)	16
STEPHEN (Sir J. F.)	14, 16, 27
STEPHEN (J. K.)	16
STEPHEN (L.)	5
STEPHENS (J. B.)	19
STEPHENS (W. R. W.)	5
STEVENS (C. E.)	16
STEVENSON (F. S.)	6
STEVENSON (J. J.)	2
STEWART (A.)	49
STEWART (Balfour)	33, 34, 45

	PAGE
STOKES (Sir G. G.)	34
STORY (R. H.)	4
STONE (W. H.)	34
STRACHEY (Sir E.)	25
STRACHEY (J. St. L.)	37
STRACHEY (Gen. R.)	11
STRANGFORD (Viscountess)	47
STRETTELL (A.)	19
STUBBS (Dean)	45
STUBBS (Bishop)	40
SUTHERLAND (A.)	11
SWAINSON (H.)	2
SWETE (Prof. H. B.)	39
SWIFT (Dean)	15
SYMONDS (J. A.)	5
SYMONDS (Mrs. J. A.)	6
SYMONS (A.)	19
TAGGART (W. S.)	38
TAINSH (E. C.)	17
TAIT (Archbishop)	6, 45
TAIT (C. W. A.)	14
TAIT (Prof. P. G.)	33, 34, 45
TANNER (H.)	1
TARR (R. S.)	11, 34
TAVERNIER (J. B.)	47
TAYLOR (E. R.)	3
TAYLOR (Franklin)	30
TAYLOR (Isaac)	32, 45
TAYLOR (Sedley)	30, 34
TEGETMEIER (W. B.)	9
TEMPLE (Bishop)	45
TEMPLE (Sir R.)	4
TENNANT (Dorothy)	48
TENNIEL (Sir John)	48
TENNYSON (Lord)	17, 19, 20, 26
TENNYSON (Frederick)	20
TENNYSON (Lord H.)	15, 49
THEODOLI (Marchesa)	24
THOMPSON (D'A. W.)	8
THOMPSON (E.)	12
THOMPSON (H. M.)	36
THOMPSON (S. P.)	34
THOMSON (A. W.)	10
THOMSON (Sir C. W.)	50
THOMSON (Hugh)	14
THOREAU	28
THORNE (Dr. Thorne)	29
THORNTON (J.)	7
THORNTON (W. T.)	32, 37, 46
THORPE (T. E.)	6, 9
THRING (E.)	10, 28
THRUPP (J. F.)	38
THURSFIELD (J. R.)	5
TODHUNTER (I.)	6
TORRENS (W. M.)	5
TOURGÉNIEF (I. S.)	24
TOUT (T. F.)	5, 14
TOZER (H. F.)	11
TRAILL (H. D.)	4, 5, 36
TRENCH (Capt. F.)	37
TRENCH (Archbishop)	45
TREVELYAN (Sir G. O.)	14, 26
TREVOR (G. H.)	20
TRIBE (A.)	8

	PAGE
TRISTRAM (W. O.)	15
TROLLOPE (A.)	5
TRUMAN (J.)	20
TUCKER (T. G.)	46
TUCKWELL (W.)	14
TUFTS (J. H.)	32
TULLOCH (Principal)	45
TURNER (C. Tennyson)	20
TURNER (G.)	1
TURNER (H. H.)	34
TURNER (J. M. W.)	15
TURPIN (G. S.)	9
TYLOR (E. B.)	1
TYRWHITT (R. St. J.)	3, 20
TYRRELL (R. Y.)	16, 28
VAUGHAN (C. J.)	39, 40, 41, 45
VAUGHAN (Rev. D. J.)	26, 28, 45
VAUGHAN (Rev. E. T.)	45
VAUGHAN (Rev. R.)	45
VELEY (M.)	24
VENN (Rev. J.)	33, 45
VERNON (Hon. W. W.)	17
VERRALL (A. W.)	17, 46
VERRALL (Mrs.)	2
VICKERMAN (C.)	38
VICTOR (H.)	24
VINES (S. H.)	8
VIOLLET-LE-DUC (E. E.)	10
WAIN (Louis)	48
WALDSTEIN (C.)	2
WALKER (Prof. F. A.)	36
WALKER (Jas.)	8
WALKER (Louisa)	38
WALLACE (A. R.)	7, 30, 36
WALLACE (Sir D. M.)	37
WALPOLE (S.)	36
WALTON (I.)	15
WARD (A. W.)	4, 5, 16, 25
WARD (H. M.)	7, 8
WARD (S.)	20
WARD (T. H.)	21
WARD (Mrs. T. H.)	24, 49
WARD (W.)	6, 28, 41
WARE (W. R.)	3
WATERS (C. A.)	35
WATERTON (Charles)	30, 47
WATSON (E.)	6
WATSON (R. S.)	47
WATSON (W.)	20, 25
WAY (A. S.)	46
WEBB (W. T.)	18, 20
WEBSTER (Mrs. A.)	20, 49
WEISBACH (J.)	5
WELBY-GREGORY (Lady)	41
WELLDON (Rev. J. E. C.)	45, 46
WEST (M.)	24
WESTCOTT (Bp.)	38, 39, 40, 41, 45
WESTERMARCK (E.)	1
WETHERELL (J.)	32
WHEELER (J. T.)	14
WHEWELL (W.)	6
WHITCOMB (L. S.)	3, 16
WHITE (A.)	28
WHITE (Gilbert)	15, 31

	PAGE
WHITE (Dr. W. Hale)	29
WHITE (W.)	34
WHITNEY (W. D.)	9
WHITTIER (J. G.)	20, 26, 28
WHITTUCK (C. A.)	45
WICKHAM (Rev. E. C.)	45
WICKSTEED (P. H.)	36, 38
WIEDERSHEIM (R.)	35, 49
WIESER (F. von)	36
WILBRAHAM (F. M.)	41
WILKINS (Prof. A. S.)	2, 16, 45
WILKINSON (S.)	30
WILLEY (A.)	7
WILLIAMS (C. M.)	32
WILLIAMS (C. T.)	29
WILLIAMS (G. H.)	11
WILLIAMS (H.)	14, 31
WILLIAMS (Montagu)	6
WILLIAMS (S. E.)	16
WILLIAMSON (M. B.)	45
WILLINK (A.)	45
WILLOUGHBY (E. F.)	14
WILLOUGHBY (F.)	49
WILLS (W. G.)	20
WILSON (A. J.)	36
WILSON (Sir C.)	4
WILSON (Sir D.)	1, 4, 17
WILSON (E. B.)	50
WILSON (Dr. G.)	5, 6, 28
WILSON (Archdeacon)	45
WILSON (Mary)	16
WINCHESTER (Bishop of)	6
WINDELBAND (W.)	32
WINGATE (Major F. R.)	30
WINKWORTH (C.)	6
WINKWORTH (S.)	25
WINTER (W.)	15
WOLSELEY (Gen. Viscount)	30
WOOD (A. G.)	20
WOOD (C. J.)	45
WOOD (Rev. E. G.)	14, 45
WOODS (Rev. F. H.)	1
WOODS (Miss M. A.)	21, 42
WOODWARD (C. M.)	10
WOOLNER (T.)	20
WORDSWORTH	4, 6, 17, 20, 26, 28
WORTHEY (Mrs.)	24
WRIGHT (Rev. A.)	39
WRIGHT (Miss G.)	9
WRIGHT (J.)	10, 26
WRIGHT (L.)	34
WRIGHT (M. O.)	28, 31
WRIGHT (W. A.)	9, 18, 25, 40
WULKER (Dr.)	16
WURTZ (Ad.)	9
WYATT (Sir M. D.)	3
YEO (J.)	34
YOE (Shway)	47
YONGE (C. M.)	6, 8, 9, 12, 13, 14, 24, 26, 28, 32, 38, 49
YOUNG (E. W.)	10
YOUNGHUSBAND (G. J. and F. E.)	30
ZIEGLER (Dr. E.)	29

MACMILLAN AND CO., LTD., LONDON.

J. PALMER, PRINTER, ALEXANDRA STREET, CAMBRIDGE.

19/50/3/96

PLEASE DO NOT REMOVE
CARDS OR SLIPS FROM THIS POCKET

UNIVERSITY OF TORONTO LIBRARY

PR   Mason, Alfred Edward Woodley
6025   The courtship of Morrice
A79C65   Buckler

www.ingramcontent.com/pod-product-compliance
Lightning Source LLC
Chambersburg PA
CBHW032301280326
41932CB00009B/652

9 7 8 3 7 4 4 6 7 3 9 2 1